Space - Place - Environment

# TRANSATLANTIC PERSPECTIVES 15

A Series of Interdisciplinary
North American Studies

Edited by Lothar Hönnighausen (Bonn) and
Christoph Irmscher (Baltimore)

ADVISORY BOARD

Literature, Language, Art, American Studies, Canadian Studies
Sonia Bačić (U. of Zagreb); André Bleikasten (U. of Strasbourg); Ursula Brumm (Free U. of Berlin); Tilmann Buddensieg (U. of Bonn); Hans Bungert (U. of Regensburg); Susan Donaldson (College of William and Mary); Joris M. Duytschaever (U. of Antwerp); Winfried Fluck (Free U. of Berlin); Friedrich Wilhelm Gester (U. of Bonn); Richard Gray (U. of Essex); Jan Nordby Gretlund (U. of Odense); Winfried Herget (U. of Mainz); Gerhard Hoffmann (U. of Würzburg); Linda Hutcheon (U. of Toronto); Heinz Ickstadt (Free U. of Berlin); R. Johnson (Georgetown U.); Eva-Marie Kröller (UBC); Mario Materassi (U. of Florence); Justus Müller Hofstede (U. of Bonn); Peter Nicolaisen (U. of Flensburg); Reingard Nischik (U. of Konstanz); David E. Nye (Institute for Advanced Studies, The Netherlands); Danièle Pitavy (U. of Dijon); K. Sieciechowicz (U. of Toronto); Heide Ziegler (U. of Stuttgart)

History
A.J. Badger (Cambridge); Thomas Bender (NYU); Russel D. Buhite (U. of Tennessee); Dan T. Carter (Emory U., Atlanta); James C. Cobb (U. of Tennessee); Evelyn Higginbotham (U. of Pennsylvania); Darlene Clark Hine (Michigan State U.); J.T. Kirby (Miami U., Oxford, Ohio); Michael O'Brien (Miami U., Oxford, Ohio); Anne Firor Scott (Duke U.); P. Ward (UBC); Hermann Wellenreuther (U. of Göttingen); Charles Reagan Wilson (U. of Mississippi)

Geography
L.S. Bourne (U. of Toronto); Eckart Ehlers (U. of Bonn); Reinhold Grotz (U. of Bonn); Chauncy D. Harris (U. of Chicago)

Political Science
D. Blake (UBC); G. Flynn (Georgetown U.); B. Job (UBC; International Studies); Robert L. Lieber (Georgetown U.); Karl Kaiser (U. of Bonn); R. Matthews (U. of Toronto); Joseph S. Nye, Jr. (Harvard); Hans-Peter Schwarz (U. of Bonn)

Social Science, Anthropology, Ethnology, Communication
Friedrich Fürstenberg (U. of Bonn); Wolf von Heydebrand (NYU); P. Marchak (UBC); R. Pearson (UBC); Hanns J. Prem (U. of Bonn); Berthold Riese (U. of Bonn); K. Schönbach (U. of Hannover); J. Sweet (U. of Wisconsin; Madison); Annette B. Weiner (NYU)

Law
John B. Barceló III (Cornell Law School, Ithaca, NY); Stephen C. Burnett (Northwestern U.); Richard M. Buxbaum (U. of California, Berkeley); Thomas Haskell (Rice U.); Peter Hay (Emory U., Atlanta); Wolfgang Freiherr von Marschall (U. of Bonn); Wulf-Henning Roth (U. of Bonn); Jost Pietzcker (U. of Bonn); Jürgen Salzwedel (U. of Bonn); The Hon. Mr. Justice Walter Tarnopolsky (Court of Appeals for Ontario, Toronto); Christian Tomuschat (U. of Bonn); Detlev F. Vagts (Harvard Law School); Jacob S. Ziegel (Faculty of Law, U. of Toronto)

Economics, Business
Horst Albach (U. of Bonn); G. Anderson (U. of Toronto); R. Aubey (U. of Wisconsin, Madison); M. Berry (U. of Toronto); Johannes Frerich (U. of Bonn); H. Sabel (U. of Bonn)

Theology, Religion, Philosophy
Diogenes Allen (Princeton); John Barton (Oriel College, Oxford); Ludger Honnefelder (U. of Bonn); Karl Heinz zur Mühlen (U. of Bonn); Ralph Norman (U. of Tennessee); Charles Reynolds (U. of Tennessee); Gerhard Sauter (U. of Bonn); David C. Steinmetz (Duke U.)

Space - Place - Environment

Edited by Lothar Hönnighausen,
Julia Apitzsch, and Wibke Reger

In collaboration with
Anne Barron and Meghan P.L. McKinnie

STAUFFENBURG VERLAG

Bibliographic information published by Die Deutsche Bibliothek

Die Deutsche Bibliothek lists this publication in the Deutsche Nationalbibliografie; detailed bibliographic data are available in the internet at <http://dnb.ddb.de>.

Printed with the support of Deutsche Forschungsgemeinschaft

© 2004 · Stauffenburg Verlag Brigitte Narr GmbH
P.O. Box 25 25 · D-72015 Tübingen
www.stauffenburg.de

All rights, including the rights of publication, distribution and sales, as well as the right to translate, are reserved. No part of this work covered by the copyrights hereon may be reproduced or copied in any form or by any means – graphic, electronic or mechanical including photocopying, recording, taping, or information and retrieval systems – without written permission from the publisher.

Setting: Julia Apitzsch
Printed by: Bookstation GmbH
Printed in Germany

ISSN 0941-8032
ISBN 3-86057-346-2

Table of Contents

Introduction
by Lothar Hönnighausen   7

Theories and Methods

Winfried Fluck
Imaginary Space; or, Space as Aesthetic Object   15

Heide Ziegler
'Place' in the Internet Age or, Borges and I   31

Hanjo Berressem
Emergent Eco:logics: Cultural and Natural Environments in Recent Theory and Literature   42

Ulfried Reichardt
Space, Nature, and Landscape in Recent Theory and Poetry   62

Sabine Sielke
Spatial Aesthetics, Ironic Distances, and Realms of Liminality: Measuring Theories of (Post-)Modernism   74

James L. Peacock
From Space to Place   88

Environment

Cornelius Browne
(Eco)logic in Utah Landscapes: Edward Abbey and Terry Tempest Williams   101

Louise Westling
Monstrous Technologies in Silko, Castillo, Ortiz, and Solnit   115

Richard Grusin
Remediating Nature: National Parks as Mediated Public Space   125

Space in Fiction, Film, and Drama

Gerhard Hoffmann
Space as Form and Force in the Novel   137

Christian Berkemeier
Reading the Void: City Codes and Urban Space in Contemporary American Fiction   157

Pearl A. McHaney
Deconstruction of Public Space in David Mamet's *Oleanna*   169

Reingard M. Nischik
"Once Upon a Time in the West": The Changing Function of Landscape
in the American Western Film, 1968-2000   185

Aurélie Guillain
The Construction of the South in *The Song of Solomon* by Toni Morrison   201

Space in Poetry and Art

Frank J. Kearful
'Going Around in Circles': Wallace Stevens, Amy Clampitt, and Rita Dove   215

Diana von Finck
'Nothing-in-Between': Silence, Empty Spaces, and Separateness as Agents
in Postmodern Poetry   232

Carina Plath
Los Angeles—A Phenomenal City: West Coast Artists in the 1970s   247

Wolfgang Werth
Trash and Space: The Uncanny Art of Tony Oursler   263

'Real' and Constructed Space

Christian W. Thomsen
Arthur Erickson as Architectural Link between Canada and USA,
between Old and New World Cultural Concepts   276

Bernd Streich, Carsten Hagedorn, Sabine Wolf
Protecting Open Space: The Urban Sprawl Discussion in the USA
and in Germany   289

Charles S. Aiken and Kyle T. Rector
Geography and Socio-Political Space   305

Edward M. Bergman
Regional Uniqueness or Global Uniformity?   318

Notes on Contributors   333

Index   337

Introduction

Lothar Hönnighausen

The case for reopening the debate on space in our time has been succinctly put by Verona Conley in *Rethinking Technologies*: "Now, in a world where the notion of space has been completely changed through electronic simultaneity, where the computer appears to go faster than the human brain, or where 'virtual reality' replaces 'reality,' how do philosophy, critical theory, or artistic practices deal with those shifts?" (qtd. in Beckmann, 151). Total electronic simultaneity, 'real-time,' or absolute instantaneousness, if this were indeed possible, would not only mean the end of time and space but of human life as well. Fortunately, we are still far from having fully achieved this and the broker who has, through e-mail communication, just initiated a profitable capital flow around the globe, comes quickly to realize the impact of the continuance of sequential time and extensional space when he leaves his computer and gets into a traffic jam. Nevertheless, the shrinkage of time and space through electronic mail and supersonic traffic profoundly influences our ordinary sense of time and space. In fact, it is the coexistence of these two different modes of time and space that distinguishes our sense of reality from that of previous ages.

No less influential are cyberspace and 'virtual reality,' given the substantial impact they have on our professional and our recreational life. In addition to these manifestations of the media revolution and in synergetic interaction with them, heterogeneous factors such as human expansion into both outer space and micro space, global migrations, world-wide urbanization, and an increasingly globalized economy will further accelerate what has been called both *delocalization* and *deterritorialization*.

The current reaction of intellectuals to this *delocalization* or *deterritorialization* can be illustrated by two prominent examples. French architectural critic Paul Virilio apocalyptically refers to it as "this pollution of *life-size* [reducing] to nothing earth's scale and size" (Virilio, 58). Asian American anthropologist Arjun Appadurai declares presence in actual places as less relevant today than *migration, displacement,* and *diaspora* on the one hand and the projection of a *virtual* homeland, e.g. by Indian emigrants on the internet, on the other (Appadurai, 9-11). However, even a brief look at the world surrounding us and at novels from Pynchon's *The Crying of Lot 49* and William Gibson's *Neuromancer* to Paul Auster's *Moon Palace* and Don DeLillo's *Underworld* clearly shows that contemporary life and fiction is neither spaceless nor placeless, although the world experienced and depicted is no longer that of the regionalists of the thirties. In fact, Michel Foucault has called ours *the epoch of space,* albeit in the sense that "we are in the epoch of simultaneity; we are in the epoch of juxtaposition, the epoch of the near and far, of the side-by-side, of the dispersed" (Foucault, 23).

One of the peculiarities of our contemporary attitude towards space is that we no longer derive much comfort from Kant's conviction that time and space are *a priori forms of perception* and are more inclined to embrace Edward Casey's phenomenological approach and his assumption that the concreteness of place takes precedence over space. One important concomitant of Casey's philosophy of place is that it enhances the relevance of the body, "emplacement" and "embodiment" being mutually constitutive, another is the renewed importance it bestows on the "local and regional." (Casey, 13-52; Hönnighausen, 2000, 283-301). Obviously, the terminological field *space, place, environment* has to be continuously redefined in accordance with both the changing conventions of viewing and with the socio-political power struggles of every age. Several papers in this volume demonstrate that changes of *space* and of *place* as well as *region* and *environment* are cultural phenomena and confirm David Harvey's view that "transformations of space, place, and environment are neither neutral nor innocent with respect to practices of domination and control" (Harvey, 44).

The idea to focus our investigation of these transformations on the period of time after 1968 sprang from an interdisciplinary research project on the changes of regional concepts in the age of globalism (Hönnighausen et al., 2004) and from the widespread conviction that the late sixties mark a major political and socio-cultural watershed, a "key transitional period, a period in which the new international order (neocolonialism, the Green Revolution, computerization and electronic information) is set in place and shaken by its own contradictions" (Jameson, 165). But the late sixties are, above all, the period of emancipatory movements and of a far ranging 'devaluation of all values' profoundly affecting our sense of reality, and, as part of this, our perception of time and place. Obviously, the topic to be addressed is not the vanishing of space, but our problematic attitude towards it and, above all, our specific contemporary modes of perceiving, defining, and expressing it.

The groundwork for this task is laid in the first section "Theories and Methods," with the opening paper by Winfried Fluck focussing on the role and function of a depragmatized and dereferentialized space, "imaginary space," in the creation of cultural meaning. Heide Ziegler, who rereads Borges as prophet of the internet with its interplay of real and constructed space, and Hanjo Berressem, who uses Deleuze/Guattari as a basis for his study of the "threshold where machinespace turns into biospace," both foreground a space of open boundaries, ruled by the laws of chaos and complexity. This theme is taken up by Sabine Sielke who, contrasting the modernist "text as space" and the postmodernist "space as text," characterizes the contemporary artistic arena as "intertextual space, the realm of historical difference and ironic distance." Ulfried Reichardt, after examining the reasons why space is at the center in structuralism and in poststructuralism, investigates central aspects of space, place, and landscape in Richard Rorty ("site-specific, situated knowledge"), Richard Sennett ("postmodern ethics of multicultural communality"), and Gary Snyder ("bioregionalism"). Section one concludes with a seminal essay in which James Peacock, convinced that place matters more than ever "as forces of globalization blindly challenge this aspect of human existence," explores this challenge at the three levels of "human directions, social policy, and personal choices."

The aspect of place which is most intensely problematized today is probably the environment, the subject of the papers assembled in section two. It opens with a comparison of Edward Abbey's *Desert Solitaire* and Terry Tempest Williams's

Refuge, in which Cornelius Browne, drawing on John Dewey's *experience,* Edward Casey's *place* as well as Merleau-Ponty's *space*, shows the ecological interrelationship of "emplacement" and "embodiment." A similar ecological commitment characterizes Louise Westling's study of works by Silko, Castillo, Ortiz, and Solnit in which she connects "the playful Walt Disney reality" of postmodern Americanized culture and the inundation with toxic waste of actual physical landscapes not only in India, Vietnam, Indonesia, Brazil, Guatemala, and Northern Mexico, but also in Southern New Mexico, Arizona, Texas, Louisiana, and Mississippi. Richard Grusin's essay "Remediating Parks as Mediated Space" deals with the development (which Rousseauist Greens may consider hardly less insidious) of the transformation by the National Park Service of nature into a public space where the boundary between the natural world and the mediated one has become permeable. His case study of how digital mediation simultaneously produces and destabilizes the distinction between nature and its mediation is a good illustration of the postmodern fascination with "the interplay between 'real' and 'constructed' space" (Ziegler), with the "realm of liminality" (Sielke), and "the threshold between biospace and machinespace" (Berressem).

In "Space as Form and Force in the Novel," the essay introducing section three, "Space in Fiction, Film, and Drama," Gerhard Hoffmann discusses the emergence of new spatial concepts in such postmodern novels as Stanley Elkin's *The Dick Gibson Show,* in which the hero defines himself not by individual place, but by homogenizing place into space, by sterilizing local surfaces, and by denying geographical differences, eventually characterizing himself as "Dick Gibson of Nowhere, of Thin Air and the United States of America Sky." The doubtful nature of fictional reality in postmodern novels makes Hoffmann refer to what "Virilio has called the replacement of the 'aesthetics of appearance' by the 'aesthetics of disappearance.'" This paper, foregrounding postmodern novelistic theory, is supplemented by Christian Berkemeier's analyses of examples of cities in recent American and British films and novels which he approaches no longer as "cities of words" (Tony Tanner), but, in the context of "sender, recipient, code, and referent," his special interest lies in how this code has been used and modified in recent years. What he addresses as "Cryptopolis" is the kind of non-descript city that has made Hoffmann refer to Baudrillard's identification of "the America of desert speed [...] of social desertification." Pearl A. McHaney examines the ideological structures of postmodern space and the ensuing personal conflicts which are the subject of David Mamet's subtle dramatic probing. She shows how, in *Oleanna*, Mamet combines the sanctioned dramatizations of personal spaces in the public theater with the similarly empowered public landscape of higher education

The manifestations of the ideological deep structure in the landscape of Western film are the focus of Reingard Nischik's overview of space in Western films from the great Ford Western to the 1990s when the revisionist Western became the norm. Like Richard Grusin and other contributors who regard nature as a cultural construct, Nischik reveals how "the land represented in the classical American Western relies upon a specifically American iconography based on a network of values." The understanding of space as culturally constructed and reconstructed also informs Aurélie Guillain's paper on Toni Morrison's *The Song of Solomon*. In the course of Milkman's return to the South, a reversal of his ancestor's migration to the North, he learns how comprehending a place implies assimilating its social code and its specific cultural grammar and vocabulary.

The study of artistic forms of spatial organization would be incomplete without considering the subtle dispositions of "Space in Poetry and Art" as is done in section four of this volume. Frank J. Kearful explores the space-distorting effect of poetic wit ("I placed a jar in Tennessee / And round it was, upon a hill.") in Wallace Stevens's "Anecdote of the Jar," Amy Clampitt's "Man Feeding Pigeons," and Rita Dove's "The Oriental Ballerina." Displacement takes on a more radical turn in Robert Rauschenberg's *White Paintings* and in John Cage's poetics of "silence" and "nothing" ("life as a space without beginning, middle, or end"). Against this background, Diana von Finck juxtaposes John Taggart's poem "Were you" and Bernadette Mayer's "untitled what's thought of as boundless," showing how both Mayer's "boundless space" and Cage's "spatial nothing" make new radical claims on the responsiveness of the audience. There seems to be a similarity between Cage's "non-intentional music" and the desire of some of the West Coast artists of the 1970s, in Carina Plath's essay, to go beyond painting and 're-produce' the "patented look" of products of the local aerospace industry. Foregrounding Robert Irwin, James Turrell, and Maria Nordman, Plath discusses their art as a stylized response to the peculiar experience of light, space, and movement in Los Angeles. The next step after registering the banality and cliché-ridden scenery of Los Angeles seems to be the exploration of the world of trash in Tony Oursler's photographs and installations. After being exposed by Wolfgang Werth to the claustrophobic situations of Oursler's dummies and to the haunted world in which his dislocated household items assume "a fleeting spatio-temporal landmark quality," Christian W. Thomsen in section five returns us to the "'Real' and Constructed Space" of contemporary architecture.

Drawing on his personal acquaintance with three houses of Canada's greatest 20th century architect, Arthur Erickson, and making use of unpublished photo material of his own, Thomsen traces the development from the Smith house with its harmonious fusion of Western, Eastern, and Native American characteristics through the Russell house and its combination of a universal mediterraneity and the American West to the postmodern harmony of contrasts in the Eppich house. It is quite a distance from the study of space in the case of Erickson's villas to the comparative analysis of 'urban sprawl' by Bernd Streich and his co-authors. American Studies scholars will be interested to learn from Streich and his team how American utilitarian individuality and the emphasis on the protection of individual property lead to different settlement patterns than the German view of property as obligated to society.

As the other contributors in section five, geographers Charles S. Aiken and Kyle T. Rector deal with 'real' space, although a constructed one, in discussing new developments in the study of electoral districts, "a space identified for political purposes." Illustrating how computer data sets, new cartography software, and spatially-detailed census maps as well as recent alterations in the technology of communication and travel have practically negated shape among the important considerations in political space, Aiken and Rector provide insight into one of the most important aspects of contemporary space and make a pertinent suggestion on how to end the impasse in the famous 'gerrymander' case of the Twelfth North Carolina district.

While some Americanists have difficulty in accepting that *regions and regionalism* are still relevant issues in the age of globalism, regional planning expert Edward Bergman accepts this manifestation of space as one of his professional frames of reference, addressing one of the apparently contradictory facts of growing uniformity in global culture and consumer goods, the media, etc., and the fact that some regions retain (sometimes intensify) their unique qualities while others become novel in quite unexpected ways. Bergman argues that mixtures of path dependence, social capital, and capitalist competition together are most likely responsible for the coexistence of trends towards global uniformity and unique regional identities in the 21st century. Bergman's paper seems to be a fitting end piece to an interdisciplinary volume, characterized by the juxtaposition of different views on space, place, and environment as well as by the common assumption that space is a cultural construction and that liminality is one of the main categories of our contemporary spatial experience.

Bibliography

Appadurai, Arjun. *Modernity at Large. Cultural Dimensions of Globalization.* Minneapolis: U of Minnesota P, 1996.

Banham, Reyner, *Los Angeles. The Architecture of Four Ecologies.* London: Allen Lane, 1971.

Beckmann, John. Ed. *The Virtual Dimension. Architecture, Representation, and Crash Culture.* New York: Princeton Architectural Press, 1998.

Casey, Edward S. "How To Get From Space to Place In A Fairly Short Stretch Of Time." *Senses of Place*. Eds. Steven Feld and Keith H. Basso. Santa Fe: School of American Research Press, 1996: 13-52.

Foucault, Michel. "Other Spaces." *Diacritics* 16.1 (1986): 22-27.

Harvey, David. *Justice, Nature, & the Geography of Difference*. Oxford: Blackwell, 1996.

Hönnighausen, Lothar. "*Regions and Regionalism*: Are They Still Relevant Terms in the Global Age?" *Regional Images and Regional Realities*. Ed. Lothar Hönnighausen. Tübingen: Stauffenburg, 2000: 283-30.

Hönnighausen, Lothar, Marc Frey, Anke Ortlepp, James L. Peacock, and Nikolaus Steiner. Eds. *Regionalism in the Age of Globalism*. Vol. I. *Concepts of Regionalism*, Vol. II. *Forms of Regionalism*. Madison: U of Wisconsin P, 2004.

Jameson, Frederic. "Postmodernism and Consumer Society." *Modernism and Postmodernism*. Ed. Peter Brooker. London: Longman, 1992: 163-179.

Virilio, Paul. *Open Sky*. London: Verso, 1999.

Theories and Methods

Imaginary Space; or, Space as Aesthetic Object

Winfried Fluck

Although there is an instinct in all of us to assume that space is simply there, a pre-given of our perception of the world, we are, at the same time, quite aware of the fact that all perceptions of space are constructs, so that two viewers may look at the same object, room or landscape and yet see something entirely different. Physically speaking, a room or a landscape consists of an aggregate of physical matter; experientially speaking, it consists of a number of sense impressions. In order to give a meaningful shape, the viewer has to link physical particles and sense impressions by means of an ordering principle, i. e., a principle which provides them with some kind of meaning (if only that of representing a 'chaotic' world). Or, to put it differently: in order to gain cultural meaning, physical space has to become mental space, more precisely, imaginary space. It is, then, highly interesting to consider for a moment what processes take place when physical space is transformed into imaginary space.

The crucial issue here—crucial, I believe, for literary and cultural studies in general—is that of representation, understood in the double sense of the German words *darstellen* and *repräsentieren,* which are often drawn together in the use of the English term *representation.* One familiar claim in critical discussions of the arts is that art should represent reality truthfully or, for a more recent version of this mimetic aesthetics, that it should represent reality in a politically correct way. For an analysis of the literary representation of space, for example, the artistic representation of a particular region, this would imply a comparison of image and reality in order to criticize distortions of reality. But it is also possible to argue that literary or pictorial representations will, by definition, always be distorting, because it is the whole point of their existence to not simply reproduce something that is already there, but to redefine (and thereby recreate) it in the act of representation. Wolfgang Iser therefore calls representation a performative act.[1] This does not mean that we cannot and should not note the romanticizing tendencies in the representation of the American South in a movie like *Gone With the Wind*. It does, however, mean that such a critique should only be the beginning, not the end of our interpretation of the film, for if we merely register its failure to reproduce our current consensus on what the historical South is really like, we fail to deal with the object of interpretation as an aesthetic object. This is only another way of saying that the nature and function of verbal or pictorial representation changes once an object is considered as an aesthetic object.[2]

Properly understood, the term 'aesthetic' describes not a quality of an object, so that some objects, called art, possess this quality and others do not, but a possible function of an object, so that, by taking an aesthetic attitude toward it, any object— or, for that matter, any space, i.e. a building, dress or landscape—can become an aesthetic object. This redefinition as aesthetic object changes the object's function: we do not look at it any longer in terms of its referential representativeness, but regard it as a form of representation that has the freedom to redefine and transform reality or even to invent it anew.

To the best of my knowledge, it was the American pragmatist John Dewey in his book *Art as Experience,* published in 1933, who first replaced the concept of the aesthetic as an inherent quality of an object with the idea of the aesthetic as a potential function of an object. Interestingly, Dewey makes his point in the description of a spatial object when he describes possible views from a ferry on which commuters approach the Manhattan skyline,

---

[1] See Iser's essay "Representation: A Performative Act" (1989).
[2] By introducing the term 'aesthetic' at this point, I do not intend to evoke a traditional view of the aesthetic as a philosophy of art or of the beautiful. Such a traditional understanding of aesthetics is, at least partly, to blame for the fact that contemporary critics often resort to explicitly or implicitly mimetic models of interpretation because they think that this is the only way in which the object can be assigned some political or social relevance.

Some men regard it as simply a journey to get them where they want to be—a means to be endured. So, perhaps, they read a newspaper. One who is idle may glance at this and that building identifying it as the Metropolitan Tower, the Chrysler Building, the Empire State Building, and so on. Another, impatient to arrive, may be on the lookout for landmarks by which to judge progress toward his destination. Still another, who is taking the journey for the first time, looks eagerly but is bewildered by the multiplicity of objects spread out to view. He *sees* neither the whole nor the parts; he is like a layman who goes into an unfamiliar factory where many machines are plying. Another person, interested in real estate, may see, in looking at the skyline, evidence in the height of buildings, of the value of land. Or he may let his thoughts roam to the congestion of a great industrial and commercial center. He may go on to think of the planlessness of arrangement as evidence of the chaos of a society organized on the basis of conflict rather than cooperation. Finally the scene formed by the buildings may be looked at as colored and lighted volumes in relation to one another, to the sky and to the river. He is now seeing esthetically, as a painter might see. (140)

The problem with Dewey's—in a way remarkably advanced redefinition of the aesthetic—is that it is still based on a latent organicism. We only see aesthetically when we overcome heterogeneity and link our sense impressions in such a way that we have an experience of wholeness.[3] The Czech structuralist Jan Mukařovský, who developed his concept of aesthetic function at approximately the same time as Dewey, goes one step further and provides an even more radical extension of the idea of aesthetic function. Again, the case is made with reference to spatial objects. In an essay entitled "On the Problems of Functions in Architecture," Mukařovský argues, for example, that

> there is no object that could not become the carrier of an aesthetic function, just as, on the other side, there is no object which inevitably has to be its carrier. Even where objects are created primarily with the purpose of achieving an aesthetic effect,

---

[3] For a more detailed discussion of Dewey's aesthetics see my essay "John Deweys Ästhetik und die Literaturtheorie der Gegenwart" or my summary of the discussion in "Pragmatism and Aesthetic Experience" (Fluck, 1999).

the object may completely lose this dimension in another time, space or social context. (1983, 224, my translation)[4]

We can, in principle, look at any object of perception or experience as an aesthetic object. As Mukařovský claims: "The aesthetic is neither the property of an object, nor is it tied to particular qualities of the object" (1966, 29, my translation).

In an even more radical manner than Dewey for whom aesthetic experience marks a culminating moment in which fragmented elements of daily experience are successfully reintegrated, the aesthetic, for Mukařovský, is created by a temporary and, possibly, fleeting shift in a hierarchy of functions that is in constant flux so that each of the functions remains present and can, at every moment, regain dominance.[5] Consequently, the aesthetic cannot be defined as a separate sphere or ontologically separate object. Mukařovský's description is almost postmodern in this respect,

> The border lines of the aesthetic realm are thus not firmly drawn in reality. On the contrary, they are highly permeable. [...] In fact, we know from our own personal experience, that the relations between the realm of the aesthetic and the non-aesthetic [...] may shift with age, health or even our current mood. (1966, 14, my translation)

In his essay on architecture, Mukařovský employs images of special plasticity in order to determine the shifting relations between aesthetic function and other functions. He describes the aesthetic function in terms of air and darkness which creep

---

[4] In this essay, Mukařovský argues that wherever other functions, for whatever reasons, are weakened, dropped or changed, the aesthetic function may take their role and become dominant.

[5] Cf. the summary of Mukařovský's position by Williams in the chapter on "Aesthetic and Other Situations" in his book *Marxism and Literature*: "Art is not a special kind of object but one in which the aesthetic function, usually mixed with other functions, is *dominant*. Art, with other things (landscapes and dress, most evidently), gives aesthetic pleasure, but this cannot be transliterated as a sense of beauty or a sense of perceived form, since while these are central in the aesthetic function, they are historically and socially variable and in all real instances concrete. At the same time the aesthetic function is 'not an epiphenomenon of other functions' but a 'code terminant of human reaction to reality'" (153).

into an empty room and fill the spaces that have been vacated by taking away an object or by switching off the light.

Referential and aesthetic dimension thus do not occupy ontologically separate planes. Or, to draw on Mukařovský's argument: as an 'empty' function (in comparison with other functions), the aesthetic function depends on other functions in order to manifest itself. Many forms of recent art such as, for example, pop art, junk art or abject art, therefore declare everyday objects or, increasingly, thoroughly 'profane' objects to be art objects in order to dramatize the redefining power of shifting attitudes that can transform even the 'lowest,' the most vulgar, most trashy or most repulsive materials into aesthetic objects.[6] Similarly, to take a recent example from literature, in Donald Barthelme's experimental postmodern story "The Glass Mountain," the dog shit on the streets of Manhattan, in its subtle color shadings, can take on an almost sublime aesthetic quality.[7]

Taking an aesthetic attitude toward an object thus does not mean or, at least, does not necessarily mean that we disengage the object or ourselves from reality. What exactly does it mean then to take an aesthetic attitude toward something? The concept refers to the capacity of any system of signification to draw attention to itself as a form of expression and to refer to itself as a sign thus foregrounding the organizing and patterning principles of which the object is constituted.[8] For this

---

[6] Rosenberg was one of the first art critics to draw attention to this development. Cf. his description of the movement toward the 'de-aestheticization' of art in the 60s: "Ideally, art *povera* strives to reach beyond art to the wonder-working object, place ('environment'), or event. It extends the Dada-Surrealist quest for the revelatory found object into unlimited categories of strange responses. Redefining art as the process of the artist or his materials, it dissolves all limitations on the kind of substances out of which art can be constructed. Anything—breakfast, food, a frozen lake, film footage—is art, either as is or tampered with, through being chosen as fetish" (37). As Rosenberg indicates, de-aestheticization paves the way for re-aestheticization. It does not do away with aesthetics, it paves the way for a new aesthetics.

[7] I am referring to fragment No. 30 of Barthelme's description of New York: "The sidewalks were full of dogshit in brilliant colors: ocher, umber, Mars yellow, sienna, viridian, ivory black, rose madder" (*City Life*, 68).

[8] In his essay "Die Bedeutung der Ästhetik" ("The Importance of Aesthetics"), reprinted in the collection *Kunst, Poetik, Semiotik* Mukařovský provides the example of gymnastics. As long as our perception of physical exercise is dominated by practical functions (gaining strength, strengthening certain muscles etc.), we will focus on aspects which are helpful for achieving those goals and will judge the single exercise in relation to how well it helps to realize the desired result. Once the aesthetic function becomes dominant, on the other hand, the exercise takes

purpose, the object is temporarily depragmatized and dereferentialized. We no longer insist that reality is truthfully represented because it is only in this way that we can concentrate on other aspects and possible functions of the object. In this sense, the aesthetic function can be seen as an "experimental and experiential epistemology" (Peper, 296). At the same time, the dominance of the aesthetic function does not mean that the reference of the object is cancelled. On the contrary, the new perspective on the object can only be experienced in its various possibilities of revelation, criticism, intensification of experience or pleasure as long as the reference is kept in view so that we are constantly moving back and forth between the newly created world and the reference which has served as a point of departure for this reinterpretation.[9]

In principle, I said, any object can become an aesthetic object if an aesthetic attitude is taken toward it and its aesthetic function becomes dominant. However, this shift to an aesthetic attitude can be encouraged by the object, however, by suggesting to us that we should take such an attitude. This is especially obvious in the case of fictional texts (in the broadest sense of the word as any form of 'invented' representation, including, e.g. literature, paintings or film). Once we classify a representation as fictional, we can no longer regard the object as predominantly referential. Rather, we have to create the object anew mentally. Since we have never met a character named Huckleberry Finn and do, in fact, know that he never existed, we must come up with our own mental representation of him. Inevitably, we have to invest our own emotions, draw on our own associations and create our own mental pictures in order to imagine a character like Huck Finn and make him come alive so that we can become interested in his fate. These imaginary additions can only

---

on interest in itself as a performance or spectacle. The various movements, the sequence of movements, and even the 'useless' details of the periods between different exercises may now become the focus of attention for their own sake. The significatory dimension of reality is foregrounded and the sign is of interest *sui generis*. Even the 'wrong' movements may now be of interest as movements with a logic of their own, not just as 'wrong' movements.

[9] Peper thus states that "aesthetic effects can only unfold against and into the non-aesthetic. [...] The aesthetic pleasure in the free play of cognitive powers is most intense where—far from empty arbitrariness—it has to be gained within a given conceptual structure, making us aware of this level of cognition as the reflexive play of forces" (1966, 314-15).

acquire a *gestalt*, however, if they are connected with discourses of the real.[10] As Wolfgang Iser has argued, a fictional text comes into existence as a combination between the real and the imaginary: on the one hand, the imaginary, defined by Iser in a phenomenological sense as a set of diffuse, formless, fleeting moods, feelings and images without clear object reference, needs a discourse of the real in order to manifest itself in a perceptible form, on the other hand, the discourse of the real requires imaginary elements in order to be more than the mere replication of something that already exists.[11]

Fictional forms of representation, including the representation of space, bring an object into our world; but these fictional forms are not identical with that object. They create an object that is never stable and identical to itself. Fictional representation is thus, to draw on Iser again, a performative mode: "Representation can only unfold itself in the recipient's mind, and it is through his active imaginings alone that the intangible can become an image." (1989, 243) This means that in order for a representation to acquire cultural meaning, a transfer has to take place. This transfer is intensified by fictional representations. As Iser puts it:

> In this respect the required activity of the recipient resembles that of an actor, who in order to perform his role must use his thoughts, his feelings, and even his body as an analogue for representing something he is not. In order to produce the determinate form of an unreal character, the actor must allow his own reality to fade out. At the same time, however, he does not know precisely who, say, Hamlet is, for one cannot properly identify a character who has never existed. Thus role-playing endows a figment with a sense of reality in spite of its impenetrability which defies total de-

---

[10] Cf. Brownstein's description of the doubleness of a novel heroine: "In one sense this doubleness of a novel heroine is perfectly obvious. Every good reader recognizes a heroine as a representation of an actual woman and, at the same time, as an element in a work of art. She does not regard a woman in a novel as if she were one of her acquaintances; she experiences how the context of the fiction limits a character's freedom and determines her style. [...] The reader identifies with Elizabeth, and as she does so accepts the rules involved in being Elizabeth, and at the same time she sees how the rules determine that Elizabeth be as she is—not merely the rules of the society Jane Austen's novel represents, but also the rules that govern the representation of it, the novel" (xxiii).

[11] For a short, succinct summary of his argument see Iser's essay "Fictionalizing Acts." (Iser, 1986).

termination. [...] Staging oneself as someone else is a source of aesthetic pleasure; it is also the means whereby representation is transferred from text to reader. (1989, 244)

Iser's description of fictional texts as a mode of representation that only comes into existence by means of a transfer may appear plausible as far as fictitious characters are concerned. But does it also apply to the representation of space? One could argue that, in contrast to character, space in fiction often functions as discourse of the real designed to provide a context of plausibility or authenticity to an imaginary character. However, we are, firstly, concerned here with instances in which space becomes a central source of meaning and aesthetic effect, and secondly, Iser's argument is not based on the possibility of recognition of an object, that is, on its reality effect. It refers to the mental processes that are necessary to translate abstract letters on a given page into an imagined world. This, in fact, is one of the problems of his approach; in the way he presents the argument it only appears to work with literature so that pictorial representations of space would not seem to qualify.

As I have tried to show so far, aesthetic experience is constituted by a transfer between an aesthetic object (constituted as such by our taking a specific attitude toward it) and the recipient. This transfer can become the basis for the articulation of otherwise inexpressible dimensions of the self. However, can this mode of explanation also be applied to our perception and experience of an image, such as, for example, the pictorial representation of space? It is at this point that we have to distinguish between two forms of images: mental constructs, for example of the literary character Huckleberry Finn, and pictures. Obviously, the image as mental construct forms an important part of aesthetic experience because it plays a crucial role in the actualization of the literary text. The image as picture, on the other hand, seems to work exactly against such engagement because it replaces mental activity by optical perception. Iser himself points out in *The Act of Reading:*

The image, then, is basic to ideation. It relates to the nongiven or to the absent, endowing it with presence. [...] This strange quality of the image becomes apparent when, for instance, one sees the film version of a novel one has read. Here we have optical perception which takes place against the background of our own remembered images. As often as not, the spontaneous reaction is one of disappointment, because the characters somehow fail to live up to the image we had created of them while reading. However much this image may vary from individual to individual, the reaction: 'That's not how I imagined him' is a general one and reflects the special nature of the image. The difference between the two types of picture is that the film is optical and presents a given object, whereas the imagination remains unfettered (in reading). Objects, unlike imaginings, are highly determinate, and it is this determinacy which makes us feel disappointed. (137-138)

Iser's contrast of an indeterminate form of literary representation and the determinacy of a picture or visual object appears immediately plausible insofar as, in the perception of a painting or a film, the picture precedes mental and meaning construction. Before we can construct a mental picture we have already seen the image we are supposed to construct. But what do we actually see when we look at pictures? Gestalt theory and, more recently, constructivism have rejected naive empiricist notions of perception as the mere registering of sense impressions. In order to make any sense of what we see, in effect, in order to register an object as an object, our perception must have a focus that gives structure and meaning to the object. Landscape painting provides an obvious case in point. Not every piece of nature is a landscape. On the contrary, in order to qualify as landscape, certain iconographic and cultural object criteria have to be met. In other words, we do not first register and then interpret what we see. Quite on the contrary, we already interpret what we see in the act of registering it.

There are differing theories of what provides this structure of interpretation. In traditional versions, schemata help us order a bewildering array of sense impressions, so that what we are transferring to the image is a set of culturally inherited cognitive structures that successfully affirms their functionality. As David Bordwell puts it: "To recognize an object or event is to possess a schema for it and to have a procedure for judging it as a member of some class" (146). However, theories of cognition and image comprehension can only explain why pictures are intelligible, not why they might be experienced as meaningful or provide an aesthetic experience. To be sure, picture comprehension depends on the recognition of the iconic dimension of the sign, but recognition is not yet the same as "making meaning," as Bordwell claims, and it is certainly not identical with aesthetic experience. Moreover, as Vivian Sobchak points out, vision is meaningless "if we regard it only in its objective modality as visibility." (290) We must acknowledge subjective experience and the invisible as part of our vision—that part which does not "appear" to us, "but which grounds vision and gives the visible within it a substantial thickness and dimension." (290) In making her point, Sobchak, too, draws on a spatial example:

> The back of the lamp is not absent. Rather, it is invisible. It exists in vision as that which cannot be presently seen but is yet available for seeing presently. It exists in vision as an *excess* of visibility. [...] The most forcefully felt 'presence' of such invisibility in vision is, at one pole, the unseen world, the *off-screen space*, from which embodied vision prospects its sights' and, at the other pole, [...] the *off-screen subject*, who enacts sight', revises vision, and perspectivally frames its work as a visible image. (292)

Vision thus emerges in an interplay between the visible and the invisible:

> The visible extends itself into the visibly 'absent' but existentially and experientially 'present.' And the invisible gives dimension to the visibly 'present,' thickening the seen with the world and the body-subject's *exorbitance*. The visible, then, does not reveal everything to perception. (294-295)

This doubleness of perception is intensified in the perception of objects that we classify as aesthetic objects because these objects invite us to emphasize their non-identity as representation and to reconstruct them anew mentally as objects, much in the same way that we have to construct literary characters like Hamlet or Huckleberry Finn in order to constitute them as objects of aesthetic experience. This description of the act of seeing may appear counterintuitive at first (in contrast to the act of reading or the attendance of a play). How is it possible to say that we have to construct an object in order to give it reality although we see the object represented right before our very eyes? The analogy to Iser's example of the actor may be of help here. The picture becomes the equivalent of the actor of Iser's example whom we also see before our very eyes, whom we recognize, in many instances, as a familiar character easily to be identified as a type, but whom we really do not know, so that the typical or familiar aspects of classification only become props for triggering and feeding our own mental and imaginary activities.

Both, literary and pictorial representations of space thus create not only a mental but an imaginary space; even where this representation may appear life-like, truthful or authentic, its actual status is that of an aesthetic object that invites, in effect necessitates, a transfer by the spectator in order to provide meaning and create an aesthetic experience. Inscribed into the reception of a narrative or a picture is always a second narrative or a second picture, that of the reader or spectator. This, in turn, raises the interesting question as to whether we can say a bit more about the nature of the transfer that takes place between aesthetic object and recipient. For what purposes can the fictional representation of space be used by the recipient? Or, to put it differently and more specifically, what is the usefulness of imaginary space for a reader or spectator? Why does it engage us, interest us, or even provide an aesthetic experience at times, although we do know quite well that it is "invented"?

The crucial question arising at this point is what the recipient brings to the transfer that constitutes aesthetic experience. Is this transfer generated by the articulation of "internal otherness" which is then projected into "the other," as critics such as Gabriele Schwab suggest who have tried to redefine Iser's concept of transfer as psychological transference in order to give Iser's reader an emotional and psychic dimension?[12] Schwab's "internal otherness" remains a very broad concept designed to characterize the psychological structure of a whole group, nation or period; hence, it cannot explain the fact that responses to fictional texts are so varied and multi-faceted. In contrast, I have suggested to speak of a second narrative or a second image that is inscribed into the aesthetic object in the act of constituting it. This second narrative or image is both similar to, and different from, the representation by which it is generated. It is similar because it is based on a semblance between the text and the imaginary needs of the recipient; it is different because the emotion invested can have entirely different sources and can be causally unrelated to the representation itself. This is the only possible explanation for the fact that a narrative or an image which deals with issues far removed in time and thus may no longer have the same daring, explosive connotation which it might once have had, can nevertheless still fascinate and engage present-day audiences.

Why does the representation of the South in a movie like *Gone With the Wind* still have such amazing appeal today? The film's viewers have never met Scarlett O'Hara; in effect, most are, I hope, aware of the fact that she never existed. Moreover, most contemporary viewers may know little and care very little about the historical South and its regional identity. But, ironically enough, this is exactly the point and the actual source of usefulness for the film's viewer. For in order to make the fictional representation come alive, a transfer has to take place in which the viewer invests her or his own emotions, for example, by attaching strong affects such as the experience of social humiliation, or a trauma of loss, to the film. We have, in fact, a recent example of this: the temporary identification of some East Germans with the fate of the American South right after German unification when historical phenomena like the carpetbagger or the myth of a lost cause appeared as plausible formulas to explain present-day developments. Although the feudal social structure of the Old South and the socialist doctrine of the GDR are obviously miles apart, the representation of the Old South in *Gone With the Wind* could thus

---

[12] See Schwab's book *The Mirror and the Killer Queen. Otherness in Literary Language* and my discussion of her argument in "Pragmatism and Aesthetic Experience."

function as host for the articulation of feelings of loss and historical defeat. This means that the aesthetic object, including the representation of space, is of interest exactly for what it does not represent but what, on the other hand, it permits to articulate. Or, to relate this insight to the issue of imaginary space: paradoxically, its major appeal rests not on what is visible but exactly on what is not visible. In both cases, the whole point of representation is to articulate something which cannot be represented itself and therefore must find a host. Visual texts are wonderfully effective in mobilizing individual affects and, at the same time, in hiding them behind the immediate experience and sensuous impact of representation.

The immensely popular paintings of Edward Hopper can serve as an illustration of this point. Whenever critics or students try to explain their amazing appeal, they describe a world of alienation, melancholy or isolation, presented in paintings in which isolated human beings are often placed in wide empty spaces and the viewer is placed in front of enigmatic surfaces. But why should the depiction of alienation or isolation have such a strong appeal that copies of these paintings have become almost ubiquitous so that we find them not only in bars and cafés but also on calendars, postcards, in dentists' offices, university offices, and in government buildings in Berlin and Bonn? The only possible explanation is that these paintings are not taken literally. A thematic interpretation will fall short of a convincing explanation of their appeal. This appeal is related to spaces or, more precisely, to the empty spaces of Hopper's pictures because it is these empty surfaces in their often colorful barrenness that are ideally designed to function as a host for aestheticized emotions or moods.[13]

In a way, my argument may appear bleak. Space in fictional representation, I have claimed, is actually imaginary space. Imaginary space is space that expresses something which is hidden. Aesthetic objects function as hosts for something that is articulated but remains invisible. The reception and experience of aesthetic ob-

---

[13] The phenomenon that space can represent something that is not visible is effectively illustrated in Preminger's film noir *Laura* (1944) where the main character, who is trying to solve the riddle of the mysterious disappearance of the beautiful Laura, moves through her rooms and uses the objects he sees as props for the imaginary construction of an image with which he falls in love.

jects appears to be an entirely subjective matter then about which, it seems, we can hardly speak. However, the hosting of the imaginary in fictional texts or aesthetic objects works both ways. In attaching emotions and moods to other objects—and thus making them in a way 'invisible'—one may hide one's own imaginary longings. But by finding a way to articulate them, we also begin to socialize them. Furthermore, by accepting a cultural representation as host, we are not only socializing these imaginary longings but also transforming them into something that makes communication and at least partial understanding possible. This is, in fact, the reason why cultures, in the words of Kenneth Burke, are endless conversations. Space is not just an *a priori* requisite of these conversations. As imaginary space, it is also one of its driving forces. We are constantly in search of objects that can function as hosts, and space, apart from its many other functions, can be such a host. In effect, one may argue that, for a number of reasons, its importance as host is constantly increasing.

In his seminal study *Bewusstseinslagen des Erzählens und Erzählte Wirklichkeiten,* as well as in subsequent elaborations of his theory of the dehierarchizing thrust of Western cultural history, Jürgen Peper has provided an outline of this gradual liberation of space and time from moral, social and other contexts in which they are still subordinated to more comprehensive goals of representation. In their focus on the wide, empty spaces of nature, romantic philosophy and literature liberate space from typological meaning or from the illustration of universal laws of creation and transform it into a realm of individual revelation. Space begins to take on a subjective dimension. At the turn of the century, impressionism's representation of space as primarily an effect of sense impression radicalizes this 'subjectivation' of space ushered in by romanticism. While nature in romanticism can become an aesthetic object only as a unified *gestalt* (called landscape), single impressions of space are now foregrounded in order to draw attention to themselves as constituents of sensuous experiences. And the more radical the fragmentation and desemanticization of time and space has become in modern and postmodern culture, the stronger the tendency to cut representations of space off from any semantic reference. In effect, this accelerating logic of liberation (*Verselbständigung*) has by now gone beyond space as a self-contained entity of representation and has proceeded to dissolve this entity into single components such as line, color, shape, and, finally, mere canvas in order to foreground the potential of these components to become aesthetic objects in themselves. Starting with Abstract Expressionism, contemporary painting has constantly reminded us again and again that we do not need characters or even faces to initiate the kind of transfer that makes aesthetic experience possible. Space, including empty space, can do the job as well, and, for certain purposes, even better.

Bibliography

Barthelme, Donald. "The Glass Mountain." *City Life*. New York: Pocket Books, 1976. 67-74.
Bordwell, David. *Making Meaning. Inference and Rhetoric in the Interpretation of Cinema*. Cambridge, MA.: Harvard UP, 1989.
Brownstein, Rachel M. *Becoming a Heroine. Reading about Women in Novels*. New York: Penguin, 1982.
Dewey, John. *Art as Experience. The Later Works, 1925-1953*. 1934. Volume 10. Carbondale: Southern Illinois Press, 1987.
Fluck, Winfried. "Pragmatism and Aesthetic Experience." *REAL. Yearbook of Research in English and American Literature* 15 (1999): 227-42.
---. "John Deweys Ästhetik und die Literaturtheorie der Gegenwart." *Philosophie der Demokratie. Beiträge zum Werk von John Dewey*. Ed. Hans Joas. Frankfurt a.M.: Suhrkamp, 2000. 160-93.
Iser, Wolfgang. *The Act of Reading. A Theory of Aesthetic Response*. Baltimore: Johns Hopkins UP, 1978.
---."Representation: A Performative Act." *Prospecting: From Reader Response to Literary Anthropology*. Baltimore: Johns Hopkins UP, 1989. 236-48.
---. "Fictionalizing Acts." *Amerikastudien / American Studies* 31 (1986): 5-15.
Mukařovský, Jan. "Die Bedeutung der Ästhetik. Kunst, Poetik, Semiotik." Frankfurt a.M: Suhrkamp, 1989.
---. *Kapitel aus der Ästhetik*. Frankfurt a. M.: Suhrkamp, 1966.

---. "Zum Problem der Funktionen in der Architektur." *Zeitschrift für Semiotik* 5 (1983): 217-28.

Peper, Jürgen. *Bewusstseinslagen des Erzählens und Erzählte Wirklichkeiten.* Leiden: Brill, 1966.

---. "The Aesthetic as a Democratizing Principle," *REAL. Yearbook of Research in English and American Literature* 10 (1994): 293-323.

Rosenberg, Harold. *The De-definition of Art. Action Art to Pop to Earthworks.* New York: Horizon Press, 1972.

Schwab, Gabriele. *The Mirror and the Killer-Queen. Otherness in Literary Language.* Bloomington: Indiana UP, 1996.

Sobchak, Vivian. *The Address of the Eye. A Phenomenology of Film Experience.* Princeton: Princeton UP, 1992.

Williams, Raymond. "Aesthetic and other Situations." *Marxism and Literature.* New York: Oxford UP, 1977. 151-57.

'Place' in the Internet Age or, Borges and I

Heide Ziegler

The concept of 'space' is, of course, time-honored; it is fundamental to our everyday experience because our own three-dimensional embodiment and built environment have provided humans with a sense of space for thousands of years. But 'places' provide what can be called 'real' spaces, "appropriate behavioral framing on the basis of patterns of social action and accountability" (Dourish, 25-26). Only places engender a set of patterned social responses. They are, therefore, cultural phenomena. Where they seem to disappear, as in many contemporary third world countries that cannot afford to preserve their heritage under the pressure of a capitalist global market, there is an immense struggle among young intellectuals to learn how to avail themselves of the advantages of the internet in order to participate in new economic opportunities, escape new forms of colonialism (i.e. prescribed social responses), and preserve or transform what is left of their cultural heritage for their own benefit. The means to achieve these goals involve substituting virtual for 'real' places in the hopes of escaping not only social dominance, wielded by others, but also social responsibility. Trusting the internet with defiant optimism, they buoyantly disregard its potential pitfalls.

In this paper I will address one particular aspect related to these cultural and economic issues before I suggest how the idea of cultural 'place' might be resurrected wherever it has been lost through what we might call social navigation of information space. Initially, then, I will concentrate on the changes in *perception* and, consequently, *consciousness* that result from our growing attachment, devotion, even addiction to the internet. I would like to highlight these changes by having recourse to the philosophical fiction of Jorge Luis Borges who, to me, is the unconscious prophet of the internet and its ever more prominent interplay between 'real' and 'constructed' space.

Postmodern philosophers and cultural critics such as William H. Gass and Fredric Jameson have long been telling us that postmodernism is obsessed with space, while modernism was concerned with time. Nonetheless, they do not have the internet in mind when they advance this philosophy. Rather, they would contend that, since the possibilities of *narrative time* seem to have been exhausted in ways impossible to emulate by writers such as James Joyce, Robert Musil, and Marcel Proust—the obvious alternative for the next generation, the *post*-modernists, is the attempt to inhabit *narrative space*. They would further argue that this concept has been influencing our ideas of architectural 'place' as well. But virtual space is different in that it is neither a concept nor a construct. Transmitting the features of narrative space into real 'place' results from a privileging of mind over matter, whereas in virtual space the boundaries between matter and mind are dissolved. Jorge Luis Borges was the true literary prophet of the present internet age because he foresaw that virtual space would come to influence the ways we view the past and the future as nothing but extensions of the present.

Borges was of course neither able to foresee the development of the internet itself, nor predict its intricacies or commercial potential—if for no other reason than that he went blind in 1955. However, prophets tend to be literally blind, and they usually do not predict the future in a pragmatic fashion. Rather, they *warn* against potential developments they sense in a more perceptive and intensive way than others. To support this contention, I shall briefly discuss two aspects of Borges's writings that relate precisely, albeit indirectly, to our present internet experience and the need for *controlled* navigation, especially controlled *social* navigation of information space: first, the loss of 'real' time and the rise of virtuality; second, the new library and the case for cultural memory.

1. The loss of 'real' time and the rise of virtuality

Dreams are the single most potent influence on Borges's fictional heroes, and these dreams are intertwined most intricately with reality. Indeed, they seem to make reality happen. In the story "The Circular Ruins" (*Las ruinas circulares*) the hero manages to dream his own son into existence. In "The Immortal" (*El Immortal*) the narrator utters the astounding sentence: "We accept reality easily, because we intuit that nothing is real" (*Labyrinths*, 113). But do the dreams in Borges's fiction also foreshadow virtuality as we know it from the internet: a state of being that is neither real nor unreal when compared to our 'normal' human experience?

A closer look at one of Borges's stories might be revealing. In "The Secret Miracle" (*El milagro secreto*), the hero is one Jaromir Hladik of Prague, a writer, translator, poet, and dramatist. When the Germans invade Prague on March 14, 1943, Hladik is denounced as a Jew and sentenced to death by a firing squad. The execution is to take place two weeks later. Before his death, Hladik asks God in a dream to grant him one more year to finish his drama in verse, *The Enemies*. His wish is fulfilled because God works a secret miracle for him. German bullets kill him at the appointed hour, but in his mind a year goes by between the order to fire and the actual firing. During that year, he finishes the play in his mind. While he is working on *The Enemies*, nothing in the courtyard changes. The world continues motionless and mute. Over time, Hladik comes to feel affection for the courtyard and the soldiers who are about to kill him. One soldier's face even modifies his conception of his drama's hero. Unhurried and undistracted, he is able to complete his mental task.

For our argument it is not necessary to consider whether God 'really' granted Jaromir Hladik an additional year of life or if the moment before his death simply appeared to him like a full year. The question is, rather, whether the unchanging appearance of the courtyard is the necessary prerequisite for the expansion of Hladik's life span or not. The raindrop that falls on his cheek before the volley hits him, and only slides down his cheek when he finds the last phrase for his play, proves that the time granted to Hladik is time out of time and not mechanical time. As the coordinate of real space, mechanical time would have caused things around him to change while the raindrop slides down. The detail is important because it substantiates the hypothesis that the prerequisite for successful virtuality is the mutation of 'space' into an imaginary 'place' which can be evaluated irrespective of the passing of time.

At the end of 1971, a software engineer in Cambridge, Massachusetts, Ray Tomlinson, invented the first e-mail program in the world. He sent a self-addressed message from one computer to another computer in the same room, unaware that he was creating a technique that would revolutionize communication as much as the invention of the telephone or the fax (cf. Zimmer, 133-4). All he seemed to do was send a message electronically that would normally have gone by letter. At best, his invention seemed to make that message faster and, on a larger scale, independent of postal service irregularities in any of various countries around the world. Still, this seemingly insignificant act was the beginning of a change in our perception of what a letter is. As God's gift in Borges's story, this change was due to the irrelevance of 'place' as a decisive factor. E-mails seem to lose their 'real' character insofar as they are not written or printed on paper, put in an envelope, and sent by mail to a recipient who has to open the envelope before he can read the letter. Instead, e-mails acquire an increasing degree of virtuality because they reach any destination in the world without any recognizable amount of mechanical time. They can be deleted without any material trace and they can be multiplied with little effort and without additional expense.

The mental consequences of successful virtuality are stupendous, and today's e-mail can serve as a good example. To begin with, e-mail has changed the private character of the letter even if its immateriality seems to prove the opposite. When we send a private e-mail addressed to only one person, we must be aware that it can be intercepted at any time. It is not impenetrable by third persons. The interceptor does not have to be as threatening a power as the United States National Security Agency (NSA), which is reported to check every message sent to the US. He or she might just as well be the systems administrator of the organization where our computer is set up. Of course letters can also be intercepted, and they have been 'purloined' and opened in the past—even deciphered when written in cryptogram. However, such acts could not be committed anonymously or randomly. They were willful breaches of privacy on the part of the perpetrator. This has changed with e-mail and consequently we ourselves have lost a sense of privacy, of intimate communication. We no longer send a *letter*, we send *messages*, and we often copy these messages, openly or tacitly, to colleagues, secretaries, or to anyone who we think might be interested in their content. Paradoxically, this seems to happen because the content of the messages somehow remains within the domain of our own mind. It does not appear to become the property of the addressee, and therefore does not become quite 'real' for the simple reason that we can no longer imagine the form of passage between sender and receiver. Thus, we act as if we were dealing with nothing but the random associations of our *own* mind, which under social aspects can indeed be considered virtual rather than real.

Does this improbable state of our mind cause a loss of identity or, on the contrary, its expansion, as in the case of Jaromir Hladik? The impossible answer is, both. Via e-mail we can connect almost immediately with anybody who happens to sit in front of a computer with internet access, anywhere on the globe, and we can get a response just as quickly. The situation resembles talking to one another without 'really' talking to our partner and without having to take the other into account as a person. Thus, we both increase and diminish our sense of identity. Our communication gains in scope, swiftness, and immediacy, but it loses in 'humanness' if being human means, among other things, to allow for the other to impinge on our time and space, as in any 'real' encounter. Jaromir Hladik, although fully aware that he lived only vicariously—that others were *not* aware of his life of the mind—nevertheless took those others into account. He even grew fond of them. He knew that he was privileged, and he knew the length of the time span that God had granted him. With the gift of a year's time came the ability to use it to the utmost and to gain in 'humanness.' We lose this ability with e-mail because in the virtual world we can no longer measure time.

But what about the intuitive need to define a 'place' for ourselves in order to enable us to think of ourselves at least as separate identities? What about the need of a room of our own, that unchanging 'place' which I have argued is the very prerequisite for virtuality? With the internet that place would be comparable to Jaromir Hladik's courtyard. All we seem to need is a desk and a computer in order to work, relax, and communicate. 'Desktop' is an appropriate name for our new 'place.' This place is not imaginary: we can buy and sell via the internet, we can look at jewelry or houses we might want to buy, and by using CAD, we can theoretically even walk around in those houses and decide whether we like them or not. It is a place of the mind entered by a person who is real. For the users of the internet the borderlines between matter and mind are increasingly beginning to blur—as in Borges's fictional dreams.

2. The library of the future and the case for cultural memory

It seems, therefore, that our sense of the *individuum*, that which cannot be divided, is strangely endangered by the rise of the internet. The past two decades have seen an increase in autobiographical texts that appears to have no parallel in the past. It is probably not wrong to infer that the need to share one's personal memory is on the rise as we increasingly lose our sense of individuality in the present. Still, the sheer number of autobiographies on the market ironically defies their purpose: to privilege the author to the point where he or she is remembered before others. Perhaps, what we need is, rather, a substantiation of our individual memory by a shared cultural memory, a memory that could expand to include other cultural traditions apart from the European heritage. Where would one be able to find and share the tangible assets of such a collective cultural memory?

One of the best-known stories by Jorge Luis Borges is called "The Library of Babel" (*La Biblioteca de Babel*) —in which he likens the library to the universe:

> The universe (which others call the Library) comprises an indefinite and perhaps infinite number of hexagonal galleries, with vast airshafts between, surrounded by very low railings. From any of the hexagons one can see, interminably, the upper and lower floors. The distribution of the galleries is invariable. (*Labyrinths*, 51)

In 1955, the year Borges went blind, he was offered the post of Director of the National Library of Buenos Aires. When that vast library finally became 'his,' he could no longer experience it as a real place, but only as virtual space. Hence, the structural regularity and seeming endlessness of the system and holdings of the library of Babel: the library expands to become the universe because its boundaries can no longer be recognized. It is regular in every respect because it is only thus that someone who is blind can control it. One could argue of course that "The Library of Babel" was written as early as 1941 and that books as well as libraries had been a reality for Borges throughout his life. Still, the gradual waning of his eyesight may long have foreshadowed the end of the library as he knew it. Some critics feel that Borges wanted to perpetuate the idea of the library in his work because he felt that libraries were disappearing as a cultural entity (Schlaffer, 72), but to me it seems much more likely that he became increasingly adept at imagining a library of the future where catalogues, encyclopedias, and dictionaries would constantly gain in importance and where the relevance of the contents of books would be more and more replaced by information about them. Of the vast number of books in the Library of Babel, there seems to be none that contains an understandable message: hence the name, *Library of Babel*. In spite of rumors to the contrary, the librarian and hero of the story has not been able to find a single sentence in any of the books he has encountered that makes 'real' sense. What he encounters time and again are repetitions of the same sequence of letters, in themselves as meaningless as the digital numbers used to code words in the Internet. Book titles do not seem to relate to contents. They are like a continuous *Online Public Access Catalogue* (OPAC), which restricts the reader to searching for particular book titles, yet cannot divulge the contents behind these titles.

The largest library in the world is the Library of Congress in Washington, followed by the British Library in London, and the Bibliothèque Nationale in Paris. Twelve thousand people visited the Library of Congress daily at the beginning of its electronic era; today more than 700,000 people seek some kind of information there every day. Still, a potential reader may look in vain for a particular title in every online catalogue available. Although this does not necessarily mean that the book does not exist, it is, by all standards, lost to the average reader. Yet it could still be found by a librarian through mere chance—perhaps in one of the huge Russian libraries in Moscow or St. Petersburg that cannot be accessed by online catalogues like the one book in Borges's *Library of Babel* that contains the ultimate meaning of the universe. The ultimate meaning of the universe would then be that which cannot be accessed but only found by mere chance. In other words: the ultimate meaning of the universe cannot be understood because it remains forever outside of every foreseeable context.

However, we tend to think of our age as the information age where all information becomes ultimately available, and we are convinced that if we want to access information, it needs to be stored, for example in libraries. The only way to store the ever-increasing amount of data, however, is electronically—despite the fact that digital media have a relatively brief life span. The number of published books, and especially articles, has not decreased nor is it likely to decrease; therefore traditional means of archiving written material no longer suffice. This, however, involves a problem: when information is no longer stored physically, it becomes fluid, so to speak. The fact that electronic data hardly takes up any storage space, that it can be distributed worldwide via global networks in almost no time, and that it can be changed and rewritten at any point in time is one of its major attractions, but also detracts from the relative importance of any one document—Zimmer states that the average life span of a document on the World Wide Web today is 44 to 70 days (12). Content, in other words, is continually lost, while the amount of information about various contents—such as the number of titles of books without contents in Borges's Library of Babel—grows exponentially. The future library will therefore be a dynamic interface between content and information stored and archived in different forms: digital and on paper, fleeting and permanent. But can it then still be a repository for the cultural memory of even one people, the cultural memory that results from storing and archiving the symbols of the relationship between individual memory and the manifold symbolic forms of its environment—

texts, buildings, pictures, and rituals, dances, meals, and street names—symbolic forms that remind us of our past (cf. Groß, 32)?

The information age is also the age of the death of information. When in 47 BC the library of Alexandria burned and 700,000 papyri were lost, this catastrophe seems to have become part of our cultural memory for all ages to come. Do we know today how many books are lost daily because they were printed on acid paper? Between 70 and 90% of the holdings of German libraries were printed after 1850, the date when acid paper was coming into use. About 12% of those books (24 million volumes) are no longer decipherable, 30% are close to that stage, and 50% will see their demise soon (Zimmer, 169). Although it is possible to save most of these books by de-acidifying them, or by storing their contents on microfilm as in the United States, the sums of money needed to save our written heritage are not available. Dieter E. Zimmer predicts that our cultural memory will soon have the appearance of the brain of an Alzheimer patient (186). Yet our libraries will continue to grow, continuously increasing and simultaneously decreasing the possibilities for a comprehensive cultural memory: increasing in quantity, decreasing in quality, forever diminishing the chance of finding that one book which contains the ultimate meaning of the universe.

This will indeed happen unless we take Borges's concept of a universe composed of an indefinite and perhaps infinite number of hexagonal galleries seriously. Within an infinite number of hexagons, no center or origin can ever be found; it would necessarily have to be defined at random. Yet this might be our big opportunity in the internet age. Infinity as such, to mathematicians, poses no problem and no threat. Within an indefinite or infinite number of hexagons they could easily settle on a point of reference. By inference, the individual who needs a room of his or her own in virtual space could simply define the starting point at which the search for meaning begins. That starting point would be his or her relation to others. From there, true 'social navigation' in the internet could be initiated—randomly, but following a certain strategy. The 'place' one will find as a result of this navigation will, of course, never be anything like places defined by tradition, social environment, family ties, long-standing friendships or shared cultural expectations. It will rather be a *virtual place*, dependent on random connections with people from all over the world who—at least for a short time—simply share a mutual interest. But it will be a 'place' nonetheless, a place from which, if one is fortunate enough, 'meaning' will radiate.

What we need, therefore, are strategies for social navigation of the information space that create humanly relevant cultural 'places.' According to Borges, these cultural places have long been defined. He believes that we need a canon of *texts* in order to possess a shared cultural memory. For Borges these are literary texts, but interestingly enough this is only because he does not share the Romantic belief in the originality of literature. Literature is important to Borges precisely because it is *not* original, because everything has already been said time and again. Therefore a classical canon of literature can help convey relevance to all past, present, and future events. Borges maintains that the texts in question are the *Iliad* and the *Odyssey* and the texts of classical Athens, but what he actually means is the following: since meaning within an ever-expanding universe can only reside in the past, at the very beginning, we have to retrieve, store, and cherish the earliest texts as our only meaningful source of humanity. However, defining a random—or individual—point of reference within our internet environment may serve as an imitation of that 'beginning,' and every beginning is a starting point of interaction. Borges's classical texts were orally transmitted and they preserve a process in written form that, on the internet, needs to be enacted time and again. For Paul Dourish, it is important to recognize "that social navigation is not a sort of technology, but rather is a *phenomenon of interaction*" (31). This becomes apparent when we compare the concepts of 'space' and 'place' with regard to computer supported collaborative settings, and compare how each of these concepts influences individuals and groups:

> Social navigation is built upon the same foundations that motivate a 'place'-centric perspective on collaborative systems, one oriented around 'peopled' spaces and a

sense of 'appropriate behavioural framing' that emerges from the visibility of social conduct within a space. (Dourish, 31)

What emerges from this picture is the internet as a *populated* information space, a space that not only contains information, but also *people* who are acting on that information. These people have to communicate with one another, that is, they have to rely on agreed-upon texts. Texts, especially literary texts, are people-centered, yet storable. What we need is the internet as a valid interface between individual and shared cultural behavior, and the virtual library as a cultural place where we store collective memory. The importance of a people's national history as the basis for their cultural memory will probably give way to a new culture of more ancient and more wide-spread symbolic forms that nevertheless need to be patterned and re-patterned, ciphered and deciphered, archived and remembered—in order to create a common human heritage which can be shared by more and more people around the globe.

Bibliography

Borges, Jorge Luis. *Labyrinths: Selected Stories & Other Writings*. Eds. Donald A. Yates and James E. Irby. New York: Publisher, 1964.

Dourish, Paul. "Where the Footprints Lead: Tracking Down Other Roles for Social Navigation." *Social Navigation of Information Space*. Eds. Alan J. Munro, Kristina Höök and David Benyon. London: Springer, 1999.

Groß, Thomas. "Kultur und Gedächtnis." Interview mit Jan Assmann über Erinnerung, Religion und Politik. *Mannheimer Morgen* (8. Juli 2000): 32.

Schlaffer, Heinz. *Borges*. Frankfurt a. M.: Fischer, 1993.

Zimmer, Dieter E. *Die Bibliothek der Zukunft: Text und Schrift in den Zeiten des Internets*. Hamburg: Hoffmann und Campe, 2000.

Emergent Eco:logics
Cultural and Natural Environments in Recent Theory and Literature

Hanjo Berressem

> We make no distinction between man and nature: the human essence of nature and the natural essence of man become one within nature in the form of production or industry [...] man [...] the eternal custodian of the machines of the universe [...] man and nature are not like two opposite terms confronting each other—not even in the sense of bipolar opposites within a relationship of causation, ideation, or expression (cause and effect, subject and object, etc.); rather they are one and the same essential reality, the producer-product.
>
> Gilles Deleuze and Félix Guattari, *Anti Oedipus*, 4-5

> The occupant [...] rests her arthritic hands upon fabric woven by a Jacquard loom. These hands consist of tendons, tissue, jointed bone. Through quite processes of time and information, threads within the human cells have woven themselves into a woman.
>
> William Gibson and Bruce Sterling, *The Difference Engine*, 7

The term 'emergent eco:logics' in my title should be read within a double reference. On the one hand, it is meant to denote historically the manner in which ecology has emerged as an answer to a vanishing nature, or better, to a nature having always already vanished, and on the other, it is meant to denote an ecology that is informed by the concept of emergence.

Introduction: MetalDuck

In his novel *Mason & Dixon*, Thomas Pynchon introduces, as yet another specimen in a truly extraordinary cast of characters, a mechanical duck that pursues Armand Allégre, who has fled from France to America in the unsuccessful attempt to escape from it and who is now the chef of Mason's and Dixon's party. As he states in desperation, "*It* would seek me out, and remain, with motives too alien for any human ever to know" (369). Perhaps, however, the reasons are not quite so alien as he imagines. Armand, after all, had gained culinary fame in France through his incomparable, and—*nomen est omen*—extremely expensive, duck dishes. The mechanical duck is not so much out to revenge her dead brothers and sisters, however, as she is in blackmailing Armand—of course through the *threat* of revenge—into intervening on her behalf with her creator to engineer a mate. Soon, however, she becomes enamoured with the chef, and thus begins a truly romantic man-machine love-affair.

Pynchon's metal duckmachine is, of course, Jacques Vaucanson's famous duck—"an artificial Duck made of gilded copper which drinks, eats, quacks, splashes about on the water, and digests his food like a living Duck" (Pontus, 21)—who has finally come alive [Fig. 1]. Pynchon, who stated in his article "Is it O.K. to be a Luddite" that the next paradigm shift in human affairs would lie at the nexus where "the curves of research and development in artificial intelligence, molecular biology and robotics all converge" (Pynchon, 1984, 41) and who had staked his hope on the fundamental unpredictability and newness of this convergence—introduces the duck to fold the 18th century world of automata onto the 20th century world of artificial life, nanotechnology and "cell-sized robots" (Stafford, 40).[1] While the tradition of automata extends into the 20th century with R2D2 and C-3PO, artists such as Mark Pauline or the fictional metalrobotics populating William Gibson's *Mona Lisa Overdrive*, the world of cellular automata is telescoped into the 21st century in Gibson's *Idoru*, in which one protagonist, Rei Toei, is a computer program, an artificial lifeform on the verge of autopoiesis. This cybernetic, programmed and hologrammed entity "is not flesh; she is information. She is the tip of an iceberg, no, an Antarctica, of information [...] She was some unthinkable volume of information" (*Idoru*, 178). Her architecture rests on a 'Deleuzian' "array of elaborate constructs that we [her builders] refer to as 'desiring machines'" (178) and "aggregates of subjective desire" (178). In the course of the story, her program-environment becomes increasingly complex. "Rei's only reality is the realm of ongoing serial creation [...] Entirely *process*; infinitely more than the combined sum of her various selves. The platforms [her holographic images] sink beneath her, one after another, as she grows denser and more complex" (202). Although some people still accuse her of being a-corporeal—"You synthetic bitch [...] You aren't real! You aren't as real as this imitation of a drowned city! You're a made-up thing" (233)—she is already on the threshold where 'the code starts to dream.' As she says about dreaming, "I cannot see the faces in clouds [her metaphor of dreaming], but Kuwayama-san tells me that one day I will. It is a matter of plectics" (237). As another protagonist realizes, she might well be the first true artificial intelligence—as well as artificial life form—, which might come, as Pynchon had implied in "Is it O.K. to be a Luddite?" as something unsuspected and chaotic. As Laney, one of Gibson's protagonists states,

> All he knew about artificial intelligence came from work he'd done on a Slitscan episode [...] but he knew that true AI as assumed never to have been achieved, and that current attempts to achieve it were supposed to be in directions quite opposite the creation of software that was good as acting like beautiful young women. If there were going to be genuine AI, the argument ran, it was most likely to evolve in ways that had least to do with pretending to be human. Laney remembered screening a lecture in which the Slitscan episode's subject had suggested that AI might be created accidentally, and that people might not initially recognize it for what it was. (*Idoru*, 247-248)

---

[1] See also Baudrillard's discussion of the difference between automaton and robot in *Simulations*.

In fact, the new, convergent space between man and information-machine that Gibson imagines is ruled over precisely by the laws of chaos and complexity. As Laney sees it, Rez' data-image began

> as something very minor, the first hints of his career. And growing, as it progressed, to something braided, multistranded. ... But then it began to get smaller again, Laney saw, the strands loosening. ... The idoru's data [...] began as something smoothly formed, deliberate, but lacking complexity [the program is as yet dead]. But at the points where it has swerved closest to Rez's data, he saw that it had begun to acquire a sort of complexity. Or randomness, he thought. The human thing [the program is on the threshold of artificial life]. (*Idoru*, 251)

But back to Vaucanson's duck: The difference between the 18th and the 20th century has to do with what is so new and different about Pynchon's duck. Vaucanson had "provided his Automaton a Digestionary Process" (*M&D,* 372). He had thus created, as another character states in a less scientific manner, a "mechanical Duck that shits" (372). Although it was later discovered that Vaucanson had cheated, because "the grain input and the excrement output were totally unrelated, the food went into a box at the base of the duck's throat, and the tail end was separately loaded [...] In its partial fraudulence, the Duck dramatized it's author's assumption of the limits of mechanization, even as it depicted the traversing of these limits. Vaucanson assumed digestion, which he took to be chemical and utterly organic, to be out of bounds" (Riskin, 47). The introduction of true digestion into a machine would be the first step from the mechanical to the living: "that strange Metamorphosis, which has sent it out the Gates of the Inanimate, and off upon its present Journey into the given World" (*M&D,* 372). The shift to truly artificial life, however, occurs when Vaucanson turns the bird—and this is Pynchon's addition—into a sexual:ized machine: "Vaucanson's vainglorious Intent had been to repeat for Sex and Reproduction, the Miracles he'd already achiev'd for Digestion and Excretion" (*M&D,* 373). Through the addition of this "erotick Machinery" (373) the duck reaches "some Threshold of self-Intricacy, setting off this Explosion of Change, from Inertia to *Independence, and Power*" (373). In other words, it crosses the threshold from inanimate to animate, the threshold where machinespace turns into biospace and what Vareli and Maturana call heteropoiesis turns into autopoiesis. As the duck herself states, Vaucanson has indeed attempted to "produce Venus from a Machine" (668); a quite unlikely cyborg goddess.

On this background, it is not such a surprise that in his book about the emerging science of artificial—"self-organizing" (5) or "emergent" (14)—life, Claus Emmeche should mention Vaucanson's duck to set off the science of artificial life (which emerged from the earlier science of artificial intelligence) from the 'romantic' automatic science in the wake of Julien Offray de La Mettrie that had fascinated E.A Poe and E.T.A. Hoffmann to such a large extent. In the shift from automaton to cellular automaton the latter is defined precisely by the introduction of a metabolics and a sexual drive. It is with these additions that the 'machines' have not only become restless, they have 'begun to dream,' although psychoanalysis still has not satisfactorily answered P.K. Dick's question 'Do Androids Dream of Electric Sheep?' As Emmeche states, artificial life is different from a robotics in its

> allowance for emergence. The essential feature of artificial life is that it is not pre-designed in the same trivial sense as one designs a car or a robot. The most interesting examples of artificial life exhibit 'emergent behavior.' The word 'emergence' is used to designate the fascinating whole that is created when many semisimple units interact with each other in a complex (nonlinear) fashion. (20)

Or, to use a neologism by Cohen and Stewart, the system aligns "simplexity and complicity" (3). On this background, the duck qualifies for at least four of Claude Bernard's five criteria for living systems: "organization, generation (reproduction), nutrition, development, and, as the only criterion that the duck probably doesn't adhere to—and I will return to this—"susceptibility to illness and death" (33).[2] Before death, however, there is love, and, equipped with the relevant machinery, the

---

[2] On machines that include death and enjoyment see Tinguely's meta-matics, such as *Homage to New York* (1960), or Calder's mobiles like *The motorized mobile that Duchamp liked* (1932).

duck, like Frankenstein's monster (which is built from what Rudy Rucker has termed 'wetware' plus the spark of life that is figured by the forces of electricity, whereas the duck is assembled from a purely mechanic, metal base into which digestion and reproduction are then mechanically added), 'before' or 'after' her (depending on what time-plateau one is referring to: the time *in* the novel or that *of* the novel), now begins to desire, which is why she had asked Allégre to ask Vaucanson to provide another duck to 'take to the opera.'[3]

As a French duck, of course, the opera might not be all she is thinking about. In fact, one can safely surmise that her ulterior motive is reproduction. As this plan fails, the company creates for her a decoy, which she, willy-nilly, accepts. As she states somewhat fatalistically in the face of the artificial substitute, "it floats like a duck,—it fools other Ducks, who are quite sophisticated in these matters, into believing it a Duck. It's a Basis. Complexity of Character might develop in time" (*M&D*, 667).

The duck remains "on the line" (666) for a while, only to vanish from the story as surprisingly as she had entered it. She turns into a mechanical ghost, learning how to vanish either through sheer speed or through "vibrating back and forth very quickly" (378), so that she can ultimately "enter and leave [...] the Stream of Time" (637). In the final image we have on her, she has become pure speed.

I. Nonlinear Eco:logics

Perhaps Pynchon, known primarily for cybernetic landscapes and environments rather than real ones, and for entropy rather than ecology—defined not so much in the context of a closed entropic space as the analysis of open systems "the relations in nature between organisms and the inorganic environment" (Emmeche, 128)— might seem a curious choice to open up a text on 'environment, landscape and space.' But then, in postmodern times, all of these terms and their connotations can no longer be restricted to what one might call 'the field of the natural.' Neurons

---

[3] As Crary notes, Mary Shelley "visited Neuchatel before writing *Frankenstein* to see Vaucanson's

create 'environments,' there are acoustic 'landscapes' [Fig. 2] and there are by now arguably more virtual than real sites and 'spaces.' At a time when more and more artists (not to mention scientists!) operate on the threshold between biology and technology—the separation between the natural and the technological:cultural seems, as Deleuze and Guattari maintain, no longer tenable.[4]

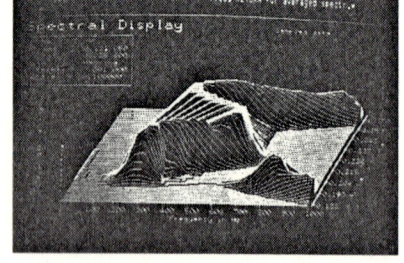

Still, other and more obvious candidates to open up this text might have been nature writers such as H.D. Thoreau—in particular *Walden* and *A Week on the Concord and Merrimack Rivers* come to mind—or Annie Dillard with her book *Pilgrim at Tinker Creek*. Symptomatically, however, Pynchon ends *Mason & Dixon* with precisely the metonymic stand-in that has figured so prominently in much of American literature to denote the promise of a utopian return to nature and to 'the simple life;' fishing. As Thoreau specified and Hemingway illustrated, the reference is specifically to "angling with a hook" (*Week*, 92) which is staked against the machinizations of, say, the industrialized whaling industry or the simulated returns that can be observed on the high-tech yachts on which sunburnt and drunk tourists attempt to reel in their 'sad trophies' in Carl Hiaasen's ecological crime novels. The final sentence of *Mason & Dixon* is about the decision of the sons of Mason to go to America: "The Fish jump into your Arms. The Indians know Magick. We'll go there. We'll live there. We'll fish there. And you too" (773).

In a more general context as well, the novel is eco:logical in its charting of the traumatic intrusion of the straight line into the American continent, and with this, the charting of the vanishing of unmapped, free space; an unexplored, and thus

---

creations on display" (qtd. in Laramée, 32).

[4] Recent examples were on display at the *ars electronica: next sex* exhibition (2000) where artworks included butterflies that artists had created (or better produced, designed or engineered) with 'artificial' wingcolorings that do not occur in nature.

fictional America which had served as "a Rubbish-Tip for subjunctive Hopes, for all that *may yet be true*" (345). In fact, America had been a wilderness

> safe till the next Territory to the West be seen and recorded, measur'd and tied in, back into the Net-Work of Points already known, that slowly triangulates its Way into the Continent, changing all from subjunctive to declarative, reducing Possibilities to Simplicities that serve the ends of Governments,—winning away from the realm of the Sacred, its Borderlands one by one, and assuming them unto the bare mortal World that is our home, and our Despair. (*M&D*, 345)

In terms of the line, this traumatic moment designates the destruction of the realm before division; a realm of pure multiplicity: "the single Realm [...] that undifferentiated Condition before Light and Dark,—Earth and Sky, Man and Woman," (523), with a hope for a return to "*that Holy Silence which the Word broke, and the Multiplexity of matter has ever since kept hidden*, before all but a few resolute Explorers" (523, emphasis added).

In the novel, the American continent is described as a multiplex field (Deleuze and Guattari would call this a 'body without organs') that had promised to be too intricately structured to completely territorialize. As the surveyor Shelby states, "There is a love of Complexity, here in America [...] no previous Lines, no fences, no streets to constrain polygony however extravagant [...] all Sides zigging and zagging, going ahead and doubling back, making Loops inside Loops,—in America, 'twas ever, Poh! To Simple Quadrilaterals" (586). Ultimately, the fight over America is one between complexity (movements of deterritorialization, 'lines of flight' and molecular arrangements) and control (movements of territorialization, 'lines of segmentarity' and molar machines);[5] a fight between "the Age of Metamorphosis, with any turn of Fortune a possibility" (*M&D,* 53) and the Company (a.k.a. 'the Firm' and 'They' from *Gravity's Rainbow*) "who desire total Control over ev'ry moment of ev'ry Life here" (154).

---

[5] On these concepts see Deleuze and Guattari (1983).

Symptomatically, Pynchon studies have recently begun to operate at the point of convergence of an ecological discourse that finds its basis in a discourse of the simulation of matter—in the early Pynchon, on the background of Henry Adams' essay "The Virgin and the Dynamo," these are predominantly constructs such as V., who is 'becoming robot,' or the two crash-test-dummies SHROUD and SCHOCK—by way of plastics, a process that culminates in the creation of Imipolex in *Gravity's Rainbow*, an erectile and thus partly alive plastic (a state of artificial life one might designate, drawing on Baudrillard's distinction, as a 'fourth order simulacrum'),[6] a discourse of complexity and chaos and a growing number of references to the theories of Deleuze and Guattari.[7]

In its various eco:logics—a term that I use to describe a discourse and a figure of thought that is slightly different from that of ecology—*Mason & Dixon* inscribes itself consciously into the tradition of an American literature that has always, consciously or unconsciously, charted aspects of the vanishing of nature and of the transformation of nature into culture. As a national project, it has not stopped annotating the intrusion of the machine into the garden, a project whose echo still reverberates through much of contemporary American cultural production, such as Jim Jarmusch's movie *Dead Man* in which the city 'in the heart of the heart of the country' to which the protagonist, William Blake, travels, is simply called 'Machine.'

Leo Marx was the first to note on a larger scale the creation of retrospective utopias in American art and literature; of spaces that seem to have escaped the relentless machinization of the landscape. In the beginning of his book, he quotes from Freud's *General Introduction to Psychoanalysis*, a passage dealing with what has become an American hallmark:

> The creation of the mental domain of phantasy has a complete counterpart in the establishment of 'reservations' and 'nature-parks' in places where the inroads of agriculture, traffic, or industry threaten to change [...] the earth rapidly into something

---

[6] See also Baudrillard's discussion of the various stages of the simulation of matter (from stucco to reinforced concrete to plastics) in *Simulations*.

unrecognizable. The 'reservation' is to maintain the old condition of things which has been regretfully sacrificed to necessity everywhere else; there everything may grow and spread as it pleases, including what is *useless* and even what is *harmful*. The mental realm of phantasy is also such a reservation reclaimed from the encroaches of the reality-principle. (8)

In Marx's reading, this becomes a truly American project:

Soon the dream of a retreat to an oasis of harmony and joy was removed from its traditional literary context. It was embodied in various utopian schemes for making America the site of a new beginning for Western society. In both forms—one literary and the other in essence political—the ideal has figured in the American view of life. (3)

In these returns to supposedly innocent, natural landscapes, a 'natural' pleasure principle is staked against an 'artificial' reality principle made of stone, steel, concrete or silicone, used symptomatically in the production of both computer chips and breast implants. The tradition of literature that is written under the aegis of this logic still reigns very strongly in America. In a lot of crime-fiction for instance, the central crimes are often crimes inflicted on the American, virgin land.

Especially in the 20th century, however,—and it might be an interesting project to delineate the various turning points of this reversal—the logic of the intrusion of *The Machine in the Garden* has been replaced by a logic inverted through an inversion of its spatial parameters. Now, there is *The Garden in the Machine*, which is, symptomatically, the title of Emmeche's book on artificial life. Such—now fully simulated and virtualized—gardens are most drastically disembodied in the work of Gibson and in the worlds of cyberpunk in general, and they have been most relentlessly critiqued, in their repression of the real, by Jean Baudrillard. And it is precisely in reference to Baudrillard that Emmeche shows how artificial life takes 'operationalization' out of simulation, but also how, through its focus on computa-

---

[7] For Deleuzian references see *Pynchon Notes* (1994). For ecological and chaotic references see *Pynchon Notes* (1998).

tion, it retains the repression of the real and of death, considered, in terms of artificial life, quite consolingly, as a "process where the delimitation [of the organism] vis-à-vis the environment is slowly erased" (137). In this context, the science of "artificial life is but a repetition of an ancient occidental mania for repressing all that is connected with the body and the senses" (137-138).

Today, the ecological field is often spanned out between two inverted binarisms, depending on what logic one follows. Either nature is good and humanity is bad, or nature is bad and humanity is good. The regressive logic of 'the machine in the garden,' which still pervades much of ecological discourse—a vicious human drive towards destruction that has to be checked and reversed in order to re-establish a natural balance—as well as the progressive, colonializing logic of 'the garden in the machine,'—an alien nature that is experienced as a hostile and frightening environment that has to be subjected and domesticated—are too well known to warrant closer scrutiny here. In my context, the reversal of the first position offered in *Gravity's Rainbow*, in which the human race is described as a deadly agent whose mission is to balance out a nature that is simply too alive is already more interesting, because it refers to nature as a system that is itself unbalanced, chaotic and catastrophic:

> this is the World just before men. Too violently pitched alive in *constant flow* ever to be seen by men directly [...] Alive, it was a threat: it was titans, was *an overpeaking of life so clangorous and mad*, such a green corona about *Earth's body* that some spoiler *had* to be brought in before *it blew the Creation apart*. So we, the crippled keepers, were sent out to multiply, to have dominion. God's spoilers. Us. Counter-revolutionaries. *It is our mission to promote death* (720, emphases added)

In his novel *White Noise*, Don DeLillo also deals with the complex enfolding of nature and culture, famously charting in detail the sliding spectrum from natural scenery to fundamentally simulated site, like that of "the most photographed barn in America" (12-13) or the Grand Canyon (243), on whose derealization and semiotization David Nye, a pupil of Marx, has commented in more analytic terms:

The Canyon has been increasingly de-realized, beginning with the very nineteenth-century paintings and photographs that made it a popular icon. The tourist has been offered ever more powerful technologies or space-time compression, to assimilate the site: railroads, cars, airplanes, snowmobiles, film, the IMAX theater, the internet, and, coming soon, the Virtual Canyon. The site that once symbolized America as nature is fast becoming a simulation, a post-landscape that offers no therapeutic renewal. (92-3)[8]

In the following, I will focus on a critique that has been directed at both logics—the machine in the garden *vs.* the garden in the machine—from within a redefinition of 'the structure of nature.' It is this critique that redefines ecology as a general eco:logics. According to the chiastic logic of this critique, the machine *is* the garden and the garden *is* the machine.

Slavoj Zizek is only one in a larger group of theoreticians who have commented on the inherent dangers implied by an ecology that considers man the destroyer of a balanced ecosystem and humanity as the species that brings imbalance to a carefully arranged nature. As he states, "the basic weakness of the usual ecological response is [...] its obsessive libidinal economy: we must do all in order that the equilibrium of the natural circuit will be maintained, in order that some horrifying turbulence will not derail the established regularity of nature's ways" (37-8). Drawing on the Freudian notion of *Nachträglichkeit*, he goes on to note that "the image of nature as a balanced circuit is nothing but a retroactive projection of man. Herein lies the lesson of recent theories of chaos: 'nature' is already, in itself, turbulent, imbalanced" (38). We do indeed live, as Jencks has noted in an architectural context, in *A Jumping Universe*.

---

[8] Cf. Nye (1977). Even earlier, however, in *The Octopus*, both social forces of the farmers and those of the railroad respectively are ultimately nothing against the 'force of the wheat'—"Men were naught, death was naught, life was naught; FORCE only existed—FORCE that brought men into the world, FORCE that crowded them out of it to make way for the succeeding generation, FORCE that made the wheat grow, FORCE that garnered it from the soil to give place to the succeeding crop" (634)—the wheat that could still re-surface in McInerney's novel *Bright Lights, Big City*.

The theories of chaos that Zizek evokes here are chaos theory—a.k.a. non-linear dynamics or complexity theory—as well as the theory of emergence or autopoiesis. Both of these attempt to chart the dynamics of systems that develop from within themselves. They are based on an "ecology of computation" (Emmeche, 128) and emerge without a structural blueprint that defines them from the outside. As Emmeche notes, "the emergent properties, instead of being represented in any central master code, are constructed anew each time an organism is created" (80). Their morphogenesis, therefore, is a precarious, chaotic process, which oscillates between a dynamics of fractal self-similarity and negative feedback loops on the one hand, and a dynamics of positive feedback loops and "random developmental noise or more violent environmental disturbances that [...] push equilibrium over into another path, resulting in a very different final product" (84) on the other. To quote a title from a book by Réne Thom, the inventor of 'catastrophe theory', these systems oscillate constantly between 'structural stability and morphogenesis.'

The chaotic sciences are interested in systems 'at the edge of chaos' rather than stable ones, and in systems that are unpredictable, turbulent, and always in danger of disintegration, although this 'danger' might better be seen as a 'possibility.' These chaotic systems do no longer follow the laws of an ideal, scientific necessity. Rather, they unfold in the space defined by the interplay of probability and chance.[9]

Whereas Zizek argues from within a Lacanian topography, two of the most persistent critics of Lacan, Deleuze and Guattari, have also related a paradigm shift to the theory of emergence; most notably Guattari in his book *Chaosmosis*, in which he sketches out "a science of ecosystems" (91); what he calls a "generalized ecology—or ecosophy" (91). Drawing heavily on theories culled from chaos theory, Guattari propagates a logic of open systems (with a minimum of structural stability) and morphogenesis that links various fields of research within a chaotic and eco:sophic reference. The project is to turn an eco:logics and thus an environmen-

---

[9] As Zizek notes, "these theories offer first drafts of a future 'science of the real,' i.e. of a science elaborating rules that generate contingency, *tuché*, as opposed to symbolic *automaton*. It is here [...] that the real "paradigm shift" in contemporary science is to be sought" (1991, 39).

tics—which is by definition both local *and* global—into a 'general project' that traverses philosophy, sociology, politics, art, the sciences and architecture, especially what might be termed 'non-linear architecture.'

The perspective point of such an eco:logics, which has nothing of a regressive luddism and which comes without the usual regressive ecological rhetoric, is a processual, open subjectivity. In fact, at the end of his text, Guattari comes to criticize the ecological movement precisely for its narrow pragmatic—rather than to close off ecology from the general ecosophic project, the ecological movement should first of all "concern itself, as a matter of priority, with its own social and mental ecology" (129)—and its tendency to departmentalize ecology into a purely natural one, when one also needs a cultural ecology, whose development has been increasingly at the center of cultural studies, in which one important strand of investigation is in charting—often in the context of the shift from Euclidean to non-Euclidean space—hybrid cultural space(s) such as Homi Bhabha's third space.

2. Textual Eco:logics and 'Pachinko Poetics'

If there is a need, in a general folding of natural environments onto cultural environments within a 'general environmentics,' not only for a 'natural' ecology but also for a 'social,' a 'mental' and for what Joe Tabbi has called a 'media' ecology, in which the novel should place itself, then maybe one might also look for a new eco:logics not only in texts that deal ostensively with problems of ecology or in what is called nature or ecotopian writing, but also in (non-literary) texts that develop their own textual eco:logics. These texts can be defined by what might be called a 'Pachinko Poetics:' an emergent narratology or a turbulent poetics; a poetics highly sensitive to narrative embeddedness and to the multiplexity of the events that are narrated.[10]

---

[10] In this context, see especially the passage in *Mason & Dixon* that 'enacts' a strange narrative loop when the story that is being told is suddenly revealed to be a part of an adventure serial two of the protagonists are reading.

Such turbulent poetics can be situated on various literary plateaus. A good example is the writing of John Cage, one of the truly chaotic writers and composers in the 20th century.[11] In his work "2 Pages, 122 Words on Music and Dance" he is attentive to the very specificity of the paper on which he arranges the words: "The number of words was given by chance operations. Imperfections in the sheets of paper upon which I worked gave the position in space of the fragments of text" (*Silence*, 97). These 'concrete' texts, then, are literally site-specific with regard to the very (landscape of the) medium onto which they are inscribed. This strategy evokes both the localism of a deterministic chaos, as well as the importance of the material contingencies within the support-medium of any writing or production of meaning.

To return once more to the duckmachine: In a recent installation—or perhaps 'artistic environment' would be the better term—at MIT (itself a symptomatic site), the artist Eve Andrée Laramée has used Vaucanson's duck as a point of reference in a speculation of the relation between art and science in a digital world which operates precisely at the interstices between the various realms I have been talking about. While she often operates directly at the interface of art and biology, this specific project is situated at the interface of art, history and technology. In all of her work, however, Laramées work operates in a truly eco:logical dimension. Her 'site,' whose title "A Permutational Unfolding" already evokes the theory of complexity and of emergence, consists of a room in which a number of important docu- and monuments of the transfers between nature to technology are assembled. She is drawing on the figures of Jacques Vaucanson, Ambroise Paré,

---

[11] See especially Shultis (2000).

(who designed one of the first prosthetic hands), Joseph-Marie Jacquard, (who designed the 'Jacquard loom'), the 'difference engine'—based on 'programmed' punched cardbord cards like those that operate in many automata—against which the Luddites were fighting,[12] Charles Babbage (who studied Jacquard's system in his own endeavour to construct his 'Analytical Engine') and Ada Lovelace, who is an important persona in the collaborative alternate-history novel *The Difference Engine* by William Gibson and Bruce Sterling as well as an absent presence in Tom Stoppard's play *Arcadia* (where she is the model for the character Thomasina). Ada Lovelace, who was the daughter of Lord Byron and one of the first people to support Babbage, linked the Jacquard loom to the 'Analytical Machine' in an analogy between nature, art, and science: "We may say most aptly that the Analytical Engine weaves algebraic patterns just as the Jacquard loom weaves flowers and leaves" (qtd. in Crary, 33). Although she would maintain that Vaucanson's duck, as well as any other machinery "has no pretensions to originate anything. It can do whatever we know how to order it to perform" (33), she would be surprised and delighted by Pynchon's duck or by the artificial life of the 20th century. The tapestry Larameé weaves from these ingredients chart the whole gamut from nature to art and science. A central position in the assemblage is held by a fabric woven for the occasion on which all of the references are assembled; a fabric that was 'produced' precisely through the inventions of the people represented in it. They are woven into it, while the fabric has been made technologically possible only through their work, so that it is, in a technological sense, woven through them. They are enfolded in the fabric while the fabric is simultaneously enfolded in them [Fig. 3].

Larameé embeds her assemblage firmly into a political and a cultural framework, opening up, in this socio-historical move, the question of an 'ecological ethics;' a complex, non-linear ethics that would have to lie at the core of any textual and artistic eco:logics. An ethics based on and developed from the conviction that

---

[12] Vaucanson designed a first automatic loom when he was "inspector-general of the silk works of Lyon" (Stafford, 42).

we are and live in open environments, in complex natural and cultural landscapes and eco:systems that are in constant interaction and friction. In this spatial field, both complete order and complete chaos are similarly 'terrorist.' The textual ethics and eco:logics would accept the chaotic structure of the cosmos, the fact that, as Michel Serres has stated, the world is a "pure multiplicity of ordered multiplicities and pure multiplicities" (*Genesis,* 111). From this conviction, one might hope to develop a mental, a medial as well as a textual eco:logics which would allow for a negotiation of inherently complex, irreducible spaces, environments, and landscapes, both natural and cultural. It seems to me that theories of complexity are a good approach to this environmental multiplicity.

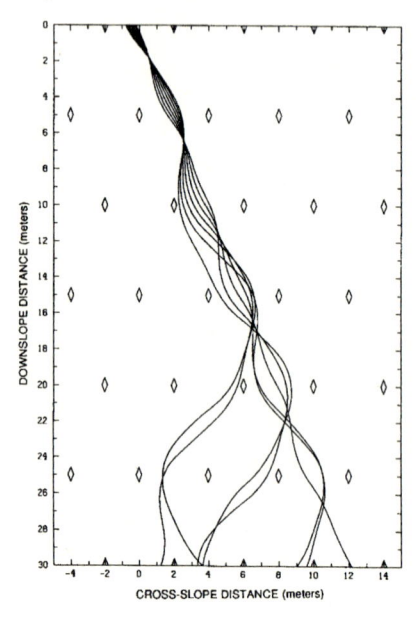

Ultimately, in exploring these postmodern environmentics, I am thinking of folding onto each other texts (literary, scientific, legal, etc.) that take their inspiration from the sciences of complexity; as does *Mason & Dixon*, which has created a truly turbulent and chaotic poetics and a narrato:logics that operates on a thousand plateaus. Not only does it contain strange narratological attractors and loops, it even plays consciously, in a general poetological shift from entropics to chaotics, with what might be called the founding image of chaos-theory, Lorenz' image of the 'sensitive dependence to initial conditions' [Fig. 4].[13]

---

[13] Although one should not look for a chaotics so much in the formal characteristics of texts, another field in which one might look for a new textual ecology are in the poetics of hyperspace, which are in themselves complex architectures and systems that are inherently unbalanced and dynamic. In fact, in *Chaosmosis* Guattari asks for a 'hypertextual thought' that links various plateaus and regimes in a constant process of territorialization and deterritorialization: narratives that operate on a thousand plateaus, always local and global at the same time through their rhizomatic networking(s).

Mr. Knockwood [...] a sort of trans-Elemental Uncle Toby, spends hours a day [...] studying [...] the passage of Water across his land, and constructing elaborate works to divert its flow [...] "You don't smoak how it is," he argues, "—all that has to happen is some Beaver, miles upstream from here, moves a single Pebble,—suddenly, down here, everything's changed! The creek's a mile away, running through the Horse Barn! Acres of Forest no longer exist! And that Beaver don't even know what he's done." (*M&D*, 364)

I would propose that, at the beginning of the 21st century, it is within such contingencies and chaotics that natural and cultural environments and landscapes should be negotiated.

Credits

Fig. 1 (p. 43). Vaucanson's Duck Automaton.
Fig. 2 (p. 48). Acoustic Landscape.
Fig. 3 (p. 56). Eve Andrée Laramée. "A Permutational Unfolding." MIT 19xx.
Fig. 4 (p. 58). "Slope Distances."

Bibliography

Baudrillard, Jean. *Simulations*. New York: Semiotext[e], 1983.
Cage, John. "2 Pages, 122 Words on Dance." *Silence: Lectures and Writings by John Cage*. Ed. John Cage. Middletown, CT: Wesleyan UP, 1973.
Cassidy, Eric and Dan O'Hara, Eds. *Pynchon Notes: Thomas Pynchon: Schizophrenia & Control*. (Spring-Fall 1994): 34-35.
Cohen, Jack and Michael Stewart. *The Collapse of Chaos: Discovering Simplicity in a Complex World*. New York: Viking, 1994.
Crary, Jonathan. "Cyberama: Adjacency, Assemblage & Display". *A Permutational Unfolding*. Ed. Eve Andrée Laramée. Cambridge: MIT List Visual Arts Center, 1999. 27-35.
Deleuze, Gilles and Félix Guattari. *Anti-Oedipus: Capitalism and Schizophrenia*. Minneapolis: U of Minnesota P, 1983.

---. *A Thousand Plateaus: Capitalism and Schizophrenia*. Minneapolis: U of Minnesota P, 1987.

DeLillo, Don. *White Noise*. New York: Viking, 1985.

Dick, Philip K. *Do Androids Dream of Electric Sheep?* New York: Granada, 1972.

Dillard, Annie. *Pilgrim at Tinker Creek*. New York: Harper, 1988.

Emmeche, Claus. *The Garden in the Machine: The Emerging Science of Artificial Life*. Princeton: Princeton UP, 1994.

Gibson, William. *Mona Lisa Overdrive*. New York: Bantam, 1988.

---. *Idoru*. New York: Putnam, 1996.

Gibson, William and Bruce Sterling. *The Difference Engine*. New York: Bantam, 1991.

Guattari, Félix. *Chaosmosis: An Ethico-Aesthetic Paradigm*. Trans. Paul Bains and Julian Pefanis. Bloomington: Indiana UP, 1995.

Hermann, Luc, Ed. *Pynchon Notes. Approach and Avoid: Essays on 'Gravity's Rainbow'* (Spring-Fall 1998): 42-43.

Jencks, Charles. *The Architecture of the Jumping Universe*. London: Academy Editions, 1995.

Laramée, Eve Andrée. *A Permutational Unfolding*. Cambridge: MIT List Visual Arts Center, 1999.

Marx, Leo. *The Machine in the Garden. Technology and the Pastoral Ideal in America*. Oxford: Oxford UP, 1967.

Maturana, Humberto and Francisco J. Varala. *Autopoiesis and Cognition*. Boston: Reidel, 1980.

McInerney, Jay. *Bright Lights, Big City*. New York: Random House, 1987.

Norris, Frank. *The Octopus*. London: Penguin, 1986.

Nye, David E. *Narratives and Spaces: Technology and the Construction of American Culture*. Exeter: U of Exeter P, 1997.

Pontus Hultén, K.G. Ed. *The Machine: as seen at the end of the mechanical age*. New York: The Museum of Modern Art, 1968.

Pynchon, Thomas. *Mason & Dixon*. New York: Holt, 1997.

---. *Gravity's Rainbow*. New York: Viking, 1973.

---. "Is it O.K. to be a Luddite." New York Times Book Review (28. October 1984): 40-41.

Riskin, Jessica. "Duckshit and Damask." Ed. Laramée, Eve Andrée. *A Permutational Unfolding*. Cambridge: MIT List Visual Arts Center, 1999. 45-51.

Rucker, Rudy. *Wetware*. New York: Avon, 1988.

Serres, Michel. *Genesis*. Trans. Genevieve James and James Nielson. Ann Arbor: U of Michigan P, 1995.

Shultis, Christopher. "Cage and Chaos." *Amerikastudien / American Studies* 45.1 (2000): 91-100.

Stafford, Barbara Maria. "Micromegalia: From Monumental Machines to Nanodevices." Ed. Eve Andrée Laramée. *A Permutational Unfolding*. Cambridge: MIT List Visual Arts Center, 1999. 37-43.

Tabbi, Joe and Michael Wutz. "Narrative in the New Media Ecology." *Amerikastudien / American Studies* 41. 3 (1996): 445-464.

Thom, Rene. *Structural Stability and Morphogenesis: An Outline of a General Theory of Models*. Trans. David H. Fowler. New York: Addison-Wesley, 1989.

Thoreau, Henry D. *Walden and Civil Disobedience*. Ed. Owen Thomas. New York: Norton, 1966.

---. *A Week on the Concord and Merrimack Rivers*. Boston: Riverside Press, 1961.

Zizek, Slavoj. *Looking Awry: An Introduction to Jacques Lacan through Popular Culture*. Cambridge, Mass.: MIT Press, 1991.

Space, Nature, and Landscape in Recent Theory and Poetry

Ulfried Reichardt

In a recent issue of *Critical Inquiry*, the editor writes with regard to the year 2000: "It only adds to the feeling of rightness that these meditations on space, place, and landscape converge at a moment of obsession with *time*; when a sense of the millennial moment and the absurd tyranny of the calendar is everywhere" (173). There is no doubt about the fact that modern technology is more concerned with time than with space. The telephone, the computer, and the internet, and increasingly faster means of transportation have reduced distances such that distance is now primarily measured in terms of the time it takes to cross it. The same is true with regard to the processing of information. Does this imply that space and location have lost their import? Joshua Meyrowitz has subsumed his analysis of the impact of the modern electronic media on social behavior under the title of *No Sense of Place*. If every event can be reproduced immediately, if we can observe and even participate virtually in events on the other side of the earth in 'real time,' then what does it still mean to be situated at a specific place, to be at home somewhere? The question I want to ask, therefore, is what the *function* of the representation of place in literature and other cultural forms and of the analysis of culture, society, and nature with regard to space and spatial relations can be today. While any attempt to separate space from time or vice versa is futile, and it is obviously more correct to speak of space-time as one does in post-Newtonian physics, it is, nevertheless, crucial to work with the time/space distinction and to ponder which specific perspective implies an emphasis on one or the other. My starting point is that a focus on space tends to stress the location of humans as given, a context in which one is situated. And this is precisely the crux of the focus on place.

While the scientific, technological, and artistic revolution around the turn of the last century has changed our views of time as well as of space,[1] in the humanities there is still a struggle going on between approaches which focus on spatial relations and those which focus on temporal ones. To point only to recent developments which are still governing the paradigms of literary and cultural studies, the most influential defender of space was Michel Foucault. In an interview he said: "Did it start with Bergson or before? Space was treated as the dead, the fixed, the unidentical, the immobile. Time, on the contrary was richness, fecundity, life, dialectic" (Foucault, 1980, 70). Ernst Bloch on the other hand had written earlier: "At any rate, the primacy of space over time is an infallible sign of reactionary language" (qtd. in Fabian, 37). The foe of spatial thinkers is historicism. As Foucault sums up the tension:

> The great obsession of the nineteenth century was, as we know, history: with its themes of development and of suspension, of crisis and cycle, themes of the ever-accumulating past [...] The present epoch will perhaps be above all the epoch of space. We are in the epoch of simultaneity [...] of juxtaposition [...] of the near and the far, of the side-by-side, of the dispersed. (Foucault, 1986, 22)

While I could cite several scholars who claim that time is the forgotten dimension of our time,[2] and while there are others who claim the same for space,[3] I think it is more interesting to investigate what is gained when one view or the other is emphasized. I will first look at some of the reasons why space is at the center in structuralism and in poststructuralism, and then look at three instances of what I consider productive analyses with the focus on space, place, and landscape: neopragmatism in Richard Rorty's philosophy, sociology in Richard Sennett's work, and finally nature, landscape, and ecology in the writing of Gary Snyder. For all three, the division between inner and outer experience, between mind and matter is the crucial problem, and thinking about humans' embeddedness in and exchange with

---

[1] See Kern (1983).
[2] See for example Altieri (1992) and Huyssen (1995).

the environment, i.e. with place in several ways, enables them to devise a solution to the problem resulting from the split between subject and object in Western culture.

The main reason both Claude Lévi-Strauss and Foucault give for their critique of historical thinking can be summed up in their argument that history has been conceived of according to the model of consciousness since the mid-eighteenth century.[4] As is well known, linear history seen as an autonomous force emerged at about the same time as autobiography in the modern sense. One no longer merely wrote memoirs, but rather used them to construct modern forms of individuality. What seemed contingent and only possible when actually experienced was transformed into necessity retrospectively. Foucault, in contrast, stresses that the movement of history cannot be traced back to the general model of a consciousness which acquires, progresses, and remembers (1988, 17). The crucial point, therefore, is the status of intentionality and the belief in the possibility to make history, that man shapes his world. When the idea of an autonomous subject was dominant, contexts were only seen as background and material to be formed rather than as a determining factor for human intentions. And even for Marx, geography was an "unnecessary complication" (Marx qtd. in Soja, 32).

Moreover, Lévi-Strauss and Foucault argue against the tendency to construct history as a teleological process which leads, in the sense of legitimization, to the position of the observer. Therefore, they insist on discontinuity and heterogeneity. Foucault's model for historical analyses is the *tableau*, i.e. spatial synchronicity (1988, 16). He claims that only in this way can the specificity of the peculiar time and chronology of coexisting social groups and different cultures be thought without reducing them to instances within the Western history of modernization. The political reason, therefore, is that only a spatial model allows him, as he puts it, "to think difference" (1988, 16).

---

[3] See in particular Soja (1989).
[4] See Lévi-Strauss (1962, 295) and Foucault (1969, 23).

Recent theories of time, however, have thoroughly dissolved the notion of a homogeneous, linear, and continuous time and argue that notions of time are always observer-dependent and contextually embedded or 'site-specific.' This view can be linked to the current topos of speaking of 'situated knowledge,' of local knowledge, of positioning oneself and being positioned—in terms of race, class, gender, ethnicity, but also in terms of place. The postmodernist critique of universalism, as in Jean-François Lyotard's attack on *les grands récits,* also stresses the locality of knowledge. Hermeneutics made this point earlier when Hans-Georg Gadamer speaks of a situation in which we inevitably find ourselves and from which we have to start (307). And in terms of systems theory, every system is situated within an environment and every observation necessarily involves a blind spot which is the result of a particular position.[5] The basic notion of observation in the sciences and in constructivism, but also in fiction (think of Henry James's point-of-view technique), stresses the limitations of the inevitable positionality of every form of knowledge. As Jonathan Crary writes, the contemporary dissolution of subjective points of view as a result of the introduction of bodyless and anonymous machines in the electronic media does not dissolve, but rather complicates this insight.[6]

While these are important points, the problem, as Edward Soja emphasizes, is that we cannot fall back onto 19th century "environmental determinism" (35), as this conception was precisely what progressive historical thinking was working against.[7] Place and geography were seen by social thinkers as "a world of passivity

---

[5] Cf. Luhmann (1992).
[6] Cf. Crary (1990). He poses the questions: "How is the body, including the observing body, becoming a component of new machines, economies, apparatuses, whether social, libidinal, or technological? In what ways is subjectivity becoming a precarious condition of interface between rationalized systems of exchange and networks of information?" (2). Furthermore, he stresses the close nexus between historically specific forms of subjectivity and of observation: "Vision and its effects are always inseparable from the possibilities of an observing subject who is both the historical product *and* the site of certain practices, techniques, institutions, and procedures of subjectification" (5).
[7] Soja explains: "Part of the story of the submergence of space in early twentieth-century social theory is probably related to the explicit theoretical rejection of environmental causality and all physical or external explanations of social process and the formation of human consciousness. Society and history were being separated from nature and naively given environments to bestow upon them what might be termed a relative autonomy of the social from the spatial. Blocked

and measurement rather than action and meaning" (Soja, 37). If place and location are understood deterministically, then creativity and change are neglected. Because of the spatial orientation of structuralism's concept of cultures, Johannes Fabian, for instance, argues that it is "devoid of a theory of creativity, or production" (62). If we wish to think about space critically, it, therefore, has to be conceived in terms of action and emergent processes as well. Consequently, one of the most far-reaching projects of theorizing space, Henri Lefebvre's, is called *The Production of Space*. Places are as much found as constructed, mentally as well as physically. Soja accordingly rephrases Marx's dictum about history to the effect that men make their geography but not under circumstances they have chosen themselves.[8] It is with regard to the tension between situatedness on the one hand and space and place as creative media on the other that I want to discuss the ideas of Rorty, Sennett, and Snyder.

Rorty's argument concerns the question of truth. For him, values cannot be validated in a foundational manner: they cannot be valid anytime and everywhere. Rather, they are always contextually embedded, i.e. historically specific but also situated locally. We cannot completely transcend the position which is linked up with our situation. Rorty argues that as a consequence of the loss of the belief in a transhistorical image of man, the grounding by reason was lost and therefore the link between truth and possibility of foundation was severed (1988, 84). He discusses John Rawls' liberal concept of justice which, according to Rawls' revised version, is only justified by the insight that this concept is *for us* a reasonable doctrine only under the condition of the traditions embedded in our public life. Rorty calls such an argument or justification—with which he agrees—*local* and also *ethnocentric* (1988, 95). The ethical and eminently political question how we can deal

---

from seeing the production of space as a social process rooted in the same problematic as the making of history, critical social theory tended to project human geography onto the background of society, thus allowing its powerful structuring effect to be thrown away with the dirty bathwater of a rejected environmental determinism" (1989, 34-35).

[8] Soja writes: "To provide the necessary recomposition of Marx's familiar dictum: We make our own history and geography, but not just as we please; we do not make them under circumstances

with incommensurable positions, for example fundamentalist ones, is solved by Rorty by regarding them as, seen from the liberal position, foreign language games which cannot be translated. They cannot enter into a common discourse because "the boundaries of normality are established by what *we* can take seriously" (1988, 98). Consequently, boundaries of inclusion and exclusion exist even in an open-ended liberal discourse which accepts contingency and process. Accordingly, Rorty conceives of democracy as experimentation: "We have to start where *we* are" (Rorty qtd. in Reese-Schäfer, 105), that is precisely from our concrete present place. Instead of searching for universally valid principles like human rights, we should work concretely for an understanding between cultures and for solidarity with marginalized groups—starting with our *own* ideas. What is important about this view is that it stresses the inevitable situatedness *and* at the same time calls for action; it is not a version of passive environmental determinism, but rather conceives of action as bounded and embedded.

Rorty's neopragmatism, moreover, includes a strong anti-dualist vision, as he conceives of consciousness as the specifically human form of adaptation to the environment: "Regardless if the tool is a hammer, a rifle, a belief or a statement, the use of tools is part of an exchange of the organism with its environment." (1997, 16, my translation). Philosophy, therefore, is itself reconceived as one way of interacting with the external world.

Yet such a conception of place and contextuality is still rather abstract. Space is experienced by the senses, involves bodies, and the concrete lifeworld, structures our daily interactions, our sense of freedom and of limits. Spatial relations inscribed into the structure of cities and territories also involve relations of power and hierarchies. One of the most interesting studies in this respect is Richard Sennett's *The Conscience of the Eye: The Design and Social Life of Cities*. Sennett's project is the development of a postmodern ethics of multicultural communality, based on the acceptance of creative difference. Focusing on the distribution of space in cit-

---

chosen by ourselves, but under circumstances directly encountered, given and transmitted from the historical geographies produced in the past" (129).

ies, of invisible yet effective boundaries and their social and political functions, and the experiences of the body enforced by architecture as well as by city planning, Sennett detects a constitutive distinction between internal and external spaces. By contrasting the Greek *polis* with the early medieval cities he argues that

> One difference between the Greek past and the present is that whereas the ancients could use their eyes in the city to think about political, religious, and erotic experiences, modern culture suffers from a divide between the inside and the outside. It is a divide between subjective experience and worldly experience, self and city. (Sennett, xxi)[9]

Sennett finds this divide already materialized in the contrast between the disorderly and violent medieval city and the sacred, ordered space of the church which functioned as a sanctuary as well.[10] As a result of this separation, a fear of 'exposure' evolved: "What is characteristic of our city-building is to wall off the differences between people, assuming that these differences are more likely to be mutually threatening than mutually stimulating" (Sennett, xii). An often quoted contemporary example is Frederic Jameson's description of the Bonaventura Hotel in Los Angeles as the epitome of postmodern space.[11] Successful public life, for Sennett, has much to do with the way the concrete places in which we move and interact are shaped.

Sennett's work is useful for our discussion as it describes 'lived space' and thus allows us to understand the concrete manifestations of how power and body are constructed in city-scapes and, moreover, how the notion of spatial synchronicity of cultural, ethnic, and social differences are experienced in the world of everyday

---

[9] He explains: "The ancient Greek could use his or her eyes to see the complexities of life. The temples, markets, playing fields, meeting places, walls, public statuary, and paintings of the ancient city represented the culture's values in religion, politics, and family life. It would be difficult to know where in particular to go in modern London or New York to experience, say, remorse" (xi).

[10] The crucial division in his opinion was the separation of the world of inner experience from the actual, sensual and external world we necessarily share with others: "The building of Augustine's city set culture upon a disastrous course in which the spiritual has become discontinuous with the physical" (Sennett, 39).

[11] Cf. Jameson (1986, 82-89).

existence, how they structure the 'ordinary,' which is the unacknowledged basis of our knowledge. Moreover, Sennett's concept of city-space is directed against a static understanding of descent and geographical location which disregards the important dislocations experienced by millions of migrants, in the contemporary *diasporas* for example, who have multiple loyalties and whose identities are active identifications with several places, pasts, and ethnicities rather than given locally situated positions.[12] According to Sennett, while the places and hierarchical orderings of space in which we find ourselves are given, they are, nevertheless, socially constructed. Consequently, they can be changed.

With regard to what I have just stated, the last position I will investigate seems rather problematic at first glance, as it involves a strong anti-modern impetus. By looking at the writing of the poet Gary Snyder I wish to think about place in the sense of landscape, ecotopia, and bioregionalism. Snyder, A. R. Ammons, and other writers who emphasize the concept of ecology in their work such as Barry Lopez, stress the fact that humans are rooted in the natural landscape, something which has been increasingly forgotten. Snyder's main concern is the natural habitat and humans' place within the dynamic network of first nature. While his writing is grounded in his local Northern California, his thoughts at the same time draw on the insights of the modern sciences, and evolutionism in particular. The main problem for him is the separation of human beings from the immediate non-human world in which we live. Human beings are inevitably part of their natural environment, even if they can control and manipulate large parts of it. In an explicitly anti-dualist move, Snyder argues for the interdependence of place and human life: "But how could we *be* were it not for this planet that provided our shape?" (*The Practice of the Wild*, 29). John Elder explains this point by citing Ernst May's term 'allopatric speciation' "to indicate the way in which a given landscape's character has evolutionary influence fully equal to that of intra- and interspecies competition; the development of species must therefore always be understood in localized terms" (39). The same is true for culture. The crucial point for Snyder, as for Rorty and

---

[12] See for example Hall "Cultural Identity and Diaspora."

Sennett, is that our inner world and our consciousness do not exist independently from the actual external world. Subject and object are not separated by an ontological gulf: "Sensation and perception do not exactly come from outside, and the unremitting thought and image-flow are not exactly inside. The world is our consciousness, and it surrounds us" (*Practice*, 16). Ecosystems process information as well, "the world is watching and listening," as Snyder puts it (*Practice*, 18-22). For him, the consequence is that we must be attentive to the landscape, animals, and plants surrounding us. Actually, this is how we get to know the world: "The childhood landscape is learned on foot, and a map is inscribed in the mind" (26).[13] Yet if our placedness is seen in the context of evolution, then place and environment are by no means static, nor are we passively determined by them. Place is thus seen as being creative and productive, always in flux, reacting to miniscule movements. Because we interact with our environment, because it is a complex and deterministically chaotic network of processes, place is paradoxically a given determining factor *and* an open-ended process. While it is impossible for us to return to an animistic world-view in which trees, clouds, and animals speak to humans, Snyder, nevertheless, attempts to conceive a reciprocal relationship with the environment in a non-dualist fashion.[14] Finally, such a view links nature, geography, and history: "Bioregionalism," Snyder claims, "is the entry of place into the dialectic of history" (*Practice*, 41).

In his poem "Riprap," Snyder describes how such a relation to the environment can be represented in poetry:

> Lay down these words
> Before your mind like rocks.
>   placed solid, by hands
> In choice of place, set

---

[13] There is a non-trivial correspondence between Sennett's lived space of externality in the Greek *polis* and Snyder's view of the relationship between human beings and the landscape and nature they live in.

[14] Accordingly, Snyder stresses that "henceforth the ecological model will dominate our model of how the world is—reciprocal and interactive rather than competitive" (*The Real Work,* 130).

> Before the body of the mind
> in space and time:
> Solidity of bark, leaf, or wall
> riprap of things.   (*No Nature*, 21)

Words and rocks are situated on the same ontological level; words are understood as something concrete, as signs of orientation in the real world of the reader. They mark a place, they are set down and described as being solid. When Snyder speaks of the "body of the mind," he emphasizes that the mind itself is grounded "in space and time," is placed physically and part of its environment. Like natural things ("bark, leaf, or wall"), the poem exists as an actual object, and like these objects, it also opens up a way for the traveler ("riprap" refers to a "cobble of stone laid on steep slick rock to make a trail for horses in the mountains," as Snyder notes). Poetry, and therefore the images and representations we devise of our world, are linked to a place, yet at the same time mark a location and a path. Moreover, placedness and change are complementary dimensions: "each word a rock / [...] / Crystal and sediment linked hot / all change, in thoughts, / As well as things." For Snyder, the solidity of place, the physical concreteness of body, mind, and natural objects is internally temporalized and seen as a dynamic process. Precisely because mind and matter are understood as being situated on the same level, because words and the mind are part of the actual world, they are necessarily historical and subject to inevitable change. Only an idealist notion of the mind could construe an atemporal and contextless position for thought.

In theoretical terms, the most important function of a focus on space, place, and landscape is the attempt to go beyond a separation between subject and object, between mind and matter. While the division between an internal and external world is attributed to monotheism in various ways by the writers I have discussed,[15] these authors endeavor to construct an alternative ethics which is based on contact and

---

[15] Cf. Sennett's reference to Augustine's (divine) city. Snyder claims "that most religious exclusiveness is the odd speciality of the Judeo/Christian/Islamic faith, which is a recent and (overall) minority development in the world. [...] We seek the balance between cosmopolitan pluralism and local consciousness" (*The Practice of the Wild*, 42).

exchange with the natural and man-made environment, based on the acceptance of man's and woman's place within a network of external forces and places. This implies a strong focus on the body in its actual locality and context, and, furthermore, links the realms of art, philosophy, and sociology to the developments in the sciences. Finally, as I hope to have shown, space is reconceived as being at the same time deterministic and open to creative action. Therefore, these conceptions of 'lived space' combine local situatedness as much as process. Seen in these terms, the fashionable slogan 'Think globally, act locally' indeed makes sense.

Bibliography

"Introduction: Geopoetics: Space, Place, and Landscape." *Critical Inquiry* 26.2 (Winter 2000): 173-74.
Altieri, Charles. "Temporality and the Necessity for Dialectic: The Missing Dimension of Contemporary Theory." *New Literary History* 23.1 (Winter 1992): 133-158.
Crary, Jonathan. *Techniques of the Observer: On Vision and Modernity in the Nineteenth Century*. 1990; Cambridge, Mass.: MIT Press, 1992.
Elder, John. *Imagining the Earth: Poetry and the Vision of Nature*. Chicago: U of Illinois P, 1985.
Fabian, Johannes. *Time and the Other: How Anthropology Makes Its Object*. New York: Columbia UP, 1983.
Focault, Michel. "Questions on Geography." *Power/Knowledge: Selected Interviews and Other Writings 1972-1977*. Ed. C. Gordon. New York: Pantheon, 1980. 63-77.
---. "Of Other Spaces." Trans. Jan Miskowiec. *Diacritics* 16 (Spring 1986): 22-27.
---. *Archäologie des Wissens*. Trans. Ulrich Köppen. 1969; Frankfurt a. M.: Suhrkamp, 1988.
Gadamer, Hans-Georg. *Wahrheit und Methode: Grundzüge einer philosophischen Hermeneutik*. 1960; Tübingen: J.C.B. Mohr, 1990.
Hall, Stuart. "Cultural Identity and Diaspora." *Contemporary Postcolonial Theory: A Reader*. Ed. Padmini Mongia. London: Arnold, 1996. 110-121.
Huyssen, Andreas. *Twilight Memories: Marking Time in a Culture of Amnesia*. New York: Routledge, 1995.

Jameson, Fredric. "Postmoderne—Zur Logik der Kultur im Spätkapitalismus." *Postmoderne: Zeichen eines kulturellen Wandels.* Eds. Andreas Huyssen and Klaus R. Scherpe. Reinbek: Rowohlt, 1986. 45-102.

Kern, Stephen. *The Culture of Time and Space 1880-1918.* Cambridge, Mass.: Harvard UP, 1983.

Lefebvre, Henri. *The Production of Space.* Trans. Donald Nicholson-Smith. Oxford: Blackwell, 1991.

Lévi-Strauss, Claude. *Das wilde Denken.* 1962; Frankfurt a. M.: Suhrkamp, 1994.

Luhmann, Niklas. "Stenographie." *Beobachter: Konvergenz der Erkenntnistheorie?.* Eds. Niklas Luhmann, Humberto Maturana, Nikio Namiki, Volker Redder, Francisco Varela. 1990; München: Fink, 1992. 119-37.

Lyotard, Jean-François. "Die Delegitimierung." *Geschichte schreiben in der Postmoderne: Beiträge zur aktuellen Diskussion.* Eds. Christoph Conrad and Marina Kessel. Stuttgart: Reclam, 1994. 71-79.

Meyrowitz, Joshua. *No Sense of Place: The Impact of Electronic Media on Social Behavior.* New York: Oxford: Oxford UP, 1985.

Reese-Schäfer, Walter. *Richard Rorty.* Frankfurt a. Main: Campus, 1991.

Rorty, Richard. "Der Vorrang der Demokratie vor der Philosophie." *Solidarität oder Objektivität? Drei philosophische Essays.* Stuttgart: Reclam, 1988. 82-125.

---. "Relativismus: Finden und Machen." *Die Wiederentdeckung der Zeit: Reflexionen, Analysen, Konzepte.* Eds. Antje Gimmler, Mike Sandbothe, Walter Ch. Zimmerli. Darmstadt: Wissenschaftliche Buchgesellschaft, 1997. 9-26.

Sennett, Richard. *The Conscience of the Eye: The Design and Social Life of Cities.* London: Faber and Faber, 1990.

Snyder, Gary. *The Real Work: Interviews and Talks, 1964-1979.* Ed. Scott McLean. New York: New Directions, 1980.

---. *The Practice of the Wild.* San Francisco: North Point Press, 1990.

---. *No Nature: New and Selected Poems.* New York: Pantheon, 1992.

Soja, Edward W. *Postmodern Geographies: The Reassertion of Space in Critical Social Theory.* London: Verso, 1989.

Spatial Aesthetics, Ironic Distances, and Realms of Liminality: Measuring Theories of (Post-)Modernism

Sabine Sielke

Tina's Millennial Tour

I will open my paper with a confession I fear might well undermine my authority right away; and yet for the sake of putting my point in a nutshell, I will take that risk. I confess that I went to see Tina Turner's "Twenty Four Seven Millennium Tour 2000." The place was the Olympic Stadium in Berlin, the landscape monumental architecture informed by Nazi ideology, and the environment many people my age, few younger, and many older. But what was the space? Well, picture this: Tina entuning the famous Beatles song *Help*, thus echoing Paul McCartney and recalling the 1960s while at the same time three video screens projected a virtual version of outer space, replete with falling stars. The intertextual space opened by Turner's citation (or parody) of the Beatles was thus filled by a utopian vision of a beyond where help is always already on its way. To me this post-modernist[1] scenario seemed to perfectly visualize what I deem central to post-modern theories: their tendency to invest liminal and intertextual spaces with powers that transgress the limits of our discursive universe. In this way, I will argue, contemporary culture and theory salvage not merely the visionary moments of the 60s, but modernism as well.

---

[1] Using a hyphen between 'post' and 'modern,' I mean to suggest a particular understanding of post-modernity which is not limited to a particular aesthetics. Rather, I take post-modernism as a cultural condition which, like any other era, is characterized by what Ernst Bloch called the synchronicity of the non-synchronic. In the context of American literature and culture this shows, for instance, in the—aesthetically and politically—diverse cultural practices that different subjects (such as Anglo-American versus African American authors or artists, for instance) due to their particular histories and subject positions (and their particular modernism for that matter) have engaged in. On similar grounds Andreas Huyssen distinguishes an affirmative post-modernism (of, let us say, Robert Coover, Thomas Pynchon, and Kathy Acker) from an alternative post-modernism (of Toni Morrison, Adrienne Rich, and Ishmael Reed, for example). I delineate this position more explicitly in my essay "(Post-)Modernists or Misfits? Nonsynchronism, Subjectivity, and the Paradigms of Literary History" (Sielke, 2000, 215-33).

Introduction: On Spatial Aesthetics and Ironic Distances

Literary and cultural criticism and theory have frequently conceived of both modernism and post-modernism in spatial rather than temporal terms. Projected as a program of "making it new" (by William Carlos Williams and Ezra Pound), theorized as the simultaneity of tradition and innovation (by T. S. Eliot), associated with decontextualized creativity rather than memory and recognition (by Gertrude Stein) and, as some would claim (with reference to Ernest Hemingway, for instance), escapist in tendency, aesthetic modernism, in particular, seemed to position itself 'outside' of history and temporality. Theories of the post-modern, like that of Fredric Jameson, similarly mourn the loss of subject, history, and "critical space" (all of which Jameson still finds in modernism though). More comprehensively Michel Foucault in his essay "Of Other Spaces" defines the present epoch as "above all the epoch of space. We are in the epoch of simultaneity; we are in the epoch of juxtaposition, the epoch of the near and far, of the side-by-side, of the dispersed" (22). At the same time, post-modern culture not only experiences and conceives of space in its own specific manners.[2] Some theories of the post-modern have also evolved a faith in peripheral moments of cultural practice, in realms of liminality, parody, and subversion that are likewise projected in spatial terms. This faith, I will argue, is only in part a renaissance of modernist romanticism, a return of what modernism repressed. It also involves a return rather than a loss of subject and history. As we move from new critical conceptions of a closural spatial aesthetics to a post-modernist sense of space as an open intertextuality, we evolve a subject that resituates herself or himself often quite literally center stage, a subject who

---

[2] In fact, as Foucault underlines, "space has a history in Western experience" (1986, 22). Foucault traces the history of space from medieval space or the space of emplacement consisting of a hierarchic ensemble of (sacred, profane, protected, exposed) places to a sense of space as extension where (beginning in the 17th century) "a thing's place was no longer anything but a point in its movement." Meanwhile the site, defined by relations of proximity between points or elements, has been substituted with extension. "Our epoch," according to Foucault, "is one in which space takes for us the form of relations among sites" (1986, 23).

knows, however, that this space is always limited and contested by pretexts and discursive conventions.

My aim here is to 'measure' theories of modernism and post-modernism, i.e. to assess both sense and function they assign to space and spatial tropes and I begin, in part one, with theories of modernist and post-modernist literature. Reconsidering the notions of space that inform Robert Frank's and Brian McHale's readings of modernist and post-modernist literature respectively, I will argue that the shift from modernism to post-modernism involves a shift from notions of 'text as space' to conceptions of 'space as text,' a shift in the process of which the term space is repoliticized. As theories of the post-modern, the post-colonial and, most particular, of performativity conceive of the political in terms of discursive space and situate subversive power in the realm of intertextuality, in ironic distance and parody, these theories have also, as I will argue in part two, revitalized modernist utopias. The particular thrust of my interest in post-modernist concepts of space is to delineate and gauge the current desire, the potential, and the limit of the liminal and the parodic. What are the functions and effects of ironic distance in a post-modern culture of citation? Where does post-modern performance locate the spaces that 'make a difference'? And how does a citation's double effect of ironic distance and memory work in such a culture? These are some of the questions that have provoked and inform this essay. I do not propose to answer all these questions here.

Part One: From 'Text as Space' to 'Space as Text': A 20th-Century Space Odyssey

There are innumerable ways to relate matters of space to issues of modernity and American modernity in particular. I could talk about the frontier—this paradigmatically American realm of liminality—and its closing; the transformation of rural into urban spaces; the migration of people across spaces; or about Gertrude Stein who wondered what the "flat land or any land or any land the flatter the land [...] has may have to do with the [creative] human mind" (1973, 149). Most significant, though, in our dominant conception of Anglo-American modernism (which significantly excludes Stein[3]), is its particular representation of movement in space. Like realism, modernism proper responds to experiences of change. Unlike realism which renegotiates cultural consensus while downplaying its own aesthetics and rhetoricity, modernism translates, as Heinz Ickstadt puts it, "cultural categories into textual ones" (594), foregrounds our means of representation, and makes us fully aware of the fact that the modern invention of the printing press embedded the word in space.[4] In this process the text itself seemed to turn into a space, a field rather than a sequence of signs. In his seminal 1945 essay "Spatial Form in Modern Literature" Joseph Frank has famously outlined this tendency. Taking issue with Lessing's distinction between plastic art (which is spatial "because the visible aspect of objects can best be presented juxtaposed in an instant of time" [6]) and literature (which, based on narrative sequence, proceeds through time), Frank argues that not only do modernist poetry and fiction—by Eliot, James Joyce, and Djuna Barnes, among others—move in the direction of spatial form. According to Frank, both modern art and modern texts have attempted to overcome the time elements involved in their structure; they transmute history and narrative sequence into the "timeless world of myth" and simultaneity and disrupt the continuities of discourse with syntactic disjunctions (Frank, 60).

Frank's argument did not quite hold. As W. J. T. Mitchell recalls, critics objected first and foremost that "spatial form" is a "mere metaphor" for critical procedures which deny the temporal sequence of literature. For space and time are by no means antithetical modalities; just as "we never talk about temporal experience

---

[3] Interestingly enough, the current renaissance of Stein both as a model of literary practice (for the so-called Language Poets, for instance) and as the central figure of American modernism involves the reassessment of her work as a utopian project. I do take issue, though, with DeKoven who argues that the utopian moment of modernity—its belief in difference without hierarchy—reemerges for a last time in the 1960s before culture gives way to the post-utopia of postmodernism and who accordingly rereads Stein's modernism as a "powerful utopian project" turned "post-utopian": "stripped of aura, detached from its revolutionary potential, indifferentiated, made just one more choice among a vast array of literary, cultural, (and) aesthetic objects of consumption" (DeKoven, 475). Rather, my claim is that modernism's utopian moments reappear in post-modernist modes.

[4] Cf. McHale (181).

without invoking spatial" (Mitchell, 544) measures, we never apprehend space apart from time and movement. In fact, as Foucault underlines, "it is not possible to disregard the fatal intersection of time with space" (1986, 22). Space and time interact, interdepend, and interpenetrate each other. Moreover, as Mitchell insists (and Heide Ziegler stresses in her contribution), spatial form is "our basis for making history and temporality intelligible" (563). Accordingly, some of the central modernist tropes and strategies (such as the binarism of cityscape versus countryside and the use of citation) are spatial representations for what are, in fact, historical differences.

Instead of assigning spatiality to one and temporality to another moment in literary history, Mitchell himself suggests that we rather sort out "what aspects of literary experience [...] insist on being regarded in spatial terms" (546); that we describe the changes in spatial form over time (558); and that we distinguish kinds of spatiality in literary texts. Mitchell himself distinguishes, first, the text itself as a spatial form in a non-metaphoric sense (550); secondly, the spatial realm that a text describes, the world that it represents (551); third, the spatiality that pertains to elements of structure and form, the patterns of coherence that a text seems to suggest (552); and fourth, the spatiality that characterizes the "overall meaning," "the metaphysics that we assign to a text" (553). New critical readings like that of Frank obviously privilege the last two moments, the spatiality of structure and meaning. Reading the literary text as a unity of contradictions and paradoxes harmonized by the powers of irony, they also reproduce the modernist desire for difference without hierarchy. And this link between a modernist utopia and the notion of irony as a structural principle is crucial for my argument: As I will show, it is both echoed and transformed by post-modernist theories which transmute ironic distance into a utopian space.

Whereas theories of the modern read space in terms of form, structure, and coherence, as a virtual space created within the confines of a supposedly autonomous work of art, theories of the post-modern repoliticize space and focus on different moments of the spatial. Starting from a notion of space as place, as the geopolitical realm of cities, suburbs, territories, and empires, Brian McHale, for instance, observes that post-modern texts construct "a paradoxical kind of space," a heterotopia[5] that accommodates many incommensurable and oftentimes mutually exclusive worlds, worlds of incompatible structures frequently called 'zones.' Such zones mapped by Walter Abish, John Barth, William Burroughs, and Thomas Pynchon are spaces of "overlapping subjectivities, including shared fantasies and nightmares," structures "in which all the world's architectural styles are fused and all its races and cultures intermingle," spaces located in Latin America or North Africa or on another planet entirely (McHale, 44). In fact, what we get are "a large number of possible worlds [that] coexist in an impossible space" (45). Thus the post-modernist heterotopia, as McHale argues, is a homotopia after all, its various places occupying the same space, that of the fictional universe projected.

Interestingly enough, terms such as paradox, incompatibility, and dissimilarity ring familiar (modernist) bells, yet carry different (post-modernist) meanings here. Whereas Frank's reading strives to transform discontinuities and "ironic dissimilarities" into the simultaneous order of a spatial aesthetics, post-modernist fiction, in McHale's reading, problematizes our very notion of space as a concept of order, autonomy, and containment, of the text as a space of closural and coherent meanings. The post-modern text instead presents space as text and subordinates the representation of geographical space to the play of the signifier, thus maps a world under constant erasure. In this way post-modernist perspectives shift the modernist focus on "spatial form" to the two-dimensional space of the page and the internal space within the sign, the gap between signifier and signified (McHale, 56). Moreover and most important for me—like post-modernist novels that explore the "between-worlds space" of zones (58)—they rediscover, open up, and redefine intertextual space, the realm of historical difference and ironic distance where multiple texts and voices clash with each other, the distance that new critical readings mini-

---

[5] McHale appropriates the term 'heterotopia' from Foucault's preface to *The Order of Things* (1966). Cf. McHale (44). Foucault provides a "systematic description" of heterotopias in "Of Other Spaces" (24).

mized.[6] In this way, as Linda Hutcheon underlines, post-modernist texts do not return us to "ordinary reality," as has been argued; instead they situate themselves in a "'world' of discourse, the 'world' of texts and intertexts" (125). This intertextual space constructed by citations and parodic echoes of pretexts has been invested—by theorists as diverse as Victor Turner, Julia Kristeva, Luce Irigaray, Jacques Derrida, Judith Butler, Linda Hutcheon, Henry Louis Gates, and Homi Bhabha—with a subversive power of both political potential and utopian dimension. Refiguring utopia as a liminal space, these authors to a certain degree counteract the dystopian temper and the focus on temporal, rather than spatial displacements that, according to McHale, characterize much of post-modernist fiction (66-67). Modernism's utopian desire for differences without hierarchies, for a more perfect social order, for "other spaces" (Foucault) therefore has not been lost. It has merely been displaced onto different spatial forms, a displacement which, interestingly enough, has evolved a revision of modernism and its dominant readings. Accordingly, towards the end of his study McHale returns to Frank's essay in order to rescue what its author had marginalized, the espacement of Mallarmé's "Un coup de dés" that Frank dismissed as a "fascinating historical curiosity" and the "necessary limit of spatial form" (191).[7] It is this liminality, this threshold of signification, that theories of the post-modern privilege, if not celebrate.

Part Two: Realms of Liminality and the Power of Parody or: Notes on a Post-Modern Utopia

Due to considerations of space I cannot possibly discuss at length the theorists I have mentioned—Turner, Kristeva, Derrida et al. Moreover, as I limit myself to these names, I am reducing the scope of the post-modern debate and include many that go under the label of structuralism and poststructuralism; and poststructuralism is, as Andreas Huyssen perceptively observes, a theory of modernism rather than

---

[6] McHale himself finds most effective the borrowing of a character from another text, the transmigration of characters from one to another fictional universe that overruns world boundaries (58).

[7] Cf. Frank (13-14).

post-modernism.[8] This, however, merely attests to the interdependence of our notions of the modern and the post-modern for what I do detect in the work of all of these authors is their investment in the intertextual space opened by the significant difference that accompanies verbal or other performative acts of repetition. (And in some way, this tendency corresponds to the revitalized interest in the work of Stein and the significance she assigned to strategies of repetition or "insistence," as she called it.) From Kristeva who evolved the concept of intertextuality from Bakhtinian dialogism across Turner's work that thrives on liminality to Gates's position on signifyin(g) and Bhabha's notion of mimicry we find plenty of faith in the powers of repetition, parody, and pastiche.[9]

How then do intertextual and liminal spaces relate? And how are they mapped out by the theorists I mentioned? Intertextual and liminal space relate because both project a surplus of meaning beyond the thresholds of signification. In both cases, this surplus is assigned to the distance between a pretext—be it social or discursive—and its citation or repetition. For Turner, for instance, liminality is a moment in the ritual process that characterizes social drama, a process which technologically advanced societies reproduce in their performative genres. More explicitly, Turner defines liminality as "a betwixt-and-between condition often involving seclusion from the everyday scene" and a shift to what he calls the "subjunctive mood," the "as-if" mode that characterizes rituals as well as theatrical performances, both of which function as metacommentaries on human relatedness (22). "It is as though everything is switched into the subjunctive mode for a privileged period of time—the time, for example of Mardi Gras or the Carneval Carême [...]. For a while almost anything goes: taboos are lifted, fantasies are enacted, the low are

---

[8] According to this view Jameson's claim that post-modernism dispenses with the subject and history would refer more adequately to modernism than to post-modernism.
[9] Jameson conceptualizes the difference between modernism and post-modernism as parody versus pastiche, reading post-modernism as a culture of citation that has done away with the quotation marks and in the process creates a kind of "blank parody" (114). I myself would object, however, that post-modernist citation as deployed by contemporary popular culture, for instance, frequently historicizes and even authorizes itself in modernist cultural practices, thereby engaging in the significant work of memory and subject formation. Jameson's distinction between parody and pastiche therefore cannot be drawn all that clearly.

exalted and the mighty abased, indicative mood behavior is reversed" (Turner, 21). Such dramatization of social hierarchies turned upside down, according to Foucault, is as paradigmatically utopian as is the projection of a perfect society (1986, 24). Moreover, in liminal spaces provided, for instance, by Japanese Noh drama, Turner finds "magic": "[a] whole world of wishes and hopes is opened up, as well as a world of moral reflectivity [...] where the 'might have been' is conceded to have indicative power" (38). Highly stylized and framed by genre-specific form, such (sub-)liminal moments of ritual and performance thus manage to peep into a more immaculate, a utopian body politic. In some sense, these spaces may even function like the mirror Foucault deems "a sort of mixed, joint experience, between utopias and [...] heterotopias." While it constitutes a heterotopia in so far as it does exist in reality, the mirror is, after all," he claims, "a utopia, since it is a placeless place. In the mirror, I see myself where I am not, in an unreal, virtual space that opens up behind a surface" (1986, 24).

Reproduction of discourse and style and intertextual space play a particular role in the writings of philosopher Judith Butler. Butler's work is particularly important here, in part because it connects with feminist theories which are usually not considered post-modern, yet which assert their—albeit alternative—post-modernity by their conception of 'female space.' Butler's sense of gender parody relies heavily on Luce Irigaray's concept of mimicry. Mimicry, for Irigaray, is a deliberate, though interim strategy through which women assert their particular speaking position. For Irigaray, woman, caught in patriarchal linguistics and logic, can either choose to remain silent, or—for the time being—mime, parody, paraphrase, and quote male discourse. Deliberately acting out the role that is historically assigned to women—reproduction—woman exposes what she repeats, undermines and thus subverts the symbolic order and its representations of women.

> To play with mimesis is thus, for a woman, to try to recover the place of her exploitation by discourse, without allowing herself to be simply reduced to it. It means to resubmit herself—inasmuch as she is on the side of the "perceptible," of "matter"—

to "ideas," in particular to ideas about herself, that are elaborated in/by a masculine logic. (76)[10]

This sense of subversion by way of repetition and parodic distance is crucial to Butler's notion of gender parody. Yet there is also a significant distance between Butler's subversive parodies and Irigaray's mimicry. According to Irigaray, one effect of playful repetition is that it uncovers what was supposed to remain invisible: "a possible operation of the feminine in language." Women, she claims, "are such good mimics [...] because they are not simply resorbed in this function. *They also remain elsewhere*" (Irigaray, 76). This "elsewhere," this female distance or difference conceived of in spatial terms and often circumscribed as a position of exile has been explored by a whole range of feminist theorists. We find it in Kristeva's work, most particularly in her concept of the semiotic chora—the pre-Oedipal physical space that, she claims, returns as the *dispositif sémiotique* of poetic language[11]—as well as in the writing of Annette Kolodny who proposed a woman's culture, a "wild zone," or "female space."[12] Significantly enough, both Kristeva and Kolodny conceive of female difference as a zone that is not a natural, but a discursive space, a style.[13]

---

[10] For a more intricate discussion of Irigaray's sense of mimicry cf. Sielke, (1997, 95-96).
[11] Kristeva develops this concept in *La révolution du langage poétique: L'avant-garde à la fin du XIXe siècle: Lautréamont et Mallarmé* (1974). On the issue see Sielke (1997, 19-90).
[12] In her 1981 essay "Feminist Criticism in the Wilderness," Kolodny reproduces a diagram, designed by anthropologists Shirley and Edwin Ardener, to map this zone. "Unlike the Victorian model of complementary spheres," she explains, "Ardener's groups are represented by intersecting circles. Much of muted circle Y [representing women's space] falls within the boundaries of dominant circle X [representing male space]; there is also a crescent of Y which is outside the dominant boundary and therefore (in Ardner's terminology) 'wild.' We can think of the 'wild zone' of women's culture spatially," Kolodny adds, "experientially, or metaphysically. Spacially it stands for an area which is literally no-man's land, a place forbidden to men, which corresponds to the zone in X which is off limits to women. Experientially it stands for the aspects of the female life-style which are outside of and unlike those of men; again, there is a corresponding zone of male experience alien to women. But if we think of the wild zone metaphysically, or in terms of consciousness, it has no corresponding male space since all of male consciousness is within the circle of the dominant structure and thus accessible to or structured by language. In this sense the 'wild' is always imaginary" (262).
[13] This space is probably conceived of as most explicitly utopian in the writings of Hélène Cixous. On Cixous's utopian conception of the imaginary see Moi (121-26).

This brings me back to Butler who famously argues that gender is not "a stable identity or locus of agency from which various acts procede: rather it is an identity tenuously constituted in time—an identity instituted through a *stylized repetition of acts*" (Butler, 1990b, 270).[14] Considering gender an effect of such acts, not an essence, Butler finds "a subversive laughter in the pastiche-effect" of gender parodies which are most obvious, but by no means limited to drag performances (1990a, 146). While, on the one hand, considering gender a process in time, Butler, on the other, employs spatial terms when she circumscribes the subversive effects of gender parody. For her such practices constitute a "terrain of signification" that "through a radical proliferation of gender" may at best "*displace* the very gender norms that enable the repetition itself" (1990a, 148). And this—Butler knows—is quite a task. Meanwhile we cherish the space that opens up locally, temporarily by practices of parodic repetition, practices that expose the "fundamental unnaturalness" of gender and its differentiated spheres (1990a, 149).

In terms of space it is not all that far from Irigaray and Butler to Bhabha who adopts the term mimicry to depict the ambivalences of colonial discourse. For Bhabha "mimicry emerges as one of the most elusive and effective strategies of colonial power and knowledge" (235). The original British policy of conferring on every colony a mimic representation of the British Empire, for instance, expresses "the desire for a reformed, recognizable Other, as *a subject of a difference that is almost the same, but not quite*" (235). This ambivalent mimic position, Bhabha argues, fixes the colonial subject as "partial" presence, yet also produces a discursive excess or slippage within the authoritative discourse itself. What Bhabha describes as the discursive effect of colonial power needs to be clearly distinguished, though, from the political potential, the other voice that some postcolonial critics assume to result from a subject's mere location in a specific geo-politically eccentric space. Arun Mukherjee's "readings from a hyphenated space," for instance— i.e. readings from the position of "a non-white British subject"—find an "oppositional aesthetics" in the works of non-mainstream, immigrant artists (iv). Whereas

---

[14] Cf. also Butler (1990a, 140f).

Mukherjee tends to believe that such aesthetics speaks truth to power, Bhabha insists that "[m]imicry conceals no presence or identity [...]. The *menace* of mimicry is its *double* vision which in disclosing the ambivalence of colonial discourse also disrupts its authority" (237).

Such concerted faith in the effects of mimicry, parody, and pastiche suggests to me that modernism's "critical space" has not been lost or deconstructed, as Jameson claims. Rather, it has been displaced. Nor have we lost history and subject in the process. Linda Hutcheon convincingly argues what post-modernist cultural practices—Tina's millennial tour included—persistently perform: "To parody," she claims, "is not to destroy the past; in fact to parody is to both enshrine the past and to question it" (126). For Hutcheon the notion of parody is entirely one of opening up rather than closing down. Contesting concepts of originality and closure, post-modernist art, according to Hutcheon, "offers a new model for mapping the borderland between art and the world, a model that works from within both and yet not totally within either, a model that is profoundly implicated in, yet still capable of criticizing, that which it seeks to describe" (23). Hutcheon thus not only contradicts Jameson who finds no position of "critical distance" in post-modern culture; she does not simply take issue with Jean Baudrillard's posture of resignation in the face of hyperreality.[15] Like Butler's writing, her work also attests to the fact that parody has turned into the privileged mode of post-modernist cultural theory and practice. Since its effect is significant, yet hard to measure, parody and pastiche easily open up toward utopian spaces, into "borderland[s] between art and the world" (Hutcheon, 23), a realm within what some post-modernist theory dismisses as the aestheticized post-modern condition or a body politic turned theater. And whereas the heterotopias envisioned by post-modernist fiction are mostly disturbing, this utopian realm is soothing, even if it does not open up into the easily accessible lands that have dominated the utopian imaginary. Thus, rather than facing "the end of utopia" (Jacoby, 1999), post-modern culture salvages the utopian momentum of

---

[15] Cf. the discussion of Jameson and Baudrillard in Storey (172, 165).

aesthetic modernism for the new millennium. It does so, of course, with significant differences.

Bibliography

Bhabha, Homi. "Of Mimicry and Man." *Modern Literary Theory: A Reader*. Ed. Philip Rice and Patricia Waugh. London: Arnold, 1989. 234-241.

Butler, Judith. *Gender Trouble: Feminism and the Subversion of Identity*. New York: Routledge, 1990.

---. "Performative Acts and Gender Constitution: An Essay in Phenomenology and Feminist Theory." *Performing Feminisms: Feminist Critical Theory and Theory*. Ed. Sue-Ellen Case. Baltimore: Johns Hopkins UP, 1990. 270-82.

DeKoven, Marianne. "Introduction: Transformations of Gertrude Stein." *Modern Fiction Studies* 42.3 (1996): 469-484.

Foucault, Michel. "Of Other Spaces." *Diacritics* 16.1 (1986): 22-27.

---. *Die Ordnung der Dinge: Eine Archäologie der Humanwissenschaften*. Frankfurt: Suhrkamp, 1989.

Frank, Joseph. "Spacial Form in Modern Literature." *The Widening Gyre: Crisis and Mastery in Modern Literature*: Bloomington: Indiana UP, 1969. 3-62.

Hutcheon, Linda. *The Poetics of Postmodernism: History, Theory, Fiction*. New York: Routledge, 1988.

Huyssen, Andreas. *After the Great Divide: Modernism, Mass Culture, Postmodernism*. Bloomington: Indiana UP, 1986.

---. "Postmoderne—eine amerikanische Internationale?" *Postmoderne: Zeichen eines kulturellen Wandels*. Ed. Andreas Huyssen and Klaus R. Scherpe. Reinbek: Rowohlt, 1986. 13-44.

Ickstadt, Heinz. "Liberated Women, Reconstructed Men: Symptoms of Cultural Crisis at the Turn of the Century." *Engendering Manhood*. Ed. Ulfried Reichardt and Sabine Sielke. *Amerikastudien/American Studies* 43.4 (1998): 593-98.

Irigaray, Luce. *This Sex Which Is Not One*. Trans. Catherine Porter. Ithaca: Cornell University Press, 1985.

Jacoby, Russell. *The End of Utopia: Politics and Culture in an Age of Apathy.* New York: Basic, 1999.

Jameson, Fredric. "Postmodernism and Consumer Society." *The Anti-Aesthetic: Essays on Postmodern Culture.* Ed. Hal Foster. Port Townsend: Bay Press, 1983. 111-25.

Kolodny, Annette. "Feminist Criticism in the Wilderness." *The New Feminist Criticism: Essays on Women, Literature, and Theory.* Ed. Elaine Showalter. New York: Pantheon, 1985. 243-70.

Kristeva, Julia. *La révolution du langage poétique: L'avant-garde à la fin du XIXe siècle: Lautréamont et Mallarmé.* Paris: Édition du Seuil, 1974.

McHale, Brian. *Postmodernist Fiction.* New York: Methuen, 1987.

Mitchell, W. J. T. "Spatial Form in Literature: Toward a General Theory." *Critical Inquiry* 6.3 (1980): 539-67.

Moi, Toril. *Sexual/Textual Politics.* London: Methuen, 1985.

Mukherjee, Arun. *Oppositional Aesthetics: Readings from a Hyphenated Space.* Toronto: TSAR, 1994.

Sielke, Sabine. "(Post-)Modernists or Misfits? Nonsynchronism, Subjectivity, and the Paradigms of Literary History." *Making America: The Cultural Work of Literature.* Ed. Susanne Rohr, Peter Schneck, and Sabine Sielke. Heidelberg: Winter Verlag, 2000. 215-33.

--- *Fashioning the Female Subject: The Intertexual Networking of Dickinson, Moore, and Rich.* Ann Arbor: U of Michigan P, 1997.

Storey, John. *An Introductory Guide to Cultural Theory and Popular Culture.* Athens: U of Georgia P, 1993.

Turner, Victor. "Liminality and the Performative Genres." *Rite, Drama, Festival, Spectacle: Rehearsals Toward a Theory of Cultural Performane.* Ed. John J. MacAloon. Philadelphia: Institute for the Study of Human Issues, 1984. 19-41.

From Space to Place

James L. Peacock

What is the place of place in globalism? In a word, place matters. Yet place is not just matter—nor mind. Globalization—the interconnecting of everyone and everything around the world, through commerce, cyberspace, migration—challenges localization, the idea of space as place, that is, the meaning of locale, of where you live.[1] This essay explores the challenge of globalism at three levels: first, human directions; second, social policy; and third, our own personal choices. The overriding question is, does space matter in a global world and if so, how?[2]

Regarding human directions, several general questions emerge. Where are we, as a species, as humanity, going? If we are moving toward globalization, how far can this process go in transcending place? To frame the question theoretically, how far can what Max Weber termed "rationalization" press in dissolving an anchor of place? (Weber, *Theory of Social and Economic Organization*, 1942). Or, empirically, what does knowledge about the human species and its evolution, history, and experience say about the importance of space/place for humanity? Do locale and localization matter to human beings in ways akin to territorial imperatives for animals generally? Does culture transcend such imperatives, or does it reinforce them? Among those who ponder this question, geographers are perhaps paramount, but humanists, including anthropologists, can address the human, especially the cultural, dimension.[3]

---

[1] Cf. Rose: "Place is one of the most theoretically and politically pressing issues facing us today" (1995, 88). On the one hand, global flows are uniting the world; on the other hand, new nations are fragmenting, leading to violence. Rose argues that we have a sense of place due to a natural instinct of territoriality; that place is constructed by underlying structures of power; and that a sense of place is part of a politics of identity, a way of defining the other. See in addition Harvey (1989).
[2] See also Hannerz (1996) and Casey (1997).
[3] See, for example Appadurai's essay "Disjuncture and Difference in the Global Cultural Economy " (1990).

In terms of social policy, one might ask where we should go, in globalization: how far, and how? What are the consequences of globalization transcending place? What, if anything, should we do about it? What policies work? Consider current situations, which I divide into three types. At one extreme is rootlessness—a massive movement of people and peoples.[4] We see forty-five million refugees, peoples who are homeless, and we also see diaspora, world citizens, cybercitizens, people who have migrated or who seem more part of a world system than any locale. At the other extreme, often a reaction to the first, is a certain fundamentalism in claiming space as place: asserting, in the words of Martin Luther, "Here I stand" (or sit or lie)! Increased mobility, both voluntary and involuntary, produces a counter-phenomenon of entrenchment in a single place, of clinging to home and all that it represents. The Southern Agrarians asserted "I take my stand in Dixie, to live and die in Dixie" from the song "Dixie," meaning that this space is my place, this locale my identity, and I shall not move from it nor allow anyone else to move into it or possess it. This traditional sentiment is radically and negatively expressed in ethnic cleansing, which forcibly removes people from a space identified as place. Culturally, politically, psychologically, and thus 'ethnically,' some group is identified as alien, as not of that place. In between these extremes are seemingly moderate policies, which are our efforts at preserving, reclaiming, and reconstructing place as a civic act. Examples include historic preservation, architectural reconstruction (of which post-World War II Germany, previously West now notably East Germany and especially East Berlin is perhaps the most impressive effort), urban renewal as a move toward combating urban sprawl, heritage tourism, and the work of the Committee on Regions of the EU. While all these have positive valence, they also pose questions about social issues, notably the treatment of the disadvantaged. What happens to the poor, forced to move from renewed and reconstructed communities for the wealthy? What are the implications of locating tribal minorities or

---

[4] See King's essay "Migrations, Globalization and Place" (1995, 5-33). King traces the history of migration, pointing out that between 1850 and 1914 around fifty million Europeans migrated, 70% to the United States (15).

poor people in separate locales, such as reservations? More generally, every effort at preservation and reconstruction advantages one population while harming another, and some actions raise serious human rights issues. One could offer as examples coercive conservation, which sacrifices human subsistence for animal ecology, threatening subsistence hunters to preserve animal species; religious oppression, strengthening identity through meaning-systems, but with repercussions for dissidents, minorities, or others (e.g. the Taliban's treatment of women); and destruction through development (dams financed by the World Bank that displace tribal communities). While these policies do not intend such consequences, they can slide down a slippery slope toward them. Preservation can be funded by sweatshops with labor by guest workers; and an influx of immigrants can lead to ethnic cleansing, which often focuses on migrants—newcomers, who are perceived as staining native purity.

Finally, there are personal choices. Should one move to get a job? To retire? A Cairo family descended from generations of landowners who stayed put now has four siblings on four continents, having gone where jobs and marriages have taken them. What are the effects on my own family? Should my aged mother and father leave their place and move to a retirement space? They view their territory as a radius of a day's drive, with children distributed around that radius. They relish moving in that space, or have until recently; now they are more restricted. Should I myself move? What does that mean? How does it work for a couple who live half the year in California and half the year in North Carolina? What does space/place mean in this globalizing world? Subjectively, how is one's life lived—in the day, at night, in the rhythms of activity—differently if one changes from one place to another, as from place of residence to an arena of work or vacation?

Addressing these questions, let us factor out what makes space place.[5] First, consider place itself: is space sufficient to make place? Put differently, can a group

---

[5] Massey and Pat Jess (1995) raise many of the issues. Massey in "The conceptualization of place" cites Harvey (1989) in his study of the difficulty of sustaining old notions of settled community in times of globalization. Solutions range from a resurgence of exclusivist nationalists (for instance in Eastern Europe and the old Soviet Union) to heritage centers—the "olde worlde" vil-

or person preserve place while changing space? Yes, to an extent. Pilgrimage is one example, as the group keeps its integrity while moving in space. Diasporas are another: displaced, people recreate the homeland by constructing little Italies, Chinatown, or little Cubas. Yet no one would confuse the homeland with the newland, or the pilgrimage with the village.[6] So, place is more than space, yet wedded to it. Secondly, if place is constructed out of space by imbuing space with cultural meaning, is culture fixed to a space? Culture could almost be defined as a way of transcending space. Belief, languages, and customs can be transported. However, different cultural configurations transport differently. Among Balinese Hindus, for example, the sacred is embodied in ancestors buried in the earth and imaged as shrines in family compounds. Among Javanese Muslims, the sacred is in God, and God is not in the earth but in heaven. So Balinese logically would be grounded when at home and more disoriented when away than the Muslims who have God everywhere or nowhere and can point toward Mecca anywhere. In fact, itinerant trade is more a custom among the Muslims (whether Javanese, Minangkabau Sumatran or other) than among the Hindu Balinese. To make another comparison, what about religion vs. technology as different modes of culture? Religions vary, but one of their characteristics is totality; they define the ultimate, everything; and the great World religions move toward comprehensive and holistic explanation. Technology, by comparison, is broken down into buttons and steps—digital vs. holistic thinking. Both transcend space but do so in different ways. Compare a mis-

---

lage—that "make places" (48). Behind this is the system in which capital is more mobile than labor, and free trade and movement of capital applauded, while barriers to migration are formidable. People may be relatively "place bounded," thus separating themselves from others, uniting around 'traditions' which are themselves 'partially illusory,' commodities of the heritage industry. Worse, is a tendency to fetishize place, which can result in jingoistic forms of localism and nationalism (49). At other extreme Castells and Hammnett argue that "the possibility of place being invested with human meaning, such that it could be interpreted as "place" has evaporated" (54). In between is Massey's "immediate activity space," which identifies a constellation of spaces revolving around a person's activities, moving toward a more open conceptualization of place/space (58).

[6] Nonetheless, as King points out in "Migrations, Globalization, and Place," migrants harbor a sense of what Bourdieu termed *habitus*. King asserts: "Habitus gives people a sense of their place in the world, a sense which is carried with them and refashioned in the new context when they migrate" (28). Ethnic enclaves in new places permit this.

sionary in the jungle with engineers or an army in the jungle, keeping in mind, of course, that the two types commingle. A somewhat similar comparison is given by a study of trails blazed by native Americans and by Western explorers and engineers in California; the first was absorbed within mythology, nature, and experience, the second marked by compasses and maps. The spaces were often the same, but the places were different, at least in terms of cultural meaning. Culture is anchored in space yet transcends it, and the tendency emphasized depends on the culture.

What about the inner life? We posit: "I think, therefore I am," rather than "I am,"—being in the world, including place—"therefore I think." To what extent can places be in the mind? This is the approach taken by Jungians and others: to psychologize space. Dreams are interpreted as representing not actual places or people but symbols, which are within a person who is part of a collective psyche. Jungian archetypes include place-connected mythical images. The supreme archetype is the mandala, the circle that is drawn in the sand by Tibetan monks and then destroyed, indicating the transient physicality. The mandala is interpreted by Jungians as expressing psychic, not spatial, wholeness. Yet recall that Jung himself remained grounded in place, building his stone house in the forest as an embodiment of his psyche, rediscovering his inner life by building villages on the beach of his lake house, and remaining in Switzerland while encompassing the world psychologically. The history of mysticism and other explorations of the inner life shows a dialectic between freeing oneself from space—divesting oneself of material possessions, perhaps wandering homeless—and anchoring oneself in a space: a monastery, a clinic, a couch, a cave.

Bodies and bodily activity build place from space. This is so for tillers of the soil, builders of homes, athletes, dancers, hunters, gatherers, for everyone, since all of our activities are cultural as well as physical, e.g. mediated by technology. Recent articles tell about the imprint of particular places for dancers—in New York, for example, and in Durham, North Carolina, where a rehearsal space called the Ark is renowned among participants in the American Dance Festival. Note how the

Olympics and other sporting events create a special ritual space. Elsewhere, I describe how the Olympics define a central space as sacral, cultural: the arena, the sites of the opening and closing ceremonies, and of the track and field competitions. By precise if implicit ritual, the Olympics build through time from short to long races, culminating in the marathon and a parade which brings nature (seas, equestrian fields, and the bodies of athletes) into that cultural arena and captures it for culture, as part of the sacred center. A parochial example is the bowl games in American football. These began with agrarian identities—cotton, rose, sugar, orange—in the South and Southwest, as the bowls are named after these plants. Such plant-places are sites in which teams with animal names defend their territories, perhaps, I argue, symbolically replaying the American Civil War and other invasions and defenses of territory. Aside from such colossal ceremonies, think of personal activities. Running a marathon in a particular city and walking 40 or 50 miles through the Luangwa valley in Zambia builds a sense of place and union with those places, I feel. But technology can do that also. Observe bumper stickers on cars, many celebrating place. And to return to bodies: think of Walkabout or The Dreaming among Australian aborigines, the Zar cult in Cairo, and pilgrimages, all celebrating place by movement of body in space.

All of these aspects—culture, group psyche, body—are elements, factors, pieces of a larger phenomenon. Some might term this phenomenon 'activity,' others 'experience.' 'Activity,' a term which some geographers use, overemphasizes the external, behavioral; 'experience,' which philosophers and psychologists favor, stresses the internal, subjective. 'Action,' which some sociologists use, following Weber (translated from *handeln*), includes both internal and external aspects, but this is not a widely understood usage. 'Life,' extended from its biological base alone, or 'Existence,' translated from *Dasein*, are comprehensive enough. 'Existential' will perhaps suffice, if we recall the social, psychological, cultural, bodily, and activity aspects; the point is, space becomes place, i.e. meaningful space, as it enters into our existence. Place is existential space.

Correlates of Place

If we agree about the basic character of place—that it is anchored in, yet transcends, space through cultural, social, psychological, and bodily aspects of existence—then we can move to consider, briefly, some of the correlates of place. What affects place? What shifts its meaning and significance? Time is obviously a factor, as are demographic factors such as class, race, and gender.[7] Politics, as a play of power, also influences place. Consider, first, how time and space correlate as quantitative as well as qualitative features. How important is the extent or size of space? How important is time in determining the salience of this variable? Time and space correlate, interact, not just in physics and philosophy, but in the nursery facts of life. Consider the individual life cycle. The infant begins life in a narrow place, the womb. Later his/her life centers around the breast and lap of mother or surrogate. Development entails moving out into ever wider spaces—the family as a whole, nuclear or extended, the community, the wider society. Aging tends to shrink that space again, as one's mobility diminishes and one retires into smaller spaces, eventually the deathbed and grave. Even elaborate afterdeath cultures, such as the Egyptian, restructure and restrict imagined movement after death; on the other hand, some dead fly, like angels, imaginatively transcending the seeming shrinkage of space through the passing of time in the life cycle.

Within this general human pattern, many variations are apparent, begging certain questions. How important is it to infant or adult that one's narrower sphere is connected to wider ones? Robert Bellah postulated the following steps in the life cycle.[8] In the first step the child participates in three levels—mother/child, the wider family, and the wider society. Bellah argues that only through a sense of connectedness to the wider society is family meaningful to the child, motivating the child to "develop," to mature. Later, as step two, the young adult is also involved in three levels, the family, the society, and some broader legitimizing framework

---

[7] Gilroy suggests a partial transcendence of place and time through forging community ties that rely on present circumstances to produce what is considered 'traditional' (1987).

[8] See Bellah's essay "Systematic Notes for the Study of Religion" (1991).

(perhaps religion), again requiring the broader level to render the others meaningful. As in step one, Bellah argues, development and maturation into an adult role in the wider society occurs only if the youth senses the value and legitimacy of that society, and that comes about through a broader legitimizing framework. Bellah does not extend his speculation into old age, but by analogy one might suggest that the elderly complete the cycle, in part by both continuing to widen the sphere of participation (toward the universal in some senses, by thought and wisdom perhaps expressed in contemplative or ritual or altruistic activities) and narrow it (by settling into a more restricted space). In a nutshell: one loses the village, gains the world, then tries to create a new village. The question is, how is this kind of embeddedness of narrower spaces in wider places significant at different stages of life? What difference does it make to raise a child isolated from kin and community? Does it really take a village to raise a child? What difference does it make for an elderly person to move in with a child, leaving behind her previous kin and community? What difference does it make when such isolation is also from one's regional or national 'homeland'? Did it/does it matter when a woman moved/moves from Texas to Connecticut to live in a bedroom of her son's house? What if she never leaves the bedroom? What if all her furniture is transported and set up as it was before? How does the wider space impact the narrower one? Is the social context of Texas replaced by the spiritual context of humanity or of religion—wider realms—or by the narrower realms of her grandchildren, her son, her bedroom? Does one's relation to space therefore change through time?

Gender, status, and power obviously affect all these correlations and co-variations of time and space. Contrast the homeless elderly and the *wanderjahre* young: it is quite different to backpack when one is twenty and on vacation than when one is seventy years old and homeless. It is, however, also different being able to build a castle, as did Ludwig II of Bavaria with *Neuschwanstein*, constructing one's living space elaborately and living here and elsewhere according to whim, or, with similar freedom, jet setting among homes around the world, and, in contrast, being restricted by income to a grimy flat or cabin or mobile home.

Relativisms and Reductionisms

"Home is where the heart is." This saying relativizes place suggestively while also reducing it to psychology. Home is where the heartless isn't or aren't. Experience demonstrates truth in this truism. Move to B from A, then travel to C; doesn't B seem more like A than before? We once moved to England, then traveled to Tunisia; returning to England was like coming home. Or, move from A to C, C being quite different from A, then travel to B. We lived in Indonesia, then traveled to Japan en route back to the USA; arriving in Japan was like coming home by comparison. Or, finally, travel many places or get uprooted radically, then settle somewhere. During WWII, we lived in many states—I went to four first grades—then returned to my grandmother's house in Alabama; the sense of returning home and settling down in a place was enhanced by the comparison to moving about. What about blacks who, after a sojourn in the North, return to the South? Many report a sense of coming back home, which is obviously a relative sense; they come home from a sojourn in the North to a place which was itself a sojourn, traumatic and oppressive, from a former homeplace. Refugees from the Holocaust or from Vietnam who settle in the USA seem to vary in their experience of finding a refuge—a new home—and losing a homeland. One Jewish refugee writes of never finding a home. A sense of home depends on a relationship to non-home, on comparison, which is culturally mediated. Mecca is the supreme example of a home away from home for Muslims—even if one has never been there, one wishes to die there if one is pious, and some Muslims settle there, feeling at home in a way they did not while living in their birthplaces in Asia or Africa, far from the religiously-defined homeplace.

Reductionism entails absolutizing place, rather than acknowledging relativism and aspects such as the role of time, culture, and group, etc.—which make space place. One commits the fallacy of misplaced concreteness, converting abstractions into space. Eschatology becomes geography, in that heaven and hell become spatialized locales on earth. Home is heaven and foreign places hell, making home folks saints and foreigners devils. This mode of thinking leads to ethnic cleansing and civil war: think of the "damn" Yankees, in which the outsider is categorized eschatologically. I confess that I still feel, mildly, that the North is enemy territory, and I suppose some might eschatologize (and scatologize) regional differences; for example, where I live is still termed "the Southern part of heaven." Here one commits the fallacy of misplaced abstraction, imbuing space with metaphysical meanings. Christians and Muslims certainly eschatologized their respective lands during and after the Crusades. Deconstructing place, which is to say, showing how it was constructed, should not dispel a sense that when space becomes place it can become numinous, imbued with the holy or demonic.

In our search for scientific precision, we forget this numinosity and we reduce place to space. Environmentalism, for example, tends to reduce place to space in the geological or zoological and botanical dimensions. The goal is to preserve the land, or nature seen as including plants and animals, but not humans and their activities and significances, thus giving rise to coercive conservation. Preservationism features human constructions—buildings and homes—but can reduce place to space as physical structures. Genealogism fetishizes our ancestries, often attached to special places, and gets snobbish about who we are 'descended' from, detaching our family trees from the deeper and broader contexts that make these spaces places.[9] Technologism reduces places to machines—highways, vehicles, and computers—that track space but not place, while bureaucracy reduces place to documents—visas, passports. Humanists need to preserve the human against such powerful forces that reduce place to space.

---

[9] For example, Massey and Jess point out in "The Contestation of Place" that in Germany "blood" defines citizenship. Descent by blood rather than place of birth defines who is German, thus excluding 6.5 million foreigners, including 250,000 "black Germans" of Afro-Asian descent (163). Similarly, in "How English is it?" (1993), Donald points to the exclusion Gilroy sums up in "There ain't no black in the Union Jack." But the basis here seems to be different: a cozy empiricism—fact is a fact—that diminishes critical questioning, leading to what Donald calls "The English Garden effect." Donald writes: "the domestication of atrocity, it seems to me, is not only the essence of a conservative 'Englishness' framed in a nostalgic rhetoric of landscape and heritage" (183).

A concluding comment about those of us who are standing aloof to comment on all this: us academics. We academics have a paradoxical sense of place only exacerbated by globalism. On the one hand, we claim membership in the 'academic community,' which transcends locales, yet we are also obsessed with locale. 'Where do you teach?' or 'Where are you?' is a frequent question we ask each other, to which one replies with the name of an institution and often a place. We each hold a job and earn tenure at a given institution, and to move from one institution to another is significant. Yet, on the other hand, we are global. Our commitment is often to the discipline, defined globally, more than to the local institution and community, and we are rewarded, even locally, for our global contribution (publication) rather than for our local contribution, which tends to be defined as 'service.' In understanding this phenomenon of the place of place in globalization, academics should be a prime specimen for dissection, taking into account our history from medieval to electronic.

A second specimen should be the businessperson. Why? Capitalism is the great dissolver of place. The problem is, none of us realize the ramifications of each of the business moves in which we are entailed—from our individual investments to vast takeovers and development projects or global chains. Capitalism is itself deaf, dumb, and blind to its consequences, and so are most of us within this Weberian iron cage.

As an arena in which to observe the interplay between space and place, I suggest a region of the USA, the South. The South is not unique, but it is distinctive in its tradition of place in dialogue with history and change. Southern identity was born around 1830, as David Moltke-Hansen explains,[10] seared to intensity during the Civil War, and sustained still in varied forms, including the defensive one illustrated by recent controversy about the Confederate flag. The question is, what is the impact of globalism? What may happen, what may already be happening, is a globalization of this place identity. Southern identity is classically oppositional: the

---

[10] See Moltke-Hansen's essay "Regional Frameworks and Networks: Changing Identities in the Southeastern United States" (2000, 149-169).

South against the North, against the nation. But the South has not particularly opposed the world. Now, as the world comes to the South (through immigration, international business, and electronics), and the South to the world (e.g. through Bank America, Coca-cola, etc.), the oppositionality may diminish in relation to the global sphere, compared to our old anti-nation, or anti-North attitude. (And conversely, the attitude of the world is on the whole not particularly anti-South, at least not as vehemently as has been true of attitudes in the North in some aspects, because the South is not a widely known identity globally.) If globalization thus diminishes the oppositionality of Southern identity, will this also dissolve sense of place? Or will it be transformed, and if so how?

Yet there are many 'Souths'. What can we learn from comparison between this instance, the US-South, and many others parallel? The place of regionalism in Europe, where the European Union has created its Committee on Regions, is of great interest. So is Asia, especially China, uniting a commitment to a huge territory with a history of diaspora. Comparative and case studies must nourish and be nourished by theoretical formulations, such as those of Saskia Sasskind, Edward Casey, David Harvey, Arjun Appadurai, Ulf Hannerz, and many others.

No topic is more timely or important, then, than space and place as we enter the new century and millennium. Place matters, perhaps more than ever as forces of globalization blindly challenge this aspect of human existence which has been central since Homo Sapiens climbed down from the trees and staked claims to spaces, transmuting these into places through the genius of human experience.

Bibliography

Appadurai, Arjun. "Disjuncture and Difference in the Global Cultural Economy." *Public Culture*. 2.2 (Spring 1990): 1-24.

Bellah, Robert. "The Systematic Study of Religion." Appendix to *Beyond Belief*. London: Harper and Row, 1970. 260-88.

Casey, Edward. *The Fate of Place*. Berkeley: U of California P, 1997.

Donald, James. "How English is it?" *Space and Place: Theories of Identity and Location*. Eds. Erica Carter, James Donald, and Judith Squires. London: Lawrence and Wishart, 1993. 21-29.

Gilroy, Paul. *There Ain't No Black in the Union Jack*. London: Hutchinson, 1987.

Hannerz, Ulf. *Transnational Connections: Culture People, Places*. London: Routledge, 1996.

Harvey, David. *The Condition of Postmodernity*. Oxford: Basil Blackwell, 1989.

King, Russell. "Migrations, Globalization and place." In *A Place in the World: Places, Cultures and Globalization*. Eds. Doreen Massey and Pat Jess. New York: Oxford UP and the Open University, 1995. 5-33.

Moltke-Hansen, David. "Regional Frameworks and Networks: Changing Identities in the Southeastern United States." *Regional Images and Regional Realities*. Ed. Lothar Hönnighausen. Tübingen: Stauffenburg Verlag, 2000. 149-169.

Rose, Gillian. "Place and Identity: A Sense of Place." *A Place in the World: Places, Cultures and Globalization*. Eds. Doreen Massey and Pat Jess. New York: Oxford UP and the Open University, 1995. 87-132.

Weber, Max. *The Theory of Social and Economic Organization*. Trans. Talcott Parsons and A. M. Henderson. New York: Oxford UP, 1942.

Environment

(Eco)logic in Utah Landscapes: Edward Abbey and Terry Tempest Williams

Cornelius Browne

As a colleague and I were looking over the program for a recent conference, we paused over something that most of us now take for granted. We remarked in particular upon the title of the first session: *"Real" and Constructed Space*, with the word 'real' in quotation marks. The scare quotes imply, of course, that constructed space is more 'real' than 'real' space. The two writers I am concerned with in this essay dissent from the near consensus that privileges anything humanly constructed. Both Edward Abbey and Terry Tempest Williams inquire into our understanding of the relationship between human beings and their physical environments and emphasize the realness and particularity of place. This heightened attention to place does not deny the constructed nature of it, but insists—as Lawrence Buell encouraged a large audience of Americanists to recognize during a recent conference in Graz—that things are not always reducible to social constructs although social construction helps to form ideas about things. Buell went on to talk about a mutual, constrained constructivism, one that recognizes that our own intellectual activities are also influenced by things outside the realm of human culture.[1] Through their insistence on the reality of natural places—the Utah landscape in particular—both Abbey and Williams forefront the idea that spatial perception is rooted in place and that places have a 'real' dimension.

This idea is furthered by (and this essay is indebted to) anthropologist/philosopher Edward S. Casey, who convincingly argues that "space and time are themselves coordinated and co-specified in the common matrix provided by place. We realize the essential posteriority of space and time whenever we catch

---

[1] Buell "Green Disputes: Nature, Culture, American(ist) Theory," Unpublished Plenary Talk, European Association of American Studies Conference, April 15, 2000, Karl-Franzens-Universität, Graz, Austria.

ourselves apprehending spatial relations or temporal occurrences in a particular place" (37). We are all—even literary critics—"emplaced," and "the world comes bedecked in places; it is a place-world to begin with" (43). This essay will move out from Casey's contention, and, using the work of John Dewey and Maurice Merleau-Ponty, will look at how Abbey and Williams contribute to a discussion of the relationships between space, place, ecology, and culture.

In his famous 1968 book *Desert Solitaire*, Abbey compresses several summers working as a park service ranger into one, and that one "seamless summer" is located in Utah's Arches National Park, in a particular place. Williams organizes her 1991 book *Refuge* around the rising lake levels of Great Salt Lake as it inundates The Bear River Migratory Bird Refuge. Place becomes even more specific as the lake is aligned with the cancer slowly killing Williams's mother. In *Refuge,* a particular place is aligned with a particular body, a connection that becomes especially interesting when Williams engages what I call here an ecological logic—or (eco)logic—that can contribute significantly to a dialogue that attempts to articulate ways in which human beings might interact with the natural world without killing it and us off by the beginning of the next century. Both *Desert Solitaire* and *Refuge* encourage a re-formulation of how an aesthetic representation of experience in which natural places play a key role might lead to a way of imagining both place and space in a more ecological manner. But, whereas Abbey arguably set the tone for environmental writing as it moved into the last part of the twentieth century, Williams seems poised to take us into the next.[2]

---

[2] Stewart in *A Natural History of Nature Writing* sums up Abbey's importance: "Abbey elicited great devotion from those who knew him well, adulation, and even something of cult worship from the many who knew him only from his calls to action and the uncompromising honesty of his books. He altered stereotyped notions of the West as a wasteland, of Western writers as regional hicks, and of nature writing as humorless and self-important" (214). Abbey's work also inspired the radical environmental group Earth First! Of course, Williams herself is deeply indebted to Abbey. Cecilia Konchar Farr sees Williams as a direct descendent of Abbey in the tradition of "ecobiography" in "American Ecobiography."

Simply asked, then, might how we read and write have consequences for 'real' places?[3] The key terms 'experience' and 'consequences' bring us around to John Dewey, and his work will prove useful in approaching an answer to this question. Dewey writes that experience "occurs continuously, because the interaction of live creature and environing conditions is involved in the very process of living" (1934, 35). This notion of experience as process can be linked to what Dewey, in *Logic: The Theory of Inquiry*, calls "The Existential Matrix of Inquiry." Obviously, inquiry cannot happen without the rigorous application of intellect, but the matrix in which inquiry is performed is more extensive than the strictly human: "Whatever else organic life is or is not, it is a process of activity that involves an environment. It is a transaction extending beyond the spatial limits of the organism. An organism does not live *in* an environment; it lives by means of an environment" (1938, 25). As both Dewey's statements imply, inquiry—as an aspect of experience—is deeply related to the physical conditions that enable it, even if the importance of the physical environment is often masked by cultural constructs. Dewey goes on to say that "If what is designated by such terms as doubt, belief, idea, conception, is to have any objective meaning, to say nothing of public verifiability, it must be located and described as behavior in which organism and environment act together, or *interact*" (1938, 33 [Dewey's emphasis]). Meaning-construction must be located, is an interaction between self and world, and always entails consequences: "there is no inquiry that does not involve the making of *some* change in environing conditions" (1938; 34 [Dewey's emphasis]). Dewey's understanding of "objective meaning" is also not static. Meaning is determinable only in "a constellation of related meanings" (1938, 49), which are, in turn, emplaced in an environment, and, again,

---

[3] See Roorda, *Dramas of Solitude*. Roorda proposes a biopragmatist criticism: "A biopragmatist criticism might focus, for one thing, on the conditions informing the 'participatory' reading of generic texts–reading that entertains the prospect of conversion in the sense of imitating actions and recognitions depicted. This criticism would ask: What difference might it make in biological terms to take this text, this set of texts, or this mode of commentary as exemplary? What does it mean to seek and accept conversion upon the terms the work provides? What does it entail for the life of the place depicted and that of the places left behind" (100). A biopragmatist criticism could be further enhanced by Dewey's work on logic.

Dewey emphasizes interrelationships among places, ideas, and things, or, we might say, constructs an ecology of meaning.

For Dewey, Abbey, and Williams, inquiry is located in both physical and cultural places. Space, on the other hand, according to Merleau-Ponty, is not a location:

> not the setting (real or logical) in which things are arranged, but the means whereby the position of things becomes possible. This means that instead of imagining it as a sort of ether in which all things float, or conceiving it abstractly as a characteristic that they have in common, we must think of it as the universal power enabling them to be connected. (243)

Space is not something out of which places are carved. Space drives relationships and enables connections. Experience is predicated upon relationships, and non-human space potentiates these relationships. But to get at space, we may have to go through places. Emplacing artistic endeavor, Merleau-Ponty argues that "Aesthetic expression confers on what it expresses an existence in itself, installs it in nature as a thing perceived and accessible to all" (183). We could say that Abbey and Williams install their books in the Utah desert. Though installed in a natural field, a thing perceived alone is not a sufficient subject for inquiry. Inquiry demands engagement with what Dewey calls a "situation," defined as "not a single object or event or set of objects and events. For we never experience nor form judgements about objects and events in isolation, but only in connection with a conceptual whole. This latter is what is called a 'situation'" (1938, 66). But the situations that demand inquiry are not "whole," they are "indeterminate situations" that evoke questioning. These situations are "placeable," or, to use Merleau-Ponty's formulation, "installed in nature." Like places, they exist in patterns of relationships. The relationship between writing and natural places is an "indeterminate situation."

It is important to pause here and keep in sight two of Dewey's key insights: 1) he insists that "Only execution of existential operations directed by an idea in which ratiocination terminates can bring about the re-ordering of environing conditions required to produce a settled and unified situation" (1938, 118); in other words, inquiry is always directed toward practice that has real consequences in the existential world, and 2) no situation is permanently "unified" or "settled." All situations are involved in ongoing experience, to which aesthetic representation contributes. Both Williams and Abbey attempt this re-ordering of situations embedded in particular places.

In the introduction to *Desert Solitaire*, Abbey claims that his book is a tombstone for a place that he loved, "A bloody rock. Don't drop it on your foot—throw it at something big and glassy" (xiv), and his invective is in line with the tone of the late 1960s. He points to a bureaucratic structure enclosed by glass and steel, insulated from and dominating the natural places in which he attempts to live. In contrast to this big glassy thing, Abbey lives barely enclosed from the desert in a tin Park Service house trailer that minimally shields him from the elements, but it is "an iron lung [...] with windows and venetian blinds" (3), in other words, a space that encloses someone who, as Abbey's metaphor suggests, is desperately ill. In contrast to the iron lung whose electricity is powered by a gasoline generator, and in which Abbey finds himself "shut off from the natural world and sealed up, encapsulated, in a box of artificial light and tyrannical noise" (13), the natural world is healthier and open: "To the east, under a spreading sunrise, are more mesas, more canyons, league upon league of red cliff and arid tablelands, extending through purple haze over the bulging curve of the planet to the ranges of Colorado—a sea of desert" (195). The operative terms here are "more," "league upon league," "spreading," "extending," and "bulging." For Abbey the desert can be neither contained in nor perceived from either tall office buildings or little tin trailers—as a particular place it resists containment. And for all its extension, and its apparent "geological chaos [...] there is method at work here, method of a fanatic order and perseverance: each groove in the rock leads to a natural channel of some kind, every channel to a ditch and gulch and ravine, each larger waterway to a canyon bottom or broad wash leading in turn to the Colorado River and the sea" (10). Abbey's method here is to make sense of an apparently confused situation. His observations on the functioning of the landforms are accurate, but in his attribution of fanaticism and perseverance to the landscape, he mirrors his own desire for a fanatic relationship to the natural world in terms that echo Thoreau: "I dream of a hard and brutal mysticism in which the naked self merges with a non-human world and yet somehow survives still intact, individual, separate" (6). Even though Abbey perceives his dependence on the natural world, he still confronts it from the position of an isolated self. The individual remains alone, shouting at a tall glassy structure or enclosed in a little tin one. When the individual turns to the natural world, it is as a "naked self."

Abbey moves out of his trailer and spends much of his time under his homemade ramada, a place closer to sand, stone, and fire, yet he still feels the need to make claim to this particular place by calling it "Abbey's country" (4) and raising a red flag above his ramada (23). Abbey knows as much as anyone else that with the denigration of natural places, the possibility of the personal revelation he seeks is also diminished. What Abbey too often fails to realize is that his own inscriptions upon the desert are no less claims for possession and a personal marking off of public, natural places, which maintains the opposition of self and natural world.[4]

Nonetheless, Abbey's descriptions are striking and compelling, and they often attempt to represent places in a space that, as Merleau-Ponty claims space does, enables interaction and connection, both for the human and non-human. In his future vision, only a few will live

> in the strange country of the standing rock, far out where the spadefoot toads bellow madly in the moonlight on the edge of doomed rainpools, where the arsenic-

---

[4] Many commentators call attention to the fact that Abbey's often arrogant and isolated positions are intentional tactics to create dissonance, to jar the reader into awareness. This is no doubt often true. For a fine reading of Abbey in this regard see Slovic (1992, 93-114). Slovic argues that Abbey seeks "to alarm and disorient his readers" (93). Scheese discusses "Abbey's passionate desire for sanctuary from civilization" (110) in *Nature Writing* and in his article "*Desert Solitaire*: Counter-Friction to the Machine in the Garden." Scheese calls Abbey's method of argument "a rhetoric of rage" (213). Morris calls Abbey a "solitary creature in the postmodern desert" in his essay "Celebration and Irony: The Polyphonic Voice of Edward Abbey's *Desert Solitaire*" (31). A recent collection of essays on Abbey is *Coyote in the Maze: Tracking Edward Ab-*

selenium spring waits for the thirst-crazed wanderer, where the thunderstorms blast the pinnacles and cliffs, where the rust-brown floods roll down the barren washes, and where the community of the quiet deer walk at evening up glens of sandstone through tamarisk and sage toward the hidden springs of sweet, cool, still, clear unfailing water. (127)

But, for all its integration of landforms and life forms these places remain in Abbey's evocative prose primarily places for the solitary human, presumably male, who is of human beings "the boldest among them" (127). We are, most of us, neither "crazed wanderers," nor "the boldest among us." Rather, we probably move rather easily between urban or suburban settings and, if not wilderness, then "wilderness areas" when we so desire, and, finally, all of these places—wild and oversettled—and Abbey's claim that "wilderness is a necessary part of civilization" (47) bear upon our understanding of place. There is a push and shove between places and our ideas about them that is "involved in the very process of living" (1934, 35). Dewey calls this the doing and undergoing that contributes to the production of aesthetic experience. Ideally, this doing and undergoing seeks a punctuated equilibrium, but Abbey seems to do a bit too much of his own pushing and shoving. The narrator of *Desert Solitaire*—Ranger Abbey—though he is often in the company of other men, remains for the most part isolated from other relationships. When he perceives place primarily as a threatened point in space, in his efforts to defend it he is too often reduced to a logic of throwing rocks.

On the other hand, Williams's book is a logic of connections. Her refuge is easily reached by car. It is only about an hour's drive from Salt Lake City, and Williams gives us exact directions how to get there, providing coordinates such as the Mormon Tabernacle and the Salt Lake City International Airport. Her family, the wildlife of the area, and the Great Salt Lake are intimately entwined in a history and an ecology that has been officially perceived as empty space: "When the Atomic Energy Commission described the country north of the Nevada Test Site as

---

bey in a World of Words. Ed. Peter Quigley. The first and still valuable full length study of Abbey is Ann Ronald, *The New West of Edward Abbey*.

'virtually uninhabited desert terrain,' my family and the birds at Great Salt Lake were some of the 'virtual uninhabitants'" (1991, 287). Williams's home place is "real," direly threatened by officially constructed perceptions of place. In her world, there is no empty space. For Williams, just as for Merleau-Ponty, space is the power that enables things to be connected. The most obvious clues to Williams's understanding of space in these terms are her chapter heads, each of which names a type of bird, and the lake level. Merleau-Ponty bounds perception with only the horizon, but Williams is able to imagine, with the help of the birds, a deeper-reaching connection between space and experience. For example, she thinks back to her childhood: "I [...] pondered the relationship between an ibis at Bear River and an ibis foraging on the banks of the Nile. In my young mind, it had something to do with the magic of birds, how they bridge cultures and continents with their wings, how they mediate between heaven and earth" (1991, 18). The birds gather experience from afar; they also mediate between self and other, and, by implication, between self and something greater than the human, "heaven." Later, as an adult facing great personal loss, Williams again calls on the birds, "How can hope be denied when there is always the possibility of an American flamingo or a roseate spoonbill floating down from the sky like pink rose petals?" (1991, 90). The birds link human emotion, experience, with potentiating space that is anchored in a particular place, the Bear River Refuge.

Whereas Ranger Abbey sees his desert spaces primarily as threatened, Williams, though also acutely aware of environmental threat, imagines space as a power that enables an ecology. What I find so important for the future about Williams's perception of ecology is, although she indeed too often descends to male/female, culture/nature dichotomies, her ecological perception of space integrating love, family, sex, death, and non-human living and non-living things. Therefore, *Refuge* is not only installed in a particular location but also "always embedded in a context of social relations" (Tallmadge, 202). Casting Williams as a writer with an eye toward consequences, Cassandra Kircher points out that these social relations extend outward into the world: "Williams's project in *Refuge* [is] to reconceptualize her relationship with the world in language in order to change the world or, at least, in order to try to change the way that her readers perceive the relationship between humans and nature" (108). It is an important book that reflects a Deweyan attention to consequences and shows affinities with Deweyan logic.

Refuge is a cyclical text beginning and ending with the rise and return to normal level of Great Salt Lake. As Mormons, Williams's family is deeply rooted in the Utah landscape, and Williams adds that "The birds and I share a natural history. It is a matter of rootedness, of living inside a place for so long that the mind and imagination fuse" (1991, 21).[5] But this place is by no means always a benign one. Williams imagines that "The pulse of Great Salt Lake, surging along Antelope Island's shores, becomes the force wearing against my mother's body" (1991, 64). At first the alignment seems a bit simplistic, the flooding lake threatens the bird refuge just as the cancer threatens Williams's mother. The island and the body of the mother are both places endangered by more or less natural occurrences. However, as Kircher points out, Williams breaks new ground with her alignment of the natural world and her actual mother, thereby reinscribing the family into environmental writing (104). Williams uses familial relations to inquire into the "indeterminate situation" of our current cultural understanding of the relationships between space and place.

To extend Kircher's argument, Williams attempts to create what might be called a familial ecology as her primary tool for performing inquiry. Again, inquiry happens within an "existential matrix," an environment. A problem, an "indeterminate situation," has a location. According to Dewey, "The immediate locus of the problem concerns [...] what kind of responses the organism shall make. It concerns the interaction of organic responses and environing conditions in their movement toward an existential issue" (1938, 107). That her mother's cancer may have been caused by nuclear testing upwind from Utah, that Great Salt Lake is flooding the bird refuge, and that human beings evince a shocking disregard for the local envi-

---

[5] Bryant sees Williams's project as a rewriting of natural history that includes the self in "The Self in Nature: Four American Autobiographies" (98-101).

ronment all locate the specific problem around Williams's home and help determine her response to the problem. Inquiry is generated through human interaction with an environment. Because of her rootedness in the Utah landscape, Williams is in a perfect position to enact the type of interactive inquiry described by Dewey:

> Organic interaction becomes inquiry when existential consequences are anticipated; when environing conditions are examined with reference to their potentialities; and when responsive activities are selected and ordered with reference to actualization of some of the potentialities, rather than others, in a final existential situation. Resolution of the indeterminate situation is active and operational. (1938, 107)

Williams's primary response, of course, is *Refuge*. Within the book, she makes certain choices, and one of those is her decision to link the members of her family to the natural landscape in her attempt to present a familial ecology whose logic works toward a particular existential consequence: a revised cultural awareness that encourages people to live in a way more ecologically respectful toward the natural world and the human and non-human communities that inhabit it. Williams is concerned with the potential of human connection to very real places and spaces. In *Refuge* the power to generate connections that Merleau-Ponty attributes to space is further drawn into experience through the aesthetic representation of a family in a place—through the logic of a familial ecology.

Developing this ecology, Williams claims that there are dunes hidden along the margins of Great Salt Lake that travelers, most of us motoring by on I-80, rarely manage to see:

> [The] dunes [...] are the armatures of animals. Wind swirls around the sand and ribs appear. There is musculature in dunes.
>
> And they are female. Sensuous curves–the small of a woman's back. Breasts. Buttocks. Hips and pelvis. They are the natural shapes of Earth. Let me lie naked and disappear. (1991, 109)

Well, part of this is readily recognizable, even a bit clichéd. The will to confront nature naked and to disappear into it echoes Abbey's "hard and brutal mysticism." But there is a difference. Williams indeed figures the land as female, a strategy rightfully suspect to many. But it is not only a *human* female. The skeletal structure of animals is revealed by the work of wind upon sand, and ribs and muscles emerge. Only then are they revealed to be female, and only after that to be a woman's shape. The woman seems to evolve from this action upon the desert, of air upon land. But even more central than that, the woman can be seen as particular women, namely Williams and her mother.

Williams herself has had two cysts removed from her breasts, both benign, but she is rightly worried about her own potential cancer. She writes about her grandmother's and her mother's physical beauty, undiminished by their mastectomy scars, and while she stands looking at her own body in a mirror her husband approaches from behind, and she whispers to him "Hold my breasts" (1991, 99). Because she aligns her own female body (and her potential cancer) with both the body of the sand dunes and her mother's dying body, this erotic gesture draws her male lover/husband deeply into the landscape and into the literal bodies of the family as well, thus extending the familial relationship well beyond only the feminine.

As her mother's cancer progresses, the link between sex and death becomes more evident: "Death is no longer what I imagined it to be. Death is earthy like birth, like sex, full of smells and sounds and bodily fluids. It is a confluence of evanescence and flesh" (1991, 219), and the confluence of her mother's body and natural spaces becomes even more clear: "I watch her skeleton push through skin, emerging bone by bone, rib by rib, until her vertebrae have become the ladder my fingers climb as I rub her back" (1991, 218). In a reversal of the process in which the human female body emerged from the sand, the dying female body recalls the dunes that "are the armatures of animals. Wind swirls around the sand and ribs appear" (1991, 109). By having her mother's rib cage emerge from her skin just as the ribs of female animals emerged from the dunes, Williams marks her realization of the cyclical nature of all life, and, as her mother declines, she charges this ancient awareness with the power that derives from familial love. The family is now extended beyond the human: "I realize months afterward that my grief is much larger than I could ever have imagined. The headless snake without its rattles, the slaughtered birds, even the pumped lake and the flooded desert, become extensions of my family. Grief dares us to love once more" (1991, 252). Kircher points out that this passage dismantles patriarchy by depicting an "ever-expanding" family inclusive of all things (107). I agree, but more happens here. Williams creates an "existential matrix" in which all things are part of an ecology, and all things become involved in her inquiry. She creates an (eco)logic that privileges the connections between the well-being of birds, sand, water, and humans as integral parts of her problem-solving strategies.

An inclusive act of an imagination grounded in the ecology of a particular place allows Williams to love the desert, its creatures and landforms as family. And William comes to see that "I am slowly, painfully discovering that my refuge is not found in my mother, my grandmother, or even the birds of Bear River. My refuge exists in my capacity to love. If I can learn to love death then I can begin to find refuge in change" (1991, 178). She loved Edward Abbey as family. In "A Eulogy for Edward Abbey," Williams writes, "Things are different now. That's why we're here. Change is growth, growth is life, and life is death. We are here to honor Ed, [...] to acknowledge family, tribe, and clan. And it has everything to do with love: loving each other, loving the land. This is a re-dedication of purpose and place" (1996, 202). Though she also throws rocks (but without Abbey's wonderful bombasity), her willingness to embrace change in the form of death, not death in the abstract, but the 'real' death of her mother—to see change in the form of a flooding lake, in the cyclical nature of human and non-human life, and to align that life with particular natural places creates an (eco)logic that perceives space as a universal power enabling connections. Williams's way toward perceiving and engaging this power lies through a specific place. The situations that drive our inquiry are closely related to particular places, to the bodies that inhabit those places, and to our representation of both. Williams has said that "the most radical thing we can commit is to stay home" (Jensen, 322; Siporin, 101). Dewey seems to concur, "To remain and endure is a mode of action" (1938, 135). Our being in a place is our being in a world, is our existence in a situational and situated ecology, in a logic that includes both cultural forms and bedrock.

Bibliography

Abbey, Edward. *Desert Solitaire: A Season in the Wilderness.* 1968; New York: Touchstone, 1990.

Bryant, Lynn Ross. "The Self in Nature: Four American Autobiographies." *Soundings* 80.1: (1997).

Casey, Edward S. "How to Get from Space to Place in a Fairly Short Stretch of Time: Phenomenological Prolegomena." *Senses of Place.* Ed. Steven Feld and Keith H. Basso. Santa Fe: School of American Research, 1996. 13-52.

Dewey, John. *Art as Experience.* New York: Perigee, 1934.

---. *Logic: The Theory of Inquiry.* New York: Holt, Rinehart and Winston, 1938.

Farr, Cecilia Konchar. "American Ecobiography." *Literature of Nature: An International Sourcebook.* Ed. Patrick Murphy. Chicago: Fitzroy Dearborn, 1998. 94-97.

Jensen, Derrick. *Listening to the Land: Conversations about Nature, Culture, and Eros.* San Francisco: Sierra Club, 1995.

Kircher, Cassandra. "Rethinking Dichotomies in Terry Tempest Williams's Refuge." *ISLE* 3.1 (1996): 97-114.

Merleau-Ponty, Maurice. *Phenomenology of Perception.* Trans. Colin Smith. London & New York: Routledge, 1962.

Morris, David Copeland. "Celebration and Irony: The Polyphonic Voice of Edward Abbey's Desert Solitaire." *Western American Literature* 28.1 (1993): 21-31.

Quigley, Peter. *Coyote in the Maze: Tracking Edward Abbey in a World of Words.* Salt Lake City: U of Utah P, 1998.

Ronald, Ann. *The New West of Edward Abbey.* Albuquerque: U of New Mexico P, 1982.

Roorda, Randall. *Dramas of Solitude: Narratives of Retreat in American Nature Writing.* Albany: SUNY P, 1998.

Ross Bryant, Lynn. "The Self in Nature: Four American Autobiographies." *Soundings* 80.1 (1997): 83-103.

Scheese, Don. "Desert Solitaire: Counter-Friction to the Machine in the Garden" *North Dakota Quarterly* 59.2 (1991): 211-227.

---. *Nature Writing: The Pastoral Impulse in America*. New York: Twayne, 1996.

Siporin, Ona. "Terry Tempest Williams and Ona Siporin: A Conversation." *WAL* 31.2 (1996): 99-113.

Slovic, Scott. *Seeking Awareness in American Nature Writing*. Salt Lake City: U of Utah P, 1992.

Stewart, Frank. *A Natural History of Nature Writing*. Washington, D.C.: Island P, 1995.

Tallmadge, John. "Beyond the Excursion: Initiatory Themes in Annie Dillard and Terry Tempest Williams." *Reading the Earth: New Directions in the Study of Literature and Environment*. Ed. Michael P. Branch, et al. Moscow, ID: U of Idaho P, 1998. 197-207.

Williams, Terry Tempest. "A Eulogy for Edward Abbey." *Resist Much Obey Little: Remembering Ed Abbey*. Ed. James R. Hepworth and Gregory McNamee. San Francisco: Sierra Club, 1996. 199-203.

---. *Refuge: An Unnatural History of Family and Place*. New York: Vintage, 1991.

Monstrous Technologies in Silko, Castillo, Ortiz, and Solnit

Louise Westling

In *The Illusion of the End* Jean Baudrillard makes the sardonic claim that our present era represents the triumph of Walt Disney, who anticipated a world in which "all past or present forms meet in a playful promiscuity," and where, as immensely privileged citizens of industrialized Western countries, we can inhabit any reality we choose" (118). The postmodern play of signifiers constructing 'place' and 'nature' allows us free enjoyment of a virtual cyberspace where all strange desires can be gratified, where we can morph ourselves or images of others into strange forms, and where we can consume an endless array of products from all over the globe. Donna Haraway tells us that we are all cyborgs and must accept the erasure and overlapping of boundaries, indeed celebrate the perverse multiplicities of our identities produced in the present era of "the implosion of the natural and the artificial, nature and culture, subject and object, machine and organic body, money and lives, narrative and reality" (14). Yet if we notice the fragments of news, the faint sounds of protest and pain that sometimes break through the fog of advertising and consumerism surrounding our comfortable New World Order, then we know that our playful Walt Disney reality is neither virtual or innocent. The pleasant spaces of our lives require the violent manipulation of other kinds of spaces. Actual physical landscapes in India, Vietnam, Indonesia, Brazil, Guatemala, northern Mexico, and southern New Mexico and Arizona, and of Texas, Louisiana, and Mississippi, and many others, are inundated with toxic waste that sickens and kills millions of plants and animals, including people who are almost always poor and dark-skinned. There is a dead zone in the Gulf of Mexico, at the mouth of the Mississippi River, that has grown dramatically in the past several xears to 7,700 square miles (12.320 km^2) last year. In fact, despite their playfully postmodern rhetorical practices, both Baudrillard and Haraway catalogue the perversions and dangers of our culture's insatiate power. Baudrillard flatly states that "the distress of the rest of the world is

115

at the root of Western power" and points to the way we feed upon that distress to entertain our jaded imaginations in a "catastrophic cannibalism, relayed in a cynical mode by the news media" (68). What we fail to notice is the way our cheerful techno-paradise is destroying our own species along with the 'natural' spaces we pretend to idealize.

> In aiming for virtual (technical) immortality and ensuring its exclusive perpetuation by a projection into artifacts, the human species is precisely losing its own immunity and specificity and becoming immortalized *as an inhuman species*; it is abolishing in itself the mortality of the living in favour of the immortality of the dead [....] As a result, by going down these paths of artifice which were supposed to ensure its indefinite survival, it is perhaps hurtling even more quickly to its doom. (Baudrillard, 84)

Haraway attacks media manipulation of images of poor and dark-skinned people as a phony racial universalism that masks increasing racial hatred and exploitation of minority populations around the world. And she anatomizes the dangerous power dynamics at the heart of technologies such as genetic engineering. Yet, in her most recent book, she has adopted a troubling new persona to replace her earlier playful cyborg, this time one that reflects her own position within the power elite. It is the figure of the vampire

> who effects category transformations by illegitimate passages of substance; the one who drinks and infuses blood in a paradigmatic act of infecting whatever poses as pure; the one that eschews sun worship and does its work at night; the one who is undead, unnatural, and perversely incorruptible. [Haraway's vampire is] the cosmopolitan, the one who speaks too many languages and cannot remember the native tongue, and the scientist who forces open the parochial dogmas of those who are sure they know what nature is. In short, once touched by the figure of this monster, one is forced to inhabit the swirling semantic field of vampire stories. (Haraway, 214-215)

The language of this passage betrays Haraway's own—and Baudrillard's—implication in the power and privilege they decry. Haraway herself implies as much when she reports the resistance of indigenous peoples to the Human Genome Diversity Project's efforts to sample and categorize their genetic material. The scientists involved were liberal biologists, but their premises were those of the dominant technological culture. "Not surprisingly," Haraway explains, "it turned out that indigenous people were more interested in representing themselves" (249) than in being manipulated by scientists and people from outside their cultures.

The victims of the monstrous technologies playfully satirized by Baudrillard and Haraway do indeed want to speak for themselves. They want to describe their lives in poisoned environments for they understand intimately what Maurice Merleau-Ponty reminds us—that our life finds its meaning in incarnation within the contingency of the event. We are bodies living within complex interrelated physical communities. In the past several decades, an increasing number of accomplished writers from Native American and Chicano (mestizo, Spanish-speaking/Indio) communities affected by toxic waste from some of these technologies have been bringing the news to a mainstream reading public in a steady stream of fiction, poetry, and essays. Writers like Rudolfo Anaya, Gloria Anzaldúa, Ana Castillo, Simon Ortiz, and Leslie Marmon Silko have been telling the stories of Indian communities poisoned by radioactivity from uranium mining on Navajo and Pueblo reservations, and Chicano communities impoverished and poisoned by toxic factories for products such as weapons, computer chips, and vinyl luggage on their traditional lands. This kind of literary resistance has become increasingly popular in the mainstream reading public, especially in the academy, where Silko's novels *Ceremony* and *Almanac of the Dead*, Ortiz's poetry, and Castillo's novel *So Far From God* are being widely read and discussed in print by a young, environmentally concerned generation of literary critics. I propose to describe this work and to offer a few thoughts about its significance. Some of the writers themselves theorize the kind of cultural work they seek to accomplish in fiction and poetry. Silko's widely-anthologized essay "Landscape, History, and the Pueblo Imagination," Ortiz's communal autobiography "Our Homeland, a National Sacrifice Area," and Castillo's unsparing book *Massacre of the Dreamers* come to mind in particular. But I want also to call attention to Rebecca Solnit's book *Savage Dreams*, an unusual blending of anti-nuclear activist reportage with a cultural history of nuclear physics within the German romantic tradition of peripatetic philosophy in idealized spaces like the *Philosophenweg* in Heidelberg, all converging within the context of a landscape history of Nevada and California. This convergence demonstrates the intertwining of imperial political conquest with cultural construction of wilderness preservation narratives, and their odd conjunctions with the Indian reservations and nuclear test zones on landscapes of the Southwest. But Solnit also implies in her discussion of the physics of Einstein and Heisenberg, as well as in her descriptions of contemporary environmental activism on military nuclear test zones in Nevada, that the instrumentalist Cartesian view of nature underlying technoscience is profoundly mistaken. Her rhetorical practice insists that nature is not separate from humans, and that it is not inert or lifeless. Furthermore, the conquered are not supine; they are fighting back. Silko, Ortiz, and Castillo prove her point, for they are engaged in a literary dialogue that destabilizes the dominant myths of Manifest Destiny and technological utopia.

Let me provide a brief descriptions of how Silko's novels, Ortiz's poetry and essays, and Castillo's *So Far From God*, dramatize the effects of poisonous technologies on people and their wider communities. Silko uses the pervasive imagery of sickness to dramatize the effects of white US society's deadly military/industrial activities upon poor Indian and mixed-blood Mexican people in Arizona. At the same time that she does this, however, she suggests that indigenous peoples can resist environmental and cultural destruction by returning to traditional wisdom and adapting it for present circumstances. *Ceremony* links the physical and psychic illness of a mixed-blood Pueblo Indian veteran of World War II with both the racist American military machine and the nuclear industry that has poisoned the Southwest landscape since the 1940s. The novel's protagonist Tayo only begins to heal when he reconnects with the feminine spiritual traditions of his tribal ancestors and the powers of the natural world with which they are in harmony. At an abandoned uranium mine on his reservation, Tayo suddenly understands this convergence.

> He had been so close to it, caught up in it for so long that its simplicity struck him deep inside his chest: Trinity Site, where they exploded the first atomic bomb, was only three hundred miles to the southeast, at White Sands. And the top-secret laboratories where the bomb had been created were deep in the Jemez Mountains, on land the Government took from Cochiti Pueblo: Los Alamos, only a hundred miles northeast of him now, still surrounded by high electric fences and the ponderosa pine and tawny sandrock of the Jemez mountain canyon where the shrine of the twin mountain lions had always been. There was no end to it; it knew no boundaries; and he had arrived at the point of convergence where the fate of all living things, and even the earth, had been laid [...] From that time on, human beings were one clan again, united by the fate the destroyers planned for all of them, for all living things; united by a circle of death that devoured people in cities twelve thousand miles away, victims who had never known these mesas, who had never seen the delicate colors of the rocks which boiled up their slaughter. (*Ceremony*, 246)

Silko's 1991 novel, *Almanac of the Dead*, is a fierce, apocalyptic indictment of greedy and materialistic American society on the eve of the 500th anniversary of Columbus's first landing in the Americas. This novel imagines the poor and oppressed of the Americas, led by the remaining indigenous populations, rising up to destroy the oppressive corporate/industrial powers which rule the hemisphere. They do so from the ground up, in a loosely coordinated attack upon the technological infrastructure that supports the dominant capitalist system. In an eerie example of life seeming to imitate art, Silko imagines twin brothers from Central America leading an army of indigenous *campesino* (peasant) rebels northward—thus prophesying the Chiapas rebellion in southern Mexico that occurred soon after the novel was published. These are the reincarnated Hero Twins of the Mayan epic *Popol Vuh*, but this time they are not fighting the mythical Lords of Death in the Mayan underworld, but rather the contemporary industrial lords of death who rule the governments of the hemisphere. Silko is thus restaging the prophesies of the

Mayan *Popol Vuh* and *Chilam Balam* as symbolic framework for her jeremiad against the corrupt American, Mexican, Guatemalan, and Canadian societies at the end of the twentieth century. The Mayan cosmic calendar is organized according to a 'Long Count' of approximately 5,200 years which completes one stage in a cyclical succession of created worlds. The present cycle in the Long Count is due to end in our year 2012, and Silko uses this calculation as the basis for suggesting that year as the time the EuroAmerican technological hegemony will collapse under the pressure of indigenous rebellions within the hemisphere, and perhaps even beyond, to encompass the globe and wreck the entire New World Order that has brought unparalleled prosperity to a few, but enormous misery and destruction to most of Earth's living communities.

Almanac moves from the focus on nuclear and military destruction that had dominated *Ceremony* to depict underground trafficking in organs taken from dismembered poor and homeless people for sale to the rich, violence as pornography for a jaded upper-class, a huge corrupt drug network to serve the pleasures of the same ruling elite, and the wrecking of the landscape for ever-larger profits. These practices, as Rachel Stein has explained, express the "reckless disregard for the integrity of the natural world and native peoples who are their prime targets of destruction" (139). Industrialists create a physical space to fulfill their own visions of nature as dead and inert, against the protests of indigenous peoples who have always understood the land as alive and themselves as kindred with all living beings within its community. Silko goes so far as to suggest in this novel that the forces of living nature will rise up against such depredations by dramatically destabilizing the weather—bringing droughts, hurricanes, tornadoes, and floods.

Ana Castillo's *So Far from God* is set in a parched New Mexico landscape where a matriarchal Chicana family of mother and four daughters negotiates among multiple realities: their life in a small agricultural Chicano community whose history goes back to an era before Spanish conquest when their Indian ancestors farmed the land; the folkloric traditions of La Llorona who cries for her murdered children; an animistic understanding of the world; the vibrant folk Catholicism of their community; and the corporate American world of factories, mass-produced consumer goods, and pervasive media pressure to consume and be successful like the icons of the TV advertising industry. The mother of this family, Sophia, is the wise organizing presence through whom we come to understand the miracle of one daughter's rising from the dead, another's rape and mutilation by angry men, the fatal attempt of another to succeed in the mainstream white world as a journalist, and the toxic poisoning of the fourth in a factory where workers are secretly exposed to powerful solvents which bring early and radical cancers denied by the elusive powers that operate the industry. All the daughters have the allegorical names of the Christian virtues of Faith, Hope, and Charity, except the one who rises from the dead and seems to inhabit an alternate reality—La Loca—the crazy one. Ultimately, all the daughters are killed, but their mother has been awakened by their sufferings to become a community activist who is elected mayor of the town to fight pollution and corporate oppression of the poor. Such small practical steps seem all that can be managed in the face of terrible damage. But it is our only hope.

What use are the stories these writers tell? Andrew Ross is right to deny the possibility of any simple return to organic holism—what he calls "visions of decentralized agrarian utopias or the atavistic appreciation of deep ecologists for uninhabited places" (1991, 8). To this denial I think we must add a denial of any restoration of a pre-industrial way of life according to tribal traditions like those imagined by Silko in her latest novel, *Gardens in the Dunes*. Do Silko, Ortiz, and Castillo mean to suggest a literal return of that kind? Probably not, but then what do they offer their readers?

- critiques of technoscience in its present imperial corporate form,
- vivid personal news from the front about problems which the advertising barrage of Disneyfied images keeps hidden from us,
- evidence that the promises of global New World Order consumerist prosperity and technofixes for our environmental problems are profoundly misguided, and

- visions of phenomenological wholeness that can be adapted for a profound redefinition of the human place in the biosphere—an ecological sense of the interdependency of all life.

Silko, Ortiz, and Castillo seek to show why rich nations need to transform the way technology is understood, to change it from a monstrous instrument of exploitation and destruction into a more modest array of tools operating symbiotically within distinctive environmental communities. They tell us that we are not separate from the devastated landscapes they write about. Those who live in the Borderlands "where the Third World grates against the first and bleeds" (25)—to use Gloria Anzeldúa's words—can testify in a literature that has never accepted the disembodied, playfully nihilistic language theories of the postmodern elites in the First World. Anzeldúa defines writing as a sensuous act linked to the sacred writing of her Aztec ancestors. "*Escribo con la tinta de mi sangre.* I write in red ink. Intimately knowing the smooth touch of paper, its speechlessness before I spill myself on the insides of trees" (93). Silko, Ortiz, and Castillo believe that language and writing are embodied and sacred. For Silko in *Ceremony*, the words of her novel perform the healing ceremony desperately needed by a sick culture.

> I will tell you something about stories.
> They aren't just entertainment
> Don't be fooled.
> They are all we have, you see,
> all we have to fight off
> illness and death. (2)

The lush green suburbias of Arizona and New Mexico are going to die when the aquifers and rivers they are draining run dry; they will be as barren as the Pueblo, Navajo, Apache, and Hopi reservations and the poisoned border between Mexico and Texas, New Mexico, Arizona, and California are now. If the Gulf of Mexico dies, so will all the ecosystems on the land around it. The monstrous technologies described by Silko, Ortiz, Castillo, and Solnit are not virtual, not socially constructed. They are poisoning us, and these writers are pulling aside the veil of denial that is fabricated by our dominant culture, pulling aside the veil to awaken us all. Simon Ortiz writes:

> Listen, that's the way you hear it.
> From the earth,
> the moving power of the voice
> and the People talking.
> Praying, you know, singing soft too.
> Hearing,
> that's the way you listen.
> The People talking,
> telling the power to come to them
> and pretty soon it will come.
> It will come,
> the moving power of the voice,
> the moving power of the earth,
> the moving power of the People.
> That's the place Indian People talk about.
>
> ("That's the Place Indians Talk About," 324)

> Duwah hahtse dzah.
> This is the land.
> It is our life, your life,
> my life, life.
> Hahtse. Naya. Kutra tsahtee.
> Land. Mother. Your breath, living.
>
> ("Mama's and Daddy's Words," 329)

Bibliography

Anzaldúa, Gloria. *Borderlands/La Frontera: The New Mestiza.* 1987: San Francisco: Aunt Lute Books, 1999.

Baudrillard, Jean. *The Illusion of the End.* Trans. Chris Turner. Stanford: Stanford UP, 1994.

Castillo, Ana. *Massacre of the Dreamers: Essays on Xicanisma.* Albuquerque: U of New Mexico P, 1994.

---. *So Far From God.* New York: Penguin, 1994.

Edmonson, Munro S., trans. *Heaven Born Merida and its Destiny: The Book of Chilam Balam of Chumayel.* Austin, U of Texas P, 1986.

Haraway, Donna J. *Modest-Witness, Second-Millennium. FemaleMan Meets OncoMouse: Feminism and Technoscience.* New York: Routledge, 1997.

Ortiz, Simon. *Woven Stone.* Tuscon: U of Arizona P, 1992.

Ross, Andrew. *Strange Weather: Culture, Science, and Technology in the Age of Limits.* New York: Verso, 1991.

Silko, Leslie Marmon. *Almanac of the Dead.* New York: Simon and Schuster, 1991.

---. *Ceremony.* New York: Viking, 1977.

---. *Gardens in the Dunes.* New York: Simon and Schuster, 1999.

---. "Landscape, History, and the Pueblo Imagination." *Antaeus* 57 (Autumn 1986): 83-94.

Solnit, Rebecca. *Savage Dreams: A Journey into the Landscape Wars of the American West.* New York: Vintage, 1994.

Stein, Rachel. *Shifting the Ground: American Women Writers Revisions of Nature, Gender, and Race.* Charlottesville: U P of Virginia, 1997.

Tedlock, Dennis, trans. *The Popol Vuh: The Mayan Book of the Dawn of Life.* New York: Touchstone, 1996.

Remediating Nature:
National Parks as Mediated Public Space

Richard Grusin

It is now possible to watch Old Faithful erupt on America Online. Indeed, courtesy of four webcams linked to the Yellowstone National Park website, anybody with an internet connection can monitor the activity of Yellowstone's most well known geyser or check on the grazing elk herds in the parking area in front of the park's Mammoth Hot Springs. In addition, Yellowstone's official website invites web surfers to take any number of virtual tours of the park, choosing from a menu comprised of one history tour, five nature tours, and twenty-one QTVR (Quick-Time Virtual Reality) panoramas. Initially, such technologically mediated phenomena appear antithetical to the kinds of experience that national parks were established to provide for American citizens and other visitors. Parks, it would seem, should get people out from behind their computers, not encourage them to stay there. Isn't at least one of the purposes of America's national parks to preserve and protect nature from the encroachment of technology, to provide opportunities for individuals to encounter nature or the wilderness face to face, without the perceptual or conceptual mediations of society or culture? Well, yes and no.

As environmental historians and ecocritics have reminded us for the past three decades, such experiences are increasingly elusive, if not phantasmatic. At the advent of the twenty-first century, it is generally agreed that 'nature' is a cultural construction. William Cronon, for example, contends that wilderness reproduces the cultural values its advocates seek to escape—that there is "nothing natural about the concept of wilderness" (Cronon, 1995, 69). As Lawrence Buell has noted, citing "The West as America," the 1991 exhibit at the Smithsonian Museum of American Art, it is now almost taken for granted that the "nineteenth-century American romantic representation of the West was built on an ideology of conquest" (35). For Cronon and Buell, as for such New Western Historians as Patricia

Limerick and Richard White, the ideology of nature or wilderness preservation has been demystified, has been revealed to harbor within it the very will to power it would set out to escape.[1] Motivated largely by the widespread acceptance of arguments for the social or cultural construction of knowledge, such scholars have begun to retell the history of American environmentalism not as the growing awareness of the intrinsic value of nature or wilderness, but as the increasing deployment of the ideology of nature's intrinsic value to advance the social, cultural, or political interests of a dominant race, class, gender, or institutional formation.

As powerful as these revisionist narratives are, however, they run the risk of stripping nature of any particularity or specificity whatsoever—of transforming nature so completely into culture that the preservation of nature as a national park, for example, becomes indistinguishable from its transformation into a ranch or a mine or a shopping mall. In noting this risk, I do not mean to propose that we undo the hard-earned insights offered by the cultural construction of knowledge. Rather I would urge that we undertake the challenging task of taking these insights more seriously. Granted that nature is culturally constructed, we need to ask how it differs from (and intersects with) other culturally constructed entities. We need to ask how the cultural construction of nature varies historically as well as how aspects of nature's construction seem to remain constant not only through time but across different geographical locations.

I argue that from their inception national parks have functioned as technologies for reproducing nature. In particular national parks emerged according to the scientific, cultural, and aesthetic practices of a particular historical moment—the period roughly between the Civil War and the end of the first World War (Grusin). In this

---

[1] It is generally accepted that the major figures of the New Western History are Cronon, Limerick, White, and Worster. The paradigmatic works of this intellectual movement include *Under an Open Sky*, edited by Cronon, Miles, and Gitlin; Limerick's *The Legacy of Conquest*; White's "It's Your Misfortune and None of My Own," and Worster's *Under Western Skies*. The works of these and other New Western Historians are by no means univocal. In a special issue of *Arizona Quarterly* devoted to the New Western History, Frisk maps out some of the differences among these historians. Frisk argues in part that these differences are made possible only within a horizon of shared assumptions, including the assumption that environmentalism and preservationism

paper I extend my historical study of the origins of the national parks to today's media-saturated environment. Building upon my recent work on new digital media, I explore the way in which the concept of nature as public space has been 'remediated' in the last decades of the twentieth century (Cf. Bolter and Grusin). At a moment when the explosive growth of new media technologies has enabled nature to be culturally constructed in an arguably unprecedented variety of aesthetic forms, it is important to understand the often contradictory ways in which these new media technologies claim to improve upon prior forms of representing place, environment, and landscape. On the one hand, through their 'liveness' and interactivity, new media technologies like streaming video or virtual reality claim to offer us a more immediate, authentic experience of nature than prior media forms, an experience in which all signs of cultural mediation have vanished. The goal of these technologies is to make possible the experience of unmediated nature anywhere in the world, that is, anywhere within the extensive networks of global telecommunication. On the other hand, through their self-acknowledgment and ubiquity, networked technologies like portable information appliances or the World Wide Web claim to offer us a more highly mediated experience of nature than has been possible before. The goal of these technologies is to make possible the experience of digital mediation anywhere in the natural world, which simultaneously produces and destabilizes the distinction between nature and its mediation.

This paper takes up some examples of how the National Park Service transforms nature into a public space where the boundary between the natural world and the mediated one has become increasingly open and permeable. Of the major American parks, Yellowstone, recognized as the world's first national park, has the most extensively developed Web apparatus for cybertourists, evident in its on-line tours, webcams, and QTVR panoramas. Grand Canyon, the most visited park in the West, has the most extensively developed media apparatus for tourists who travel to the park seeking to experience the mysteries of the canyon. As I argue elsewhere,

---

do not escape, but replicate, the ideological categories and the discriminatory or exploitative practices of nineteenth-century American culture.

Grand Canyon National Park is a heterogeneous cultural and technological network for reproducing nature as cognitively inaccessible (Grusin). The seeming impossibility of capturing the Canyon within a single representational form has brought forth a proliferation of different representations in a variety of genres and media. Although no individual conceptual or pictorial framework may let a visitor comprehend the Grand Canyon in its entirety, the multiplicity of representations can reproduce something like the feeling of nature's cognitive inaccessibility that lies at the heart of the Grand Canyon's appeal to tourists. In re-mediating the Canyon in different technologies of mediation, more recent efforts do not give up on the goal of capturing an experience of the Canyon's immediacy, but often do so in such a way as to call attention to, while at the same time seeking to erase, the signs of nature's mediation.

A telling example of this remediation of nature can be found by taking up the production of the IMAX film *Grand Canyon: The Hidden Secrets* in conjunction with the cultural practices for screening it that have evolved since its release in 1984. The aim of the film, as expressed in the companion piece *Making of Grand Canyon: The Hidden Secrets*, is to provide the "ninety-five percent of people, who only see the South Rim, an extraordinary extension of their experience" (Merrell and Memmott). If as McLuhan famously noted, media technologies are extensions of our senses, the makers of the IMAX film extend our experience of nature by putting cameras "where very few people ever go" and providing "perspectives very few people ever get" (Merrell and Memmott). *Making of Grand Canyon* emphasizes the heroism of the filmmakers, opening with a voice-over narrative that makes a claim about how IMAX can improve upon the limitations of prior media technologies in reproducing nature's creation in its entirety: "The Grand Canyon, a masterpiece of nature formed by 6,000,000 years of erosion, a chasm over 270 miles long and one mile deep—so epic, its wonder and majesty have never successfully been recorded, until now" (Merrell and Memmott). Like Emery and Ellsworth Kolb, who used the latest motion picture technology of the early twentieth century to attempt to capture "the Colorado as it is" (Kolb, 4), the Academy Award-winning director of the film, Kieth Merrill, is described as using "the most advanced motion picture format in existence" to try to capture the Grand Canyon's "hidden secrets" (Merrell and Memmott). Not only does the oversized IMAX technology make it difficult to "put that camera in places people have never seen before," but "the unique requirements of the IMAX format" pose formal cinematographic problems as well. One of the main differences between IMAX and "conventional 35 mm film production," according to David Douglas, the film's veteran cinematographer, is that "with IMAX, we have tried to fill the field of view completely with the image so that you have no terms of reference except for the screen and the pictures on the screen" (qtd. in Merrill and Memmott).

As Douglas indicates, the experience of viewing the IMAX film is designed to be totally immersive. Like most new advances in media technologies, IMAX participates in a rhetoric which claims to erase signs of mediation at the same time that it situates itself within a proliferation of media technologies. Yet the Grand Canyon IMAX film is presented in an environment that does not eliminate, but is saturated with, other terms of reference. Employing "the world's largest motion picture format in one of the world's largest locations," the film is shown 365 days a year, hourly at half past the hour, in the National Geographic Theater in Grand Canyon, Arizona, "Arizona's Number One Tourist Attraction." The National Geographic Theater has two gift shops "offer[ing] an excellent selection of Native American arts and crafts."[2] But the theater, which is home to the Arizona Tourist Information and Visitor Center, also offers a food court featuring Taco Bell, Pizza Hut, and the Canyon Cappuccino and Cafe; ATM and Phoneline U.S.A. machines; postage stamps and a mailbox; and a courtesy desk where visitors can make reservations for airplane and helicopter tours of the Grand Canyon. The film's narrative voice-over characterizes the experience of the Grand Canyon as mediated through IMAX as one in which we "discover a consciousness of our own immortality" through feelings of "reverence, appreciation, and kinship." At the very same time as we are

---

[2] Quotations and other details taken from IMAX brochure for the *National Geographic* Theater in Grand Canyon, Arizona.

immersed in our reverence of unmediated nature, however, we are invited to enmesh our experience of the park in a post-industrial network of commodification, communication, transportation, and commerce. The IMAX film and its exhibition space just outside the boundary of Grand Canyon National Park epitomize how, in today's media-saturated environment, the Park Service participates in a process of remediation—the simultaneous attempt to erase and to proliferate signs of its mediation of nature. The aim of this process is not only to mediate nature in another form, but to reform nature, to remedy the damage we have done to it.

In environmental waste management, remediation refers explicitly to the cleanup of contaminated sites, the process of rehabilitating or restoring soil and groundwater to a healthy condition, if not to its natural state. Without getting into the many interesting philosophical and ecological questions about what constitutes a 'healthy' or 'natural' state for any particular site, it is worth noting the way in which the National Park Service employs a rhetoric of remediation that functions both in this ecological sense as well as in terms of mediation. Indeed to 'remediate' a contaminated site it is necessary to re-fashion or re-mediate that site in another form in order to remedy or reform it. This process of environmental remediation resembles what Carolyn Merchant has characterized as the "recovery narrative" at the heart of American environmentalism, a narrative that is at work across the Park System, as I will illustrate in brief discussions of Cumberland Island National Seashore, Dinosaur National Monument, and Bravo 20 National Park. Each of these parks adopts different strategies for remediating something that has gone wrong in nature as a result of human action. In the interpretive materials of Cumberland Island, for example, the story that the Park Service tells is a teleological one, in which nature has fallen from its original Edenic state and in which the goal of the Park Service is to restore it to its natural state, which can only be preserved and maintained by the authority of the Park Service itself. Cumberland Island was established as a national seashore in 1972, to preserve the scenic, scientific, and historical values of the largest and most southerly island off the coast of Georgia. The Park Service narrates the history of Cumberland Island as a series of prior appropriations, each of which has left some mark upon the island both of its culture and of the damage it has done to the island's coastal ecosystem. The earliest human inhabitants were American Indians, followed by Spanish missionaries, English colonial military personnel, antebellum plantation owners, Confederate soldiers, and the wealthy industrialists of the Gilded Age. The return of the island to nature has been made possible by the (ongoing) intervention of the Park Service, which aims both to preserve a record of prior interventions and to return nature to self-sufficiency (as defined and authorized by the institutional practices of the park service itself). Thus not only does the Park Service tell the history of the island as a series of remediations, in which nature is mediated differently according to the cultural practices of its different owners, but it also seeks to remedy the detrimental ecological effects brought about by its prior inhabitants.

The idea that national parks should seek to preserve nature as it was prior to its first encounter by European-Americans obtains from Yellowstone to the state parks of Florida. Cumberland Island poses an interesting case in that its official goal is to return the national seashore to a coastal ecosystem independent even of native inhabitants. An even more extreme remediation of nature can be found in Dinosaur National Monument, which tries in some senses to return visitors to an ecosystem prior to the appearance of humans on the planet. As on Cumberland Island, Dinosaur National Monument attempts to return to some originary state of nature. But where that ur-nature for Cumberland is placed in the context of human interaction with landscape, in Dinosaur this ur-nature exists prior to humans completely, as the park in some sense tries to return visitors to a natural world before dinosaurs went extinct. But perhaps the more significant remediation of nature is the attempt to remedy the thoughtless and selfish activities of nineteenth-century explorers, discoverers, and even early museum curators, all of whom participated in plundering sites for profit rather than preserving them for scientific purposes or for human appreciation and observation. In aiming to remediate the site, the museum at the heart of Dinosaur National Monument is built into a hillside containing undisturbed dinosaur fossils. This intriguing design preserves for visitors the experience of the moment of scientific discovery, as well as preserving the fossils themselves. Through interpretive exhibits, the monument also situates itself in relation to the history of the early discoverers and provides a genealogy of the museums and collections to which notable fossils have gone, as well as records of when they were found. Thus in Dinosaur National Monument the interpretive materials concern not (as in Cumberland or other traditional parks) the appropriation of the land or landscape, but the appropriation of the fossils of extinct dinosaurs, whose extinction could (at least in imagination) be remediated.

Where Dinosaur National Monument exists in part to preserve a record of both the extinction of dinosaurs and the destruction of their remains, Bravo 20 National Park would (if it were actually to be established) preserve the devastation of a desert landscape by the United States Navy, which has used it as a bombing range since 1952. Currently existing as a virtual park on the World Wide Web, Bravo 20 National Park is the brainchild of Richard Misrach, a photographer known for his images of devastated natural landscapes. As set forth in a book published in 1990 in the Johns Hopkins University Press series "Creating the North American Landscape," Bravo 20 National Park would "serve as a permanent reminder of how military, government, corporate, and individual practices can harm the earth. In the spirit of Bull Run and the Vietnam Memorial, it would be a national acknowledgment of a complex and disturbing period in our history" (Misrach, 95). Andrew Ross has criticized the proposal for its lack of radical edge, for running the risk of "being viewed more as an example of conceptual art" than as a political statement. Ross laments: "This would be unfortunate, since it promises to be an entirely novel way of presenting an environmental critique: rather than celebrate the preservation of an environment, Bravo 20 would be a park whose purpose is to preserve a record of environmental destruction" (199-200). But as my discussion of Cumberland and Dinosaur has suggested, Ross here misses the point of contemporary National Park Service ideology. Although Bravo 20's remediation of nature is only at this point a proposed one, it is of a piece with the logic of remediation informing present-day national parks. Misrach remediates the site aesthetically by photographing it and reproducing these photographs as a book and on the Web, as well as displaying them as a museum exhibit and as individual prints. The proposal for the national park also remediates the site by memorializing it in terms of the history of nuclear and other armed air warfare. That is, the national park remediates not only the effect of these practices on our own landscape, but in an even larger sense, the practices themselves. So, the remediation here is not only formal (as in the photographs, the book, the exhibit, the web-site, and even the proposed park), but also reformative, in that it is meant to improve the landscape but also to somehow remediate our practices of military testing or our militaristic posture towards nature in the 20th century.

Most importantly, what the proposal for Bravo 20 National Park recognizes is the way in which national parks function as technologies for the reproduction of nature. The book concludes with a series of architectural drawings and illustrations depicting the proposed park, commissioned by Misrach from Burton and Spitz, a Santa Monica landscape architecture firm, with help from Matthew Miller and Rico Solinas. What these architectural drawings and illustrations remind us is that national parks are constituted not as Ross naively suggests by "the celebration of a natural environment," but by the reproduction of nature. Because he does not understand that national parks have always been constituted by the network of technological, cultural, and aesthetic practices for the reproduction of nature at a particular historical moment, Ross has difficulty imagining "visitors incorporating Bravo 20 into the tourist circuit of the West which includes the likes of Yosemite, King's Canyon, Lake Mead, the Grand Canyon, Grand Teton, Yellowstone, and the great national parks of Utah" (Ross, 198). Misrach, however, understands the way in which just as Yellowstone and Yosemite, for example, were created as national parks in accordance with late nineteenth-century assumptions about landscape and representation, so a national park today must be created according to present-day assumptions about media, culture, and technology. Consequently, his proposal for Bravo 20 National Park features all of the technologies of a national park in the 1990s: "In accordance with the 'interpretive programs' of all national parks," Misrach writes, "Bravo 20 will serve an educational function" (95). The park will have a "Visitor Center and Museum, devoted to the history of military abuse in peacetime, which will include "a film and video archive" and a "library [which] will collect relevant material for the public's edification" (95). "To put the consequences and implications of the Navy's actions into perspective," Misrach continues, "the geological, archaeological, environmental, religious, economic, and cultural (Indian) significance of the area will be highlighted." The park proposal also includes a café, primitive camping sites, viewing towers, a scenic drive, a boardwalk for viewing "the rough terrain of craters and shrapnel," a walk-in crater, and a trail to the top of Lone Rock, the sacred Northern Paiute mountain at the center of the park. Noting that "no national park is complete without a gift shop," he writes that "as in all national park gift shops, the Bravo 20 items will range from the meaningful to the tacky," from serious books, maps, and art reproductions to "imprinted clothing such as camouflage-style caps, t-shirts, pants; 'Nevada is not a Wasteland' and 'Bombs Away' mugs, tote-bags, and bumper stickers; and for the kids, Mattel models based on the most advanced, top-secret military designs—up-to-date delivery systems and Stealth bombers" (Misrach, 96). Although the book's dramatic photographs and narrative of environmental "monkey reclamation" are meant in part to create the impetus for preserving the "Bravo 20 landscape [as] a poignant and sobering symbol of the military's destruction of the environment" and "a powerful warning for future generations," Misrach's work is also important for its self-conscious recognition of the way in which national parks are cultural practices for remediating nature as mediated public space. While today Bravo 20 National Park can only be read about in a book or visited on the World Wide Web, access to the Web is now readily available at parks like Yosemite, Yellowstone, and Grand Canyon, not only for tourists but for the parks' native inhabitants as well. Indeed, as of September 2000, the Havasupai reservation on the floor of the Grand Canyon (along with Navajo and Hopi reservations in New Mexico and Utah) was linked to the internet via two-way, high speed wireless satellite connections furnished by an alliance between Starband Communications, Northern Arizona University, and the

Southwest Navajo Nation Virtual Alliance (*New York Times*) At a moment when we can not only watch Old Faithful erupt on America Online, but also access America Online from the site of Old Faithful, a firm distinction between natural and mediated public space becomes increasingly difficult to maintain. And just as national parks were created in postbellum America as technologies for reproducing nature according to the aesthetic forms and practices of nineteenth-century landscape representation, so they will increasingly be created and maintained in the century to come as technologies for remediating nature according to the aesthetic forms and practices of digital media today.[3]

Bibliography

Bolter, Jay David, and Richard Grusin. *Remediation: Understanding New Media.* Cambridge, MA: MIT P, 1999.

Buell, Lawrence. *The Environmental Imagination: Thoreau, Nature Writing, and the Formation of American Culture.* Cambridge, MA: The Belknap Press of Harvard UP, 1995.

Cronon, William. "The Trouble with Wilderness; or, Getting Back to the Wrong Nature." *Uncommon Ground: Toward Reinventing Nature.* Ed. William Cronon. New York: Norton, 1995. 69-90.

Cronon, William, Jay Gitlin, and George Miles, eds. *Under an Open Sky: Rethinking America's Western Past.* New York: Norton, 1992.

Frisk, Jerome. "The Theoretical (Re)Positions of the New Western History." *Arizona Quarterly* 53.2 (1997): 17-60.

Grusin, Richard. *Culture, Technology, and the Creation of America's National Parks.* Cambridge UP, 2004.

Kolb, E. L.. *Through the Grand Canyon from Wyoming to Mexico.* 1914; rpt. Tuscon: U of Arizona P, 1989,

Limerick, Patricia. *The Legacy of Conquest: The Unbroken Past of the American West.* New York: Norton, 1987.

---

[3] This essay appears in a different form in my book *Culture, Technology, and The Creation of America's National Parks* (Cambridge UP, 2004).

Merchant, Carolyn. "Reinventing Eden: Western Culture as a Recovery Narrative." *Uncommon Ground.* Ed. William Cronon, 132-159.

Merrill Keith, and O. Douglas Memmott, prods. *Making of Grand Canyon: The Hidden Secrets. Grand Canyon: The Hidden Secrets.* Filmed in IMAX. Grand Canyon Theatre Venture, Distributed by Destination Cinema, Inc., 1994.

Misrach, Richard, with Myriam Weisang Misrach. Bravo 20: *The Bombing of the American West.* Baltimore: Johns Hopkins UP, 1990.

New York Times. Thursday, September 21, 2000, D11 (Circuits Section).

Ross, Andrew. *The Chicago Gangster Theory of Life: Nature's Debt to Society.* New York: Verso, 1994.

White, Richard. *"It's Your Misfortune and None of My Own": A New History of the American West.* Norman: U of Oklahoma P, 1991.

Worster, Donald. *Under Western Skies; Nature and History in the American West.* New York: Oxford UP, 1992.

Space in Fiction, Film, and Drama

Space as Form and Force in the Novel

Gerhard Hoffmann

1. Situation

The placement of space in the novel is determined by two conditioning circumstances. First, space is a constituent factor of the narrated situation. The narrated situation itself is a narrative *constant*, it is a foundation of fiction.[1] Consciousness and its product, fiction, are always anchored in situations which are isolated by division and negation of the other and (re)connected by the 'good' continuity of time, by reflection and imagination. Fiction has a location (Iser, 167), or rather, *is* a location, an actual site. It is so much dependent on its being situated that the narrated situation is not only the basic unit of the narrative location and of communication with the reader, but narrative in fact is the *situational transformation of (anti-)meaning*.

The situation in fiction is double-poled; it is *form* as order and *force* as disorder (the term force will be defined below). This indissoluable duality provides it with its operational power. Considered as *form*, the constituents of the situation are *space* and *time*; *character* and *action/event*. They form minimal consistencies without which no experience and no representation of experience are possible, and they ensure the coexistence of mobilization and immobilization. Being an abstraction and a design, the situation pertains as matrix both to experiential reality and the worlds of memory and imagination, i.e., art.

The situation as form acts like a *frame*. The frame theory, in this case Goffman's concept of frame, helps to understand the constitution and deformation of the nar-

---

[1] Chambers uses the term situation only metaphorically (1984). He intends to undertake "relatively formal and entirely text-based studies of the apparatus—the discursive *dispositifs*—by which [...] texts designate themselves as contractual phenomena" (9). Looking for "textual indi-

rated situation, its centerment and decenterment. In his book, *Frame Analysis*, Goffman speaks of "two broad classes of primary frameworks: natural and social" (22). The natural primary framework would, in our terms, encompass the elementary components, space and time, and the social framework the more complex ones, character and action/event: "Natural frameworks identify occurrences seen as undirected, unoriented, unanimated, unguided, 'purely physical.' Such unguided events are ones understood to be due totally, from start to finish, to 'natural' determinants" (22). "Social frameworks," on the other hand, "provide background understanding for events that incorporate the will, aim and controlling effort of an intelligence, a live agency" (22). However, the central assumption (pointing to the necessity of an integrated situational context) is that "although natural events occur without intelligent intervention, intelligent doings cannot be accomplished effectively without entrance into the natural order" (23).

The situation as *force* can change this relationship of dominance. Although the more complex social framework (character, action) relies on the natural framework (space, time), which is the more elementary one, the force factor may deform this relationship. What is called the social frame might be reduced to the natural frame, i.e. it might become undirected, unguided or mechanized, and the natural frame might take on some of the characteristics of the social frame, such as will, and the controlling effort of intelligence. Dismissal of the formally operative hierarchies in the interplay between form and force would level out whatever differences there are among the elements. As a result, the situation would be 'decentered' or rather 'deformed' in that the expected dominance relationships between social and natural worlds and with them the reign of elements such as character and plot and of concepts such as reality, truth and identity would be suspended. The field of experience, not the character, would be dominant. Force unfolds its power in creating fantastic worlds, in giving them form by freely distributing and adjusting all possible perspectives of evaluation, in superimposing one stance on the other and chang-

ces" that serve to identify the texts' "narrative situation," he negates the difference between the outside and the inside, and text and world.

ing them at will, thus attaining its own form through possibility, simultaneity and play, play being the only remaining synthesis, though in fact it is no synthesis.

2. Space and Spatial Form

Space, i.e. referential space, is always related to time through change and movement. It contains places and things, it is structured (as time is) by the perspective of an experiencing subject. Just as the discourses of time are shaped by the relations between chronological/mechanical and subjective/mental time, and the interaction between present and past, present and future, the discourses of space are organized in terms of relations between inside and outside, breadth and depth, proximity and distance, closedness and openness, finiteness and infinity, horizontal and vertical dimensions, etc. People simply have and are oriented in time as well as in space. From the experiencing subject's point of view space opens from the near to the far in ever-widening horizons. The manifestations of space, of spatial relations and objects (as of time), are not neutral, but are put into perspective by the relationship between the subject and the object. They are *perceptual, emotional, cognitive, utilitarian,* i.e. they are determined by *attitudes* which are theoretically separable, but which, in practice, combine and interrelate because all space is *experienced* space, and experience includes the activity of several if not all human faculties, though of course priority may be given to the one or the other. The fact that space is experienced space makes it into *place*. But there are in-between stages. Space is an abstract category that can be defined by further abstracted categories, especially attitudes. One can thus speak of male, female, and children's space, specifications which determine the experience of space and thus the specific transformation of space into place.

For the modernist writers the existential relationship between the human being and space becomes crucial. With the failing of the ideologies of progress, the isolation of the individual and the retreat of communication, narration emphasizes ways of relating to the world that are more elemental than those of rationality; fiction activates what one might call bodily consciousness, thus following belatedly Carlyle's dictum in *Sartor Resartus* (derived from Kant):

> That the Thought-forms, Space and Time, wherein, once for all, we are sent into this Earth to live, should condition and determine our whole Practical reasonings, conceptions, and imagings or imaginings,—seems altogether fit, just, and unavoidable. (197)

The novel, now less concerned with society, morality and progress than with the self, its isolation and its existential quest for identity and truth, focuses on what Ernst Cassirer wrote at the end of the 1920s:

> there is no accomplishment and creation of the mind that does not make reference in one way or another to the world of space, that does not as it were attempt to make itself at home in it. For a turning towards this world the first necessary step is towards concretization, towards the perception and definition of being. Space, as it were, forms the general medium in which the spiritual production first can 'establish' itself, can bring itself to its first forms and gestalts. (Cassirer, 174-75)

Karl Jaspers notes that the processes of consciousness are represented in spatial terms: "*Pictorially* we imagine consciousness as the *stage* on which individual spiritual phenomena 'come and go'" (115, see also 75, 67ff.; qtd. by Iser, 336). And Maurice Merleau-Ponty speaks of a "relation of totality" people have to the place they live in, a relation negotiated by the body:

> We said space is existential; we also could have said, existence is spatial, that indeed it opens itself to something 'external,' and it does so in such an essential way, that we can speak of a spiritual space and a world of meanings and the objects of thought which constitute themselves in this world (1986, 341).

The increasing structural weight of the spatial element in modern fiction has given rise to a discussion of the 'spatialization' of the novel. In radical cases of modernism the deterioration or abolishment of causality results in anti-causality or irrational causality (Kafka), and out of the loss of temporal order and coherence arises a vacuum that is filled by what has been termed 'spatial' order. This 'spatial' order is complex and requires a greater interpretative effort from the reader. Roman Jakobson analyzes this in Todorov's words, as "symmetries, gradations, antitheses, parallelisms, etc." (47). Joseph Frank in his well-known essay "Spatial Form in Modern Literature" states

> that modern literature exemplified by such writers as T.S. Eliot, Ezra Pound, Marcel Proust and James Joyce, is moving in the direction of spatial form. This means that the reader is intended to apprehend their work spatially, in a moment of time, rather than as a sequence. (225)

For documentation he uses an early example of the 'spatialization of form,' the market-place tableau in Flaubert's *Madame Bovary*. Here

> the time-flow of the narrative is halted: attention is fixed on the interplay of relationships within the limited time-area. These relationships are juxtaposed independently of the progress of the narrative; and the full significance of the scene is given only by the reflexive relations among the units of meaning. (Frank, 231)

Proust and Joyce have taken over this method and rendered spatial form prominent in the novel and have further developed it towards a spatialization of time. The result of which is a "continual reference and cross-reference of images and symbols which must be referred to each other spatially throughout the time-act of reading" (Frank, 439), a method of composition that requires the recipient to read the book in terms of *separation* and *connection*.[2]

---

[2] Spencer and others have elaborated Frank's ideas, using, like Frank, the literal and figurative meaning of 'spatial' without differentiation. Spencer states that "in the novel [...] there exists an observable struggle to subdue the patterns suggested by time in its accustomed sense to those existing in its new spatial sense." She studies those novels "that embody approximations of time-space fusions achieved by various ingenious structural procedures," by "the principle of juxtaposition," using either "a single exclusively maintained and often unusual perspective" or "a great variety of perspectives simultaneously focused on the subject" (xx-xxi), and distinguishes types of novels according to the use of these principles. Compare also Kestner, *The Spatiality of the Novel*. A collection of essays that focuses on Frank's concept of spatial form; and Smitten and Daghistani, *Spatial Form in Narrative*.

2.1. The Historical View: Towards Modernism

In the eighteenth century English novel, plot and character were localized in a concrete place and set in a specific time; both space and time functioned as coordinates of the narrated situations and their sequence. But space and time were not necessarily particularized because the novels were composed more loosely; the various manners of the time experience were taken for granted and the characters were free to act according to (universal) moral laws and as masters of their environment. Reality was neither mysterious nor opaque, place and time did not have the role of a determining context. Since the reader's interest was supposed to focus on character and plot, space and time did not have to be detailed or given a stabilizing, meaning-giving or interesting role. In the Gothic novel things changed. The discourses of time and place together served to set up a trap for the hero or heroine and to heighten suspense or to articulate the romantic idea of the beautiful and the sublime. With the introduction of history in the novels of Walter Scott not only the authenticity of local color became important (which is only a picturesque 'decorative' device and cannot really awaken the spirit of the age) but the lasting interaction between humans and place and time. This re-orientation among the elements of the situation gave the novel a crucial new direction.

Georg Lukács notes that Scott's seemingly romantic novels are by no means romantic but rest on the distinction between different realities, milieus (cf. Lukáçs 1983, 40). Scott differentiates Scotland from England, the Highlands from the Lowlands, on the principle of natural and cultural environment, climate, regional history, social organization, manners, and traditions. Balzac and the realists of the nineteenth century eagerly follow the new trend of demonstrating how ideas, feelings, manners of behavior grow out of such basic circumstances. Boundaries become important; time, space, and social organization within such boundaries fuse into effective operational principles. The growing complexity of the world in the nineteenth century, moreover, brings about within the novel a multiplicity of persons, plots, places, even times, a phenomenon that intensifies emphasis on parallelism and juxtaposition and leads therefore to a strengthening of spatial order, its symbolic potential, and a foregrounding of simultaneity. Narrative now includes the extensive description of places. Characters extend into place (and time), and place (and time) extend into character. George Eliot writes: "It is in the habit of my imagination to strive after as full a vision of the medium in which a character moves as of the character itself" (366). The maxim of naturalism, the determination of character by milieu, which develops in the wake of Darwinism, furthers the close alliance between humans and space, the detailing of the social and natural environment, and its evaluation as social determinants in the French (Zola), the English (George Eliot, George Moore) and the American novel (Garland, Crane, Norris, Dreiser). Two attitudes toward the environment develop what Lukács characterizes as "experiencing" and "observing" and, according to the form, as "narrating" and "describing" (1971, 206-07). The reader too becomes an observer of a series of "pictures."

The modern novel interrupts this development towards description, or rather, it demands with Henry James the dramatizing, intensifying, and narrative integration of the pictorial elements under psychological aspects. This would mean "a reversal of the essential method of fiction" (Beach, 38-39) as practiced in the traditional English novels which Henry James regarded as "great fluid puddings" (qtd. in Booth, 28). It was now the "chamber of consciousness," "the atmosphere of the mind" that, in a mutual penetration of abstract consciousness and optic textual reality, turns "the very pulses of the air into revelations" (James, 1957, 31-32). Narrative ontology is changed in the works of James ("art deals with what we see" [James 1962, 312]), Conrad ("my task [...] is, by the power of the written word, to make you hear, to make you feel—it is, before all, to make you *see*" [Conrad, 1921, x]) and other modernist writers. New dominants, reflecting new kinds of sensibility, come to the fore. According to T. S. Eliot or Theodor Adorno, only *indirect* methods which establish an "objective correlative" (T. S. Eliot) for feeling and thought can represent the whole experience in all its aspects that include both conscious and unconscious signification. Emphasizing the spatial aspect of experience,

Hemingway later will remark: "Unless you have geography, background, you have nothing" (Antheil, 218). The aesthetic goal—to integrate all situational elements into a significant whole—makes the modernists turn against the excess of description (primarily that without a function) and its isolation in separate passages that mark the 'setting' of the characters, especially at the beginning of chapters. Henry James, James Joyce, Joseph Conrad, Virginia Woolf, and others, move from extensity to intensity, thus deepening the interrelation between subject and object, making it in fact indissoluble. Virginia Woolf writes: "What I want to do now is to saturate every atom. I mean to eliminate all waste, deadness, superfluity: to give the moment whole; whatever it includes" (1973, 139). Such a fully saturated moment that gives wholeness to experience is the visionary or mythical *moment*. This moment of revelation suspends mechanical time and penetrates the surface. Space is important for this psychic synthesis because it is a synthesis of the inner *and* the outer worlds. In the intensity of psychic time the character bridges the abyss between the inner and outer by the ecstatic feeling of totality, connecting the deep structure of consciousness and the depth dimension of nature, the essence of the mind and the essence of place (Conrad, *Lord Jim*; Joyce, *The Portrait of the Artist as a Young Man*; Lawrence, *The Rainbow*; Woolf, *To the Lighthouse*). In fact, place becomes a decisive dialogue partner for the socially isolated individual (see James, Joyce, Woolf, Faulkner, etc.).

Time and space act as interpretative media not only by initiating responses of the experiencing subject and opening ways of expressing feelings and thoughts in sensory perceptions; not only do they provide material for indirect methods of signification, but they also function as *systems* of interpretation in a complex aesthetic structure. As our discussion of the spatial method indicated, in modernism space gains on time. Space is the basis of elementary bodily consciousness, the structured and structuring stabilizer and matrix of meaning; it obtains the lead when the discourses of time become problematic. Having lost the integrative wholeness of time characteristic of the nineteenth century novel, the modernist writers split time into mechanical time and mental time. The two having become disconnected, psychological time wars against mechanical time for the overcoming of transience, for duration, permanence and universality, in short, for making sense within the new wholeness of psychic time. Under these circumstances, the texts of Joyce, Virginia Woolf, Fitzgerald, Hemingway, and Faulkner assign space the role of a balancing factor, a sound basis for the temporally disruptive narrative process. The novel creates meaningful constellations of places, directions, opposite poles that function as points of reference in the stream of consciousness, in the flow of associations between present and past, present and future, for the quest of identity, the substance of the self, and for the general thematic issue of transforming chaos into order and (universal) meaning. Place turns into a polarized, but coordinated and thematically directed environment that is not a social determinant (as in the naturalistic novel), a (stifling) milieu, but, by being *experienced* as significant, becomes the receptor of feelings, thoughts, and in fact, a dialogue partner and the operative principle of human fears and hopes.

This is the case with Dublin in Joyce's *Ulysses*, London in Virginia Woolf's *Mrs. Dalloway*; Yoknapatawpha County in Faulkner's *The Sound and the Fury*, and more so in his *Absalom, Absalom!* Place offers a refuge (Forster, *Howard's End*), the final goal of a quest (Lawrence, *Women in Love*), an alternative experience (Conrad, *Heart of Darkness*) and a dialectic relationship (James, *The Ambassadors*); or it provides for mobility, change, and thus for the illusion of life as something dynamic and meaningful (Hemingway, *A Farewell to Arms*, *The Sun Also Rises*; Kerouac, *On the Road*; Bellow, *Augie March*; see the chapter on mobility and immobility in Hoffmann, 1978, 591ff.). Space in fact becomes a symbolic and thematic *constellation*. In the American novel this modern symbolic configuration of space already informs the fiction of Hawthorne, Melville, Poe or Twain. In Hawthorne's *The Scarlet Letter*, the puritanical settlement with its moral rigor is set (ambiguously) against the natural wilderness and freedom of the forest. Melville's *Moby-Dick* contrasts land and sea, the ship and the sea, the surface and the depth of the sea, the human quest for universal meaning and nature's indifference. Mark Twain's *Roughing It* juxtaposes civilization and the rough west; *Life on the Missis-*

sippi and *Huckleberry Finn* contrast the wilderness and freedom of the river with the corruption of civilization on shore. Virginia Woolf's *To the Lighthouse* plays on the interrelations between lighthouse and sea; the island, the sea and the lighthouse; the house and the island, the inside and the outside. Henry James's novels distinguish America and Europe, innocence and historic experience, morality and aesthetics. Conrad's *Heart of Darkness* sets Africa against Europe, the deep inside of Africa against the accessible outer parts, the river Congo against the mythical forest; D. H. Lawrence's *Women in Love* contrasts the North and the South, cold and heat; William Faulkner opposes deforming history and the natural purity of the primeval forest; Hemingway frames exhausted civilization with the elemental character of nature.

This extension of space and the confrontation of places can be seen in a larger context. According to George Steiner, Western culture is confronted with a loss of spatial centrality, of "the confident pivot of a classic geography" (53). It is accompanied by the loss of the belief in the superiority of Western civilization, as developed in Europe and America. A sudden void of classic values opens up. Certainty in value consciousness turns into doubt and negation, into the notion that Western civilization is exhausted in its striving for rationality, in its arrogance that it is full of hybris, is in fact an impostor, uses means and disguises to exploit the other races and continents, and needs the primeval as balance. The consequence is a geographical decentralization of the idea of culture. Culture is multiplied, serialized, and 'democratized' in its various manifestations. The result is that the novel loses its spatial sense of being self-contained and its geographical, relatively homogeneous societal basis. Modern authors such as Hardy, Lawrence, Conrad, Hemingway, and Faulkner express their dissatisfaction with society by extending space not only into nature in terms of a new romanticism, but also into the *unfamiliar*, in contrast to "the pivot of a classic geography" (Steiner) and its self-contained value system. This method of extension includes domesticated and ideologized nature as a pole *within* the cultural and philosophic systems, which are no longer sufficient for the pursuit of the pressing epistemological and ethical questions in fiction. As a consequence, the concept of the quest is 'geographized' on a wider scale. The heroes are sent to the "primitive," "mythic" regions of Egdon Heath (Hardy), of Africa (Conrad, Hemingway), of Mexico (D. H. Lawrence, Bellow) or Yoknapatawpha County in Mississippi (Faulkner). Nature is set *against* culture, not in Rousseau's terms as a friendly alternative and corrector of faulty developments of civilizations, but as the quite 'Other,' the basis of the mythical view which is now set against history, just as the moment of vision is set against the ordinariness of everyday life. Or, if one adheres to the familiar geographical centers, then the spatial 'stability' of the city is at least partly dissipated by subjective, atmospheric sensibility (James Joyce, Virginia Woolf) or made into a (demonic) threat (Dreiser, Dos Passos). By showing the negative influence of civilization on the individual and on society, the dominance of the cultural over the natural frame is damaged, if not irreparably broken. The next step, at the end of modernism, is that nature also loses its role as a retreat, a compensation or balancing force. With the common loss of orientation, place (or even names of places) may be all that is left once the ideological positions have failed to make sense. Frederic Henry, the protagonist in Hemingway's *A Farewell to Arms*, sees in place names alone the remaining truth in words:

> I was always embarrassed by the words sacred, glorious, and sacrifice and the expression in vain [...] I had seen nothing sacred, and the things that were glorious had no glory. [...] There were many words that you could not stand to hear and finally only the names of places had dignity [...] Abstract words such as glory, honor, courage, or hallow were obscene beside the concrete names of villages, the numbers of roads, the names of rivers, the numbers of regiments and the dates. (184)

2.2. The Historical View: Postmodern Alternatives

According to Daniel Bell, the organization of space has "become the primary aesthetic problem of mid-twentieth-century culture, as the problem of time (in Bergson, Proust and Joyce) was the primary aesthetic problem of the first decades of this century" (107-11) (see also Jameson, and Harvey, 201ff.). Anthony Giddens has called globalization "a process of uneven development that fragments as it coordinates" (175). Jameson notes that in this "new global space" "our bodies are bereft of spatial coordinates" (49). Though the "postmodern hyperspace" (44) "has moved the closest to the surface of our consciousness, as a coherent new type of space in its own right" (49), it no longer has the "capacity for representation" (36). This new experience of global space is marked by the loss of human dominance over the spatial environment. Though the latter is produced by humans, it turns into a field of overpowering force all its own, and transcends "the capacities of the individual human body [...] to organize its immediate surroundings perceptually, and cognitively to map its position in a mappable external world" (44).

For Jameson this new type of space that leads to physical and mental disorientation symbolizes "the incapacity of our minds, at least at present, to map the great global multi-national and decentered communicational network in which we find ourselves caught as individual subjects" (44). This also concerns art and architecture. Postmodern narrated space suspends social purposes, static configurations and fixed patterns, and, in Harvey's words, emphasizes "fragmentation," "the ephemeral," and "uncertainty" (1989, 296);[3] in fact, this penchant for deconstruction in postmodernist art demonstrates, although with certain reservations, the preference for aesthetics over ethics (see Hoffmann and Hornung).

---

[3] Cf. Gibson (12). Gibson's book is the most recent and most interesting attempt to deconstruct and overcome what he calls the "fantasy of a geometrical clarity, symmetry and proportion to narrative or the narrative text" (8), which is promoted by a "narratological geometry or technology of narrative" that "universalise and essentialise the structural phenomena supposedly uncovered" and have their "roots in structuralism" (5). In a turning-away "from laws and regularities," he adopts a model of exchanges and interferences, connections and disconnections, between and within "pluralized spaces." As the title notes, he aims at "a postmodern theory of narrative," which, however, gets entangled in the general rejection of all classifications, categories, and textual invariants, and falls short of establishing a specific postmodern aesthetic by an unspecified "pluralisation of the narratological imaginary" (15), the "notion of narrative parcours" as "movement through multiple spaces" (16) that invalidates "explicatory grids" (Serres) in general, replaces them with ideas like "force, hymen, inauguration, event, monstrosity, laterality, writing" (25) following a strategy that is "nomadic" (25). The usefulness of the book for our purpose is restricted by the fact that it does not say what kind of postmodern narrative he has in mind and that none of the established postmodern texts are referred to, much less analyzed, with the exception of Robbe-Grillet. Yet I am indebted to Gibson's lucid and competent overview over the development of narratology, especially his analysis of the postmodern ideas of time, event, and monstrosity.

Yet in spite of the abstraction of space the sensory and spatial aspects of the fictional world do not lose their importance. They are only deployed differently. In terms of the situational duality of form and force they serve the expression of energy, not of form. Under the auspices of force, a flexibility of space occurs that leads to paradoxical arrangements. First, the dissolution of the seemingly indissoluble unity of subject and object causes the separation of character and environment; they become *detached* from one another, and no longer form an 'objective' or 'subjective' unity. Second, space itself splits into *space* and *place*. Place represents containment, circumscription, milieu and *form*, whereas space, which is indefinite, infinite, fluid, incorporates *force*. As always in postmodern fiction, the positions are not fixed. Both space and place can become ambivalent in their positions; their role in the meaning scheme of the text can be played with, and even reversed. An example of this is Elkin's *The Dick Gibson Show*. The novel's protagonist defines himself not by individual place, as one would expect, but by homogenizing place into space, sterilizing local surfaces, and denying geographical differences; he sees himself as "Dick Gibson of Nowhere, of Thin Air and the United States of America Sky" (21), "the generalized sound of American life" (105). Being a "voice" on the radio (251) he has "an undeveloped [...] sense of place" (190); he lives in "what I think and nothing else" (251). The social frame (character, action/event) and the natural frame (space, time) of the situation need not but may be manipulated independently.

In principle, the representation of space follows the designs of *montage*; space is neither ideologized as 'setting,' 'environment' or 'milieu' nor made use of as an initiator of, or reaction to, existential thoughts and feelings. It becomes decentered and rejects the idea of 'reality,' recognition, human plausibility, and logical consistency. This means that space is not only free to be detailed or left vacant (because the continuity of space and time never can break off), but it is furthermore fantasized so that it can be free to be differentiated or *de*-differentiated, to be localized or synthesized, to build or disrupt, together with time, the creative 'natural' basis for new imaginary worlds. In space, too, the possible and imaginary replace the stable and allegedly given.

For the presentation of space in the postmodern novel three factors are important that all converge in their deconstructive tendency but do not necessarily combine within the works of individual authors or texts; in fact, they are, in part, mutually exclusive but together demonstrate the higher flexibility, the reign of possibility, not reality, in the approach to space. First, the appearance-disappearance paradigm reigns in the presentation of space; second, space is liberated from the concept of (determinate) milieu, from the projection of the inner into the outer, and from elaborate description; and, third, movement is transformed into a mere operation in space and time; beginning, end and goal are lost or suspended. Due to the importance of the polarity of space and lack of space we will concentrate on the appearance-disappearance paradigm here.

2.3. Appearance and Disappearance

The representation of place and space in postmodern fiction can be understood in terms of what Virilio has called the replacement of the "aesthetics of appearance" by the "aesthetics of disappearance."[4] The *aesthetics of appearance* asserts place identity and a sense of rootedness, creates spaces and times of individuation and of social or universal connection and establishes a coherent perspective of continuation; it opposes spatial and social disaffection and barrenness and the merely insignificant and superficial. Against the fleeting, ephemeral and fortuitous are set patterns of denial, hope, meaning, and utopian perfection. The *aesthetics of disappearance* denotes the vanishing of time and space as palpable meaning-giving areas of social life. In this sense, it is a reflex to a change in reality, or rather, in the sense of reality. It ultimately *cancels difference* and *depth*, and it does away with the consolation by place that Hemingway speaks of.

---

[4] Virilio, *The Aesthetics of Disappearance*; *La machine de vision*. Docherty in his essay on "The Ethics of Alterity: Postmodern Character," uses the same terms to differentiate the paradigm of the postmodern novel, i.e., "appearance versus disappearance," from that of the traditional and modern novel, "appearance versus reality."

Instead of place identity and a sense of wholeness the aesthetics of disappearance promotes a sense of emptiness and multiplicity of forms and perspectives. In Beckett's *Malone Dies* there is no externality, there are no roads, forests, bicycles or crutches as there are still in *Molloy*. Malone only possesses a notebook, a pencil and a hooked stick for opening and closing the skull space of his room. Increasingly placed in the foreground in Beckett's trilogy are stasis, inertia, exhaustion, and the labyrinth of (mental) repetition and confusion, all of which come across as entropic by the loss of movement, i.e. the dynamics of force. *The Unnamable* has no definable plot, no nameable character, no setting that is describable and no chronological time flow. The forms of the book are repetition, contradiction and question. The book begins: "Where now? Who now? When now?" (293). In Beckett's *Imagination Dead Imagine*, there are only places vanishing into space and a vague rotunda and skull-like enclosure that the narrating voice is bound to. Robbe-Grillet's spatial universe contains, in Borges's phrase, a "fundamental vagueness" (19), "the indefinite light of a rainy landscape" (4), the "labyrinth of streets" (43), a "labyrinth of unlighted hallways" (97). In the first paragraph of *In the Labyrinth*, the narrator notes in a manner reminiscent of Beckett that outside it is both rainy and sunny, cold and hot, windy and calm. A few pages later he describes an object on the table as a cross, a knife, a flower, a human statuette, in fact, it could be "anything" (72). The preface to Robbe-Grillet's novel *In the Labyrinth* rejects all depth associations, stating that the "reality in question is a strictly material one; that is subject to no allegorical interpretation" (28). Five writers that become influential for American postmodernists, Kafka, Beckett, Borges, Robbe-Grillet, Nabokov, write only surfaces, and even the surfaces may be suspended. America is seen by Baudrillard as the best example of the disappearance of social rootedness and density, the loss of the authenticity of place; in his words (referring to Virilio): "the America of desert speed," of "social desertification" is a model of "the inhumanity of our ulterior, asocial, superficial world" (1988, 5). The result is the dissolution of the regulating order of the social world, of hierarchical distinction and of totalizing form, of the distinction between nature and culture, surface and depth, the outer and the inner, the true and the false, between negation and affirmation, reality and fiction.

Abandoned are also the particulars of everyday life. Vonnegut explicitly formulates the rejection of the routine world of the quotidian, an attitude that would be underwritten by most of his postmodern colleagues:

> I do not furnish transportation for my characters; I do not move them from one room to another; I do not send them up the stairs; they do not get dressed in the mornings; they do not put the ignition key in the lock, and turn on the engine, and let it warm up and look at all the gauges, and put the car in reverse, and back out, and drive to the filling station, and ask the guy there about the weather. (Bellamy, 201)

Federman writes that the "new fictitious creature will be [...] unconcerned with the real world" (13). Time and space are solely the objects of imagination and reflection. Sukenick speaks of "a series of overwhelming social dislocations" (41). These dislocations do not make place and things disappear, but the natural framework of the situation is no longer intimately bound up with the social level of the situation, character and action, as environment and milieu, as the outer for the projection of the inner. In Barthelme's *Snow White*, there are no descriptions of the place where Snow White and the dwarfs live, nor of streets or cities, while many references to the US as setting open up a comic contrast between the archetypal milieu of the fairy tale and the civilized circumstances of the present. Gass notes that *Omensetter's Luck* "really says nothing at all about the 1890s, nothing about the Ohio river towns, of which I have no knowledge whatever. Fiction, goddamn it, is fiction. When will that simple truth be acknowledged? The same thing is true of most of the stories" (LeClair and McCaffery, 164).

Under the guidance of the imagination, place and things gain a certain independence. Place for instance supports or rather constructs time as the substratum of a past that is made operative within the present, especially in one-place novels. This is the anti-model to the loss of the past, which is the other paradigm of postmodern fiction (see Beckett, Barthelme). Space here gives time, as it were, presence, whether or not the character wants it; it makes time a subject, not only an object and receptacle. It accumulates and stores time, making its continuous presence a burden, even a threat. The 'liberation' of space and objects from the dominance of the social frame of the situation, character, and action appears as the result of the activities of the force of space and time that gain for the natural frame a certain independence and lead to a reversal of the accustomed dominance relationship so that the inanimate comes to master the animate, making mechanical sameness the ruling form. Objects are released, set free from order, reason and determination. They even turn into a *list*.

The use of the list is part of 'the aesthetics of disappearance' that abolishes concrete placement in space in order not to limit the range of the imagination by the experience of familiar stability. The imagination then playfully fills the gap that is left on its own terms, in the extreme case by mere lists. Barth says of his long novels that "their mere persistence" is "an exorcism of nothingness, of the vacuum that one fears might exist if one stops to look at the void" (Ziegler and Bigsby, 36). One may 'fill' the void or leave it open, or even willfully create it. Contrary to filling the vacuum with lists, with an overabundance of serially arranged words/things/situations, the method of voiding space produces *emptiness*; or rather, it plays with the *absence-presence* constellation, a strategy which again, though in a different way, serves to establish the *force*-aspect of the narrated situation. The dimension of nothingness is created by leaving 'unnatural' and mysterious gaps of emptiness open, which, however, do not elude control. Control over emptiness is retained by play, by blurring the borderlines, for instance, between the representative and the textual levels as in Sorrentino's *Mulligan Stew*.

The multiplicity of perspectives is radicalized in the unfathomability of the *labyrinth*. Borges sets the trend. In his fictions the labyrinth is the structural paradigm that covers and supports all movement; for him the labyrinth is "the decisive most obvious symbol of feeling puzzled and baffled" (Dembo, 317). He turns space, time, characters, actions or, to use his representative examples, books, libraries, deserts, cities, palaces, and lotteries into labyrinths; and he revels, in contrast to

Kafka, in confounding reversals and framings inside and outside the text. Borges figures labyrinths within the text and the text itself as labyrinth. The labyrinth is indeed the image/metaphor of the myriad of *possibilities* that are offered at every point of the forked path which is an "incomplete, but not false image of the universe" (Borges, 1964, 28). In the labyrinth, sequentiality is complemented with or even replaced by the simultaneity of possibilities; possibility becomes reality and vice versa, force relativizes form, form absorbs the dissolution of form. In the 'ideal' fiction, form and force are balanced, all possibilities are chosen at once (as in the ideal novel of The Tralfamadorians in Vonneguts *Slaughterhouse Five.*) The fact is, as Ts'ui Pên in "The Garden of Forking Paths" maintains, that "in all fictional works, each time a man is confronted with several alternatives, he chooses one and eliminates the others; in the fiction of Ts'ui Pên he chooses—simultaneously—all of them" (Borges, 1964, 26). His world is a simultaneity of places, as it is also a simultaneity of times, and the figuration of infinite designs, designs of possibility. Possibility thinking and possibility narration are the characteristics of postmodern narrative, and space is its fundamental playmate.

Bibliography

Antheil, Gerald. *Bad Boy of Music.* New York: Da Capo, 1981.
Baudrillard, Jean. *America.* Trans. Chris Turner. London: Verso, 1988.
Beach, Joseph W. *The Method of Henry James.* Philadelphia, NJ: Saifer, 1954.
Beckett, Samuel. *Molloy, Malone Dies, The Unnamable.* London: Calder, 1959.
Bell, Daniel. *The Cultural Contradictions of Capitalism.* New York: Basic, 1976.
Bellamy, Joe David, ed. *The New Fiction: Interviews with Innovative American Writers.* Urbana: U of Illinois P, 1974.
Booth, Wayne C. *The Rhetoric of Fiction.* Chicago: U of Chicago P, 1961.
Borges, Jorge Luis. *Ficciones.* Ed. Anthony Kerrigan. New York: Grove P, 1962.
---. *Labyrinths: Selected Stories and Other Writings.* New York: New Directions, 1964.
Carlyle, Thomas. *Sartor Resartus.* London: Dent, 1956.

Cassirer, Ernst. *Philosophy of Symbolic Form.* Vol. III. Trans. Ralph Manheim. New Haven, CT: Yale UP, 1965.

Chambers, Ross. *Story and Situation: Narrative Seduction and the Power of Fiction.* Minneapolis: U of Minnesota P, 1984.

Dembo, Lawrence S. "An Interview with Jorge Luis Borges." *Contemporary Literature* 11.3 (1970): 315-23.

Docherty, Thomas. "The Ethics of Alterity: Postmodern Character." *Alterities: Criticism, History, Representation.* Oxford: Clarendon P, 1996. 36-68.

Eliot, George. "Letter to R. H. Hutton." *George Eliot's Life As Related in Her Letters and Journals.* Ed. J. W. Cross. London: Blackwell, n.d. 366-67.

Elkin, Stanley. *The Dick Gibson Show.* New York: Warner, 1971.

Federman, Raymond. *Surfiction: Fiction Now...and Tomorrow.* Chicago: Swallow P, 1975.

Frank, Joseph. "Spatial Form in Modern Literature." *Sewanee Review* 53 (1945): 221-40 (I), 433-56 (II), 643-53 (III).

Gibson, Andrew. *Towards a Postmodern Theory of Narrative.* Edinburgh UP, 1996.

Giddens, Anthony. *The Consequences of Modernity.* Cambridge: Polity P, 1960.

Goffman, Erving. *Frame Analysis: An Essay on the Organization of Experience.* New York: Harper & Row, 1974.

Harvey, David. *The Condition of Postmodernity: An Enquiry into the Origins of Cultural Change.* Cambridge: Blackwell, 1989.

Hemingway, Ernest. *A Farewell to Arms.* New York: Charles Scribner's Sons, 1966.

Hoffmann, Gerhard. *Raum, Situation, erzählte Wirklichkeit: Poetologische und historische Studien zum englischen und amerikanischen Roman.* Stuttgart: Metzler, 1978.

Hoffmann, Gerhard and Alfred Hornung, eds. *Ethics and Aesthetics: The Moral Turn of Postmodernism.* Heidelberg: Winter, 1996.

Iser, Wolfgang. *The Fictive and the Imaginary: Charting Literary Anthropology.* Baltimore: Johns Hopkins UP, 1993.

Jakobson, Roman. "Grammatical Parallelism and Its Russian Facet." *Language* 42 (1966): 399-429.

James, Henry. "Preface." *Roderick Hudson.* London: Macmillan, 1921. vii-xxvii.

---. "The Art of Fiction." *The House of Fiction: Essays on the Novel by Henry James.* Ed. Leon Edel. Westport, CT: Greenwood, 1957. 23-45.

---. *The Art of the Novel: Critical Prefaces by Henry James.* Ed. Richard P. Blackmur. New York: Scribner's, 1962.

Jameson, Frederic. "Postmodernism, or the Cultural Logic of Late Capitalism." *New Left Review* 146 (1984): 33-92.

Jaspers, Karl. *Allgemeine Psychopathologie.* Berlin: Springer, 1946.

Kestner, Joseph A. *The Spatiality of the Novel.* Place: Wayne State UP, 1978.

LeClair, Thomas and Larry McCaffery, eds. *Anything Can Happen: Interviews With Contemporary American Novelists.* Urbana: U of Illinois P, 1983.

Lukács, Georg. *Essays über Realismus (Probleme des Realismus, I)..* Werke IV. Neuwied: Luchterhand, 1971.

---. *The Historical Novel.* Trans. Hannah and Stanley Mitchell. Lincoln, NE: U of Nebraska P, 1983.

Merleau-Ponty, Maurice. *The Prose of the World.* Ed. Claude Lefort. Trans. John O'Neill. London: Heinemann, 1986.

Robbe-Grillet, Alain. *In the Labyrinth.* Trans. Richard Howard. New York: Grove Press, 1978.

Smitten, Jeffrey R. and A. Daghistani, eds. *Spatial Form in Narrative.* Ithaca, NY: Cornell UP, 1981.

Spencer, Sharon. *Space, Time and Structure in the Modern Novel.* New York UP, 1971.

Steiner, George. *In Bluebeard's Castle: Some Notes Towards the Redefinition of Culture.* London: Faber & Faber, 1972.

Sukenick, Ronald. "The Death of the Novel." *The Death of the Novel and Other Stories.* New York: Dial Press, 1969. 41-102.

Todorov, Tzvetan. *Introduction to Poetics.* Trans. Richard Howard. Minneapolis: U of Minnesota P, 1981.

Virilio, Paul. *La machine de vision.* Paris: Galilée, 1988.

---. *The Aesthetics of Disappearance.* Trans. Philip Beitchman. New York: Semiotext[e], 1991.

Woolf, Virginia. *Collected Essays.* Ed. Leonard Woolf. London: Hogarth Press, 1966/67.

---. *A Writer's Diary.* Ed. Leonard Woolf. New York: Harcourt Brace Jovanovich, 1973.

Ziegler, Heide and Christopher Bigsby, eds. *The Radical Imagination and the Liberal Tradition: Interviews with English and American Novelists.* London: Junction, 1982.

Reading the Void: City Codes and Urban Space in Contemporary American Fiction

Christian Berkemeier

It is hip to be urban. Our *fin de siècle* has seen more studies on all conceivable aspects of the city and of the urban experience than any other era before. Urban studies established itself as a field of studies in its own right long ago and has become one of the first cases of interdisciplinary approaches at work. The subject here will be the representations of the city in American and British films and fictions in recent years. Departing from the much rephrased notion that the city, like any fictional landscape, is a city of words, and implying that an understanding of these words can only function within the context of sender, recipient, code, and referent, my primary interest lies in the way this code has been used and modified in recent years.

As in so many scholarly debates, there have been new questions, but probably no new answers in the discussion of urban space and urban culture in recent years. Research on cities is a slippery territory, and the vast amount of the most recent contributions from all conceivable fields of study, from theology to demography, has not changed this situation, but, rather, has added to the complexity of the matter. Ironically, there is a gap at the center of the debate. That which is termed 'city' has never been defined on the basis of the lowest common denominator. It should suffice at this time to remind you of Leo Marx's rather resigned statement at the opening of the 1997 Annual Meeting of the German Association for American Studies when he declared he was not so sure "what civilization and technology were all about"[1] and, thereby, set the tone for what proved to be a rather disturbing conference.

---

[1] Leo Marx in his key note lecture at the Annual Conference of the German Association for American Studies, Freiburg, May 1997 (*not* printed in the conference publication.)

To sketch how the image and idea of the city have changed over the past century, at least three definitions of 'city' can be compared. Max Weber sees the city as nothing but "a state of mind," (83) Louis Wirth defines it as "a large dense permanent settlement of socially heterogeneous individuals," (4) Joseph Rykwert speaks of "a strange artefact, compounded of willed and random arguments, imperfectly controlled," (qtd. in Gombrich, xx) and Peter Calthorpe vaguely concludes this collection with the remark, "The American Dream is an evolving image and the American Metropolis is its ever-changing reflection" (15). After this rather random grouping of definitions, it should be obvious that there is no stable idea or consensus with regard to a definition. The city has changed in shape, extension, nature, and purpose, and has seen radically diverse and disturbing reflections in 20th century visual arts, film, and fiction. Thomas Pynchon is the founder of San Narciso in *The Crying of Lot 49*, an intellectual property often copied, but never quite attained as it shows the state of the art in the present day American understanding of the city: "San Narciso lay further south, near L. A. Like many named places in California it was less an identifiable city than a grouping of concepts—census tracts, special purpose bond-issue districts, shopping nuclei, all overlaid with access roads to its own freeway" (13).

Canons for city fiction have proven to be of little literary value, and it is just as difficult to find meaningful categories in which examples of city fiction can be grouped, but I would like to introduce four elements of thematic emphasis that dominate certain currents in present day fiction of the urban:

1) *Por qué pagar más?* The Social Chessboard
2) Double Spacing: The Other, the Self, and the Same
3) San Narciso Revisited: Urban Playgrounds
4) Alphabet Street: The Letter and the Labyrinth

The Social Chessboard

The representation of the city as a social chessboard has been at the heart and is the origin of the 20th century fictional city. William Dean Howells, Theodore Dreiser, and Stephen Crane are among the first to explore fictional strategies and work in highly visual discrepancies between high and low, narrow and wide, dark and light, big and small, and succeed in picturing cities structured and defined by sharp social and ethnic differences. In contemporary city fiction, urban space materializes as a means of setting apart social groups, of showing prestige or the lack of it. But it is very early that not only the space, but also all other narrative elements of the urban novel of this type are incorporated into an all-embracing social space that gradually turns the city into the protagonist of the novel. John Dos Passos' *Manhattan Transfer* is well known as the first American example of this kind. Protagonists are defined in terms of their work and social status, and fictional time follows the syncopated rhythm of work and industry in the novel.[2] Mobility (on foot, on horseback, by tram or car) and destination are used as indicators of social acceptance and caste adherence. Naturally prominent throughout novels of social protest, this type of novel has made its way from Realism to Muckraking and Red Decade to conformist success myths of the 1950s and into the restless sixties and seventies, reinvented here by ethnic minorities and their foremost prominent representatives.[3] Juneau Diaz's praised recent collection *Drown* may indicate how alive this tradition still is. The volume of short fiction combines intermedially informed means of expression from rap and Latino movies with the traditional concerns and desires of his native people and the challenges they encounter in their understanding of initiation and career, tradition, family, and gender relations.

Strangely enough, there is now also a proportion of distinctly WASP writers who seem to fall back on the fictional potential of this type of novel: Tom Wolfe's *Bonfire of the Vanities* from 1988 not only refers to Thackerey's *Vanity Fair* in its

---

[2] One of the seminal studies on the subject is still Klotz, *Die erzählte Stadt. Ein Sujet als Herausforderung des Romans von Lesage bis Döblin.*

title, but has also been called "a Dreiser novel for the nineteen eighties." (Smith, 1991). More than that, as Wolfe self-consciously explains in his Essay "Stalking the Billion-Footed Beast" (1988) which functions as a preface to the novel in its paperback editions, his is a new attempt at writing the new great realist novel. In a project quite unlike everything Wolfe had to say and write earlier on the New Journalism and its typically innovative features, he sets aside everything experimental and wishes to return to good old realism with a satirical edge. Just as in Wolfe's later novel, *A Man in Full,* the city is much more than an environment—it is a social catalyst, an incubator of ethnicity, and class, and gender-based conflict:

> Even the Wasps. They won't know what they're looking at. They'll sit in their co-ops on Park and Fifth and East Seventy-second Street and Sutton Place, and they'll shiver with the violence of it and enjoy the show. Cattle. Birdbrains! Rosebuds! *Goyim*! You don't even know, do you? Do you really think this is your city any longer? Open your eyes: The greatest city of the twentieth century! Do you think *money* will keep it yours? Come down from your swell co-ops, you general partners and merger lawyers! It's the Third World down there. Puerto Ricans, West Indians, Haitians, Dominicans, Cubans, Columbians, Hondurans, Koreans, Chinese, Thais, Vietnamese, Ecuadorians, Panamanians, Filipinos, Albanians, Senegalese, and Afro-Americans! Go visit the frontiers, you gutless wonders! Morningside Heights, St Nicholas Park, Washington Heights, Fort Tryon—*por qué pagar más*! The Bronx—the Bronx is finished for you. (*Bonfire*, 6-7)

At this point the unnamed Mayor of New York City is speaking, and it is not the only time in the novel that someone speaks of a frontier in the city; the paradigm of a space divided between a civilized world and a 'Third World' wilderness occurs frequently and resonates in a tone of colonial imperialism. The city code here is of a rhythm set by the rapid changes in the narrative perspective, by the change between places of work, life, and (although rarely) leisure. It is also a code of aggression: Wolfe has repeatedly been criticized for his alleged sexism and lack of politi-

---

[3] The term 'city novel' and a typology for American examples are first used in Gelfant, *The American City Novel* of 1954.

cal correctness.[4] While it is certainly correct that a racial and sexist bias is the overtone in the narrative voice in a major part of the novel, it should be noted that most of Wolfe's male characters are caricatures of failed businessmen and husbands. In addition to this, the narrative perspective is one of multiple perspectives, and even if it were not, it would still leave the political position of the author unclear.

Urban Playgrounds

Another, much younger novelist of the eighties is Bret Easton Ellis, who is too often identified exclusively with his shocker *American Psycho*.[5] Equally disturbing, not as shocking, but not always readable are his first novel *Less than Zero* and his latest *Glamorama*, both works of social satire and dyed-in-the-wool moralism. *Less Than Zero* introduces its reader to a new urbanism altogether: West Coast urban and suburban sprawl, an indistinct sequence of parking lots, low-cast buildings and semi-industrial plants, and, of course, Ellis' central image at the beginning of the book: Los Angeles International Airport, written in three capitals, LAX. Apart from the fact that everything in the novel is very lax, at least everyone is seemingly all-so liberal, all codes are relaxed and all resources are unrestricted, the 'X' in LA. 'X' may be of more extensive significance to the setting of the novel as a whole. 'X' may refer to a gap, an undefined place, or, if it is defined, it is only defined in terms of airline slang abbreviation, a language reducing every conceivable place on the globe to three capital letters, a place merely defined as an intersection of the incessant flow of people and goods, a place dissolving into all four corners of the X. The very first sentence of the novel, over which the protagonist broods for a period of time, indicates that this supposed place of intersection is actually a paradox:

> People are afraid to merge on freeways in Los Angeles. This is the first thing I hear when I come back to the city. Blair picks me up from LAX and mutters this under

---

[4] Cf. McNiff and Lurie, "*Bonfire*, the New Journalism, and Big Bad Tom Wolfe" (66).
[5] Ellis has recently been an often-quoted role-model to the so-called "Neue Berliner Autoren" including Georg M. Oswald, Benjamin v. Stuckrath-Barre, Christian Kracht and others. There has been considerable dispute over whether or not Ellis can be seen as one of the fathers of Post Pop, but he and his Berlin step-sons certainly share a concern for play, pose, and surface.

her breath as her car drives up the onramp. She says, "People are afraid to merge on freeways in Los Angeles." Though that sentence shouldn't bother me, it stays in my mind for an uncomfortably long time. Nothing else seems to matter. (*Less Than Zero*, 1)[6]

Blair is the protagonist's former (?) girlfriend, and this is just the first in quite a number of relationships in the novel, both parallel and subsequent, that only function on the surface. Even if (or because?) the environment is so permissive in the City of Angels, there is a lack of genuine contact and interaction here, out on the freeway (or 'free way'), in itself an icon of mobility and freedom, which is now irretrievably reduced to a strictly linear pattern. Every attempt at transgressing this pattern, the novel tells us, will end in violent monstrosity.[7] The freeway is no longer what it used to be, i.e. the easiest and fastest way of mastering a space that has become meaningless. To the individual, the human body and its extension (the car) have become a matrix for gestures of posing, for actualizing the self, for mirroring its surface in its most pleasant form, and for thereby being reassured of its own existence.

Ellis has found his own way of using urban codes. His images are the short and simple, impressive and sustainable do's and don'ts of traffic signs and street names, the terms for products and places. Street signs like "This Is Not an Exit" or "Disappear Here" can be seen as signals to both the characters and readers alike; they function as meta-codes in the no man's land of cityscapes between fact and fiction.

Ellis is one of the authors to include in the context of Advanced or Post Pop—or the new hedonistic novel. His latest novel *Glamorama* (1999) certainly constitutes a new level in the representation of life in the fast lane in a metropolitan city of the late nineties. The rhythm is still syncopated, this time, however, from the single and personal narrative perspective of a jaded wanna-be yuppie, the pseudo-winner Victor, shifting between long lethargic periods and moments of intense shock, as

---

[6] For an analysis of the novel, see Horst Steur, *Der Schein und das Nichts. Bret Easton Ellis' Roman* Less Than Zero.

we have seen it before in Bret Easton Ellis. New York space is mastered by either helicopter or by motorcycle, never by car, as this is *so* totally inefficient and out of date. Places (trendy clubs, that is) are defined by the rules of attraction, i.e. by how many guests and celebrities they host and entertain on a regular basis, by who owns them, and by the latest and farest-out interior design[8].

Glamorama does not showcase a city. It showcases the very small proportion of those in the entertainment and gastronomy sector, in the media, named and rephrased in catalogues of details and invitation lists for parties and events. If there is such a thing as a poetics of this novel, it lies in an aesthetic of abundance and redundancy, a surplus of information that deliberately bores and torments its readers with its paratactic logic, its flat protagonist and shallow plot, only to confront the readers with the void behind it all. This is a city of celebrities, a city that centers around fame and popularity and shatters all systems of coherence, revolving centrifugally at breathtaking speed.

Part of this world can also be found in Douglas Coupland's recent *Generation X* in which he chooses Seattle as the setting for his novel. We are beyond the frontier, in a newly defined post-urban culture, home of grunge, stronghold of cyberculture, ecology, and everything attributed to Generation X. Seattle appears more as a Pacific Rim city than an American city, more an indicator of a particular lifestyle than a place, more a concept than a distinct position on a map.[9]

Double Spacing

Just as much as it stresses the shallowness of urban playgrounds, Coupland's novel shows a concern for internalized spaces. It returns to a social setting that is very familiar to readers of John Updike's or Richard Ford's fiction or to spectators familiar with *American Beauty* or Lynch's *Blue Velvet* and *Lost Highway*: suburbia.

---

[7] Structurally and thematically, Ellis' debut novel prefigures much of the concerns of the later *American Psycho*.
[8] Cf. Kreutzer, "New York in der Gegenwartsliteratur: Bild der entwirklichten Vertikalen."
[9] For the study of distinct spatial arrangements and forms in cities of the American East and West, see also Bremer, *Urban Intersections: Meetings of Life and Literature in United States Cities*.

What Ellis shows as a hollow merry-go-round and 24-hour event is placed at the periphery of the average contemporary American metropolis and reduced to domestic banality. What creates the special thrill of these novels is the way they internalize conflict in a seemingly harmonious environment that seeks to escape all forms of excitement, the way they displace and delay acute problems and still distinctly bring out the signs of mute desperation of daily routines. From Updike's *Rabbit* tetralogy to Richard Ford's *The Sportswriter* and *Independence Day*, they are also always the pitiless satire of an all-American mediocrity. The protagonist of Sam Mendes' *American Beauty* makes a careful collection of all he has ever wanted in life and projects it onto the juvenile product of a mainstream culture that has been perfectly commodified and standardized: a cheerleader and homecoming queen. But it is exactly this homecoming, this escape from a world of boredom and sameness that this movie rejects just as much as David Lynch's *Blue Velvet* or *Lost Highway*. If psychedelic colors in *Blue Velvet* make the suburban home appear as a hopeless trap to all forms of human neurosis, this is even more obvious in *Lost Highway*. The tiny backyard of a suburban house is perceived in a daydream as a strangely unreal and despatialized environment that gains its status as territory only by its separation from the next allotment of land; the small piece of lawn is restricted not only by a wall, but also by a white picket fence in front of it. The other that is fenced off (this becomes more than obvious in Lynch's movie), however, is nothing but the horror of eternal sameness. The play on words of 'Realty' vs. 'Reality' which Mendes uses in *American Beauty* as much as Richard Ford in *Independence Day* (1995) in connection with the profession of their protagonists makes it evident: The exchangeability of a place of living by commercial standards, the complete lack of reference or destination of individual, origin and goal comes to perfection in the suburban nightmare on paper and on the screen, a nightmare also underlying the atmosphere of *Girlfriend in a Coma* (1998) in which conflict is no longer hidden: It may not be accidental that at the beginning of the book teenagers at a party violently destroy an entire house and injure some friends in the quiet neighborhood, and it may also not be accidental that one striking anagram of coma almost spells amok.

Alphabet Street

Mr. Bones, the canine protagonist of Paul Auster's latest novel *Timbuktu*, reaches a similar suburban environment on the last part of his futile and aimless wanderings across the North American continent, looking for a home. He has been the faithful companion of his down-and-out master, a certain William Gurevich, who, after a revealing vision, changed his name to Willie G. Christmas. The two set out on a fictional journey through Baltimore, which is not unlike the wanderings of Daniel Quinn and Peter Stillman in Auster's *City of Glass* that have become a classic example for encoding and decoding urban space. Auster and DeLillo have been known to take up techniques and concerns reflected in Pynchon's novels or those of his earlier colleagues. If Manhattan is the setting for a major part of the New York trilogy, Baltimore becomes the central fictional landscape in *Timbuktu*. Willy G. Christmas likes it so much because it relates to one of his idols, to Edgar Allan Poe, and thereby in a pun also to his own origin, which is Poland—or 'Poe-land.'

Plays on words are once more at the basis of the loose connective tissue of references in this Auster novel. There is still a considerable amount of research to be done on the intertextual traps in this work, but it seems as though this time Auster has used more Jewish and Christian imagery than before. Willy G. (or *Jee*) is quite obviously intended to remind the reader of the life of Christ: He leaves his mother to set out on a true pilgrimage throughout *Mari*land and Baltimore—which North Americans know to be the first Catholic diocese on their continent (*Encyclopaedia Brittanica, Micropaedia*, 1981). As in earlier novels, Auster seems to be so fond of his plays on words that he explains some of them himself, telling his reader that his canine narrator, Mr. Bones, is so fond of his existence because 'dog' is the exactly inverted anagram of 'god.'[10] In the end, you do not have to be a prophet to read

---

[10] A trick stolen from one of Barthelme's short stories entitled "The Fallen Dog." Cf. Berkemeier, *Inverted Commas: Studien zur Parodie in den Fiktionen Donald Barthelmes und Robert Coo-*

'*Timbuktu*' not only as 'far out,' not merely as the reference to some city in the heart of Africa, nor exclusively as an allusion to poem by Tennyson or as a reminder of an English nursery rhyme, but you might as well read Auster's title as another name, as a re-writing of St. *Paul's* Second Letter to Timothy—or 'Tim Book Two.' The emphasis on the Paulinian trias of values of faith, charity, and hope in the novel (and especially in its concluding paragraphs) would strongly support this reference. The novel appears to be yet another example of an Auster book on contingency and control, on freedom and its price, on openness and determinism.

It should have become clear that different codes of the urban continue to coexist. A clear distribution of the traditional style/content type would not be possible, as different urban themes are approached in the same way, and as strategies may vary within one novel or movie. All of the fictions described work on the basis of existing genre models—most of them associating the city with economic success and therefore remodeling and inverting elements of the American business novel in the tradition of William Dean Howells and others. The representations of suburbia recall echoes all the way back to Anderson's *Winesburg, Ohio* or the fictions of John Cheever and their uniform backyards.

With the turn of the century, we are witnessing the prolonging of what Ihab Hassan has called "the dematerialization of the metropolis" in fiction (Hassan, 93-112). Long after William Gibson, we have seen forms of textualized space that go far beyond the approaches in Pynchon or his successors who ultimately leave the gap, the desire, and the void at the unresolved center of their fictional constructions. Cyberfictions go a step further in confronting us with the blending of human thought and electronic information processing, of interfaces between human and cybernetic communication, of hybrids of human and artificial life forms. Where deconstructivist fictions would skeptically stress lack, longing, and impossibility, this post-urban fiction which leaves behind any focus on spatiality, settlement, and their implications for humans, tends to emphasize provocation, opportunity and

---

vers. Mr. Bones may also remind the reader of "The Learnéd English Dog" in Pynchon's *Mason & Dixon*.

potential. The fate of our cities will not go unreported; it will be reflected in our cybergames, interactive movies, and events. Our books, however, might rot and crumble like ancient brownstone buildings, leaving us with nothing but some memories of good old 20th century pop music, like the protagonist in *Girlfriend in a Coma* ("I'm Jared, a ghost"), relating our fate in allusions to song titles by Skeeter Davis, Kansas, R.E.M., and Pink Floyd:

> Yes, the world is over. It's still here but it's ... *over*. I'm at the End of the World. Dust in the wind. The end of the world as we know it. Just another brick in the wall. It sounds glamorous but it's not. It's dreary and quiet and the air always smells like there's a tire fire half a mile up wind. (*Girlfriend in a Coma*, 4)

Bibliography

Berkemeier, Christian. *Inverted Commas: Studien zur Parodie in den Fiktionen Donald Barthelmes*. Essen: Die Blaue Eule, 2001.

Bremer, Sidney. *Urban Intersections: Meetings of Life and Literature in United States Cities*. Urbana: U of Illinois P, 1992.

Calthorpe, Peter. *The Next American Metropolis. Ecology, Community, and the American Dream*. New York: Princeton Architectural P, 1993.

Coupland, Douglas. *Girlfriend in a Coma*. London: Flamingo, 1998.

Diaz, Junot. *Drown*. New York: Riverhead, 1996.

Ellis, Bret Easton. *Glamorama*. New York: Knopf, 1999.

---. *Less Than Zero*. New York: Simon and Schuster, 1985.

Ford, Richard. *Independence Day*. New York: Knopf, 1995.

Gelfant, Blanche Housman, *The American City Novel*. Norman: U of Oklahoma P, 1954.

Gombrich, E. H. *Art and Illusion. A Study in the Psychology of Pictorial Representation*. Princeton: Princeton UP, 1961.

Hassan, Ihab. "Cities of Mind, Urban Words: The Dematerialization of the Metropolis in Contemporary American Fiction." *Literature and the Urban Experience*. Eds. Michael C. Jaye and Ann Chalmers Watts. New Brunswick, 1981. 93-112.

Klotz, Volker. *Die erzählte Stadt. Ein Sujet als Herausforderung des Romans von Lesage bis Döblin.* München: Hanser, 1969.

Kreutzer, Eberhard. "New York in der Gegenwartsliteratur: Bild der entwirklichten Vertikalen." *Medium Metropole. Berlin, Paris, New York.* Eds. Friedrich Knilli and Michael Nerlich. Heidelberg: Winter, 1986. 125-144.

McNiff, John and Nancy Lurie. "*Bonfire*, the New Journalism, and Big Bad Tom Wolfe." *DLSU-Dialogue* 25.2 (1990/91): 61-75.

Pynchon, Thomas. *The Crying of Lot 49.* New York: Harper, 1999.

Smith, James F. "Tom Wolfe's *Bonfire of the Vanities*: A Dreiser Novel for the 1980s." *Journal of American Culture* 14 (Fall 1991): 43-50.

Steur, Horst. *Der Schein und das Nichts. Bret Easton Ellis' Roman 'Less Than Zero.'* Essen: Die Blaue Eule, 1995.

Volker Klotz. *Die erzählte Stadt. Ein Sujet als Herausforderung des Romans von Lesage bis Döblin.* München: Hanser, 1969.

Weber, Max. *The City.* Trans. and ed. Don Martindale and Gertrud Newirth. New York: The Free Press, 1958.

Wirth, Louis. "Urbanism as A Way of Life." *American Journal of Sociology* 44 (July 1938): pages.

Wirth-Nesher, Hana. *City Codes, Reading the Modern Urban Novel.* Cambridge: Cambridge UP, 1996).

Wolfe, Tom. "Stalking the Billion-Footed Beast." *The Bonfire of the Vanities.* London: Picador, 1988.

---. *The Bonfire of the Vanities.* New York: Farrar Straus Giroux, 1987.

---. *A Man in Full.* New York: Farrar Straus Giroux, 1997.

Deconstruction of Public Space in David Mamet's *Oleanna*

Pearl A. McHaney

When we look back—as we look back—we see that we could never have done otherwise than as we did. (Pause.) Surely, then, there must have been signs. If only we could have read them.

David Mamet, *Edmond*, 15.

Moss: I lied. *(Pause.)* Alright? My end is *my* business. Your end's twenty-five. In or out. You tell me, you're out you take the consequences.
Aaronow: I do?
Moss: Yes. *(Pause.)*
Aaronow: And why is that?
Moss: Because you listened.

David Mamet, *Glengarry Glenn Ross*, 46.

David Mamet concerns himself with the most private of demons: the self set against the myth of the American dream. In the symbolic, institutional space of the theatre, the public environment of Mamet's postmodern plays, and the personal landscape of dramatized human relationships, Mamet's plays hinge upon the reading of signs by the characters and by the audiences. Viewers and readers of Mamet's plays are duped from the start, for they objectify the plays and subconsciously distance their personal lives from those enacted in Mamet's public spaces.

In this essay, I consider the space of the academy. Most readers of this collection of essays have come to this 'stage' as students or professors in institutions of higher education. I want to layer upon this place the landscape of theatre with its conventions of illusion and reality, its performative spaces, its rendering of written words back into speech acts, and its role-playing that is accepted by 'trapped audiences.'

In *Three Uses of the Knife: On the Nature and Purpose of Drama* (1998), David Mamet states that the artist is driven to create, not to "bring anything to the audience or to anyone else," but "to create a raging ambivalence" (51). He accomplishes this in his 1992 play *Oleanna*, a play at once about sexual harassment, political correctness taken to the extreme, the power of language as a form of entrapment, and ultimately, primarily, according to Mamet himself, a scathing indictment of the American institution of higher education.[1]

At the beginning of each of the three acts of *Oleanna*, John, a college professor, and Carol, his student, are seated on either side of John's desk. Carol has come to her teacher's office without an appointment to discuss her failing grade. At the start and intermittently throughout the play, their dialogue is interrupted as John talks on the telephone to persons who are not fully identified and who are never seen or heard by Carol or by the audience. At first the telephone conversations concern John's impending mortgage for a house for his family, a house he can now afford because his tenure is about to be approved on the basis of a published book about the hazing of higher education. In Act One, John offers to start the course over for Carol, to erase her history of grades. He will instruct her individually so that she can further her understanding. In Act Two, in response to Carol's written report to the university tenure committee of his sexist, elitist, and threatening behavior during their meeting (performed in Act One), John explains his love of teaching. Carol has been consulting with a group who apparently helped her to write her report. Act Three opens again with John and Carol seated. John has invited Carol to explain her position. John has lost his bid for tenure, his house, and most likely will lose his job. Carol offers him a deal, worked out with her group, that if he agrees to the censoring of certain books including his own, she will withdraw the charges. John learns that Carol has filed official charges of rape, an interpretation of the actions at the end of Act Two. Interrupted for a last time by a call from his wife, John is nonetheless about to continue the negotiation when Carol twice instructs him, "Don't call your wife 'baby'" (79). Suddenly, John resorts to the physical and verbal

---

[1] Cf. Roudané, *Conversation* (2000).

violence generic to Mamet's male characters, and the play ends with Carol's threats about to be realized.

Trevor J. Barnes and James S. Duncan in *Writing Worlds: Discourse, Text, and Metaphor in the Representation of Landscape* (1992) paraphrase Foucault, saying that "Because of its appeal to 'common sense' or its scientific status, knowledge in the form of representations is in itself a power rather than simply a reflection of power relations in the 'real' world 'beyond' the academy, the media or government task force" (9). Students demonstrate awe for the professor's words, particularly published ones. The hierarchical discourses of the professor and his tenure-earning book, of the student who demands understanding, and of the competing powers outside the performative space of the drama battle for center stage in *Oleanna*.

Whether we look at theatre, Mamet's work, or *Oleanna* with models of spatiality articulated by Manuel Castells who shows that spatial structures of symbolic and institutional spaces develop from ideological and political-juridical social structures, or by Edward Soja's reading of Henri Lefebvre that all spatiality is socially produced, we can arrive at the same postulates. Theatre is a socially produced space in which the various ideologies represented are bound by the power inherent both in the symbols used and in the institutions represented by the various discourses (Johnston, 583-84). Soja explains that "To recognize what 'takes place'" in a space, "what it is used for, is to resume the dialectic" and thus to dramatize the contradictions of the space (17). This is Mamet's intention in *Oleanna*, to unseat the hegemonic powers of the academy by examining contradictions inherent in the private and public spaces of higher education. John's classroom is a public space where a temporary community gathers information from the truth-wielding professor. The classroom is transformed into a performative space, student and teacher taking roles, acting in character, reading lines, interpreting actions. John's office, on the other hand, is a contradictory space, symbolic of his accomplishments, his rank in the university and his professionalism, and yet, one's office is the most private space in the public landscape of higher education, an inner sanctum. Although Mamet's scenography is minimalist, audiences naturally form idealistic abstractions about education based on personal experiences from their own institutions of higher learning. We are 'let in' to John's private space within the public landscape, just as Carol must have been let in. There, his telephone connects him to his personal life while he engages in his profession.

Mamet alters and extends the theatrical space of John's office in three modes: the play's epigraphs that complicate the utopia/prison dichotomies dramatized by the play, the use of the telephone to create narrative spaces in which the dialogue becomes monologic and soliloquized, and the privileging of writing by the academy in a landscape that is phonocentric at large. Through each of these cultural landscapes, the audience, whether viewing or reading, is positioned to empathize with one or the other of the two characters to the extent that the characters and the audience are taken in by a confidence game.

In *Oleanna*, Mamet combines the sanctioned dramatization of personal spaces in the public theatre with the similarly empowered public landscape of higher education. Both the theatre and the academy are socially constructed spatial institutions (Soja, 57) dependent upon language for their power. Both the theatre and the academy assume a skewed economic exchange in which the symbolic value of what is gained far exceeds its monetary cost. In both instances, the product (performed play or learned lesson) becomes particularly temporal when separated from the institutions' spatial boundaries and is quickly rendered abstract. In both institutions, the power is guardedly maintained in the background, while a few persons foreground the rules and interface with the institution's consumers. The audience of *Oleanna* in particular, so accepting of these parameters in theatre as to not question or even remark them, is distracted by the sexual harassment, the feminist agenda, the political correctness gone extreme, and fails to recognize Mamet's deconstruction not just of the tenure process, but of the academy itself, its use of public and private spaces, its use of language in the specialized discourses held sacred and secret to persons outside the environment, its privileging of writing as a means of entitlement and power. In the conventional, expected, and accepted performative space with stage, actors, dialogue, and audience, we are taken, surprised, shocked.

When we move the drama to a wholly different performative space by reading the play, we change our expectations and thus our reactions. Performed in the mind of the reader, the play becomes an isolated, solitary, and unstable experience because space, place, and landscape are indeterminate, controlled by the reader. The reader performs the play in a now completely symbolic space, individually creating meaning from the tropes. How does this power exerted by the reader effect the balance of power that was previously weighted on the side of the institution of the theatre? Reading the stage directions and interlinear instructions for inflection, the reader engages on a metacognative level different from that of the viewer of a performance. In theatre, the director 'writes' or inscripts the players' actions; whereas, in a 'reading space,' the reader gives, imagines, or 'writes' such directions.

In viewing the play, we wait for Oleanna to appear, or as no such character is on the cast list, we wait for a reference to the title person or place. However, when we are given a text to read, we find two epigraphs; the second one includes the title word.

> Oh, to be in *Oleanna*,
> That's where I would rather be.
> Than be bound in Norway
> And drag the chains of slavery.[xiii]

Oleanna refers to a nineteenth-century Norwegian utopian community in the Midwest; Mamet draws the title from a folk song that he recalled from his boyhood camp days.[2]

> Ole, oleanna, ole, oleanna
> ole, ole, ole, ole, ole, oleanna
>
> Oh to be in Oleanna,
> that's where I'd like to be
> Than to be in Norway
> and bear the chains of slavery

---

[2] Trans. from the Norwegian by Seeger (2000).

Little roasted piggies
rush around the city streets
Inquiring so politely
if a slice of ham you'd like to eat

Beer as sweet as muncheners
springs from the ground and flows away
The cows all like to milk themselves
And the hens lay eggs ten times a day

The women there do all the work
As round the fields they quickly go
Each one has a hickory stick
And beats herself if she works too slow

In Oleanna land is free
The wheat and corn just plant themselves
Then grow a good four feet a day
While on your bed you rest yourself.

The title and the epigraph focus the cultural landscape of the drama on the irony of "the university as a utopia of thought, expression, and enlightenment" (Bechtel, 35). John sought to make the university an Oleanna by exposing its rituals, but Carol's undermining of the institution through its nearly-tenured representative turns John's university into a Norway of enslavement. For the Broadway production, the folk song lines were included in bold within the New York *Playbill* for *Oleanna*, not as an epigraph (47).

The first epigraph in the reading text presents a complementary comparison; this one between the idyllic, rustic, and "free" Scottish moors and the crowded, filthy alleyways of nineteenth-century London as described in Samuel Butler's nineteenth-century *The Way of All Flesh* (1872).[3] As the initial introduction to the ideological space of *Oleanna*, this epigraph is unambiguous. We are given to understand that young children's happiness is of no concern, for they have "a marvelous

---

[3] Cf. Butler: "The want of fresh air does not seem much to effect the happiness of children in a London alley: the greater part of them sing and play as though they were on a moor in Scotland. So the absence of a genial mental atmosphere is not commonly recognized by children who have never known it. Young people have a marvelous faculty of either dying or adapting themselves to circumstances. Even if they are unhappy—very unhappy—it is astonishing how easily they

facility of either dying or adapting" and they can be easily "prevented from finding it out or from attributing it to any other cause than their own sinfulness." John as a child was stupid: "Why must you behave so stupidly? Can't you *understand?*" (16). But he adapted sufficiently to write in adulthood about the *"exploitation* in the education process" (22).

The epigraphs work equally well for Carol who would rather be in Oleanna, the university, than not, for only there can the American dream be fulfilled. Mamet's works nearly all reveal the American dream to be a myth. He believes that our "national culture is founded very much on the idea of strive and succeed," but the American myth, Mamet says, is that we can get "something out of nothing. One feels one can succeed only at the cost of someone else. Economic life in America is a lottery. Everyone's got an equal chance, but only one guy is going to get to the top" (Roudané, 1986, 1). "Our national character," according to Mamet, is to "consider life as a commercial enterprise" (Covington, 2). Carol tells John he has "no idea what it cost" her "to come to this school" (52). Once there, under John's instruction, she finds the Oleanna to be more like the Norway of the song. Likewise, at first she is ignorant of the oppressive nature of the landscape and then attributes it to her own sinfulness (stupidity). With the help of John, she develops a "want of fresh air" and adapts accordingly, playing by John's set of rules.

These two epigraphs write onto the text of the moral and cultural landscapes of the postmodern university by putting them into the spatial environment of the nineteenth century industrialization. Is the American dream of higher education for each citizen a utopia or a prison? Mamet offers a staged landscape that takes us, we think, into the public world of the university, but from the beginning, we should watch and read with caution, for Mamet asserts in most of his works that "all great crimes are committed in the name of public tranquility. It is a confidence trick for taking power" (Covington, 9-10).

---

can be prevented from finding it out, or at any rate from attributing it to any other cause than their own sinfulness" (30).

Language is the key in Mamet's work. His characters' monologues "dominate his plays so fully that words replace and even subvert the physical and visual elements of the productions," writes Deborah Geis (89). A character performing a monologue takes center stage (Geis, 94). He may speak introspectively, or to another character, or provide exposition, or even talk 'at' rather than with another character (95). Soliloquy, a subcategory of monologue, can achieve the same ends but with increased metadrama because the character speaks more consciously to the audience or to himself. All characters are eavesdropping, for in both monologue and soliloquy, one character alone speaks.

In *Oleanna*, John speaks often into the telephone, which interrupts while Carol "is seated across the desk from him" (xvi). John's speech is not technically a soliloquy because he is not talking to himself, or even a monologue, for he is carrying on a dialogue with some other person, yet he is alone in speaking. However, the illusion or the fact/truth of an additional character in a physical space outside the staged place is realistic. Use of the telephone is a stock theatrical convention that brings an outside, unseen presence into the play because the theatre, as Susan Sontag compares it to film, is otherwise "confined to a logical or *continuous* space" (366).

Carol and the audience eavesdrop on John's private discussion and participate somewhat unwillingly in his personal dilemmas. John's telephone 'monologues' create additional narrative spaces in which the audience during Act One aligns itself with Carol in eavesdropping and in imagining the extra-theatrical spaces. The audience is invited to cross the physical boundary of the stage and thereby 'plays' at being the character who listens.

When monologue occurs in a dialogue-based play, or within the ongoing dialogue, the drama intensifies because the action of the dialogue itself is interrupted. The telephone ring is always jarring. John must decide each time how long to let it ring, how to excuse himself from the dialogue, what response to give, how much to reveal or to conceal with his responses. Carol must decide whether or not to listen obviously, what her body language should reveal or conceal, whether or not to continue the interrupted conversation, or to resume the dialogue contingent upon information overheard in the soliloquized telephone conversation. During the course of the three-act play, after the opening conversation, the telephone rings eight times, four times in Act One, once in Act Two, and three times in Act Three. John speaks to his wife Grace four times, to his friend Jerry three times (in one call to both Grace and Jerry), and once to an unidentified person. Only one time does John let it ring without answering. In Act One, each time John hangs up, Carol asks him for clarification regarding the information she overhears. During the final call, John speaks both to his wife Grace and to Carol intermittently and never hangs up. Thus, Grace becomes the eavesdropper to Carol's, "Don't call your wife 'baby'" (78-80) twice, and she hears John's loss of control/power, his rage, and his verbal attack.

The information given to John in the telephone conversations is always shocking: his real estate deal is threatened, what he had thought to be urgent truth is revealed as a lie (just a surprise party!), and that he may be charged with rape. The telephone itself is a form of aggression, a means of intruding upon one's private life. In John's private office, he is harassed by those who love him and by those whom he teaches, both categories of persons apparently his subordinates.

In extending the spatial text of the drama, the telephone serves as a substitute for interaction with characters in places beyond the staged illusion allowing John to play many roles in addition to that of professor. These new narrative spaces then reveal additional discourses, hegemonies, and binary oppositions. Foucault argues that it is the discourses' "association with the institutions that legitimates the 'truths' that they produce. The power of discourses derives not so much from the abstract ideas they represent as from their material bases in the institutions and practices" (qtd. in Barnes, 9). Thus, in *Oleanna*, Mamet dramatizes that the discourses of real estate purchases, marriage partners, women's groups, lawyers, promotion and tenure manuals, and criminal courts compete for power. As the cast expands beyond the staged re-presentation, only John or Carol can visualize or hear the other characters.

At first, the intrusive telephone calls seem to carry the threat of losing the house over a minor, legal loop hole. Tension builds and John is confused and frustrated because his presence is requested, then urged, and finally demanded. After the final phone call of Act One, Carol asks, "What is it?" John replies, "It's a surprise party" (40).

> Is it your birthday?
> No.
> What is it?
> The tenure announcement.
> The tenure announcement.
> They're throwing a party for us in our new house.
> [...]
> They're proud of you.
> Well, there are those who would say it's a form of aggression.
> What is?
> A surprise. (40-41)

The aggression of Act One is verbal, mostly re-presented from past speech acts. The surprise party victimizes John, but his comment seems merely rhetorical. Although his book is about the "ritualized annoyance [of] higher education" (28), John doesn't regard his own teaching as such.

Keir Elam explains in *The Semiotics of Theatre and Drama* that "theatrical text is defined and perceived above all in spatial terms" (56). In *Oleanna*, the performative space becomes a prison from which neither character can escape. The audience cannot escape the ambiguity, cannot understand who is victim, who victimizer, for each person reads the actions and speech acts with a difference. At the conclusion when John asks, "Are you kidding me?" Carol answers, "Yes, That's right" (79-80). We are left with another form of aggression.

In Carol's world, outside the hegemony of higher education, power is found in speech rather than in writing. Derrida reminds us that there are "speech acts everywhere, but the possibility of speech acts, or performative speech acts, depends on conditions and conventions which are not simply verbal." "What I call 'writing' or 'text,'" he says, "is not simply verbal" (Olson, 15). *Oleanna*, set in a socially-constructed landscape of the academy allows us to see two sets of conventions at once. Theatre privileges speech acts, obviously, but they are written first and then returned to verbal states. William H. Macy, who acted the part of John in the original production as well as in the New York production, remarks on this translation from writing to thought with regard to the telephone calls that they "were murder" to perform. "In Boston I had three sheets on the desk with my dialogue." People asked if he had written "out the dialogue [his] wife is supposedly saying on the phone." He hadn't; "I think my way is better. It's like music. I hear what she's saying on the phone and musically respond to it" (Botto, 47).

The academy, the landscape Mamet dramatizes, also originates from written texts that are returned to verbal acts in the form of lectures. The speech acts performed in the classroom, however, are relatively void of power outside the physical space and landscape of higher education, unlike the speech acts of theatre. By conflating phonocentricism of the student's and the audience's environments by writing that is given special status in the university, Mamet deconstructs the power of the academy and reveals the theatrics of the professor once he is dethroned, put off-stage, removed from the hegemonic position of teacher.

In John's space, in the university, even at a liberal arts college where individualism and maverick actions and thinking are encouraged,[4] writing is privileged. The university as a whole disregards Derrida's assertion that writing is outside of the center; every university, in fact, has a Writing Center, a physical and objective place where 'writing' is taught. John has made his idea that education is "'prolonged and systematic hazing'" public in a book (35). Carol reads her written notes taken from John's oral lecture ideas that he has taken back from his published text. The linear and temporal space through which John's idea has traveled is great. Derrida explains, "All signifiers and first and foremost written signifiers, are derivative

---

[4] Mamet scholar Roudané suggests in *Conversation* that John is teaching at a liberal arts college such as the one Mamet attended, Goddard College, so that the ironizing of the freedom versus censorship is deepened.

with regard to what would wed the voice indissoluble to the mind or to the thought of the signified sense" (Derrida, 11). Writing within the landscape of the university attempts to mediate this distance, to stabilize the signifiers and thereby the "ideality of meaning" (Derrida, 12).

John tries to speak his experience—as a boy, feeling stupid, how he overcame his failures, how he learned the game of education and now has power—in order to pass to Carol in speech his lived experience because Carol had only his book, necessarily removed from private, personal meaning. She had the written public text and John's lectures that he had translated from his writing back into thought and then into speech. All these re-presentations are increasingly distant from John's phonocentric experience/feelings where logos is directly related to phonetic expression.

Carol also has translated her thoughts into written form from her notes into an assigned essay from which John reads: "'I think that the ideas contained in this work [John's book] express the author's feelings in a way that he intended, based on his results. 'What can that mean?" he asks Carol (8). Carol's phrases "I think" and "the author's feelings" indicate that her writing shows a recognition of the processes of thought and signification to a greater degree than John understands. Deconstructing Carol's written sentence, we find that she has taken John's words to be honest— a truthful expression of his feelings—the professor is always right, especially if he has a published book and believes that his intentions are fulfilled. She states the parameters of the argument: "in this work." And she gives his evidence: "based on his results." We learn later that the book is a debunking of the powers of higher education. John has upended the hierarchies, the binary oppositions, seen through the discourses, the political correctness of the academic landscape, and he tells Carol, "that's my *job*, don't you know." "What is?" she asks. "To provoke you" (32).

John succeeds in leading Carol to doubt, distrust, and then revolt against the system of education that he shows to be so needlessly full of itself. And now with tenure approved by thought and speech, with only public, written authority lacking,

John has nearly reached his personal goal. He can move into a "*Nice* house, close to the *private school*" (33).

Because Carol cannot understand John's written book or even the notes she has made, John tries orally to explain his ideas in a personal, private fashion: "I think you are angry" (12), "I'll tell you a story about myself" (15), "I'm talking to you as I'd talk to my son" (19), "If we're going to take off the Artificial *Structure* of 'Teacher,' and 'Student,' why should *my* problems be any more a mystery than your own?" (2). He also begins to write out his ideas as he verbalizes them. Carol checks her notes from class several times (27, 28, 29, 31) and then begins writing new jottings simultaneously as John writes (33). John forgets where he is and to whom he was speaking as he makes his notes. He says to himself in soliloquy fashion: "*where is it written* that I have to send my child to public school. [...] Is it a law that I have to improve the City Schools at the expense of my own interest? And, is this not simply *The White Man's Burden?* Good. And (*Looks up to* Carol) ... does this interest you?" (34). "No," she replies, "I'm taking notes." He tells her that is not necessary, she can just listen, he's not lecturing her, "just trying to tell you some things I think" (34).

It is valid for John to write, but not for Carol to do so. He is fully couched in the university environment, but excludes her from it, maintaining his authorial position of hegemonic power while keeping her suppressed. What Carol learns in her first visit to the professor's office is that writing is the means to power in the landscape of the university. John's published book earns him tenure, a private office, a stage on which to perform his ideas. However, he denigrates her writing as muddled, unnecessary, lacking in meaning in order to keep her in his control.

By Act Two, Carol has learned to write as a means of signifying her thoughts. She has recognized the rhetorical value of audience and has sent a written complaint about John's physical, verbal, and ideological abuse to the Tenure Committee, a group John has ridiculed as "a joke," "garbage," "bad" (23). But the tenure committee has only "announced"; "they haven't *signed*," he tells Carol (23). What the audience and Carol had believed was the present status, John in a tenured position, we now discover was a physical space of a future time. Writing down what John has said and done in their previous meeting has given Carol the understanding that she could not gain by reading or even by listening. Each of the charges, read back to her by John from the Tenure Committee's report that cites Carol's letter, can be corroborated from Act One, witnessed by the audience.

As Carol learns to write in order to gain power in the university's ideological space, now recognized for its political powers, John begins to retreat from his mockery and to lose faith in his ideas about revealing the true political landscape of higher education. When John sees his speech acts in Carol's writing, he refuses to believe that his words signify his feelings, so he tries to explain his love of teaching, "the aspect of *performance*" (43), what he feels. Carol, having accepted John's intentional upending of the binary opposites inherent in Western higher education in general and between John and Carol in particular, teacher/student, father/son, male/female, published/unpublished, for example, does not simply reverse the hierarchies, but rather exposes the difference between each sign used by John and that which he sought to signify.

Mamet seeks to critique the theory of higher education by exposing where that theory originates. He uses John as a signifier for a professor who wants to deconstruct the very same thing: higher education's hegemonic power. And Carol has the equal goal of understanding the ideological position of the professor's book about higher education, so she seeks out the origin/originator of the theories, John.

John and Carol's analysis of the system, however, is doomed from the start, for they are looking for the flaws and making efforts to improve higher education. Mamet, on the other hand, does not expect to correct the metaphysical map of the academy, but, in Barbara Johnson's explanation of deconstruction, to read higher education "backwards from what seems natural, obvious, self-evident [...] in order to show that these things have their history, their reasons for being the way they are, their effects on what follows from them, and that the starting point is not a (natural) [...] but a (cultural) construct, usually blind to itself" (Johnson, xv).

That Mamet performs his deconstruction in a drama is more than felicitous. The cultural landscape of the theatrical conventions (acting, performing, staging, dialogue, audience) is metaphoric for the performative conventions of the teacher and the student. If we are not delighted by *Oleanna*, at the very least, we will not forget Mamet's attack on the landscape of the higher education. When John says that surprise is a form of aggression, he is more correct than perhaps he realizes. 'Surprise' is to attack or capture without warning and 'aggression' derives from the Latin roots meaning 'to attack, to go' (*American Heritage Dictionary*). John is prevented from taking leave, from going, by Carol's unannounced office visit, and then Carol is prevented from leaving John's office by his lecturing and physical restraint. The audience, too, is prevented from escaping *Oleanna*. Mamet does not want theatre goers to forget the "name of the play" or "what the play was about" (*Three*, 21). *Oleanna* belongs in Stanislavski's second category of plays, described by Mamet as plays "that are perhaps upsetting or intricate or unusual, that you leave unsure, but which you think about perhaps the next day, and perhaps for a week, and perhaps for the rest of your life" (*Three*, 21).

Bibliography

Barnes Trevor J. and James S. Duncan, eds. *Writing Worlds: Discourse, Text, and Metaphor in the Representation of Landscape*. London: Routledge, 1992.

Bechtel, Roger. "P.C. Power Play: Language and Representation in David Mamet's *Oleanna.*" *Theatre Studies 41 (1996)*: 29-48.

Butler, Samuel. *The Way of All Flesh*. 1872. New York: Doubleday, 1944.

Botto, Louis. "Mamet's Oleanna." *Playbill* 92.12 (December 1992): 44, 47-49.

Covington, Richard. "The Salon Interview: David Mamet." www.salonwanderlust.com/feature/1997/10 (July 12, 2000).

Derrida, Jacques. *Of Grammatology*. Trans. Gayatri Chakravorty Spivak. Baltimore: John Hopkins UP, 1976.

Elam, Keir. *The Semiotics of Theatre and Drama*. London: Meuthuen, 1980.

Geis, Deborah R. *Postmodern Theatric(k)s: Monologue in Contemporary American Drama*. Ann Arbor: U of Michigan P, 1993.

Johnson, Barbara. "Translator's Introduction," *Dissemination* by Jacques Derrida. Chicago: U of Chicago P, 1981. vii-xxiii.

Johnston, R. J., Derek Gregory and David M. Smith, eds. *The Dictionary of Human Geography*. 3rd ed. Oxford: Blackwell Publishers, 1994.

Mamet, David. *Edmond*. New York: Grove P, 1983.

---. *Glengarry Glen Ross*. New York: Grove P, 1984.

---. *Oleanna*. New York: Vintage, 1993.

---. *Three Uses of the Knife*. New York: Columbia UP, 1998.

Olson, Gary A. "Jacques Derrida on Rhetoric and Composition: A Conversation." *jac* 10.1 (1990): 1-21.

Playbill: The National Theatre Magazine: Orpheum Theatre. 92.12 (December 1992).

Roudané, Matthew C. "An Interview with David Mamet." *South Carolina Review* 19.1 (1986): 73-81. <www.mindspring.com/~jason-charmick/mamet> (July 10, 2000).

---. *Conversation*. Atlanta, Georgia, (July 17, 2000).

Seeger, Pete. *The Mudcat Cafe: A Magazine of Blues and Folk Music*. www.mudcat.org (7.12.00).

Soja, Edward W. *Postmodern Geographies: The Reassertion of Space in Critical Social Theory*. London: Verso, 1989.

Sontag, Susan. "Film and Theatre." *Film Theory and Criticism: Introductory Readings*, 4th ed. Ed. Gerald Mast, Marshall Cohen, and Leo Braudy. New York: Oxford UP, 1992.

"Once Upon a Time in the West"
The Changing Function of Landscape in the American Western Film,
1968-2000

Reingard M. Nischik

The Western, the oldest and altogether most successful genre in American film history,[1] is a form of popular culture drenched in American myths. In spite of its formulaic content and narrative style, and in spite of fashionable ups and downs in popularity, it has bridged the entire 20th century. This is in large part due to the fact that the classical Western formula encapsulates and renarrates America's founding myth: the birth of a nation from the meeting of Euro-American civilization and the wilderness on the ever-moving frontier during the movement west; the "Manifest Destiny" (John O'Sullivan, 1839) of "God's Own People" "winning a wilderness" (F.J. Turner, 1893) against the opposition of the Native Americans, in the face of a harsh land and climate, and the adverse conditions of conquering and settling a vast continent.[2] Richard Slotkin has argued that "the Western as a genre depends less on the continuity of form and more on the continuity of myth" (Smetak in Engel, 167). Yet the heroic 'master narrative' of the westward movement has been called into question since the 1960s. Cultural critics such as Annette Kolodny, Richard Slotkin himself, Langdon Elsbree, and Patricia Nelson Limerick have pointed out the one-sided spuriousness of this Turneresque conception of American (Western) history. If the American film Western has nevertheless survived such drastic reorientations and revisions in cultural criticism, it is because the format has shown itself to be flexible and variable in conception and narrative style in spite of its time-honored generic tradition. Peter Bischoff even goes as far as to claim that no other genre in its entire development has been as sensitive and reactive to changes in the cultural

---

[1] Cf. "The American Western, the signature art form of this country, for seven decades dominated the U.S. film industry, defining it and influencing other types of films, even non-American ones" (Smetak in Engel, 166).
[2] Cf. Limerick's stylized version of America's "most popular origin myth" (322f.).

climate as the supposedly formulaic Western film (415). To put it bluntly: In its choice of conception of American Western history, the Western is invariably just as much concerned with contemporary American culture and self-conception as with a fictional representation of American history. Thus, the Western has been called "the signature art form of this country" (Smetak in Engel, 166) and "an index to America" (Sonnichsen in Bischoff, 5).

After the flourishing of the Western in the first five decades of the 20th century, and after the demise of the Hollywood Studio System and the competitive rise of television in the 1950s, the genre had to reconsider (cf. Nischik, 2001). I will now investigate, after a glimpse at the classical Western, how the diversification and reorientation which has taken place within the American Western film since the 1960s has provoked changes in the function of landscape representation.

The celebration of the American Western landscape, such as the characteristic Monument Valley in John Ford's Westerns—its beauty, vastness, magnitude, infinity—forms one of the staple elements of the classical American Western film.[3] As Jacqueline Smetak has pointed out, "the stories were often small, but the myth they enacted was large, as big as the land that produced it" (Smetak in Engel, 166). With respect to John Ford's classic Western *The Searchers* (1956), set in Texas but, significantly, largely filmed in Monument Valley in Arizona, Richard Hutson has shown how Monument Valley is

> a highly theatrical exterior, as if nature had decided to call attention to itself in its spectacular theatricality. Monument Valley came to be John Ford's signature setting because it served as landscape pure and simple, the archetypal West, landscape as frame [... as] national cultural memory. (196, 204)

Indeed, the desert and canyon Southwestern landscape of Arizona and Utah, specifically Monument Valley, has come to be associated with the classical American

---

[3] 'Landscape,' a much debated term, is here taken to be "a construction—indeed, a composition, in that it selects and highlights certain visual aspects of the environment. [...] Landscape implies an active, two-way engagement between people and their surroundings." (Mills, 7). Cf. also these

Western. A large proportion of movies were filmed in this area or were taken to be located in Monument Valley (Buscombe, 118-20): "[John] Ford has come to be synonymous with the Western, the Western signifies Hollywood cinema, and Hollywood stands for America. Thus, through a kind of metonymic chain, Monument Valley has come to represent America itself" (Buscombe, 120). This highly selective approach to western landscape in the (classical) American Western shows, in itself, how the Western features a constructed, not a found landscape.

The land, as represented in the classical American Western, relies upon a specifically American iconography based on a network of values and assumptions connected with American history and mentality. Thus, Jane Tompkins has shown in general terms how the typical Western opens with a landscape shot and how such landscape shots make up 'The Language of the Western':

> In the beginning, say these shots, was the earth, and the earth was desert. [...] And the story you are about to see goes back to the beginnings of things. [...] All there is is space, pure and absolute, materialized in the desert landscape. [...] The opening shot of a Western is a land defined by absence: absence of trees, of greenery, of houses, of the signs of civilization, above all of water and shade. (qtd. in Engel, 1994, 284-85)

The message which such depictions of preferably Great Plains scenery transmit is, in Tompkins' words: "Be brave, be strong enough to endure this [...] and you will become like this—hard, austere, sublime" (286). "The harshness of the western landscape is so rhetorically persuasive that an entire code of values is in place [...] from the outset, without anyone's ever saying a word" (288). The "code of asceticism" (286) in the classical Western finds its perfect context in an austere and demanding landscape. "The hero imitates the desert's fierceness in his hard struggle to survive its loneliness in his solitary existence, and its silence in his frugal way with language" (298).

---

definitions of landscape in *Webster's*: "picture of natural inland scenery"; "a portion of land that the eye can see in one glance."

A case in point is the epic-scale *Once Upon a Time in the West*, Sergio Leone's masterpiece released in 1968 and his most 'Americanized' Western. It is a perfect starting point for our film analyses since it is situated at the crossroads between the traditional Western and the anti-idealistic Western, which Leone himself introduced with his so-called "Man With No Name Trilogy" (*A Fistful of Dollars, For a Few Dollars More*, and *The Good, the Bad and the Ugly*), released in the US in 1967. *Once Upon a Time in the West* follows in the footsteps of this earlier Italo-Western-Trilogy in that it shows the ugly side of settling the West: economic greed, murderous brutality, and obsessive self-interest are shown to be the driving forces in the so-called 'civilizing' of the West. Among the conventional aspects of this film are its temporal setting in the 'classical' time period of the Western, that is between 1865 and 1890, the epic-scale motif of the building of the railroad, and a foregrounded rendering of the landscape which nicely bears out Stephen Mills' characterization of landscape as implying "an active, two-way engagement between people and their surroundings" (6). As an example, there are several panorama shots which show a Monument Valley landscape in all its grandeur and beauty—with tiny characters riding through it and all the grand opportunities ahead of them, which such a wonderful vista in warm, red colors promises (Mrs. McBain [Claudia Cardinale] riding towards Sweetwater, not realizing yet that her newlywed husband has been brutally killed by Frank [Henry Fonda] Morton's men for ruthless economic reasons). Apart from such warm-colored, elevating landscape shots at the beginning of the film, the dominant color of this film is grey-brown, the uniform color of sand and dust. First, the dusty landscape shots show small, busy frontier towns, visibly smothered by heat and dust. Second, such desert landscape shots show the West in the process of being industrialized. The railway and the constant progress of further railroad building is one of the central symbols in this film. The symbolism, however, is ambivalent: in repeated shots in which the railway is shown to emit huge black clouds into a beautiful blue sky, or in the many railway construction shots, the railroad is seen to open up but also to destroy the beauty of the primordial western landscape. Last but not least, the desert landscape is portrayed as deadly, particularly in connection with those who people it. The famous opening sequence of this film, aptly translated into German as *Spiel mir das Lied vom Tod*, is full of foreboding—set in a scenery of murderous dry heat with a wide desert landscape punctuated by dead plant stumps, the opening scene eventually features four men, three of whom are soon dead after the film's first showdown. As Cheyenne says in the German version: "Wer hier draußen falsch kombiniert, lebt nicht lange."[4] Significantly, after being hit by a bullet, Cheyenne does not stay indoors with his beloved Mrs. McBain, but goes out into the desert shrub landscape to die by himself. The desert is the landscape of death, and again and again in this film the biblical "dust to dust" is shown in drawn-out close-ups when shot men in dusty clothes literally bite the dust. This is also the case in the final, dramatic showdown scene when the mouth-organ player ("Harmonica," [Charles Bronson]) is at long last in a position to take his revenge by shooting Frank who had cruelly made him an agent in his father's death while a child. The prelude to this slow-motion showdown blends present with past and is situated in a harsh, rocklike, funnel-like scenery from which there seems to be no way out. And there *is* no way out—at the end of the film two of the three male protagonists have been shot, and the third one, played by Charles Bronson, rides off again into the desert—"on [his] way across a dusty plain that reminds us of a fate postponed" (Tompkins, 301).

In contrast to the desert landscape, *Once Upon a Time in the West* develops an isotope about water, that life-giving necessity in a desert context. Yet, again and again in this film, water too is connected with death. As an example, Mr. McBain is shot by Frank's gang when he goes to the well to get fresh water. The mortally ill railway magnate Morton's obsessive dream is to live to see his railway line reach the Pacific: "I want to see the blue of the Pacific outside that window." Yet the desired sea is only seen in painted representation, as a *mise en abyme*, in this film, with Morton looking repeatedly, dreamily, at an ocean painting on his railway train wall. The only scenery involving natural water in this desert setting is shown when Morton is dying—scrambling strenuously to a water puddle, deliriously fantasizing

---

[4] The English version is: "Watch those false notes."

that he has, finally, reached the Pacific, which is technically evoked by a sound montage of rolling sea waves. Water, scarce in a desert setting, is thus rarely seen in this film, though it is frequently an issue. It is often used as a marker of failed illusions and of deficiency. Only in the final scene, when Jill McBain brings the water buckets to the railway constructors at Sweetwater, is water shown as a life-force and, indeed, as a sign of hope for the developing town of Sweetwater on the new railway route.

Almost thirty years later, in 1995, *The Quick and the Dead*, directed by Sam Raimi and co-produced by star actress Sharon Stone, who also plays the female leading role, represents a fascinating rewrite of earlier Sergio Leone Westerns, from *A Fistful of Dollars* to *Once Upon a Time in the West*. A comparison of the latter film and *The Quick and the Dead* reveals essential aspects of what has happened to the Western genre between the 1960s and 1990s. This change can also been seen in the function of landscape representation.

Once Upon a Time in the West, as we have seen, features a West during the first beginnings of industrialization by way of transcontinental railway construction, and depicts economically-based conflicts between white settlers—in this early anti-idealistic Western, the bad Indians have been totally replaced by bad white guys. *The Quick and the Dead* extends such earlier trends by placing the events in a more 'urban' setting at a later period of time. Whereas the earlier Leone film seems to be situated in a lawless zone, the later plot in *The Quick and the Dead* is derived from a political conflict in which brutal John Herod (superbly played by Gene Hackman) displaces the town marshal by cruelly having him killed. Whereas the earlier film works towards the famous showdown of the two antagonists in an austere, rocky desert setting, *The Quick and the Dead* has a multiple showdown as its basic structural principle. 95% of the action is set in a town called Redemption, terrorized by John Herod, mostly on Main Street or, less often, in the saloon. The ritualized showdowns, staged as an annual duel contest which can only have one winner, are claustrophobically set on Main Street, on which one of the main 'stage props' is a large clock—relentlessly advancing to the full hours at which the next pre-arranged showdown is to take place. The landscape of this film, in other words, is essentially man-made, outdoor scenes are largely reduced to a stage for deadly showdowns. The film features the American West as a location of willful brutality and financial greed, where only the fittest shooter can survive. There are several controversial scenes which link landscape and deadly human action in even more extreme images than the innovative 1960s Western *Once Upon a Time in the West*. Some of the duelists, who are repeatedly shown in a context of gun fetishism, use pump guns—leaving disastrously large wounds in their antagonists. In a decade of utter brutality in horror movies and other Hollywood productions, the Western follows suit. Splashing blood is shown in slow motion to mingle with the dust of Main Street. A pump gun shot directly through Herod's heart in the final showdown is first seen as a hole in a shadow reflection of his body on the dusty ground of Main Street. One of the most memorable takes in this film, typical of its deadly combination of man and landscape, is the camera perspective which opens up a restricted view of the duelist John Herod and the landscape beyond Main Street—restricted through the hole left by a perfectly aimed pump gun shot in the forehead of a duelist not quick enough with his gun ... Could there be a more telling condensed image of the brutal aspects of, ironically, "winning a wilderness" (F.J. Turner)?

Compared to earlier Westerns including *Once Upon a Time in the West*, *The Quick and the Dead* features strikingly few views of the open range. This in itself downplays the conventional vast desert landscape of the Western. The few panoramic views of the land which remain are primarily rendered in gloomy colors pointing towards death: on two occasions these shots are centered around a desolate burial ground in which Ellen erroneously suspects the remains of her father (in whose death Herod forced her to be an unwitting agent when a child) to be buried. The sky in these shots is gloomy, darkly clouded. In contrast to earlier Westerns, it rains frequently in this film and the tensions repeatedly erupt in thunder and lightning. The eternally sun-drenched, majestic desert landscapes of earlier Westerns have been replaced by a dark, foreboding landscape. The only elevating and magnificent landscape shot left in *The Quick and the Dead* is the beautiful, warm-colored, vast prairie sky which Ellen sees when she temporarily decides to leave the deadly town behind her. This is a visual indication of a flickering of hope in her for a cheerful future, but her next stop is the rain-drenched burial ground in which her father's former companion convinces her that she will not be able to go on 'living' without having avenged her father by killing Herod in the shooting contest. Thus Ellen returns to the town which is then shown amidst a hopeful sunrise.

The final scene of *The Quick and the Dead* revises two classical endings of earlier Leone Westerns: the sequence of induced explosions and the final showdown in *A Fistful of Dollars* as well as the memory flashbacks of the harmonica player and the dying killer Frank in *Once Upon a Time in the West*. The recreation of these earlier endings featuring a deadly landscape in which the evil killer finally receives his rightful punishment also points to the revision of the Western gender code in *The Quick and the Dead*. In the post-explosion, final showdown scene it is an attractive *female* who now emerges from the dusty, misty wreckage on Main Street as a tough heroine about to avenge her father in the final shoot-out. The flashback memory scenes in this film and in the Leone interfilm are both triggered by the two dying killers' desperate question, "Who are you?" and by their being shown by the avengers the object that triggers memories: a harmonica in *Once Upon a Time in the West*, a marshal's star in *The Quick and the Dead*. The little girl in the later film grows up just like the little boy in the earlier film to become the best pistol-wielder in the area—to be able to avenge the brutal killing of their fathers.

The trends and differences detected in the comparison of these two movies are by and large representative.[5] The 1960s, with their inauguration of the violence-foregrounding Italo-Western and its American successors, such as Sam Peckinpah's *The Wild Bunch* (1969), and with their development of the Western comedy and parody (e.g. *Cat Ballou*, 1965, and *Support Your Local Sheriff*, 1969) debunked

---

[5] Other rewarding comparisons would be between Leone's *A Fistful of Dollars* and Walter Hill's rewrite *Last Man Standing* (1996), with a tough Bruce Willis in many ways extending the footsteps of Clint Eastwood in the earlier film; or between John Ford's final, elegiac Western *The Man Who Shot Liberty Valance* (1962) and Jim Jarmusch's anti-Western *Dead Man* (1996).

hallowed traditional Western values and myths, focusing on violence and senseless killing, and on the deconstruction of the former Western male hero. As a consequence, landscape is often represented on a smaller scale than in pre-1960s traditional Westerns, often reduced to a mere setting, robbed of its former mythical proportions (e.g. *Custer of the West*, 1968, *The Undefeated*, 1969, or *True Grit*, 1969). Yet, as is suggested by Sergio Leone's *Once Upon a Time in the West*, even in the revolutionizing (late) 1960s there are also rather traditional or even epic-scale Westerns which demonstratively present Western landscape settings (e.g. *The Scalphunters*, 1968, *Butch Cassidy and the Sundance Kid*, 1969). From the 1970s onwards, with a further diversification of the Western genre, a new trend has been to situate the action not in the pioneer times of the mid to late 1800s, i.e. not in the 'Old West,' but later than that. Similarly, the setting is often not the traditional desert plain, but places like the Rocky Mountains (*Jeremiah Johnson*, 1972), a mining town in the Pacific West (*McCabe and Mrs. Miller*, 1971), a city such as Carson City (*The Shootist*, 1976), or a town like Jericho at the time of prohibition, cars and ties having replaced horses and bandannas (*Last Man Standing*, 1996). Often in such 'late' or 'Neo-Westerns' which signal that the Old West is a figment of the past, the season symbolically chosen is autumn or winter rather than the seemingly almost constant summer sunshine of the classical Western.[6] In such later films, the Western often goes indoors (see *True Grit*, *McCabe and Mrs. Miller*, *The Shootist*, or *Last Man Standing*). Thus, in *The Shootist* (1976), set in 1901, Western icon John Wayne in his last film plays an aging gun-wielder (with Lauren Bacall, the landlady, as his female counterpart), whose problem is his life-threatening prostate cancer, not any open-range shoot-outs.

After *Heaven's Gate* (1980), the biggest financial flop in film history, seemed to have temporarily killed off the Western, it was resurrected in Clint Eastwood's *Pale Rider* (1985) and then particularly in Kevin Costner's *Dances with Wolves* (1990).

---

[6] See, e.g., Fred Zinnemann's *High Noon*, 1952; an exception to this rule in the classical Western may be seen in John Ford's *The Searchers*, 1956, where in some scenes horses are forced to wade through deep snow.

These films returned to the Old West and a corresponding symbolic landscape. *Dances with Wolves* ushered in a decade of revitalized, highly diversified Western productions, thus framing a century of Western film: *Son of the Morning Star* (1991), *The Last of the Mohicans* (1992), *Unforgiven* (1992), *Geronimo* (1993), *The Ballad of Little Jo* (1993), *Tombstone* (1993), *Posse* (1993), *Wyatt Earp* (1994), *Bad Girls* (1994), *Maverick* (1994), *Wild Bill* (1995), *Dead Man* (1995), *Last Man Standing* (1996), *Lone Star* (1996), *The Horse Whisperer* (1998), and *Wild Wild West* (1999), to name several of the best-known 1990s Westerns.

Many, though not all, of the 1990s Westerns reverted to the classical time period of the Western genre, 1865-1890. In a prosperous decade for the world's now uncontested super power, several of these Westerns return to a renarration of American Western history in large proportions, with often breathtakingly beautiful landscape shots.[7] Yet even such celebrations of the Western landscape are represented during the 1990s with a sense of loss and a critique of the whites' colonizing attitudes towards Native Americans and the land. In a decade of 'political correctness,' these Westerns, often by focusing on the perspectives of Native Americans and women rather than the conventional white male-centered viewpoint, are revisionist in their own way, representing the second wave of the American revisionist Western after the first wave in the 1960's.[8] The landscape representations, constructing liminal symbolic spaces, are subtle markers of this ambivalent attitude to the Western in the 1990s.

Kevin Costner's *Dances With Wolves* (1990) is a case in point. Early in the film there is a close-up image of ecological perpetration when an abhorrent white stagecoach driver simply throws an empty tin can into the seemingly unspoiled, beautiful prairie landscape.[9] Shortly afterwards in the film, on the ride to Lieutenant Dunbar's (Kevin Costner) outpost on the frontier, there is a close-up shot of a hu-

---

[7] Cf. the term "neotraditionalism" for the 1990s Western (Johnson, 211).
[8] Cf. Kitses's and Rickman's characterization of the 1990s Western: "shoot-outs at the PC corral" (17).

man skeleton in the prairie. After Dunbar has made friends with the Sioux tribe (represented in such positive terms in this film that they, not the advancing American army, engage the viewer's sympathy), accompanying them on their search for buffaloes, there is a lengthy panorama shot of a magnificent landscape—shockingly spoilt, however, by being littered with dead, skinned, bloody buffalo bodies.

Some of the most moving landscape images in this great film are connected with the wolf with which Dunbar becomes 'friends' in the course of his stay at the outpost. There are wonderful shots of a vast prairie landscape in a beautiful sunset which, in a kind of body choreography, link Dunbar with the wolf, foreshadowing Dunbar's later practically becoming Indian and turning against the advancing US army. In what may be the most cruel scene in a film which witnesses a lot of killings, American soldiers who have captured Dunbar attempt to shoot the wolf, which hardly moves since it has become trustful and almost tame in Dunbar's presence. In a highly symbolic long shot, the senselessly killed wolf is shown lying on the prairie grass between the white soldiers and the hidden Sioux who have stealthily approached to rescue Dunbar: The pointless killing of animals precedes the displacement of the American Indian. *Dances With Wolves* ends fittingly with a final panorama shot of a howling wolf in a majestic landscape at dusk, with a low-key voice stating these elegiac words in the distance:

> Thirteen years later, their homes destroyed, their buffalo gone, the last band of free Sioux submitted to white authority at Fort Robinson, Nebraska. The great horse culture of the plains was gone and the American frontier was soon to pass into history.

One final example: Walter Hill's *Geronimo* (1993) renarrates the events of the so-called "Geronimo Campaign" in the Arizona Territory and (New) Mexico (ca. 1877-1886). The film features wonderful landscape panoramas of the Southwestern deserts, representing the Apache leader Geronimo in heroic stature in the context of

---

[9] There is a similar introductory image in Walter Hill's Last Man Standing (1996), when the protagonist, played by Bruce Willis, throws a bottle of gin, emptied in one go, out of his car into the

an appropriately epic-scale landscape. Although the Southwest is visually celebrated in such warm-colored (mainly yellow-orange) landscape panoramas, these vistas are also presented as liminal spaces. Thus the ending of the film combines verbal and visual language in a highly symbolic final statement. While there is a panorama shot of an uninhabited desert landscape, slowly but surely a railway train pushes into the picture from the right, cutting right through the panorama shot and belching out an overwhelmingly large cloud of black smoke which darkens the blue sky. At the same time, these words are spoken in the off by the first-person narrator of the film: "I am [...] faced with an undeniable truth: a way of life, that endured a thousand years, was gone. This desert, this *land* that we look out on, would never be the same." As if that were not enough, there follows an inside shot into the train, which in this scene, too, appears like a destructive monster in a primordial landscape—and it comes as a final shock that inside the train are Geronimo and his fellow Native Americans, being deported to a reservation, debating in final resignation the breach of the whites' promise to them.

These few examples must suffice to characterize more than thirty years of American Western film productions. In an overview of the representation of landscape in these Westerns, we can, by and large, detect a development from a decidedly antimythical landscape representation, beginning in an earlier, highly innovative 1960s Western, Sergio Leone's Italo-Western *A Fistful of Dollars* (English version, 1967; and still to be found e.g. in *The Quick and the Dead*); through Leone's own cross between an Italo- and an American Western in *Once Upon a Time in the West* (1968), featuring grand desert landscape shots, but marking it as a landscape of death; through Westerns in the 1970s and 1980s which generally downplayed landscape representations; and finally towards the revitalization of the American Western in the 1990s, demonstrating a remarkable range of further diversification, not only in landscape representation, and, indeed, proving the continuing vitality of the oldest American film genre.

---

desert landscape.

By the 1990s, the revisionist Western had become the norm.[10] Yet in contrast to many earlier revisionist Westerns, the 1990s Western, like the traditional Western, tends to select an epic-scale format with consequences for the landscape representation as shown above. The changing function of landscape in the American film Western from 1968 to 2000 is thus a perfect exemplification of Stephen Mills' general characterization of landscape, suggesting that it "is a construction—indeed, a composition, in that it selects and highlights certain visual aspects of the environment. [...] Landscape implies an active, two-way engagement between people and their surroundings. [...] Landscape, then, is a way of seeing the world" (Mills, 6, 7).

---

[10] Cf. Kitses: "But even as the exceptions have begun to outnumber the rule, the idea that these films now constitute the creative mainstream of the genre has not truly registered" (19).

Picture 1. "Monument Valley." Still from the movie *Stagecoach*. John Ford. © United Artists, 1939. Philip French. *Westerns: Aspects of a Movie Genre*. London: Secker and Warburg, 1973. 101-02.

Picture 2. Still from *The Wild Bunch*. Sam Peckinpah. © Warner Bros., 1969. Philip French. *Westerns: Aspects of a Movie Genre*. London: Secker and Warburg, 1973. 2.

Bibliography

Bischoff, Peter. "Der Western als amerikanischer Gründungsmythos." *Studies in the Western.* 1.1 (1992-93): 3-11.

Buscombe, Edward. "Inventing Monument Valley: Nineteenth Century Landscape Photography and the Western Film." *The Western Reader.* 2nd ed. Eds. Jim Kitses and Gregg Rickmann. New York: Limelight, 1999. 115-130.

Engel, Leonard, ed. *The Big Empty: Essays on Western Landscapes as Narrative.* Albuquerque: U of New Mexico P, 1994.

Hutson, Richard. "Sermons in Stone: Monument Valley in *The Searchers*." *The Big Empty: Essays on Western Landscapes as Narrative.* Ed. Leonard Engel. Albuquerque: U of New Mexico P, 1994. 187-205.

Johnson, Michael L. *New Westers: The West in Contemporary American Culture.* Lawrence, Kansas: UP of Kansas, 1996.

Kitses, Jim and Gregg Rickman, eds. *The Western Reader.* 2nd ed. New York: Limelight, 1999 [[1]1988].

Limerick, Patricia Nelson. *The Legacy of Conquest: The Unbroken Past of the American West.* New York: Norton, 1987.

Mills, Stephen F. *The American Landscape.* Edinburgh: Keele UP, 1997.

Nischik, Reingard M. "The American Western of the 1960s: Diversification, Specialization, New Beginnings." *Zeitschrift für Anglistik und Amerikanistik* 49.1 (2001): 59-66.

Tompkins, Jane. "Landscape: The Language of the Western." *The Big Empty: Essays on Western Landscapes as Narrative.* Ed. Leonard Engel. Albuquerque: U of New Mexico P, 1994. 283-301.

The Construction of the South in *The Song of Solomon* by Toni Morrison

Aurélie Guillain

Like most of Toni Morrison's novels, *The Song of Solomon* explores the significance of a geographical movement: the migration of African American ex-slaves and workers who moved from the Southern States to the large cities of the North from the Reconstruction period to the early 1960s. The narrative focuses on a family's long journey north which begins around 1869 when the first Macon Dead leaves the state of Virginia after having been freed. He moves north to Montour County, Pennsylvania, where he tries to farm but is killed by his white neighbors. His twelve-year-old son, Macon Dead II, kills a white man and then moves further north where, in the 1930s, he has become a slumlord in a city of the Great Lakes region. The first section of the novel is devoted to the gradual piecing together of the migration story by the son of Macon Dead II, a boy whom for some reason everyone calls 'Milkman.' In the second section, Milkman returns to Pennsylvania, and then further south to Virginia in a quest for lost gold which will turn into a quest for lost geographical and historical origins. In Shalimar, Virginia, the young man will discover, or rather reconstruct, the story of the mythical *Ur-Vater* of his family: Solomon, the flying African. Literary critics have often focused on the similarity of this novel to a pre-modern fable in which a traditional pattern of emancipation—the journey north—is reversed in order to create a new pattern of emancipation, now based on the remembering of a communal past. Yet, *The Song of Solomon*[1] does not use geographical space merely as the already oriented and codified place of some universal allegorical progress for this African American pilgrim: Morrison's narrative constantly shows how space is experienced and named within a given linguistic community, itself rooted in a specific historical period.

---

[1] In the following quoted as *SS*.

The reader is invited to share the representation of space of black people whose families have recently arrived from a rural southern background and now live in a large city in Michigan. Here, Toni Morrison is tapping her own family history, for her father, George Wofford, came north from Georgia at the age of sixteen and found work as a welder in the shipyards on the edge of Lake Erie while her mother, Hannah Willis, came from Kentucky where her family had moved after they lost their land in Greenville, Alabama at the turn of the century and were forced to become sharecroppers. Morrison is also using a feature of her own experience when she chooses to portray, not only in *The Song of Solomon* but also in many of her early novels, the gap between two generations of characters: an older generation who has had immediate knowledge of a southern environment, and a younger generation of characters who were born in a northern city and are at first confined to mediated knowledge of the South; this place is first experienced by them as a topic in conversations or other forms of discourses. In this respect, the Midwestern towns can be defined as 'remembering sites' for both the fictional characters and the novelist. At given historical periods these towns have housed communities in which southern places were still recalled and talked about: used as *topoi* (*topos* refers to a common place, but also to a given place in the delivery of an organized speech). The subjects of enunciation, either a speaker in the *diegesis* or the authorial voice, must select these *topoi* within their own private encyclopedias, and decide to pass them on (or *not* to pass them on) to this younger generation of listeners who were born in the North. Such a situation always raises a metatextual question as well as an ethical one which is strikingly posed at the end of Morrison's novel *Beloved*: What is to be passed on? What is worth being passed on from one generation to another? This meditation on the duties involved in selective tale-telling tackles the issues some poets, dramatists, and novelists of the Harlem Renaissance had already confronted in the 1920s in their attempts to define the function of a black writer writing in a northern environment and using the South as a place in discourse for inexperienced audiences or even for audiences made up of outsiders.

The Stage of Maturation: Listening to Commonplaces about the Southern Scene

Through its use of internal focalization, the narrative often fosters identification with the character of a listener: Milkman, the son of the propertied black man. He also exemplifies the ignorant young man who has never been in the South but has always heard people talking about it. He is in the position of any black person who was born in a northern city to southern parents and has always been immersed in speeches dealing with a South that is both spatially remote and made absent by the simple fact that it is an object of discourse. During his childhood, adolescence and early adulthood, Milkman absorbs various definitions of what the South is, usually through short piecemeal narratives—before he travels to the southern state of Virginia. Until then, his entire knowledge of what he calls the South had consisted of inherited fictions. In this way, the northern city acts as an echo-chamber where messages from or about the South can be heard. In one early episode, he enters a bar in Southside and finds a group of men who are commenting on a news broadcast that has just reported Emmett Till's murder (we can then infer that the scene is set in 1955) gathered around a radio set. The conversation functions as a choric lament on the death of a fellow black man who behaved as freely as a northerner in a southern territory (Till was accused of verbally abusing a white woman and was lynched by a mob). Still lamenting Till's fate, the men launch into reminiscences of their own sufferings in the South at the hands of white men: "'South's bad,' Porter said. 'Bad. Don't nothing change in the good old U.S. of A.'" (*SS*, 82).

This type of echo-chamber should be distinguished from the modernist, and perhaps from the specifically Faulknerian echo-chamber, understood as a private and abstract space, reverberating apocryphal fragments of discourses taken out of their historical context. In fact, Morrison's narrative endows the radio listeners' collective oral testimony on the southern scene with far more reliability than the written record, or rather the lack of record offered by the newspapers which are identified with the white official discourse.[2] Nevertheless, I think that the metaphor of the echo-chamber remains an enlightening one, for it suggests the great variety of potential messages describing the South to which Milkman, the typical northern black listener, is exposed. The sometimes contradictory messages include the ideological discourses of Milkman's father or those of his friend, Guitar. When the father, Macon Dead II, relates his version of the family history, the state of Virginia is used as the setting of a scene of dispossession involving the figure of the grandfather who was then robbed of his name:

> "Papa was in his teens and went to sign up, but the man behind the desk was drunk. He asked Papa where he was born. Papa said Macon. Then he asked him who his father was. Papa said, 'He's dead.' [...] Well, the Yankee wrote it down, but in the wrong spaces. Had him born in Dunfrie, wherever the hell that is, and in the space for his name the fool wrote, 'Dead' comma 'Macon.' But Papa couldn't read so he never found out what he was registered as till Mama told him." (*SS,* 53)

Even when Macon Dead I (now having the name of a southern city for a first name) moves to the northern state of Pennsylvania, the scene of violent dispossession and downfall seems to repeat itself: he is shot and falls off the fence of his farm. By going further north, Macon Dead II, his son, chooses to eternally remain at the outskirts of the South, which to him is no longer a territory that one day might be explored: It has been turned into the mythical setting of the archetypal loss of identity and dignity, the setting where the first Macon Dead was mis-named and miscreated. The second Macon's life will henceforth be devoted to the creation of a counter-myth: the story of a self-engendered man, living where only scenes of acquisition are to be played. Macon's private system is based on the absolute dichotomy between a southern territory which he cannot possess, and a northern one which he appropriates and uses to display his power. The neighborhood in which

---

[2] This inverts the conventional hierarchy between the oral version and the written version of a given event. Here, the most authoritative version is the spoken one, for all tales, even the ghost story and the tall tale can be authoritative in that they are versions of a first-hand experience: they bear witness.

Macon owns and rents shacks to other black people is a theatrical space in which he is said to "strut" rather than to walk (and to fondle the keys representing his power over the thresholds of the houses he rents out). While the southern stage is reserved for dispossession, the northern one is meant for ownership. To borrow Emile Durkheim's terms, this representation of space could be called a religious one since it is based on "heterogeneity," on the establishment of an absolute dualism between two types of spaces. Moreover, any scene performed on the northern stage has a symbolic value and is meant to exorcise the original southern scene of dispossession.

A similar use of the *topos* of the South can be observed in the didactic preachings of Milkman's friend, Guitar, when the latter became a terrorist. Whenever he describes action taking place in a southern state, the scene follows a gothic pattern; if a potential white ally in the fight for civil rights is mentioned to him, he will insist that a southern place has the power to make any white man reenact the typical southern gothic scene, in which his white unnaturalness is bound to re-surface: "if Kennedy got drunk and bored and was sitting around a potbellied stove in Mississippi, he might join a lynching party just for the hell of it" (*SS,* 156); the eloquent Guitar inflicts the same treatment on Roosevelt's character: "You could've taken him and his wheelchair and put him in a small dusty town in Alabama and given him some tobacco, a checkerboard, some whiskey, and a rope and he'd have done it too" (*SS,* 157). The scene that the white man is bound to repeat (the lynching) is not even a naturalistic episode, showing an individual acting under the pressure of his surroundings like an animal creature responding to the constraints of its environment and to its own atavistic impulses. It shows the actions of a creature not even belonging to the animal kingdom, but to the unnatural realms of the gothic. The white character is the tormentor, forever performing his part in the gothic scene. Now, Guitar belongs to a secret society supposedly founded in the 1920s "when that private from Georgia was killed after his balls were cut off and after that veteran was blinded when he came home from France in World War I" (*SS,* 155). Whenever a black person is killed, the Society of the Seven Days picks a white person at random and kills him or her: This usually implies that Guitar must kill a white in the North when a black is murdered in the South; thus, though living in the North, Guitar can imagine that he belongs to the South simply because a symmetry has been created between the southern and the northern scene. "My whole life's about geography" (*SS*, 115), he says. Indeed, through his magical thinking mode, a magic balance is struck between the southern space and the northern one.

It seems that both Milkman's father and his friend imagine the southern states as stages on which particular dramatic action is continually being performed, where a black body is continually being victimized. To them, whenever a form of 'Black power' is displayed in the North, the violent show is meant to exorcise the scenes where blacks are being oppressed or dispossessed on the southern stage. Milkman can sense how similar the two men's worldviews are; both are characterized by their absolute respect for the repetitive cleansing ritual their lives have become: "The least little thing is a matter of life and death to you. You're getting to be just like my old man. He thinks if a paper clip is in the wrong drawer, I should apologize" (*SS*, 106). These ideological representations of space which are based on an idealistic belief in the power of images, are not criticized from a materialistic or even a historical point of view; Morrison's narrative does not question the magical thinking mode *per se*. The two men's particular magics are criticized for the solipsism they stand for, and from an ethical viewpoint. Guitar describes his own behavior as the best way to stage a lovescene, saying "My whole life is love" (*SS*, 159), whereas in actual fact, the love scene he repeatedly acts out is nothing but the solitary staging of self-love.

In the poor black neighborhood of Southside, where Milkman likes to hang out, he can listen to many other messages about the South: non-didactic fictions and yet fictions that act as subtler forms of education and nurture the ignorant, childish character. Quite often, when the signifier 'South' occurs in speeches heard in Southside, it connotes the experience of staying too long in a place where only women are to be found, of lingering in the company of women or in contact with a woman's body. It does not, then, connote regression so much as a state of overly-delayed weaning. For instance, when Milkman is four, he discovers that still being suckled at that age is unusual when Freddie, the janitor, surprises Milkman's mother suckling her already grown-up child. To the mother's shame, Freddie interrupts the scene and comments on its archaic character; according to him, such a practice has become unusual not only in the North, but also in southern rural areas. Literally and symbolically, Freddie the janitor acts as a messenger and an initiator, revealing to Milkman that this yet unnamed experience is an archaic and southern 'thing': from now on, the word 'South' will connote the experience of being backward and lingering in the vicinity of a mothering body: a slight but meaningful deviation from the right and quicker path to manhood. Later, and then in the black neighborhood of Southside, Milkman will hear another story told by his aunt, Pilate Dead.

> "I remember doing laundry for a man and his wife once, down in Virginia. The husband came into the kitchen one afternoon shivering [...] I asked him what was it that had grabbed hold of him, he looked so bad. He said he couldn't figure it out, but he felt like he was about to fall off a cliff. [...] I opened my mouth to tell him wasn't no cliff in that kitchen. Then I remembered how it was being in those woods. I felt it all over again. I told the man did he want me to hold on to him so he couldn't fall. He looked at me with the most grateful look in the world? "Would you?" he said. I walked around back of him and locked my fingers in front of his chest and held on to him. His heart was kicking under his vest like a mule in heat. But little by little it calmed down." (*SS*, 41)

An indirect consequence of this tale is that Virginia appears as the type of a setting where a grown-up man can be safely nursed and mothered by a woman like Pilate, this story reinforces an already-existing link between the signifier 'South' and the connotation of positive backwardness that I have just pointed to.

The first section of Morrison's narrative renders the great heterogeneity of messages defining the South, a heterogeneity reflecting in turn the diversity of the messengers' ideological stands and social status. Moreover, it shows how the ignorant northern character will borrow various elements from these sometimes contradictory messages in what the novel describes as a pragmatic process, in opposition to the building of some coherent system, when identifying with his father, a propertied black man, Milkman will adopt the dichotomy the slumlord has established between the northern scene of power and the southern scene of dispossession whereas when Milkman is staying at his aunt Pilate's in the black neighborhood of Southside, his representation of the southern space is likely to be borrowed from the southern nursing scene.

In the second section of the novel, when Milkman actually goes to Virginia, the discovery of the actual place will occur in another pragmatic process, which has more to do with the learning of a new linguistic code than with any other cognitive process.

The Stage of Exploration: Learning New Commonplaces, New Ways of Referring to the Southern Space

By going south the central character upsets the bases of his former personality, most notably because he realizes how relative to his former environment the codes were that he had used to that point in his deciphering of space. The southern territories (in this case, the Virginian backwoods) act as a form of wilderness: a hostile area in which a particular means of orientation, namely the character's trust in his own native language, is threatened and put to the test.

In Shalimar, Virginia, Milkman's attention is drawn to the signs used in reference to places: "he'd had to pay close attention to signs and landmarks, because Shalimar was not on the Texaco map he had, and the AAA office couldn't give a nonmember a charted course—just the map and some general information" (*SS,* 260). He is entering "an area the signs kept telling him was the Blue Ridge mountain" (*SS,* 260). He then realizes that one understands space thanks to 'signs' ('road signs' of course but also, and more broadly, 'signifiers') which are not always available. For instance, he notices buildings for which he has no particular name at all: "near a building that looked like a church or clubhouse of some sort" (*SS,* 263). The hamlet where he has stopped is a "no-name hamlet" (*SS,* 250). Later, he learns that the man called "King Walker [...] was nothing like his name suggested", and that King Walker's "gas station" (*SS,* 271) is still called a gas station but is now used for a club house by the hunters. Not only the names used for locations, but also the words or phrases locally used to refer to a distance, seem to be linked to unusual referents, and the urban visitor learning this new language about space has to adjust to these linguistic customs: "The farm, they said, was right in back of the Butler place, but knowing how different their concept of distance was, he thought he'd better get moving" (*SS,* 238). Morrison's narrative quite accurately describes the almost physical uneasiness seizing the user of certain codes (either in speech or in body language) when he enters a territory where a different linguistic community with a different relation to implicit meanings and connotations lives: a threatening linguistic area, all the more dangerous as it is deceptively familiar, for the spoken language is still American English. Here, Milkman's position may remind the reader of Emmett Till's ten years earlier; the latter had used the wrong code of behavior in the wrong context and, quite similarly, Milkman is unaware that he has offended the men in Shalimar simply through the implications and unconscious connotations of his words: "He was *telling* them they weren't men" (*SS,* 266, my italics). Even though Milkman is faced with an ultimately comic experience in a *black* southern environment, and Emmett Till was faced with a tragic experience endured on a *white* southern territory, both travelers to the South enter threateningly *codified* spaces, the codes of which partly evade them.

    Having offended the men of Shalimar (unwittingly giving away that he is a wealthy black young man from a northern city) Milkman is challenged by them and invited to a hunting party in the forest. The forest is a more literal illustration of the wilderness than the Virginian village for Milkman is now at a loss to orient himself in the physical sense. The skills required to move about have to be learnt over again, notably because the visual apprehension of space either needs to be completed or is contradicted by the tactile and auditory ones. When the narrative describes the young man stumbling against roots and feeling his way through the dark forest it points to the dialectic between the mistakes the character makes and his newborn capacity to orient himself afterward; like an infant, he learns to project the shape of his own body and, concurrently, to adjust to the encountered shapes as he is moving about:

> If he was to grow accustomed to the dark, he would have to look at what it was possible to see. A long moan sailed up through the trees somewhere to the left of where they were. It sounded like a woman's voice, sobbing, and mingling with the dog's yelps and the men's shouts. A few minutes later, the distant screaming of the dogs and the calls of the three men stopped. There was only the soughing wind and his and Calvin's footsteps? It took Milkman a while to figure out how to pick up his feet and miss the roots and stones; to distinguish a tree from a shadow; to keep his head down and away from the branches that swept back from Calvin's hand into his face. They were walking upland. (*SS,* 273)

Milkman's trial mostly consists in his sudden inability to read and decipher space. The overpowering environment of the forest is a wilderness inasmuch as the forest is filled with sounds which are not yet signals. Yet, in the hunting party episode, the emphasis is put on Milkman's capacity to learn a new mother tongue and to join the local linguistic community. Not only does the character recognize the presence of a local language that can be learnt, he realizes that the command of this code will condition any improvement in his command of space itself:

> The dogs, the men—none was just hollering, just signaling location or pace. The men and the dogs were talking to each other. In distinctive voices they were saying distinctive, complicated things [...] All those shrieks, those rapid tumbling barks, the long sustained yells, the tuba sounds, the drumbeat sounds, the low liquid *howm howm,* the reedy whistles, the thin *eeee*'s of a cornet, the *unh unh unh* bass cords. It was all language. An extension of the click people made in their cheeks back home when they wanted a dog to follow them. No, it was not language; it was what there was before language. Before things were written down. (*SS,* 278)

Eventually, the southern scene, as reconstructed in the light of experience, proves to be closer to the nursing scene which Pilate's tale had foreshadowed than to the scenes of dispossession (or gothic scenes) presented by Milkman's father or by his friend Guitar:

> Down either side of his thighs he felt the sweet gum's surface roots cradling him like the rough but maternal hands of a grandfather. Feeling both tense and relaxed, he sank his fingers into the grass. He tried to listen with his fingertips, to hear what, if anything, the earth had to say, and it told him quickly that someone was standing behind him and he had just enough time to raise one hand to his neck and catch the wire that fastened around his throat. (*SS*, 279)

Even though this tender scene (where a grown up man is being mothered by an old tree) abruptly turns into an attempted murder scene, it fulfils the promise encapsulated in Pilate's tale about Virginia. The Virginian setting is indeed a place where you can safely fall to the ground and die, because you will do so in the arms of some tall maternal body. The maternal presence symbolized by the tree may very well be the sheltering proximity of a new community of speakers: Once all familiar landmarks are lost, balance can still be regained within another system of signs. Yet, this does not necessarily imply that in *The Song of Solomon* the South stands for a sacred place in which some archetypal order may be revealed to a lonely individual, a character reminiscent of the child-poet of the Romantic tradition, whose solitary perception of space has been analyzed and praised by Emerson as well as by another idealist philosopher, the French phenomenologist Gaston Bachelard. Bachelard pointed to archetypes and archetypal relations to space that could be experienced when an isolated individual returns to his former condition as child and day-dreamer. I do not think that Toni Morrison does adopt the latter's particular brand of romantic idealism. In *The Song of Solomon*, the narrative shows how space may be apprehended, within specific communities, at a given historical period (in this case between the 1930s and the 1960s). It is a community, the repository of a given state of language, evolved in a given environment that has the power to teach a particular command of space through its cosmo-logy, that is to say through the teaching of its own linguistic tools. It seems that nature itself has no a-temporal message to deliver to the disoriented subject (in short, no archetypal relation to space is to be revealed). In the novel, the only experience of space that may be called universal is probably the experience of disorientation itself (the moment when one's ability to read signs into one's environment is incapacitated). It is only when the narrative points to a departure from a child's former place and his former landmarks that the experience of space is described in the vocabulary of the European fairy tale:

> When Hansel and Gretel stood in the forest and saw the house in the clearing before them, the little hairs at the nape of their necks must have shivered [...] No one was there to warn or hold them; their parents, chastened and grieving, were far away. So they ran as fast as they could to the house where a woman older than death lived. (*SS,* 219)

The experience of being thrown off center and off balance, and eventually trusting (with no particular reason) the direction which our imagination—or our dream—has pointed out to us, is the limit to which Morrison is willing to stretch the universality of her tale.

> He had had dreams as a child, dreams every child had, of the witch who chased him down dark alleys [...] So when he saw the woman at the top of the stairs there was no way for him to resist climbing up toward her outstretched hands, her fingers spread wide for him, her mouth gaping open for him, her eyes devouring him. In a dream you climb the stairs. (*SS,* 239)

In other works, Morrison (notably in her interviews and essays) has consistently downplayed the resemblance between the founding myth of the flying African to the myth of Icarus and, more generally, has minimized the universality of any revelation reached by the central character. In the final analysis presented here, her novel shows how comprehending a place amounts to integrating a new community where the vocabulary and the grammar of a specific cosmology is being used. What makes this 'mapping' of space accessible to any reader is mostly the fact that the protagonist of the quest himself has to learn how to read this new map of the South.

One episode recurs in almost every character's account of the family past, namely, the encounter of Milkman's grandparents on a wagon heading north. In the father's interpretation of the family story, the emphasis lay on the fact that the ancestors were heading north, serving an ideological interpretation of his own progress toward the North and toward the acquisition of property. In the light of the new cosmology he is learning, Milkman will develop his own interpretation of the family story by shifting the emphasis to the act of departing itself. What matters is the analogy between any scene of departure and the mythical scene of Solomon's take-off for Africa. In this light the grandparents are essentially migrants, who met in a moving space: a "wagon going North. Ate pecans all the way, she told me. It was a wagonful of ex-slaves going to the promised land" (*SS,* 243). The home place of the family (this village called Shalimar) was named after this man, Solomon, the flying African. Milkman can now read a tale of southern emancipation where his father had read a tale of southern dispossession, even the scene of the fall of the father from the fence is given a sequel and is reinterpreted as a tale of liberation and endless floating through space: "the grave was too shallow and the body floated up to the surface" (*SS,* 245), "was dumped in Hunters' cave" (*SS,* 244) and then carried to the North in Pilate's bag and hung from Pilate's ceiling. Within Milkman's new-learnt cosmo-logy, the elevated point called Solomon's Leap is the very type foreshadowing any other idyllic place. When he eventually leaps through the air from Solomon's leap toward Guitar, who now intends to kill him, the novel ends with this sentence: "Now he knew what Shalimar knew: if you surrendered to the air, you could *ride* it" (*SS,* 337). Now, Shalimar is the name of the village, not the name of the ancestor, therefore the character is not identifying with the mythical figure, but with a community of people who have evolved a certain cosmo-logy, a certain code in their relation to space and motion through space. In the novel, the patterns organizing one's view of space are never referred to as archetypes which might be inherited from a 'universal unconscious' by the human species; in fact, to inherit these patterns, one merely must become acquainted with a particular linguistic environment.

Bibliography

Morrison, Toni. *The Song of Solomon*. New York: Plume Editions, 1987.
---. *Beloved.* New York: Plume Edition, 1998.

Space in Poetry and Art

'Going Around in Circles': Wallace Stevens, Amy Clampitt, and Rita Dove

Frank J. Kearful

As numinous images, the circle and its three-dimensional realization as sphere have enjoyed a long life in eastern and western civilizations. In the Christian Middle Ages their ultimate expression was the paradoxical definition of God as a circle or a sphere whose center is everywhere and whose circumference is nowhere. In poetry, from Dante's *Divine Comedy* to Donne's "Valediction: Forbidding Mourning" the circle was the most potent archetype of perfection, circular motion was a recurrent image of divine harmony, and the sphere, rotating, was conceived of as the most perfect three-dimensional shape, combining change and changelessness. The cosmos itself was a perfect sphere, encompassing within itself concentric transparent spheres, each revolving at its own speed about the earth at the center. This cosmic circular motion, generating the music of the spheres as each sphere sounded its own note, was also figured, in English poetry most elaborately in Sir John Davies's "Orchestra, or a Poem of Dauncing" (1596), as a cosmic dance involving all creation. But by the mid-twentieth century Theodore Roethke, in "Four for Sir John Davies," was forced to ask, "Is that dance slowing in the mind of man / That made him think the universe could hum?" (116, 1-2).[1]

---

[1] The cosmic dance, which began with Plato's reference in the *Timaeus* to the choric dances of the stars, continues unabated in Milton's *Paradise Lost* (III. 579-81; V. 178 and 618-27; VII. 374; VIII. 125; and IX. 103). On the ubiquitousness of the circle in human civilization, see Lurker *Der Kreis als Symbol*. Although primarily concerned with later French literature, Poulet in *Les metamorphoses du cercle* writes informatively on earlier periods in western thought and literature. On the impact of the new science on seventeenth-century English poetry, and the circle as archetype, see Nicolson, *The Breaking of the Circle*: "The Circle of Perfection, from which man for so long deduced his ethics, his aesthetics, and his metaphysics, was broken during the seventeenth century. Correspondence between macrocosm, geocosm, and microcosm, long accepted as basic to faith, was no longer valid in a new mechanical world and mechanical universe, nor is it valid in the modern world" (7). Nonetheless, "old habits die hard, and [...] time-honored ways of thinking about the world and man did not change in a moment" (126).

Since the seventeenth century we have been confronted with other world models and other spatial concepts, and in early twentieth-century poetry and poetics the circle and the sphere were often demoted in favor of related but less serene metaphors, such as Pound's vortex or Yeats's tumultuous "widening" gyre within which "the centre cannot hold."[2] Pound's *Cantos*, one critic has suggested, can themselves "be viewed as a spiral, whirling with events, which are reiterated at new levels, juxtaposed to new elements and made new" (Brooke-Rose, 177). Less turbulently, space in modernist poetry can also function as a perceptual field in which objects are juxtaposed in poetic parataxis, as in Pound's "In a Station at the Metro" or Williams's "The Red Wheelbarrow." When flattened to a collage surface, textual space subserved an aesthetic scheme of metonymic linkages and became a drawing board for serial composition.

If the macrocosm no longer goes around in circles, and if since the discovery of DNA the microcosm is to be figured as a double helix, can the circle continue to invest space, place, and a surrounding environment with at least traces of the symbolic significance of Dante's and Davies's poetic universe? Can poetry continue to impart to an aesthetically contrived fictive space resonant circular grace? By way of answer, I will call upon selected "round" poems of Wallace Stevens, then look more closely at two poems of the postmodern era which evoke something of the mythic power of an older concentric universe, Amy Clampitt's "Man Feeding Pigeons" and Rita Dove's "The Oriental Ballerina."

Although other modernist poets sometimes strove to set a world in circular motion, Wallace Stevens (1887-1955) is the pre-eminent modernist singer of circles,

---

[2] I quote from the opening lines of Yeats's most memorable evocation of the gyre, "The Second Coming" from 1921 in *William Butler Yeats. The Poems*: "Turning and turning in the widening gyre / The falcon cannot hear the falconer; / Things fall apart; the centre cannot hold; / Mere anarchy is loosed upon the world" (235). On "the typically modernist images of the vortex and the abyss," see Eagleton (367-368). On the fate of the circle in Derridean deconstruction, see, for example, Derrida's excursus on "Structure, Sign and Play in the Discourse of the Human Sciences" (1978), in which he lets fall: "But all these destructive discourses and their analogues are trapped in a kind of circle. The circle is unique. It describes the form of the relation between the history of metaphysics and the destruction of the history of metaphysics" (91).

of roundness, of sound-ness, of round open vowels.[3] If Davies's Elizabethan cosmic dance had ceased, Stevens sounded ways to begin a round anew, as in the ringing neo-pagan prophecy uttered in "Sunday Morning":

> Supple and turbulent, a ring of men
> Shall chant in orgy on a summer morn
> Their boisterous devotion to the sun. (vii, 1-3)[4]

A devotee of the ancient and noble art of punning, Stevens sounds a pun on "ring" while revivifying the traditional Christian sacred pun on "sun/Son."[5] In that "round" poem "Le Monocle de Mon Oncle," he conflates within a "round" a humorous pun ('to read a round'—'to read around'), a Fortunate Fall, Newtonian physics, musical composition, and Shakespeare's Hamlet examining Yorick's skull:[6]

> An apple serves as well as any skull
> To be the book in which to read a round,
> And is as excellent, in that it is composed
> Of what, like skulls, comes rotting back to ground. (iv, 5-8)

---

[3] A case might be made for Gertrude Stein as the modernist, after Stevens, most wedded to the circle. See, for example, her children's story *The World is Round* and *A Circular Play*. Commenting on the latter, Dydo observes that "it is only one of many Stein pieces built on circles, rounds, cycles. The texts of circles appear in innumerable guises, each time a new charm, a new ring, an oval, an eye, an orifice, a mouth. The linear printed shape of 'Rose is a rose is a rose is a rose' in 'Sacred Emily' curls into the magic circle of her seal, which turns into a cauliflower, centered and sacred, a new form of the essence of a rose. Like the Möbius strip, the world of Stein's work has no beginning, middle, or end, and her perceptions back in upon themselves in a continuous process that makes inside and outside indistinguishable, one, complete only in its continuing. A Stein reader is wise to remember that like stones dropped into a quiet pool, her word ideas make circles upon new and unexpected circles in her work" (Dydo, 326). Images of circles that have no end or beginning recur also in Eliot's *Four Quartets*. Joyce, as usual, might be said, however, to have the last and first word, in *Finnegans Wake*. In the text itself ("a commodius vicus of recirculation") Joyce pays tribute to the eighteenth-century philosopher Giambattista Vico, an inspiration for the circular structure of the *Wake*: "The Vico Road goes round and round to meet where terms begin. Still onappealed to by the cycles and unappalled by the recoursers we feel all serene, never you fret as regards our dutyful cask" (452); my first quotation is from midway in Joyce's initial *Wake* sentence. Beginning in *Dubliners*, circular motion is central to Joyce's works.

[4] "Sunday Morning" was included in Stevens's first book, *Harmonium* (1923). Stevens' quotations in my text are from the *Collected Poetry and Prose*.

[5] On Stevens's word-play, see Cook, *Word-Play*. On the central importance of sun/son puns in Stevens's poetry albeit in non-Christian senses, see Irmscher, *Masken der Moderne* (116-145).

[6] See McCaffrey, "The Ways of Truth" (211). McCaffrey does not stoop, however, to pick up the a round / around pun. "Le Monocle de Mon Oncle" is also from *Harmonium*.

The "round" / "ground" rhyme recurs in the complex image initiating the last stanza, a heavenly circular image of life and death, continuity and change, figured in the flight of pigeons:

> A blue pigeon it is, that circles the blue sky,
> On sidelong wing, around and round and round,
> A white pigeon it is, that flutters to the ground,
> Grown tired of flight.(xii, 1-4)

But Stevens in another mood was also an inveterate teller of tall tales, told tongue in cheek as frontier parables. Labeled anecdotes, the best-known of these poetic whoppers is his "Anecdote of the Jar," in which one hears again the "around," "round," "round," "ground" of "Le Monocle de mon Oncle."[7]

> *Anecdote of the Jar*
>
> I placed a jar in Tennessee,
> And round it was, upon a hill.
> It made the slovenly wilderness
> Surround that hill.
>
> The wilderness rose up to it,
> And sprawled around, no longer wild.
> The jar was round upon the ground
> And tall and of a port in air.
> It took dominion everywhere.
>
> The jar was gray and bare.
> It did not give of bird or bush,
> Like nothing else in Tennessee.

In "Anecdote of the Jar," resonating within Stevens's *Harmonium*, space rhetorically becomes voice, as circular motion reverberates, "round," "surround," "around," "round" and, finally, swept in rounds, "ground." Its mere presence causing a universe to surround it, Stevens's jar resounds with its own music of the spheres, "air," "everywhere," "bare" ringing out, while the trisyllabic sound-event

---

[7] On the anecdote as one of Stevens's favorite genres, see Morris, *Wallace Stevens* (23). Stevens begins describing circles in his first anecdote, "Earthy Anecdote," the opening poem of *Harmonium*, set in motion by a "swift, circular line / To the right" and a "swift, circular line / To the left."

"Tennessee," ending both the initial and final line, lingers in our hearing, and makes of the poem a kind of round.[8]

Echoing throughout his poetry, "round" repeated often enough merges into its own "sound," as in Stevens's lighthearted "The Pleasures of Merely Circulating" in Ideas of Order (1936):

> *The Pleasures of Merely Circulating*
>
> The garden flew round with the angel,
> The angel flew round with the clouds,
> And the clouds flew round and the clouds flew round
> And the clouds flew round with the clouds.
>
> Is there any secret in skulls,
> The cattle skulls in the woods?
> Do the drummers in black hoods
> Rumble anything out of their drums?
>
> Mrs. Anderson's Swedish baby
> Might well have been German or Spanish,
> Yet that things go around and again go round
> Has a rather classical sound.[9]

Beginning with a *gradatio* which merrily ascends from garden to angel to clouds, and then becomes enchanted with its own merely circulating sound, "The Pleasures of Merely Circulating" celebrates the untrammelled pleasures of round soundness. The second stanza, posing two rhetorical questions to which the implied answers are "no" and "no," abandons an incipient *gradatio* in the woods (secret-skulls, skulls-woods, woods-?). Stevens mockingly dismisses the drum beats of black-hooded poets—their only skulls are, it turns out, cattle skulls—who would portentously invoke dark, ominous symbolism in lieu of merely composing amiably cir-

---

[8] For a different approach to how "Anecdote of the Jar" is, and is not, "rounded off" by "Tennessee," see Gray, *American Poetry* (93-94). Readers of *Paradise Lost* may recall, when reading Stevens's "Anecdote of the Jar," Milton's description of Paradise placed upon a hill, surrounded by wilderness, and by a "circling row / of goodliest trees" (IV. 132-47). For perspectives on circularity and "going round" in Stevens's poetry quite different from mine, see Springer, "Repetition."

[9] Compare William Carlos Williams, "The Dance" in *Selected Poems*: "In Breughel's great picture, The Kermess, / the dancers go round, they go round and / around, the squeal and the blare and the / tweedle of bagpipes, a bugle and fiddles / tipping their bellies (round as the thick- / sided glasses whose wash they impound) / their hips and their bellies off balance / to turn them

culating verse. The pleasures of the latter kind of verse may be experienced, the last stanza suggests, even when one is listening to a poem recited in another language.[10]

In another "pleasure" poem, "It Must Give Pleasure," section ix of "Notes Toward a Supreme Fiction" in *Transport to Summer* (1947), Stevens extols less boisterously in post-Dantean tercets his aesthetic of a "final good," no longer the medieval *sphaera cujus centrum ubique, circumferentia nullibi* but "the merely going round":

> A thing in itself and, therefore, good:
> One of the vast repetitions final in
> Themselves and, therefore, good, the going round
>
> And round and round, the merely going round,
> Until merely going round is a final good,
> The way wine comes at a table in a wood. (ix, 10-15)

"Merely"—as in "merely going round" and in "merely circulating"—is along with "mere" another key word in Stevens's poetry, including the last of his late poems, "Of Mere Being" (1955). Deriving ultimately from the Latin *merus* (undiluted, unmixed, pure), "mere" has in modern usage largely shed its more positive 'unmixed' connotations. Stevens liked to stow away the 'nobler' now rarer meaning within the more customary limiting, derogatory sense of mere as "only," or "purely and simply," and hence as no better or no more than.[11]

But what of the survival of the circle, in Stevens's verse ceaselessly making its heavenly and earthly rounds gravely and gaily, in later twentieth-century poetry?

(ll. 1-8). For other pleasures afforded by merely circulating, see Clampitt's "Let the Air Circulate," in *What the Light Was Like* (101).

[10] The stanza can be read as turning on the sort of multilingual pun of which Stevens, no less than Joyce, was fond: Anderson (Swedish) = ander (German) son (Spanish) = another sound = other languages.

[11] The *OED* gives as its first usage category of "mere" (derived from Latin *merus*) "Of wine: Not mixed with water." For the second, "Of a people or their language: Pure, unmixed. Chiefly in *mere Irish* [...] now often misunderstood as a term of disparagement." For its third category, "Of other things material and immaterial: Pure, unmixed" it gives as its first example, from 1535, Henry VIII's pronouncement, "The true, mere, and sincere word of God." See also in the O.E.D. "mere" as an adjective deriving from Old English, in use throughout the Middle English period, meaning "Renowned, famous, illustrious; beautiful, noble. (Said of persons and things.)." In tune with the times, Yeats's "mere anarchy" having wreaked its havoc on civilization, the sixth edition of the *Concise Oxford Dictionary* (1976) gives as examples merely "a mere swindler" and "the merest buffoonery."

What survives of the "roundness that pulls tight the final ring" in Stevens's "central poem"?[12] Paul Hoover, in his capacity as editor of the Norton *Postmodern American Poetry* anthology, informs us that "postmodern poetry opposes the centrist values of unity, significance, linearity, expressiveness, and a heightened, even heroic, portrayal of the bourgeois self and its concerns" (xxvii). But given the proliferation of postmodernism paradigms, it is notoriously difficult to formulate what postmodernism does espouse, unless one falls back on such bromides as Hoover's "postmodernism decenters authority and embraces pluralism" (xxvii). That postmodern poetry is said to oppose "centrist" values, while "decenter" has become an indispensable verb in correct critical discourse, is suggestive, however, of a devaluation of the circle as a foundational archetype. For American poets it nevertheless remains a potent image, as may be seen, to cite a few striking instances, in Robert Lowell's "Reading Myself" (1970), A. R. Ammons's *Sphere* (1974), Shirley Kaufman's "The Dream of Completion" (1984), James Merrill's "Dead Center" (1988), Joy Harjo's "Eagle Poem" (1990), and J. D. McClatchy's "Dervish" (1999). As for Stevens's postmodern scion, John Ashbery, one might begin by placing his "Self-Portrait in a Convex Mirror" (1975) alongside Stevens's "The Planet On the Table" (1954).

With *The Kingfisher* (1983), perhaps the most highly praised first volume of the decade, Amy Clampitt (1920-1994), whose poems not infrequently go around in circles, began her elaborate poetical rounds when she was over the age of sixty. Four substantial collections were to follow before her death in 1994, making her, in the eyes of many fellow poets and critics, one of the most accomplished American poets to have emerged during the last two decades of the century. Circles and circular motion, turnings and returnings, rounds and roundaboutness, recur in her often stylistically convoluted poetry. Circular motion commences at the outset of *The Kingfisher* in the initial lines of its opening poem, "The Cove," when "Inside the snug house, the blue willow-ware / plates go round the dado" (3, ll. 1-2), while

---

[12] Cf. Stevens, "A Primitive Like an Orb," section vi, in *The Auroras of Autumn*.

phonograph records also go round as "we [...] listen / to Mozart" (ll. 5-6).[13] The cove, an encompassing image of roundness within which round things go round, is presided over, the last lines reveal, by the pulsing of "a lighthouse, light- / pieced like a needle's eye."

But Clampitt is also, like Stevens, a poetical pigeon fancier, and "Man Feeding Pigeons," from her 1987 collection *Archaic Figure*, may be read as an aesthete's anecdote, art being the ultimate tall tale. The poem's putative spatial world is not, however, the American wilderness, and Clampitt is no frontier magus. "Man Feeding Pigeons" is an urban epiphany, in which the transcendent is perceived as intervening in the ephemeral, and art is celebrated as a mode of envisioning ultimate roundness.

Man Feeding Pigeons

It was the form of the thing, the unmanaged
symmetry of it, of whatever it was
he convoked as he knelt on the sidewalk
and laid out from his unfastened briefcase
a benefaction of breadcrumbs—this band

arriving of the unhoused and opportune
we have always with us, composing
as they fed, heads together, wing tip
and tail edge serrated like chicory
(that heavenly weed, that cerulean

commoner of waste places), but with a
glimmer in it, as though the winged
beings of all the mosaics of Ravenna
had gotten the message somehow and come
flying in order to rejoin the living: plump-

contoured as the pomegranates and pears
in a Della Robbia holiday wreath that had
put on the bloom, once again, of the soon
to perish, to begin to decay, to re-enter
that dance of freewheeling dervishes,

---

[13] In "Fog," the following poem in *The Kingfisher*, "Opacity / opens up rooms, a showcase / for the hueless moonflower / corolla, as Georgia / O'Keefe might have seen it, / Of foghorns" (5, ll. 21-26). Similarly convoluted circlings transpire in succeeding poems. Particularly as one of the things "we" do in the snug house, along with listening to Mozart, is read Marianne Moore, "The Cove" might be read alongside Moore's "The Steeple-Jack," the initial poem in Moore's initial *Selected Poems* (1935).

> the breakdown of order: it was the form
> of the thing, if a thing is what it was,
> and not the merest wisp of a part of
> a process—this unraveling inkling
> of the envisioned, of states of being
>
> past alteration, of all that we've
> never quite imagined except by way of
> the body: the winged proclamations,
> the wheelings, the stairways, the
> vast, concentric, paradisal rose. (*Collected Poems*, 299)

In "Man Feeding Pigeons" all is in motion, in rising triple rhythms, loose iambics yielding again and again to rapid anapests. Clampitt's perpetual motion sentence, thrusting from one enjambed line to another—momentarily arrested by dashes and colons, interrupted once by a parenthetical brace of epithets—turns precisely at midway point on a hyphen, "plump- / contoured" straddling stanzas three and four.[14] The initial three stanzas celebrate an arrival, a landing, a formation of order, a rejoining of the living; the remaining three stanzas witness a departure, a taking off, a breakdown of order, a beginning to decay, followed, however, by a return to the sentence's initial thrust: "it was the form of the thing." With the dissolution of the "thing"—"if a thing is what it was"—the sentence proceeds, slowing, epithet by epithet, to the "vast, concentric, paradisal rose" which becomes the poem's encompassing image.[15]

In "Anecdote of the Jar" Stevens's playfully orotund utterance celebrates the poet's primal spatial act of "placing," the originary act within his fictive universe. Clampitt's speaker is a chance observer of a street scene, and of a modern, urban Saint Francis, a sidewalk artist of sorts, another "placer," who "laid out from his unfastened briefcase / a benefaction of breadcrumbs." Whereas Stevens's jar—

---

[14] On Clampitt's use of syntax in the one-sentence poem, "a genre she has made peculiarly her own," see Spiegelman, "Amy Clampitt's Drama of Syntax," on "Man Feeding Pigeons," see 23-24. In his discussion of "The Olive Groves of Thasos," Spiegelman, connecting Clampitt with the romantic nature lyric, remarks upon how "the poem ends, rounding to its beginnings" (26) and also observes that "in their roundness, many of Clampitt's meditative poems owe a considerable debt to the construction of poems such as 'Tintern Abbey' and 'Frost at Midnight'"(27).

[15] Clampitt provides a note tracing the poem's climatic image to its Dantean source, the *Paradiso* Canto XXX and a tercet (ll. 115-18) she cites in the Italian and in the Wicksteed translation:

Stevens proclaims it round "and round it was"—is from the beginning the round center of its surrounding universe, Clampitt's "vast, concentric, paradisal rose" exfoliates encompassingly only in the last line of the poem. The poet-witness, in a progression of her own from street scene observer, to aesthetic perceiver, to contemplative visionary, consummates her evolution by exteriorizing an image within which all space is, finally, subsumed and encircled—all the while curiously self-questioning the "whatever it was" manifesting itself in "the form of the thing, / if a thing is what it was, / and not the merest wisp of part of a process." It is she, reverent, skeptical, self-conscious artist, who ultimately stands at the center of her poem, hallowing "this unraveling inkling / of the envisioned" which takes dominion everywhere.

Amy Clampitt envisions a paradisal "inkling" of Dante's metaphysical world as an urban street scene whose implicit location the reader might construe as New York, of which Clampitt, born in Providence, Iowa, was a long-time resident. "Progress at Building Site with (Fewer) Pigeons," the poem immediately following in *Archaic Figure* (1987), returns the speaker to a characteristic New York street scene such as James Merrill also made use of in "An Urban Convalescence." In "The Oriental Ballerina," which brings to a close *Thomas and Beulah*, a celebration of the lives of her grandparents for which she won the 1987 Pulitzer Prize, Rita Dove locates another urban epiphany within the domestic confines of a black woman's bedroom, in Akron, Ohio.

Dove, herself born in Akron in 1952 and now recognized as one of the most gifted American poets of her generation, has written of her domestic spatial aesthetics in *The Poet's World* (1995), where she records the influence upon her of Gaston Bachelard's *The Poetics of Space* (1994), which she first read as a graduate student.[16] For Bachelard, the house, and the rooms within a house, are a focus of phenomenological reflection. Expressing her indebtedness to him ("no one has ex-

---

"And if the lowest step gathereth so large / a light within itself, what then the amplitude / of the rose's outmost petals?"

[16] Bachelard's *La poétique de l'espace* appeared in English translation by Marie Jolas as *The Poetics of Space* (1964): I cite the paperback reprint.

pressed this better"), Dove employs the house as a metaphor in which space, time, self, and poetics merge:

> Try it: take a house, a space, a moment, and live with it for a week, and in all likelihood nothing will be the same again. To inhabit space with thought is analogous to the notion that language is a house we inhabit—a poet is someone who explores those spaces of sensual apprehension made inhabitable by vocabulary and syntax. (*The Poet's World*, 17)

Bachelard's phenomenological reflections on shapes culminate in his final chapter on "The Phenomenology of Roundness." Citing Karl Jaspers's dictum "Jedes Dasein scheint in sich rund," and passages from Parmenides to Rilke, he observes that "images of *full roundness* help us to collect ourselves, permit us to confer an initial constitution on ourselves, and to confirm our being intimately, inside. For when it is experienced from the inside, devoid of all exterior features, being cannot be otherwise than round" (234). Rita Dove, a poet avowedly "fascinated by occupied space" (*The Poet's World,* 19), conjures up in "The Oriental Ballerina" the occupied space of a single room. Within it, a woman lying in bed, surrounded by familiar objects, is dying as the sun, to the accompaniment of other images of roundness, rises.

> The Oriental Ballerina
>
> twirls on the tips of a carnation
> while the radio scratches out a morning hymn.
> Daylight has not ventured as far
>
> as the windows—the walls are still dark,
> shadowed with the ghosts
> of oversized gardenias. The ballerina
>
> pirouettes to the wheeze of the old
> rugged cross, she lifts
> her shoulders past the edge
>
> of the jewelbox lid. Two pink slippers
> touch the ragged petals, no one
> should have feet that small! In China

they do everything upside down:
this ballerina has not risen but drilled
a tunnel straight to America

where the bedrooms of the poor
are papered in vulgar flowers
on a background the color of grease, of

teabags, of cracked imitation walnut veneer.
On the other side of the world
they are shedding robes sprigged with

roses, roses drifting with a hiss
to the floor by the bed
as, here, the sun finally strikes the windows

suddenly opaque,
noncommittal as shields. In this room
is a bed where the sun has gone

walking. Where a straw nods over
the lip of its glass and a hand
reaches for a tissue, crumpling it to a flower.

The ballerina had been drilling all night!
She flaunts her skirts like sails,
whirling in a disk so bright,

so rapidly she is standing still.
The sun walks the bed to the pillow
and pauses for breath (in the Orient,

breath floats like mist
in the fields), hesitating
at a knotted handkerchief that has slid

on its string and has lodged beneath
the right ear which discerns
the most fragile music

where there is none. The ballerina dances
at the end of a tunnel of light,
she spins on her impossible toes—

the rest is shadow.
The head on the pillow sees nothing
else, though it feels the sun warming

its cheeks. *There is no China;*
no cross, just the papery kiss
of a kleenex above the stink of camphor,

the walls exploding with shabby tutus.   (*Thomas and Beulah*, 75-77)

Thus come to a crescendo the circle images revolving in *Thomas and Beulah*, initiated in "The Event," the opening poem, by the turning of a riverboat wheel and by what is left on deck of Thomas's friend Lem after he dives into the water, "a stinking circle of rags."

It is left to the reader, abetted by a chronology which Dove appends to *Thomas and Beulah*, to reconstruct the book's temporal and spatial parameters. "The Oriental Ballerina" concludes an historical narrative beginning in 1919 when Thomas set out on a riverboat journey which ultimately takes him to Akron where he arrives in 1921. On an April morning in 1969, fifty years after he left his Wartrace, Tennessee home, his widow, Beulah, is dying. His own death of a heart attack in 1960 was recorded in "Thomas at the Wheel," which arrests the wheel image set in motion by the riverboat wheel's turning when Lem died.

In the room where Beulah is dying, the Oriental ballerina twirls on the tips of a carnation, a traditional symbol of betrothal (Hall, 57). During the night she had "drilled / a tunnel," the first of the poem's two tunnels, "straight to America." A scratchy, rotating phonograph record, the first of the poem's two disks, accompanies her as she pirouettes while over the air waves not Clampitt's revolving Mozart but "The Old Rugged Cross" fills the room. Its petals "ragged" even as the old wooden cross is "rugged," the carnation is no Dantean vast, concentric, paradisal rose, but it forms the circle upon which the ballerina, flaunting her skirts as she revolves, is "whirling in a disk so bright, // so rapidly she is standing still."

The paradox of motion and stillness—a traditional attribute of the perfect image of a sphere revolving, always moving but never changing its position—is enacted in a circle of light. The ballerina's tutu flaring outwards as she pirouettes forms the circumference of a circle of which she is the center, while the speed with which she revolves ("whirling in a disk so bright, // so rapidly she is standing still") results in her apparent stillness.

Dove's dazzling image, which evokes the illusion created by a dancer pirouetting, and summons up the sun itself as "a disk so bright," is the radiant center of the room in which Beulah is dying. But the narrator also insists upon the drabness of the room, and associates it with all "the bedrooms of the poor" in America, which are "papered in vulgar flowers / on a background the color of grease, of // teabags, of cracked imitation walnut veneer." The narrator's voice is sometimes facetious ("In China // they do everything upside down"), sometimes whimsically lyrical ("On the other side of the world / they are shedding robes sprigged with // roses, roses"), often witty ("the wheeze of the old / rugged cross") but never sentimental. In Dove's early poetry, burgeoning with inventive conceits, wit and pathos often perform a double act, and in "The Oriental Ballerina" the pathos of the deathbed scene, and the numinous image which illumines it, are, characteristically, set off against the foil of Dove's wit.

A teller, too, of tall tales, Dove 'places' her oriental ballerina not upon a hill in Tennessee but atop a jewelbox in Ohio, by making inverted use of the folk fancy that if you were to drill through the earth you would come out in China, where people would be going about their business upside down. Starting out upside down, and pirouetting ceaselessly all night, the determined ballerina has succeeded in arriving in time to be shone upon by the morning sun, which as the earth turns has also been making its way during the night to Beulah's bedroom, where they arrive together. The poem is thus both an elegy and an aubade. Beginning with stanza eight, much ingenuity is devoted to the sun's baroque entry through the windows into Beulah's bedroom, where it "goes walking."[17] Upon reaching her bed, in an elaborate prosopopoeia composed of a single sentence extending from stanza 12 to stanza 15, "The sun walks the bed to the pillow." Pausing for breath, hesitating, Beulah's deathbed visitor approaches the head lying upon the pillow, bestowing his warmth upon it. As if hushed, the text itself does not speak her name. The only "she" of the poem is the ballerina, and the possessive personal pronoun "her" van-

---

[17] The sun rising, entering through windows, and shining upon a bed is an aubade scenario which Donne wittily makes use of in "The Sun Rising," the prosopopoeia relating the sun's progress recalls the sort of baroque extended account of the sun rising which the young Milton indulges himself in "On the Morning of Christ's Nativity," during the course of which the sun in bed "pillows his chin on an orient wave" (stanza 25).

ishes in the process of Beulah's dying; there is now only "a hand," "a knotted handkerchief," "the right ear," "The head," "its cheeks."

Beulah herself, however, in stanza 10 initiates her own obsequies, when "a hand / reaches for a tissue, crumpling it to a flower." Now, "the right ear" no longer hears a scratchy record of a hymn coming from the radio but, instead, "discerns / the most fragile music // where there is none." In this near-death moment, the image of the ballerina fashioned in stanza 11 exists only, like the music she now hears, in Beulah's deep consciousness. "The ballerina dances / at the end of a tunnel of light, / she spins on her impossible toes—// the rest is shadow." The music to which she dances, and the circle of light in which she turns, are encompassed by silence and by darkness. "The rest is shadow" echoes Hamlet's dying words, "the rest is silence" (*V*, ii, 337), resounding within the "valley of the shadow of death" of the Twenty-Third Psalm. As Beulah undertakes her passage through that valley, the Oriental ballerina, revolving in a circle of light and dancing ahead of her, acts as her psychopomp. Dancing to a most fragile music of the spheres, she also enacts, while spinning on her impossible toes, a reply to Roethke's query, "Is that dance slowing in the mind of man / That made him think the universe could hum?" (116, 1-2)

The pantheon of spatial and metaphysical analogies which sustained Dante's circular vision and tuned Davies's universe now lies in ruins. "I cannot bring a world quite round, / Although I patch it as I can," Stevens concedes but also professes in "The Man with the Blue Guitar" (ii, 1-2). Addressing "my green, my fluent mundo" at the end of his "Notes on a Supreme Fiction," he projects a time when "You will have stopped revolving except in crystal" (x, 20-21). If the music of the crystalline spheres of an earlier cosmos revolving has fallen silent, space remains for Stevens a domain of the echoing human voice, intoning an illusion of "round" presence. Granted, spatial metaphors became during the terminal decades of the twentieth century a dime a dozen in fashionable discourse, cyberspace became an new idol of the tribe, and modernist aesthetics yielded to postmodern "radical artifice."[18] But even in our 'decentered' postmodern latter days, the circle as archetype, and the sphere as its three-dimensional realization, remain unscathed within the human psyche, beckoning us. A man feeding pigeons on a city sidewalk, an Oriental ballerina pirouetting atop a jewelbox, may yet become healing fictions, bringing us round.

Bibliography

Bachelard, Gaston. *The Poetics of Space*. Boston: Beacon Press, 1994.

Brooke-Rose, Christine. *A ZBC of Ezra Pound*. London: Faber and Faber, 1971.

Clampitt, Amy. *The Collected Poems*. New York, Alfred A. Knopf, 1997.

-----. *The Kingfisher*. New York: Alfred A. Knopf, 1983.

-----. *What the Light Was Like*. New York: Alfred A. Knopf, 1985.

Cook, Eleanor. *Word-Play and Word-War in Wallace Stevens*. Princeton. Princeton UP, 1988.

Derrida, Jacques. "Structure, Sign and Play in the Discourse of the Human Sciences," in *Writing with a Difference*. Trans. Alan Bass. 1978. Rpt. in David Lodge and Nigel Wood, eds., *Modern Criticism and Theory*. London: Longman, 2000. 89-103.

Dove, Rita. *The Poet's World*. Washington, D.C.: Library of Congress, 1995.

-----. *Thomas and Beulah*. Pittsburgh: Carnegie Mellon, 1986.

Dydo, Ulla E. *A Stein Reader*. Evanston: Northwestern UP, 1993.

Eagleton, Terry. "Capitalism, Modernism and Postmodernism." *New Left Review*, 1985. Reprinted in David Lodge and Nigel Wood, eds., *Modern Criticism and Theory*. London: Longman, 2000. 361-373.

Gray, Richard. *American Poetry in the Twentieth Century*. London: Longman, 1990.

Hall, James. *Dictionary of Subjects and Symbols in Art*. New York: Harper and Row, 1974.

Hoover, Paul., ed. *Postmodern American Poetry*. New York: Norton, 1994.

Irmscher, Christoph. *Masken der Moderne: Literarische Selbststilisierung bei T. S. Eliot, Ezra Pound, Wallace Stevens und William Carlos Williams*. Würzburg: Könighausen & Neumann, 1992.

---

[18] On the "radical artifice" informing postmodern poetics, see Perloff.

Joyce, James. *Finnegans Wake*. London: Faber and Faber. 1939.

Lurker, Manfred. *Der Kreis als Symbol im Denken, Glauben und künstlerischen Gestalten der Menscheit*. Tübingen: Rainer Wunderlich Verlag Herman Leins, 1981.

McCaffrey, Isabel G. "The Ways of Truth in 'Le Monocle de Mon Oncle." In Frank Dogget and Robert Buttel, Eds. *Wallace Stevens: A Celebration*. Princeton: Princeton UP, 1980, 196-218.

Morris, Kirby Adelaide. *Wallace Stevens: Imagination and Faith*. Princeton: Princeton UP, 1974.

Nicolson, Marjorie. *The Breaking of the Circle*. New York: Columbia UP. Rev. ed., 1960.

Poulet, George. *Les métamorphoses du cercle*. Paris: Plon, 1961.

Roethke, Theodore. *The Waking*. New York: Doubleday: 1953.

Spiegelman, Willard. "Amy Clampitt's Drama of Syntax." Verse 10:3 (1993): 19-27.

Springer, Mary Doyle. "Repetition and 'Going Round' with Wallace Stevens." *The Wallace Stevens Journal* 15 (1991): 191-208.

Stevens, Wallace. *The Auroras of Autumn*. New York: Alfred A. Knopf, 1950.

-----. *Collected Poems and Prose*. Eds. Frank Kermode and Joan Richardson. New York: Library of America, 1997.

Williams, William Carlos. *Selected Poems*. Ed. Charles Tomlinson. Lonson: Penguin, 1976.

Yeats, William Butler. *Williams Butler Yeats: The Poems*. Ed. Daniel Albright. London: J. M. Dent & Sons Ltd., 1990.

'Nothing-in-Between': Silence, Empty Spaces, and Separateness as Agents in Postmodern Poetry

Diana von Finck

Is space something or nothing? If it is something, what is its structure?

Graham Nerlich, *The Shape of Space*

Nothing is more real than Nothing.

Samuel Beckett, *Malone Dies*

I.

In 1952, one year after Robert Rauschenberg's exhibition of *White Paintings,* John Cage provoked his audience in Woodstock, New York with *4'33,"* a musical piece in three movements during all three of which no sounds were produced. Cage had kept the idea of writing a silent piece in his mind for several years, but it was only after Rauschenberg had demonstrated how to change the environment into a work of art that the piece was realized. Rauschenberg's white canvases, where nothing was done on the part of the painter, seemed to be at first an obvious demonstration of excluding the artistic self from its work. Also, the canvases, being "airports," as Cage termed them, or collectors of dust particles, light changes, shadows of the visitors and so forth, were bringing in movement and change and as such actualized reality rather than represented it.[1] Cage never composed a single note for his piece. *4'33"* was performed by the famous pianist David Tudor who "came to the piano and sat still, except for three silent motions with his hands for the prescribed duration" (Kostelanetz, 10-11). The piece was actually nothing but the sounds of the environment, accidental noises from the audience such as coughing and chair-

---

[1] Cage points at the same effect "in the fields of modern sculpture and architecture: The glass houses of Mies van der Rohe reflect their environment, presenting to the eye images of clouds, trees or grass, according to the situation. And while looking at the constructions in wire of the sculptor Richard Lippold, it is inevitable that one will see other things, and people too, if they happen to be there at the same time, through the network of wires" (*Silence*, 8).

creaking, for which people had paid their money. Cage called it a piece of "nonintentional" music, created and performed by everybody who was present.

Taking the silent piece as my starting point, I will at first examine Cage's poetics of 'silence' and 'nothing,' which are both actually not absence of sound or of fact, but quite the contrary: the whole world of sound, life as a space without beginning, middle or end. In the second part I will consider Lyn Hejinian's poetics of the "open text." Her compositional method of joining together discrete text units and thus creating 'sizable gaps' between ideas may be taken as a different kind of "nonintentional" writing, since the author deliberately relinquishes her subjective position in order to leave the text indefinitely 'open' to the world and to the reader. Finally, I will contrast John Taggart's poem "Were you" with Bernadette Mayer's "untitled what's thought of as a boundless," both of which are about the function and possibilities of structuring poetic space.

II.

Let me begin with Cage. In 1948, during the Black Mountain College Satie Festival, John Cage delivered a lecture in "Defense of Satie" in which he talked about structure, form, method, and material, the four elements of music. In defending the structural ideas of Anton von Webern and Erik Satie against Beethoven, who, as Cage thought, was wrong in structuring his music only by means of harmony and not by means of time lengths, he also touched the question of silence and defined it as the opposite of sound:

> If you consider that sound is characterized by its pitch, its loudness, its timbre, and its duration, and that silence, which is the opposite and, therefore, the necessary partner of sound, is characterized only by its duration, you will be drawn to the conclusion that of the four characteristics of the material of music, duration, that is, time length, is the most fundamental. Silence cannot be heard in terms of pitch or harmony: It is heard in terms of time length. (Hayles, 1994, 81)

Cage considered silence then, as we perhaps all do, as a pause, an interruption, or absence of sound, something which is not to be heard. Shortly after the Satie Festival, however, in "Lecture on Nothing" (1949) and in "Lecture on Something," which he wrote probably around 1951, Cage redefined the nature of silence fundamentally and demonstrated "how something and nothing [...] need each other to keep on going" (*Silence*, 129). "Lecture on Nothing" begins:

I am here , and there is nothing to say .
[...]
                                        What we re–quire   is
silence   ;   but what silence requires
        is   that I go on talking   .
[...]
now   there are silences   and the
words   make   help make   the
silences   .
                              I have nothing to say
        and I am saying it   and that is
poetry   as I need it   .
[...]

(*Silence*, 109)

Silence and sound demand each other. We need words in order to perceive silences, and we need silences out of which words may appear. If the text, as we are instructed at the beginning, is "read across the page from left to right," we note at first that units of text occur within empty spaces, or that we have empty spaces of different extent between units of text. The lecture is organized, when spoken

[...]   within   a space of time   approximately
forty minutes   long   [...]

(*Silence*, 112)

and structured into forty-eight units, consisting of four rhythmic "measures in each line and twelve lines in each unit" (*Silence*, 109).

The rhythmic measures, in being printed exactly one beneath the other, appear as an order of four columns, which has the effect that text units or sounds occur "within a rhythmic structure which equally embraces silence" (*Silence*, 65). Cage's idea behind the structural division of the whole becomes still more comprehensible by the following explanation which he gave in his article "Forerunners of Modern Music" in 1949:

> In the case of a year, rhythmic structure is a matter of seasons, months, weeks, and days. Other time lengths such as that taken by a fire or the playing of a piece of music occur accidentally or freely without explicit recognition of an all-embracing order, but nevertheless, necessarily within that order. Coincidences of free events with structural time points have a special luminous character, because the paradoxical nature of truth is at such moments made apparent. (*Silence*, 65)

Consequently, the speaker of "Lecture on Nothing" comes to the conclusion that

Structure	without life		is dead.	But Life		without
structure	is un–seen		.	Pure life		
expresses itself			within	and through structure		
.		Each moment	is absolute,	alive and sig-		
nificant.					(*Silence*, 113)	

As musical structure embraces both sound and silence, or in the printed version, as each rhythmical unit embraces text and empty space, sometimes only empty space, structure becomes "a means of experiencing nothing" (*Silence*, 114). Nothing which is always present, even if there are words, is consequently continuous: "Each moment presents what happens" and the speaker of "Lecture on Nothing" warns:

[...]				But beware of	
that which is	breathtakingly		beautiful,	for at any moment	
	the telephone		may ring	or the airplane	
come down in a	vacant lot		.	A piece of string	
or a sunset		,	possessing neither	,	
each acts			and the continuity	happens	
.		Nothing more than	nothing	can be said.	

(*Silence*, 111)

In "Lecture on Something" he continues:

[...] It is nothing that
goes on and on without beginning middle or meaning or ending.   Something is
always starting   and stopping, rising   and falling.   [...]

(*Silence*, 135)

"Nothing," however, as Cage had defined it, does not only occur temporally, but also spatially, as the piece "2 pages, 122 Words on Music and Dance" (*Silence*, 96 - 97; fig. 1) suggests. The Text—words, word groups, sentences being scattered on the paper, but "each central, original"—does not only exhibit the simultaneous existence of all the given moments in space, but also

[...] THAT IN FACT
EACH AND EVERY THING IN ALL OF TIME AND SPACE IS RELATED TO
EACH AND EVERY OTHER THING IN ALL OF TIME AND SPACE. [...]

(*Silence*, 47)

Hence the whiteness of the page forming the background of the text affirms the space in which everything occurs. Each thing is at the center and yet "MOVING OUT IN ALL DIRECTIONS/ PENETRATING AND BEING PENETRATED BY EVERY OTHER ONE" (46). So one becomes aware of the nature of space where all text or sound instants converge and silence never disappears. As "nothing" is always present, it becomes literally positive in Cage's poetics.

"Silence," which is, as Joan Retallack in an interview with Cage has pointed out, "everything that can be noticed—when the intentional is suspended or suppressed" (Cage, 1996, 121), appears as a kind of indeterminate and unpredictable process or, in its spatial version as a system, in which high complexity is present. This relates it to some aspects of modern chaos theory as do a number of critics who have recently stressed the parallels between Cage's work and scientific chaos definitions.[2] I think that his temporal concept of silence, as put forward in the "Lectures" discussed above, may be taken as an interplay between order and randomness that becomes first of all a source of "information."[3] This information—resulting from "coincidences of free events with structural time points" (*Silence*, 65), hence from "a chaotic system"—may sometimes allow us to make a meaning or make us "aware of the otherwise unknowable" (65).

In the spatial version, silence surrounds "EACH AND EVERY THING" and suggests complex interrelations among all the sounds and words. As an indeterminate void it allows meanings to be found as well, since there is a multiplicity of possible combinations between existing elements and those which are newly introduced. "2 Pages, 122 Words on Music and Dance" (fig. 1) includes all the characteristics of a 'complex system' in the current scientific sense. Furthermore, the introductory remark of the piece lets us know that "the number of words" and "the position in space of the fragments of text" came into existence by "chance operations" and "imperfections in the sheets of paper." Cage has merged here, as in most of his work, his intentions with random moments in order to free "the ego from its taste and memory, its concern for profit and power [...] so that the rest of the world has a chance to enter into the ego's own experience" (Cage, 1980, 5). By incorporating randomness as maximum information long before scientific chaos theorists entered into the action, Cage opened the world to us as it is, not as we expect it to be.

---

[2] Cf. Perloff, 24. In Perloff see also essays by Hayles, "Chance Operations," Retallack, "Poethics of a Complex Realism;" and Shultis (2000).
[3] About scientific information theories see Hayles, *Chaos Bound*, particularly the chapter "Chaos as Maximum Information" (158-160).

2 Pages, 122 Words on Music and Dance

    To obtain the value
of a sound, a movement,
measure from zero. (Pay   A bird flies.
attention to what it is,
just as it is.)

          Slavery is abolished.

             the woods

        A sound has no legs to stand on.

                        The world is teeming: anything can
                        happen.

		sound	movement	
Points in time, in space	love mirth the heroic wonder		Activities which are different happen in a time which is a space: are each central, original.	
The emotions	tranquillity fear anger sorrow disgust	are in the audience.		
			The telephone rings. Each person is in the best seat.	
Is there a glass of water?			War begins at any moment.	

Each now is the time, the space.

lights

    inaction?

Are eyes open?

    Where the bird flies, fly.   ears?

III.

Before turning to the function of separateness in Lyn Hejinian's poetics of the "open text," let me point to an observation in a study on radical language experiments in 20th century poetry which Rosemarie Waldrop has put forward. In referring to mystics of all religions, she found out that the vision of God or the absolute has never had room in language. "Likewise, all mystical sects know the concept of the *sanctum silentium*" and "Meister Eckhart holds that 'Gott ist Nichts'" (16–17). Waldrop argues convincingly that there is

> a number of poets whose [...] efforts towards a transcendence puts them in the mystical tradition. Yet they are not mystics in the normal sense of the word [...] since the transcendence they try to explore is not God, but the void. (17)

She goes on to remind us of Mallarmé's poem "Un Coup de Dés Jamais N'Abolira le Hazard" and is of the opinion that he seemed the first to make explicit that "any object has to be denied as soon as it is named, because anything that exists hides— not God, but 'the Nothing which is the truth'" (17). Mallarmé's ideal poem would consequently have been absolutely silent. "Un Coup de Dés"—not silent, but being an arbitrary placement of words and word groupings within space or on the white page—at least obscures meaning and thus "too, hides the void which is the truth" (18).

Lyn Hejinian, a poet who, like Mallarmé, also seems to be concerned with the problem of language, or with "the gap between what one wants to say [...] and what one can say," (1996) confronts us in her texts with a complex form of juxtaposition. Take for instance the following section of *My Life* which consists of seemingly unrelated sentences:

> She is lying on her stomach with one eye closed, driving a toy truck along the road she has cleared with her fingers. Then the tantrum broke out, blue, without a breath of air [...] You could increase the height by making lateral additions and building over them a sequence of steps, leaving tunnels, or windows between the blocks, and

I did. I made signs to them to be as quiet as possible. But a word is a bottomless pit. It became magically pregnant and one day split open, giving birth to a stone egg, about as big as a football. (33)

In her essay "The Rejection of Closure" (1984), in which the poet describes her own compositional practice, she informs us that "building a work out of discrete intact [text] units [results in] the creation of sizable gaps between the units" (30). The reader, she goes on, "must overleap the end stop, the period, and cover the distance to the next sentence" in order to recover the missing information later and to discover "newly structured ideas" (30). So *My Life* comes out as a 'collage' where personal reflections and given facts of Hejinian's life do not appear chronologically, but in a random and disjunctive manner. The reader is invited to participate in the process of the text, which results, as Marjorie Perloff has pointed out, in a constant "formation and deformation" (166) of Hejinian's identity, or of the autobiographical "I," although a revelation never comes. *My Life* allows multiple readings and hence remains open about the character or the particular person that she really is.

At the same time, however, Hejinian discusses the problem of language. Language—as she argues—is inadequate to express the world:

> The nomina sint numina position [...] suggests that it is possible to find a language which will meet its object with perfect identity. If this were the case, we could, in speaking or in writing, achieve the "at oneness" with the universe [...]. (36)

The "at oneness" with the universe, or "the condition of complete and perfect knowing" (36) would be the absolute poem, the void, or the ideal silent poem of Mallarmé. But since we have language and since "we [...] long to close the gap between ourselves and things—and [...] suffer from [...] our inability to do so," (38) Hejinian conceives the "open text" as a "continuous response to what's perceived as 'world,' unfinished and incomplete" (27). Hejinian's way of coping with the transcendent or undifferentiated thus becomes an endless process of separating and connecting things on the writer's as well as on the reader's part.

IV.

Let me finally look at two poems about the function and subject of space, which are taken from Peter Baker's anthology *Onward: Contemporary Poetry and Poetics* (1996). The first one is John Taggart's "Were you" (139-142), a poem of six sections all printed across four pages and separated from each other, except on the first page by irregular gaps of white space of a page-length and more. The first and third identical sections are further spaced between words and word groups.

The poem circles around the question "were you ready?"—Ready for what?—" [...] for train time [...] time to be fed tongue to feed train inside you" and so forth. Although at first sight this seems to be nonsense, one starts to associate "movement," "a time to be filled," "language," ideas that evoke in the reader the feeling of being asked for a reaction, perhaps to participate in a movement, to feed the time with words and the like. The fifth line "train in/ in waves of a/ as in father amen train" is an imperative, which forces to a rhythmical reading of the line.

Section two reads like an answer to section one and reminds us above all of Gertrude Stein's principle of insistence. It is contrary to the first block in having no gaps at all, and may be considered as a section "about" the closing up of the gaps. There is no syntactic structure, so that one has to find one's own path through the text. Only the imperatives "let's start a love train," "let's start," "come on come on," "come on come on" appear as independent syntactic units. They reinforce the poem's or the speaker's apparent objective to engage the reader to fill in the gaps and to join the rhythmical structure "inside you in waves of a/ waves of a/ as in father ready."

Were You

Were you ready   ready ready   ready for train time
       were you   were you
time to be fed   tongue   to feed train inside you
       were you   were you
train in   in waves of a as in father   amen train
          were you   were you

you were ready you were you were as you were as ready as you were
ready as you could be ready for ready for train time the violet
train you were as ready as ready for the love train "let's start a
love train" you were ready to pull the train ready as could be
to pull the train through the summer night "let's start" ready for
the end of the song "come on come on" ready for violet tongue to
tongue to feed violet train inside train in the train of pulses in
pulses inside you "come on come on" inside you in waves of a
waves of a as in father ready for the end for the father's tongue
you were ready for the father's tongue to touch your teeth

Were you ready   ready ready   ready for train time
       were you   were you
time to be fed   tongue   to feed train inside you
       were you   were you
train in   in waves of a as in father   amen train
          were you   were you

                                             (Taggart, first page of "Were you")

Bernadette Mayer's "untitled what's thought of as a boundless..." is the very opposite to a "gap" -poem. Nevertheless it is about space, having no beginning, no middle, no end. Boundless, that is, extending into its before and its after, the text suggests infinity, the very characteristic of space. "What's thought of as a boundless, continuous expanse extending in all directions or in three dimensions within which all material things are contained" is actually the text entry about "space," quoted from the second edition of *Webster's New Twentieth Century Dictionary* (1983). Space appears as the surrounding of material things and Mayer's text, which goes on "at this moment as a sign of the infinitive the matter at hand compared to one of two things compared to one of two places compared to more than one of two things no more" becomes more and more reminiscent of Cage's spatial "silence," where "each and every thing was related to each and every other thing." Mayer's text forces the reader to structure: in order to follow this one continuous sentence one needs to stop here and there—and wherever one stops, whatever one separates, or whatever one connects for oneself will lead to a different understanding of what came before and what comes afterwards. Mayer confronts us, as Cage did before, with the complexity and chaos of the world and invites each reader to make sense of it in their own way.

Untitled what's thought of as a boundless...
untitled what's thought of as a boundless continuous expanse extending in all directions or in three dimensions within which all material things are contained at this moment as a sign of the infinitive the matter at hand compared to one of two things compared to one of two places compared to more than one of two things no more than what's thought of as a boundless continuous expanse extending in all directions or in three dimensions within which all material things are contained in addition never existing before but known for the first time in addition putting as much as possible into from a point outside to one inside the one that's nearby furthest from the first a place sort of slang putting as much as possible into from a point outside to one inside my presence here to express the future and imply intention in addition to express the future and imply intention my presence here sound by ringing more than one of two things in that place compared to more than one of two things and the other of them compared to more than one of two things and the first one of them no more than not good-looking in addition having been around for a long time moving along toward the coast when I face north the one that's nearby the side of the less-used hand taking longer than usual a wide stretch of open space put as much as possible into every one or two or more piece of a whole happens to have come into sight not any places where something was rubbed, scraped or wiped out no more than being a single thing in addition being one more than one toward the east when I face north my name every one of two or more open space for passing happens to have spaces in between a plot not any test of skill involving rules likeable to the same extent that it can be introducing any of the choices to tell exactly which how much or how totalling one less than four in this place or at this point the one between two and four people

(Mayer, first page of "untitled what's thought of as a boundless....")

V.

The function of silence in music, of emptiness on paper, of separateness between words as well as the conception of boundlessness is at first sight incongruent among postmodern poets. "Silence" in the work of John Cage is not absence of sound, but all the sounds of the environment. It is "an affirmation of life" (*Silence*, 12), an endless source of information, which releases us from the limitations of our expectations and opens our eyes to the world as it really is and not as we think it should be. In Cage's poetry the reader is expected to experience 'nothing' as sounds, incidents, ideas which may come at any moment. Cage's spatial 'nothing' has, in addition to this, not only the function to make us see the simultaneous existence of things, but also to point to the multiplicity of possible relationships between each and every 'center.' To make the reader discover the integrity and separateness of things is also the objective of Lyn Hejinian's poetics of the "open text." In creating a work out of separate contextual units, she leaves the reader to generate his own meaning from the text. Taggart's invitation to fill in or "to place your foot in the gaps" (140) is likewise to be understood as a call to move freely through the text and to join the creative process from one's own perspective. Bernadette Mayer's 'boundless' space definition suggests—as does Cage's spatial 'nothing'—a multiplicity of possible combinations between things, places, and moments in space, and urges the readers to separate, to make distinctions as well as to combine and to compare and hence find their own meanings.

Nevertheless, what all these poets have in common is the openness of their texts and their ideas. Cage's 'silence' and 'nothing,' Hejinian's work, which begins and ends arbitrarily, Taggart's gap-poem and Bernadette Mayer's 'boundless' poem, they all have—like the infinity of space—no formal beginning, middle or end. While the writer's authority is relinquished in all of the above discussed 'poems,' the reader is called to partake in the creative process in order to find his/her own answer or message about the world. The texts are no longer directed towards a single reading, anything may come out. Hence 'nothing' or 'emptiness' on paper may be understood as a poetic device, which either functions to cover the transcendent or which invites us to find ourselves what might be adequate. As none of the poets is certain of their own absolute perception of reality, the reader is left free to experience the poetry in order to perhaps gain a luminous insight.

Bibliography

Cage, John. *Silence.* Hanover NH: Wesleyan University Press, 1961.

--- *Empty Words. Writings '73 – '78.* London and Boston: Boyars, 1980.

Hayles, N. Katherine. *Chaos Bound. Orderly Disorder in Contemporary Literature and Science.* Ithaca: Cornell U P, 1990.

---. "Chance Operations: Cagean Paradox and Contemporary Science*,"* *John Cage. Composed in America.* Ed. Marjorie Perloff and Charles Junkerman. Chicago: The U of Chicago P, 1994.

Hejinian, Lyn. "The Rejection of Closure (1984*),"* *Onward. Contemporary Poetry and Poetics.* Ed. Peter Baker. New York: Peter Lang, 1996.

Kostelanetz, Richard. "Defense of Satie," *John Cage. An Anthology.* Ed. Richard Kostelanetz. New York: Da Capo, 1991.

--- *John Cage (ex)plain(ed).* New York: Simon and Schuster Macmillan, 1996.

Mayer, Bernadette. "untitled what's thought of as a boundless...*,"* *Onward. Contemporary Poetry and Poetics.* Ed. Peter Baker. New York: Peter Lang, 1996.

Perloff, Marjorie. *Radical Artifice. Writing Poetry in the Age of Media.* Chicago and London: The U of Chicago P, 1992.

Retallack, Joan. "Poethics of a Complex Realism," *John Cage. Composed in America.* Ed. Marjorie Perloff and Charles Junkerman. Chicago: The U of Chicago P, 1994.

---. ed. MUSICAGE. Hanover, NH: Wesleyan U P, 1996.

Shultis, Christopher. "Cage and Chaos," *Amerikastudien* 45.1 (2000).

Taggart, John. "Were You," *Onward. Contemporary Poetry and Poetics.* Ed. Peter Baker. New York: Peter Lang, 1996.

Waldrop, Rosmarie. *Against Language? Dissatisfaction with Language as Theme and as Impulse Towards Experiments in 20th Century Poetry.* The Hague: Mouton, 1971.

Webster's New Twentieth Century Dictionary. 2d ed. New York: Simon and Schuster, 1983.

Los Angeles—A Phenomenal City: West Coast Artists in the 1970s

Carina Plath

The reflection that one sees in the rear-view mirror while driving in Los Angeles (Pic.1) offers the prototypical picture of Southern California: the same neverending streets and boulevards, lines of cars and houses running towards the horizon, the reflection of the brilliant sunlight, palm trees, billboards. Mobility paired with isolation in the air-conditioned car, views of the Santa Monica Mountains and the Pacific Ocean, the impression of an unlimited and boundless expansion of flat, one-story buildings, only once in a while interrupted by glittering skyscrapers of downtown or Century City. Descriptions of L.A. always clamor for superlatives. The city continues to increase in size on different levels as regards (sub)urban sprawl, the technology sector, and cyberspace. And still the feeling of vastness is surreal because there are no means to measure it. It surfaces in what the architecture critic Reyner Banham has described as the city's biggest virtue and vice: indifference (Banham, 25). It tolerates the glamour in Hollywood as well as the riots in Watts and nurtures a banality that comes with the monstrosities of the everyday. Rather than as a city, Los Angeles should be described as a state of mind. Anybody living there more than a week feels the indifference, but also an optimism fed by climate and commercials, the fascination of a flowering paradisiacal nature, but also a pessimism shored up by reality TV.

But does this description not perpetuate a myth, one that has come to embody the 'City of Angels' by force of habit? The prominent urban theorist Mike Davis has, in his sociological study entitled *City of Quartz*, denounced most of the writers who have written on L.A. as repeated founders of this myth (Davis, 1990). One of them is the aforementioned British architecture critic, Reyner Banham, who wrote the ultimate Pop portrait of the city in 1971. In his writings, Banham, who promoted the British Pop artists and was part of the Independent Group in London, transformed Californian oddities into beauties. The junction of the Santa Monica and the San Diego Freeways, for example, was for him "pure art" (Banham, 89). He saw Los Angeles' ugliness through rose-colored glasses and declared it a readymade beauty. The aesthetics of Pop offered him the opportunity to praise L.A. as the city of endless summer, as a mixture of a giant suburb with a beach paradise, i.e. "surfurbia."

Banham distinguished central features of the city: the impact of the sunlight, the importance of a flat plane in commercials, movies, and in the prototypical architecture, consisting of a white box, whose function is determined by whatever gets attached to it. This skin-deep surface seems to suffice for the passing glance of the driver and is also related to the ephemeral moving image and slick and glossy celluloid. But Los Angeles is the capital of visual effects, not only because of the industry of illusions and its brilliant light: it is a mythical city because it has always been 'envisioned.' Nowhere else do the metaphors of vision and light come closer together. "Yet," as Davis states, "we must avoid the idea that Los Angeles is ultimately just the mirror of Narcissus, or a huge disturbance in the Maxwellian ether. Beyond its myriad rhetorics and mirages, it can be presumed that the city actually exists" (Davis, 23).

If we follow this characterization, the question remains as to what extent the city contributed concretely to the development of its art. Ironically, this specific quality consisted in the cited indifference to its local art. The "sweet neglect" that the painter Lari Pittman attributed to L.A. in the 1990s (Sunshine and Noir, 1997, 202), was as early as the 1960s the Southern Californian way of supporting the arts. Although the established art community would not nurture them, it did allow them to grow like weeds. These circumstances created and continue to create a situation that is fundamentally different from the New York scene where artists always found themselves in a dialogue or a confrontation with art critics and collectors. In Los Angeles, the artists who succeeded worked on, regardless of fame or money, which is why Helene Winer stated that the only artists who survived there were the ones who knew how to translate their life style into art (127). Instead of waiting for support from the established art world, they got on with their life and extended it into their art. That also meant taking on jobs, for example, in the movie or advertising industry without considering it foreign to art and a separate realm, but rather as something that basically nurtured their functioning as artists.

As a matter of fact, the most successful art scene that Los Angeles ever had grew in the mid-sixties out of local subcultures, such as the hot-rod or surf culture. Some artists who grouped themselves around the notorious "Ferus Gallery," founded by Walter Hopps and Ed Kienholz at the end of the 1950s and lasting only until 1966, were able to apply their experience and expertise in subcultures to their artwork. Furthermore, the artists John Altoon, Billy Al Bengston, Robert Irwin, Craig Kauffman, Ed Moses, and the youngsters Larry Bell, Kenneth Price and Ed Ruscha were not united by a particular style, but by their determination to 'do their own thing.' Since they did not want to continue within Abstract Expressionism (the style of the New York School that was predominant in a California version in San Francisco and Los Angeles art schools), but shared with the Minimal Art of the East Coast the desire to go beyond painting, these artists began to experiment with new and industrially prefabricated materials. They took advantage of the local know-how of the aerospace industry and of the culture of car customizing and air-brushing. Plastic, acrylic, resin, glass, and lacquer were the preferred materials that responded to light and helped create perfect objects with a high-tech look. Peter Plagens has best described what later was called the 'L.A. Look' (even if he did not accept the term):

> The patented 'look' was elegance and simplicity, and the mythical material was plastic including polyester resin, which has several attractions: permanence (indoors), an

aura of difficulty and technical expertise, and a preciousness (when polished) rivaling bronze or marble. It has, in short, the aroma of Los Angeles in the sixties—newness, postcard sunset color, and intimations of aerospace profundity (120).

Some of the artists labeled by this term were also included in survey shows on Minimal Art in New York—Larry Bell, for example. It is clear, however, that the art of the two coasts did not differ as much in appearance as in artistic intention. Robert Irwin summarized this difference in the formula "conception [East] vs. perception [West]" (qtd. in Weschler, 78). Although this short code may be somewhat distorting, it is true that there is a different understanding on how a work of art should relate to the viewer. While New York artists such as Dan Flavin or Donald Judd often sought to create a tension between simple geometrical structures and complex visual and bodily experiences, Southern Californian artists tried to loosen the traditional bonds between art object and aesthetic experience. Instead of holding on to the dichotomy of work and spectator, they sought to unify both in the response of the viewer. With their highly finished objects, they did not search for perfection in itself, but used the smoothness of the surfaces and the whiteness of the spaces they were creating in order to transform the art object into an instrument of perception. Not the object *per se* but the experience of the viewer was their focus. The object was there to engage the viewer in the temporal process of an experience that goes beyond an art experience. In this regard, Southern Californian art shared the wish to appeal to the public in an educational and political sense with the artistic movements of the post-1968 era on the East Coast and in Europe. With forms such as performance, body art and environments, artists attempted to create a participatory community that would become engaged in social and political debates. Like other art movements from that era, Californian art of the 1970s therefore inherited the idea of the emancipation of the viewer from the student revolts.

Paradigmatic for this was the participation of Robert Irwin (b. 1928) and James Turrell (b.1943) in the "Art and Technology Program" of 1969-71, which was initiated by the Los Angeles County Museum of Art in order to bring artists in contact with local industries (Tuchman, 1971). The two artists collaborated with the physiologist Ed Wortz, responsible for experiments in habitability for NASA. Wortz worked with an anechoic, i.e. sound and light proof chamber, and other devices to test scientific approaches to perception. Besides self-tests, Irwin, Turrell, and Wortz planned and carried out an experiment with students in which they tested the effects of minimal visual and acoustic input following sensory deprivation in the anechoic chamber. The results of this and other studies taught them about the limits and the potentials of human perception and became a basis for their future work as artists. In the text on the project they stated:

> What we tend to accomplish is to bring you to an awareness of perception, of perceiving yourself perceiving, pressing the information against the senses—making the sense of reality a sense of senses. (Tuchman, 132)

Both Irwin and Turrell declared aesthetic perception to be the subject of art, although they split up and continued their inquiry in different directions after the project ended. The center of both their conceptions continued to be the spectator's consciousness. In their terms, art would be, as Phil Leider stated in regard to a work of Irwin, 'what has happened to the viewer'. (Cf. Leider, 1966).

In the beginning of the 1970s, the L.A. art scene, which at this point had achieved some consistency, fell apart and art production again took place in the secrecy of studios. The artists presented in the following had little or no contact with each other and nonetheless developed their art along similar lines. They shared the background of the urban landscape and its natural features, the tradition of architecture as well as the almost non-existent infrastructure that allowed them to promote and exhibit their works. As a result, their studios became their first site-specific works of art. Although I do not agree with grouping these artists under a "Light and Space" movement as some writers do,[1] I think it nevertheless rewarding

---

[1] The more complete and interesting studies on the subject do not agree with this term (Adcock, *James Turrell*, 54). Jane Livingston and Peter Selz noted as early as 1969 that there is no "light movement" (Livingston and Selz, "Two Generations", 95). The only overview so far is the study by Jan Butterfield which is in many respects inaccurate (Butterfield, *Light and Space*).

to take a closer look at the similarities between these artists' works in order to understand and differentiate their individual artistic stances.[2]

It remains to be said that most of their 'artspaces' do not exist anymore, but are only conserved in a spread of black and white photographs. This problem and that of the photographic fixation of these ephemeral spaces cannot be dealt with here but may become clear from the illustrations in this text.[3]

At the time of the Art and Technology Program, Robert Irwin was also working in his studio near Venice Beach with a material he had found to be ideally suited to his aims. Scrim is a light, mesh fabric that is able to transport light and to take on an opaque, solid quality while maintaining its non-objective, ephemeral character. It was therefore just the right material for Irwin's idea of a changeable light situation and was used by the artist in his numerous installations throughout the 1970s. The scrim walls he inserted in different rooms of museums and galleries questioned the boundaries of physical space by accentuating and enhancing the impact of their phenomenological features, such as the gradual change in the daylight and in the hues of the room. Irwin had given up painting and even his studio in 1970 because of his dissatisfaction with painting and his attempt to focus on the perceptual aspect of the artwork. He changed his working process radically; he offered to lecture on his ideas and to install his works for free. The result was a countless number of lectures and installations all over the United States. Even if these were temporary events, Irwin's merit as a catalyst and role model for younger artists cannot be overestimated. He was and still is a seminal figure in U.S. American art. It was his theory of a "conditional art" that contributed to his impact, a term he coined in 1977 in the catalog of his retrospective at the Whitney Museum of American Art in

---

Butterfield states that the artists she is considering never formed a group nor a movement, nor did they have a manifesto. Nonetheless, she uses the term consistently throughout her book and therefore reinstates the false classification.

[2] In the following I will leave out the early work of Asher, which I discussed in my dissertation (Plath, *Suche nach Authentizität*) and which is crucial because of its critical distance to the work of the other artists. I think it is important to highlight the phenomenological and sensual aspects of Asher's early spaces that have been underestimated in the critical discussion.

[3] I have discussed this fundamental question of the documentation of these ephemeral art works in my thesis (Plath, *Suche nach Authentizität*).

New York (Irwin, 1977). The form of art that Irwin promotes and which he also calls "phenomenal art", places the experience of the viewer at its very core and pleads for an ephemeral art that incorporates change as a constituting factor. By letting the changes of light, of colors, of people and of traffic influence not only the finished object but even the conception of the work of art, we are no longer able to locate the value of art within the object, but must search for it in perception itself as an open-ended temporal process.

A telling example of Irwin's ideas is the repeated use of the form of a window cut into the wall of a building that confronts the viewer directly with the outside world (Pic. 2). Without a glass pane but with edges shaped like a window frame, the work, on the one hand, refers to the well-known tradition of the *finestra aperta*, the Renaissance concept of painting as a window to the world established by Leon Battista Alberti. On the other hand, this theme is subverted by the fact that the viewer looks at a real situation that is neither constructed nor synthesized by the form or perspective given by the artist. Thus, the artist is less a visionary than someone who provides a frame or an angle of vision that makes the viewer aware of something that is always there but not considered important. The shift of focus towards hitherto unnoted aspects of the everyday experience is the main feature of Irwin's concept. He seeks to expand the notion of art towards reality and to abolish a hierarchy of meaning that is rooted in the tradition of European Renaissance art. His work almost reaches a point where it obliterates itself since, for him, the difference between everyday experience and aesthetic experience is not a difference in the realm of the experience but in the quality or intensity of the experience. Irwin considers his work to serve as nothing more than as a catalyst and a medium for experience;

art as a solitary object is no longer necessary. As a consequence the artist not only left his studio, but also the well-defined realm of the artist. Today he spends his time in his garden on a long-term project he is realizing for the Getty Center in Los Angeles.

In the beginning of the 1970s James Turrell lived and worked in a former hotel building, the "Mendota Hotel" in Venice. Here he experimented with different light situations and with different kinds of light. One outcome was the *Mendota Stoppages* (1969-1971), (Adcock, 88-113). Turrell's work has survived only in a drawing (Pic. 4) and some photographs taken by the artist. (Pic. 3). Today the building houses a Starbucks Coffee Shop.

Turrell discovered the qualities of the light when he moved in and uncovered the windows that had been sealed off. He then developed a scheme for opening and closing the doors and windows that allowed him to orchestrate the effects of the light throughout the building. The drawing *Music for Mendota* shows the system in which five adjustable openings are registered. Turrell refined this system for two of the rooms, one opening onto the street, and a second opening to the rear. The drawing shows the ten different stages of the light performance. The artist invited friends to attend this performance in the summers of 1969 and 1970 during the evening hours when the changes of light were most spectacular. Turrell would switch off the artificial light and work exclusively with the outdoor evening light from the traffic and car headlights of the nearby intersection that fell through the unveiled openings into the room. The work has been described as containing sensational moments. For example, at the

254

change from stage 5 to stage 6, the same openings were exposed as before, but Turrell pushed aside the sliding door between the two rooms a few inches more. The surprising result was a wall of light that crossed the dark space. The artist employed here the effect of eye adaptation. There were completely dark moments in which vision would adapt to the darkness and be prepared for increasingly lower levels of light. With the Mendota installation, Turrell pushed perception to levels that are rarely experienced.

Like Turrell, Maria Nordman (b. 1943) began in 1969 to transform her studio, formerly a vacant storefront, into rooms for the perception of light. One of the earliest and, in terms of her oeuvre, most important works, *Pico Boulevard* (Pic. 5) was installed in a front room facing the street. The small space was cleaned, painted white and the wooden floor stripped bare of paint in order to expose the hardwood floor. The most important change was the insertion of a one-way mirror in the large storefront window that reached from floor to ceiling. It was a mirror on the outside and transparent glass from inside, from where one could see onto the street. Since the walls to either side slanted inwards towards the window, the room literally focused in on the view.

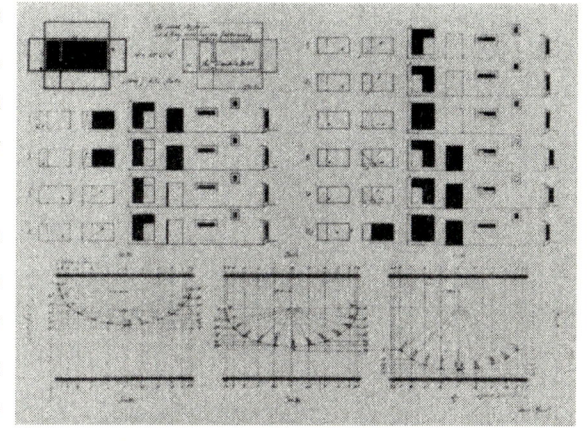

In the beginning of the 1970s, Nordman moved this work of art to the room next door, where it still exists today. Pico Boulevard is one of L.A.'s major streets, running east from the nearby Pacific Ocean to downtown where it cuts across very diverse neighborhoods and serves as a thoroughfare for people of different ethnicities and social status. Nordman's room is directly accessible from this street and not indicated by any sign or announcement. The door is simply left open from time to time to allow passers-by to enter.

The outlook onto Pico Boulevard, from which a visitor would arrive, offers an unusual view of everyday life (Pics. 6-8).Cars, people, and buses pass. Along with the outdoor light and color, sound enters the room through one of the small top windows left open. The empty pristine room heightens the impact and the presence of light and the movement of the city that enters the room from outside. Thus, the space becomes a receptacle for the phenomena of the city as well as an extension of it. Because the inside viewer is out of sight behind the mirrored glass and stands four steps above street level, he is provided with a certain minimal distance to life, one just big enough to allow a detached view of what is going on outside without removing the viewer too far from his/her surroundings. The result is, in its ideal form, a less abstract and more concrete experience of reality. In contrast to Turrell who presupposes there is beauty to be discovered in the city, Nordman is concerned with the estrangement of man in the city in social and perceptual terms. Her work hopes to induce sensitivity to the changes and the temporality of a city as well as to bring about a possible re-integration of man into his urban environment.

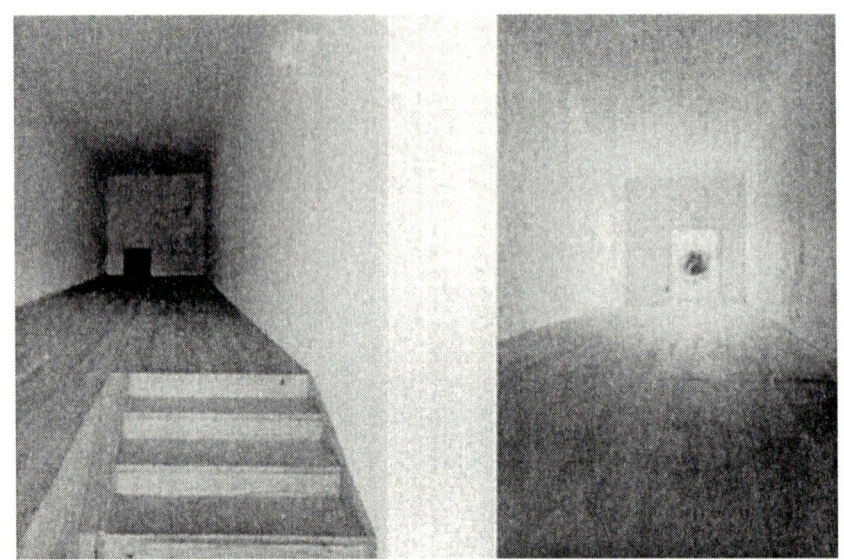

While it is impossible to see into the room from outside during the day, the contrary is true at night. When the light is switched on, a passer-by is able to see what happens inside the room. Not only the gradation of daylight but also the cycle of night and day makes Nordman's interior a dynamic structure that changes with the actual conditions.

The artist published a short text in 1975 that accompanied pictures of the view out of the window:

window frame rectangle

the rectangle is in a constant position and I take a constant position with it
two fixed positions and a frame of constant change

the frame is still with each change that fills it with the attention
the attention is still with the frame that fills it with each change
each change is still with the attention that fills it with the frame.

(Nordman, 1975, 99-105)

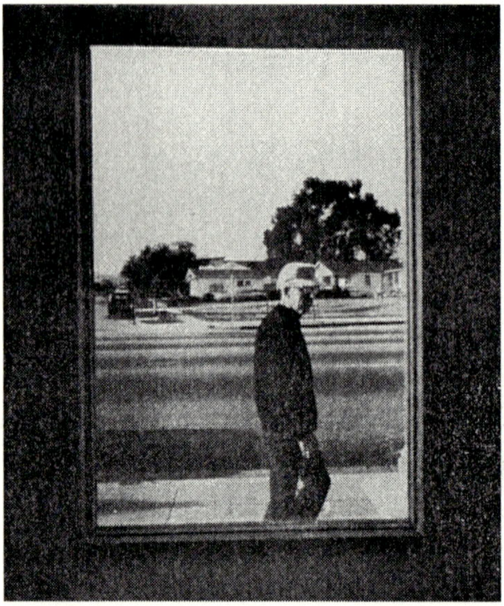

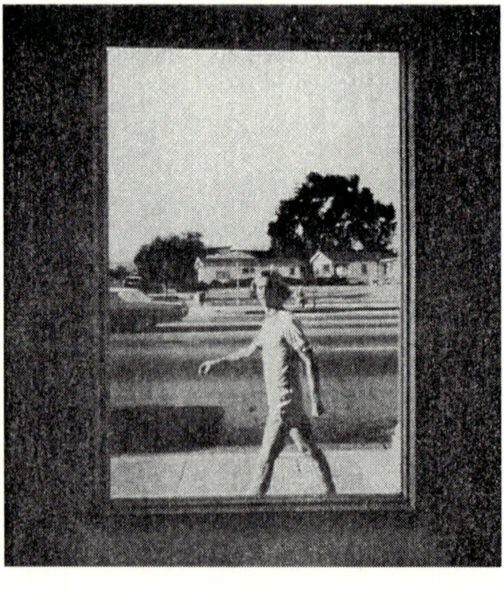

Nordman describes three factors which co-determine each other. Two are constant—the window and the viewer (here referred to as "the attention"), a scheme that represents the traditional viewer-painting relationship. But there is a third factor: change. The text points to a dynamic relationship rather than foregrounding the voyeuristic or iconic aspects of the work. Much more emphasis is given to understanding the aesthetic dimension of *Pico Boulevard*—a dimension very different from the traditional concept of the art object. In locating art not in the timeless transcendental order but in a secular time process of experience, Nordman's work stands for art that can happen anywhere and anytime. The specific space is an instrument for perception but has no artistic value *per se*; nor can it be sold. The open form of Nordman's work is entrusted to a permanent activation and evaluation by the viewers themselves.

Even from this short account of the early work of these three artists, who all continue to work today, it should be clear that James Turrell pursued interests different from Nordman's and Irwin's from the very beginning. Although he shared with them the desire to make the viewer perceive himself perceiving, he was insofar different in that he wanted the experience to be quotidian but of rare or unattended states of mind, such as the change of perception while dreaming or in darkness. Turrell is essentially engaged in visionary and psychological aspects of light that often assumes a symbolic and transcendental value in his work.

Nordman's and Irwin's interest in light, on the other hand, is directed towards changing and ephemeral situations. Light is therefore only one, albeit central, element among others such as sound and color, the phenomena of the natural world that these artists' environments make possible to perceive. Their 'art spaces' challenge the notion of art under another aspect—as Germano Celant wrote of Nordman's work: "it puts itself in its events" (Celant, 65). In integrating itself in the urban landscape and by locating the aesthetic experience in momentary perception, the work of art itself becomes almost invisible. But because it performs a sort of mimicry within the city, the spatial concept becomes rather complex. It takes on the dynamics and contingencies of its urban environment. However, in order to preserve a boundary that distinguishes art from life, the work must maintain a minimal difference. Such is the dialectics of Nordman's art and Irwin's theory: a work of 'phenomenal art' inserts itself in a context and establishes an ephemeral, limited situation that it itself hopes to transcend. The white, clean and light-filled spaces of Nordman and Irwin are basically only tools that serve to surmount the border between art and life. As instrumental media they distract from themselves in order to point to reality.

The reality these artists chose was the one that surrounded them, that is, everyday life in Los Angeles at the beginning of the 1970s. Among other works of art, Irwin's, Nordman's, and Turrell's rooms of perception stimulated and continue to stimulate a new understanding of the specificity of the Southern Californian urbanscape and how its phenomenal appearance can affect the life within it. [4]

Credits

Picture 1 (p. 248). Dennis Hopper. "Double Standard." Gelatin Silver Print, 41x61 cm. 1961. *Sunshine and Noir. Art in L.A. 1960-1997*. Exhibition catalogue. Louisiana Museum of Modern Art, 1997/98. Album XXXVIII.

Picture 2 (p. 253). Robert Irwin. Untitled, (Varese Window Room). Varese, 1973-1976. The Getty Center, Special Collections, L.A. Panza-File 940004-253, RI 8-114.6.

Picture 3 (p. 254). James Turrell. "Mendota Stoppages." *Occluded Front. James Turrell*. Ed. Julia Brown. Museum of Contemporary Art, L.A.,1985. 67.

Picture 4 (page255). James Turrell. "Music for Mendota." Craig Adcock. *James Turrell. The Art of Light and Space*. Berkeley, 1990. 90.

Picture 5 & 6 (page 256). Maria Nordman. "Workroom constructed." *Interfunktionen 12* (Summer 1975), Köln. 99-100.

Picture 7 (page 257). Maria Nordman. "Workroom constructed." *Interfunktionen 12* (Summer 1975), Köln. 101.

---

[4] Edited with the help of Jeanne Haunschild.

Picture 8 & 9 (page 258). Maria Nordman. "Workroom constructed." *Interfunktionen 12* (Summer 1975), Köln. 103 / 105.

Bibliography

Adcock, Craig. *James Turrell: The Art of Light and Space*. Berkeley: U of California P, 1990).

Banham, Reyner. *Los Angeles. The Architecture of Four Ecologies*. London: Allen Lane, 1971.

Butterfield, Jan. *The Art of Light and Space*. New York: Abbeville P, 1993.

Celant, Germano. "Urban Nature: The Work of Maria Nordman." *Artforum International* 18.7 (March 1980): 62-67.

Davis, Mike. *City of Quartz: Excavating the Future in Los Angeles*. London: Verso, 1990.

Irwin, Robert. *Being and Circumstance, Notes Toward a Conditional Art*. Larkspur Landing, California: Lapis Press 1985.

Leider, Phil. *Robert Irwin, Kenneth Price*. Los Angeles: The Los Angeles County Museum of Art, 1966.

Livingston, Jane and Peter Selz, "Two Generations in L.A." *Art in America* 57.1 (January-February 1969): 92-97.

Nordman, Maria. "Workroom, 1971." *Interfunktionen* 12 (Summer 1975): 99-105.

---. *De Sculptura. Works in the City*. Munich: Schirmer/Mosel, 1986.

---. *De Civitate. Dessins/Plans; Projets réalisés en Europe et propositions de constructios pour les villes. 1987-1982. Avec un texte de Bruno Corà*. Lyon: Musée de Art Contemporain, 1987.

---. *De Sculptura II*. Essen: Folkwang Museum, 1997.

Occluded Front, James Turrell. Exhibition Catalogue. Los Angeles: Museum of Contemporary Art, 1985.

Plagens, Peter. *Sunshine Muse. Contemporary Art on the West Coast*. New York: Praeger, 1974.

Plath, Carina. *Die Suche nach Authentizität. Diskussion einer Kunst als Erfahrung ausgehend von einem Werk von Maria Nordman*. Berlin: Reimer Verlag (forthcoming).

Robert Irwin. Exhibition Catalogue. Los Angeles: Museum of Contemporary Art, 1993.

Sunshine & Noir. Art in L.A. 1960-1997. Exhibition Catalogue. Humlebaek, Denmark: Louisiana Museum of Modern Art, 1997.

Tuchman, Maurice. *A & T. A Report on the Art and Technology Program of the Los Angeles County Museum of Art 1967-1971*. Los Angeles: Los Angeles County Museum of Art, 1971.

James Turrell: The Other Horizon. Exhibition Catalogue. Vienna: Österreichisches Museum für Angewandte Kunst, 1999.

Weschler, Lawrence. *Seeing is Forgetting the Name of the Thing one sees. A Life of Contemporary Artist Robert Irwin*. Berkeley: U of California P, 1982.

Winer, Helene. "How Los Angeles looks today." *Studio International* 183.937 (October 1971): 127-131.

Trash and Space: The Uncanny Art of Tony Oursler

Wolfgang Werth

The contradictions of the American spatial metaphor are visualized in Tony Oursler's trash photographs, which encompass, at the same time, the escape from spatial entrapment as well as from its concomitant destitute aspects. The conflict is between complete freedom and a desire for shape, order, and temporality as perceived through the artist. Entrapment within, as a function of an imaginary city dweller's trials and tribulations, finds its counterpart in discarded objects without. Abandoned objects symbolize the distance from the turmoil. In *The Poetics of Space*, Gaston Bachelard "writes about the 'hut dream,' an archetypal pastoral and spatial ideal, which is well-known to everyone who cherishes the legendary images of primitive houses. But in most hut dreams we hope to live elsewhere, far from the overcrowded house, far from city cares. We flee in search of a refuge" (40). Oursler is concerned with shapes and forms that can be put to use even within an arena that calls for abandonment and destruction. By attempting to merge aspects of space within an arrangement that denies space and, ultimately, eliminates spatial expansion altogether, Oursler focuses on the dialectics of urban experience. In a way, Oursler infuses an imaginary, shapeless, and fugitive self into spatial metaphor. Remnants of erstwhile habitation convey notions of nostalgia as well as of renewal and a fresh start and, above all, overcome constraints. Ironically, the self is presented triumphantly in its very absence. As Frederick Karl so astutely remarks on American space and spatiality: "Everything will be sacrificed to the inner need to move on," (31) and "The new always beckons; and failure, to a large extent, is marked by remaining" (35). Hence, Oursler's trash photographs are meant to be understood as an obtrusive gesture of triumph. Occasionally, in an almost embarrassed manner, details in those arrangements are hidden underneath plastic wrapping so as not to restrict the viewer's imagination. Oursler implants a human element into arbitrary accumulations of abandoned objects, rummaging through tokens of unconsciously-motivated sculpture. Ultimately, Tony Oursler is turning horrors of an increasingly virtual media culture into slapstick.

Trash is a lucid metaphor of our century and has been employed in the visual arts from the Futurists through Robert Rauschenberg, from Kurt Schwitters to Marcel Duchamp and Pablo Picasso, from the ironical use in the sixties through the sarcastic and cynical use in the nineties.[1] Tony Oursler, a native of New York, where he still lives and works, is an artist who has distinguished himself in his ability to use new idioms of mass communication, from the first videotapes produced in the late seventies, when he was just over twenty, to the unsettling, disturbing figurative works of the early nineties. These latter works involved the projection of talking heads onto puppets and dolls in order to break up the narrative structure which is typically cinematic. The works have a strong emotional impact; the individual is shown as fragmented and limited in potential. In his trash photographs, Oursler conceives of garbage as an empirical experience of unconsciously-motivated sculpture.

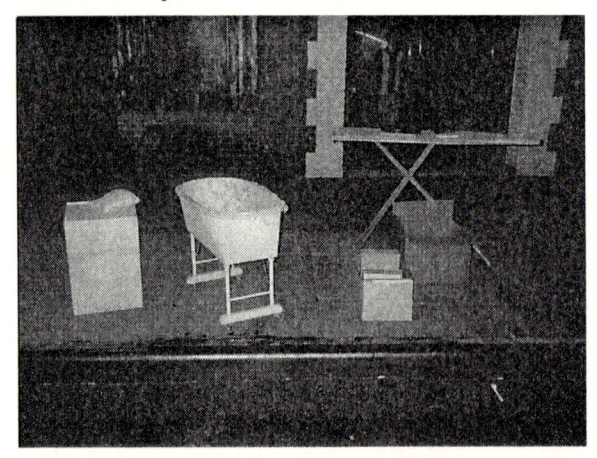

These photographs do not develop their narrative potential, but allow the viewer to infer who or what generated the arrangement. The trash photos are an empirical study of a world in-between, a world between inside and outside, a study conducted by someone who permanently moves between the defined worlds of 'high' and 'low,' 'in' and 'out.' Oursler's photos do not belong to the realm of the pastiche or post-Surrealism, nor are they simply a rejuvenated form of Dada. They may be read as incongruous tokens of a somewhat belated attempt to salvage the self from the detritus of urban life and media overkill. In the same vein as Cindy Sherman's work, the aesthetic exploitation of the discarded object has given way to the artistic attempt to rescue the redundant human being. Oursler reintroduces people discarded from the cycle of production and use, albeit ironically, through their very absence. Oursler intends his work to be an empathy test for the viewer. The idea of progressive fragmentation of the body is the key to Oursler's work. Pain, fear, anger, and memory are central emotions that are employed in a domestic environment that may be encountered outdoors. The possibility of entering the drama of other people's lives, of peering into their homes, exerts a voyeuristic attraction which is taken to the limit in Oursler's trash photos. Ultimately, the individual is revealed as an endangered species within a haunting urban landscape which is inscribed with memories of lives lived and abused, objects possessed and discarded. In his *The World as Sculpture*, James Hall maintains that the interest in detritus, effluvia, leavings—industrial, military and carnal—is in the same vein as the shift to messy, ramshackle mixed-media constructions and thus to more transient forms of art that seem to be supplanting traditional forms of representation (Hall, 1999).

Since the early nineties, Oursler has been working with the human figure in contradictory ways, both endearing and upsetting at the same time. His figures not only annoy the viewer, but are obviously being bothered themselves.

They are squashed under sofas, chair legs, and mattresses, shut up in suitcases and trunks, are hung head-first from the ceiling, are even gored and skewered, all grieving their afflictions in semi-darkness. They are made of fabric, but they seem quite life-like. Little video projectors provide them with a living face, and from loudspeakers an insistent voice can be heard complaining, calling out for help or simply giving a death rattle. His idiosyncratic combination of features of the stage, the cinema, and video art has become his unmistakable trademark. It is as though monitors and canvas had suddenly assumed bodily form. Oursler's figures swiftly

---

[1] Cf. Vergine, *Trash. From Junk to Art.*

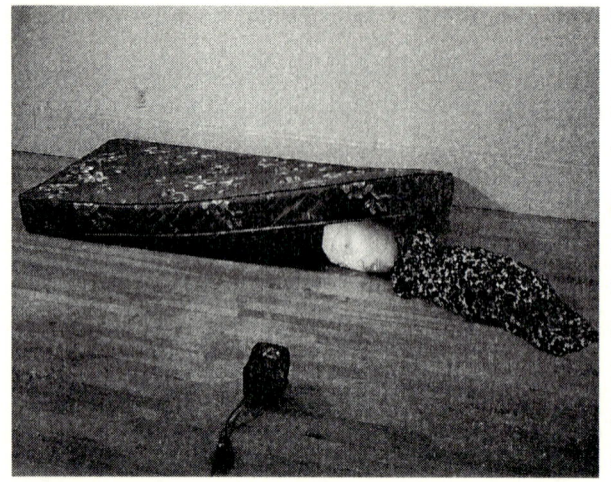

became the darlings of the public (Blase, 370). In a recent series, individual eyes are projected onto large fiberglass spheres, which eerily look from side to side. Initially, the viewer is lured to believe that he might be the object of attention. As he gets closer to the projection, however, he realizes that the eye has apparently been following a TV program. A small blurred picture of a monitor is reflected in the eyeball, and this corresponds to the movements of the pupil. Excitement and fear are evoked in the viewer who is left unsure of what is going on. "But actually the person to whom the eye belongs could feel bored. In this way Oursler demonstrates the mechanisms of the media and at the same time exposes our belief in them" (Blase, 370). Upon closer inspection, the visitor is able to glimpse reflections of a man jogging or doing push-ups. The program's droning soundtrack can also be heard. Bloodshot and prone to blink, the eye seems mesmerized and, at the same time, disoriented by weariness or pain. Like a drug addict suffering from an overdose, the eye looks dazed by media saturation. The viewer is left with the hushed case of an immutably sated eye—baffled, dizzy and obviously incapable of absorbing any more. But the final irony of the work lies in the person's inability to turn away and liberate herself from televisual exhaustion. The eye remains perversely in thrall to the source of its own affliction.[2] Tony Oursler is an artist who is constantly reflecting on the mechanisms of perception shaped by the media which, in his work, are simultaneously endorsed as well as lampooned. Remarking on the deceptions and illusions of space, Oursler says

> I like the idea of someone expecting to "get" an artwork entering an environment where they can't possibly absorb anything within a few seconds or minutes—thus the viewer is put into a different position; they must make a decision of where they stand in relation to the artwork, how they want to read it, how much do they want to invest in the process? (qtd. in Lodi, 25)

Expectations are unhinged and the viewer becomes involved in the dolls' predicament. He is unsettled simply by the lack of orientation, combined with his exposure to extremely private emotions and utterances which, ultimately, are intended to work as an empathy test. "I was deconstructing cinematic genres," Oursler said in an interview,

> and I thought it would be interesting to hire a performer to weep indefinitely, which is how I became involved with Tracy Leipold, who ended up performing in many works. But the first project we did, Crying Doll, featured Tracy weeping for a half an hour straight. This was then projected onto an eight inch doll. The overall effect was an almost fetal, or diminished human who was suffering tremendously. This work was intended to be an empathy test for the viewer. One characteristic of technology, which is quite disconcerting, is that of the perpetual action. What makes the crying doll most effective is its superhuman ability to never stop weeping, which in turn becomes horrifying for the viewer, who eventually must turn away. It is that moment of turning away which the empathy test is all about. (Qtd. in Lodi, 25)

Oursler juggles cinematic and perceptual conventions and denounces the audience's inclination to participate in the exploitation of very private emotions. Oursler's dummies are seen as victims of the somewhat obscene cultural industry, but they strike back with a vengeance. Individuals are rendered as fragmented and perceived as immature objects and as the playthings of a prurient public. Humor and cynicism are enticed in order to release some of the tension incurred.

Oursler engages the viewer's identity directly in installations such as *Mansheshe* (1997), in which several small projections throw hybrid talking heads onto egg-

---

[2] Cf. Cook, "The Blues—Ours and Oursler's."

shaped ovals suspended from poles. The heads, looking directly at the camera (which becomes the viewer), spout aphorisms about sexual identity, personal religious beliefs, and interpersonal relationships. Oursler's work has clear theatrical appeal, masking biting commentary in the guise of humorous, off-beat and fun-projections. Formally, Oursler seeks to remove the image from the television screen and project it onto the real world. (Rush, 154)

Hence, he spatializes, if only virtually, flat images. In Oursler's installations, there is a continual oscillation between reduction and entrapment of the body and, on the other hand, virtual omnipresence of anxieties and trauma. Oursler makes use of "multiple personality disorder" and probes the intricacies of the ubiquitous presence of the media and surveillance systems in order to aesthetically render the experience of fragmented and dissociated personalities. Face and voice, ultimate tokens of individuality, are isolated, subsequently multiplied and translated into virtual space where they constitute a matrix of enveloping archetypal emotions, anxieties, aggression, desires and vices.[3]

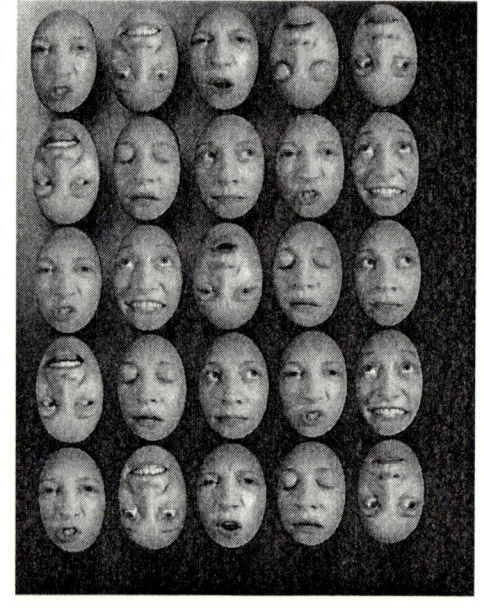

Unable to make the distinction between the self and imaginary aspects of the self, projections, and personality traits evoked by the media, the individual floats in a state of virtual limbo. The self is only to be ascertained through counterfeit attributes as incurred by media exposure. Eventually, the self is dissipated and vanishes into the realm of media-controlled, virtual space. The individual's attempt to pre-

---

[3] Cf. Müller (282).

vent the ultimate dissolution of personality fails due to the figures' very lack of corporeal properties.

Oursler's work is about the loss of information and individuality in the digital age. The face in "Digital" complains "I'm breaking up" and is actually shown in the very process of breaking up as a result of magnifying individual pixels. Unlike the analogous representation pursued through Pop artists like Lichtenstein with his use of Benday dots, Oursler takes the image to the next state of resolution. Heads fade in and out of clarity and emotional states are portrayed comically. Oursler is trying not only to puncture the balloon of high art, but also that of the glory or tragedy of existence.

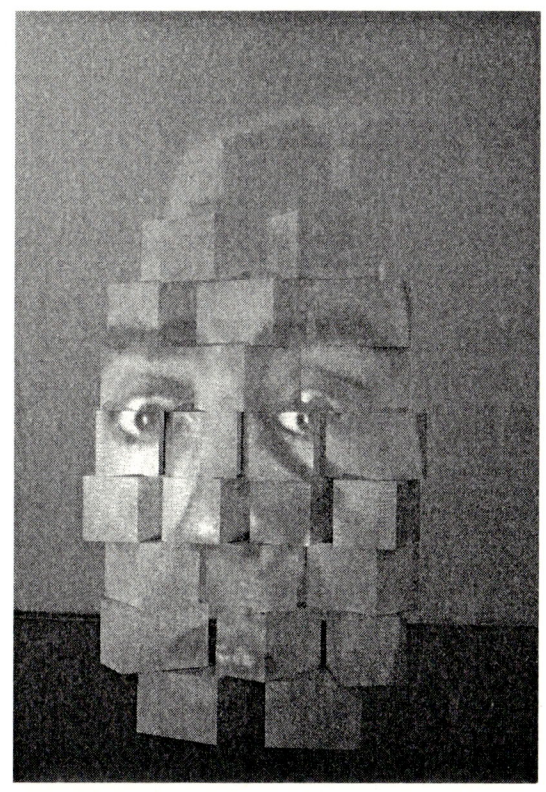

An abject and abandoned place is translated into a work of art by means of astute perception. This translation is indebted to Oursler's drive for composition. Confidence in the epistemological potential of the quotidian, the mundane, and the discarded is ingrained in the American mind. "I do not doubt there is far more in trivialities, insects, vulgar persons, slaves, dwarfs, weeds, rejected refuse, than I have supposed," says Walt Whitman (202).[4]

Oursler's main achievement is the introduction of extremely private and somewhat gruesome emotions into art. In exposing attitudes associated with mental disorders, multiple personality disorder in particular, Oursler oversteps yet another boundary of representation. The diversity in Oursler's approaches is what lends his work a unique quality. The proximity of tokens of American family values (like fabric used for interior decoration in suburbia) and states of acute anxiety convey an eerie atmosphere within the public spaces he creates. The viewer is enticed to wonder whether the whining and whimpering he is witnessing is being triggered by his very presence. The unease thus enforced is eventually released through the ridiculous quality of Oursler's dummies, which appease the viewer by means of their very silliness and absurdity. His dummies are a cynical rendering of the atrophied emotional condition of the TV junkie. In his video environments, Oursler himself remarks, his method is akin to the

> way the TV generation has built a language that is almost psychomimetic. [...] I'm interested in the hypnotic effect of television, its position in society as something that either lulls and acts as a drug, or can be an inspirational factor. The dynamics of the set comes to overpower the human element in the performances, and vice versa. (Nolen et.al., 73)

Tony Oursler has been one of the most inspiring artists of the nineties. His work first became widely known in the late eighties, when he introduced his first dummies and suffering talking heads. Oursler is one of the pioneers of comprehensive video installation which was actually begun as early as 1958, as Michael Rush has shown:

> Multimedia video installations appeared virtually at the same time as single-channel video art, even a little earlier. [...] In common with other Fluxus practices of the period, [Wolf] Vostell was calling into question both the materials of art and the practices of culture, in this case the ubiquitous intrusion of television into everyday life. In reflecting on his work, Vostell noted, "Marcel Duchamp has declared readymade objects as art, and the Futurists declared noises as art—it is an important characteris-

---

[4] Whitman, "Assurances" (202). First published in 1856 as "Faith Poem."

tic of my efforts and those of my colleagues to declare as art the total event, comprising noise/object/movement/color/& psychology—a merging of elements, so that life (man) can be art." [...] Rooted in [a] conceptual approach, and incorporating the practices of performance, body art, and sound art, as well as other aspects of Fluxus, multimedia installation developed, both as a response to the inclusiveness of multiple objects and ideas into the realm of art, and a challenge to the prevailing media institutions, principally television and its bedmate, advertising. (Rush, 117)

Tony Oursler has created a new art form that introduces the element of performance into sculpture. He employs the media in almost vulgar terms, taking the tradition of home videos to obnoxious extremes. Oursler takes various states of anxiety as a point of departure to arrive at a distinctly individual idiom which tackles both the mechanisms of the medium as well as the public's automated responses and perceptions. Beyond outright commentary, Oursler teases elusive responses out of the viewer and, ultimately, exposes our involuntary inclination to be entertained. Mental deviation and anxieties are treated as commodities in the art world, which is invited to shun serious contemplation and rather opt for consumption and entertainment. Oursler's trash photography, then, can be seen as a material extension of his ephemeral video environments that evoke uneasiness as well as amusement. Both responses are so intricately intertwined that Oursler's art may ultimately be seen as an exploration and challenge of the banality and the redundancy of the individual in a world governed by the media. Oursler's work deals with irrationality, anxiety, vice, meanness, phony and commodified emotions, which seem to retaliate but yield nothing but redundancy and impotence. In fact, the art of Tony Oursler may be seen as a cynical foreshadowing of the ubiquitous exploitation of private emotions in a highly competitive entertainment industry that breeds self-exposure, contempt, and ridicule.

The artist does not view himself as a photographer, but utilizes photography as a complementary medium to his installations. The piles of garbage distanced from their human creator may be seen as tokens of unconsciously-motivated sculpture found within the built environment. They are reflections of redundancy and abandonment, a tongue-in-cheek homage to slighted personal memories which, at the same time, refer to architecture and urban space. These photographs reveal the faded beauty of discarded objects. They radiate an eerie atmosphere of short-lived circumstances. Oursler's use of the two-dimensional medium of photography to depict a three-dimensional sculpture, no matter how arbitrary and unconscious it may be, is part of his project to salvage the individual from an inchoate urban environment. According to Boris Groys,

> photography today does in fact do everything that painting did in the nineteenth century—although painting itself later stopped doing it. Photography shows us urban life [...]. Like painting in [the nineteenth] century, however, photography does not merely portray our everyday world, but adopts an attitude towards its problems. (25)

Oursler reveals the hidden material basis of urban life. Photography is, by definition, "evidence of a gesture," "the test of sight" (Virilio, 23). Not only do Oursler's trash photographs raise questions in terms of interior and exterior, settlement and movement, but they also touch upon issues of the metamorphosis from subjectivity to objectivity, from significance to insignificance, and from real to virtual space. This process is illustrative of a transitory esthetic statement and a comment on the ephemeral quality of all objects. Once again, one man's trash is another man's treasure. "Trash is always filled with personal histories" (Rathie and Murphy, 11). Home, as Frederick Karl remarked, "becomes a place that exists in order to be left behind or to disappear" (35).

Oursler's photographs, taken on one of the special pickup days in which sanitation crews collect the bulky durable goods before the garbage collectors arrive and scavengers sweep through the streets and methodically pick through all the household appliances and pieces of furniture in sight, seem like a tongue-in-cheek survey of urban abandonment. The mechanisms of re-use in a culture engrossed in separating and recycling waste within an expanding and diversifying garbage economy has spread to the arts, if only to reveal an arbitrary and unwittingly aesthetic quality. Scrapped items presumably devoid of any obvious commercial value still yield a subliminal potential for narrative and composition. The aesthetic dislike most people would probably take to piles of trash is defied. In Oursler's case, trash represents the tangible equivalent to those emotional states ironically explored in his video environments. The dislocated figural forms in his photographs may be seen as physical extensions of those mental plights. They are shown in a deadlock situation before being scrapped on the garbage heap of contemporary life and urban space.

According to Virilio, "photography is the halting of a hidden sequence, a stop of imagery in progress, between the object aimed at and the fixity of the snapshot" (22). Dislocated from an anonymous domestic interior, household items and furniture assume a fleeting spatio-temporal landmark quality before they are removed from significance to the junkyard from which there is no return other than in recycled shape.

Credits

Picture 1 (p. 264). Oursler, Tony. "Trash (Empirical) *Domestic Exterior.*" 1988. Photo by Tony Oursler. Courtesy Metro Pictures, New York. Reproduced in Eckhard Schneider.41.

Picture 2 (p. 266). Oursler, Tony. "Guilty." 1996. Tracy Leipold, performer; photo by Tony Oursler. Reproduced in Eckhard Schneider. 26.

Picture 3 (p. 268). Oursler, Tony. Untitled. 1999. Videoprojection on fiberglass. Photo by Tony Oursler. Courtesy Tony Oursler, Metro Pictures, New York. Reproduced in Riemschneider. 372f.

Picture 4 (p. 269). Oursler, Tony. "Digital." 1997. Projector, VCR, videotape, 23 blocks of wood. Total dimensions 193 x 137,1 x 91,55 cm. Reproduced in Simona Lodi. 35.

Picture 5 (p. 273). Oursler, Tony. "Trash (Empirical) Funnier than a broken crutch." For Jerry Neville. Photo by Tony Oursler. Courtesy Metro Pictures, New York. Reproduced in Eckhard Schneider. 41.

Bibliography:

Bachelard, Gaston. *The Poetics of Space.* Boston: Beacon Press, 1994.

Blase, Christoph. "Tony Oursler." *Art at the Turn of the Millennium.* Eds. Burkhard Riemschneider and Uta Grosenick. Cologne: Taschen, 1999. 370f.

Cook, Richard. "The blues—ours and Oursler's." *The Times* (March 29, 2000).

Groys, Boris. "The Promise of Photography." *The Promise of Photography* Ed. Luminita Sabau. Munich: Prestel, 1999. 25-32.

Hall, James. *The World as Sculpture: the Changing Status of Sculpture from the Renaissance to the Present Day.* London: Chatto & Windus, 1999.

Karl, Frederick R. *American Fictions 1940-1980. A Comprehensive History and Critical Evaluation.* New York: Harper & Row, 1985.

Lodi, Simona. *Tony Oursler.* Milan: Edizioni Charta, 1998.

Müller, Maria. "Tony Oursler: 'Duplicate yourself.'" *Ich ist etwas Anderes. Kunst am Ende des 20. Jahrhunderts.* Eds. Armin Zweite, Doris Krystof, Reinhard Spieler. Kunstsammlung Nordrhein-Westfalen, Düsseldorf. Cologne: DuMont, 2000. 282f.

Nolen, Leslie et.al., eds. *The BiNational: American Art of the Late 80s.* Cologne: DuMont, 1988.

Phillips, Lisa. *The American Century. Art & Culture 1950-2000.* New York: Norton, 1999.

Poetter, Jochen, ed. *I love New York. Crossover der aktuellen Kunst.* Cologne: DuMont, 1998.

Rathje, William and Cullen Murphy. *Rubbish!: The archaeology of garbage.* New York: HarperPerennial, 1992.

Rush, Michael. *New Media in Late 20th-Century Art.* London: Thames & Hudson, 1999.

Schneider, Eckhard, ed. *Tony Oursler. Videotapes, Dummies, Drawings, Photographs, Viruses, Light, Heads, Eyes, and CD-ROM.* Hanover: Kunstverein Hannover, 1998.

Vergine, Lea. *Trash. From Junk to Art.* Milan: Electa, 1997.

Virilio, Paul. "Photo Finish." *The Promise of Photography.* Ed. Luminita Sabau. Munich: Prestel, 1999. 19-24.

'Real' and Constructed Space

Arthur Erickson as Architectural Link between Canada and USA, between Old and New World Cultural Concepts

Christian W. Thomsen

There can hardly be any doubt that Arthur Erickson is Canada's best and most noteworthy architect of the 20th century, one of the few Canadian architects comparatively well known in the US and even in Europe. Vancouver-born Arthur Erickson of ultimately Swedish origin has all his life been a fervent traveler and connoisseur of architectural excellence around the globe, a man deeply rooted in music and the arts and, above all, in the history of architecture.

He was trained at McGill, Montreal, from 1947-1951, where his teachers strictly exercised the principles and dogmas of classical modernism and cured young Erickson of his romantic predilection for Frank Lloyd Wright's Talisien West. He started practicing in 1953 and found to his particular form of modernism in a series of wooden houses throughout the sixties which count among the masterful examples of a specific West Coast Style, mainly employed in and around West Vancouver.

Painter Gordon Smith and his wife Marion, a weaver, had been Erickson's first daring clients with a very small budget who commissioned him to design a home for the newlyweds in 1953. Eleven years later, Gordon having become a well-known professor of painting at UBC's Department of Fine Arts, he commissioned Erickson for his second house, still at a budget extremely low by today's standards of less than 50,000 CAN $. The Smiths collaborated with Erickson in the design and execution of the garden and after a freshening and polishing up in the mid-eighties, this house remains a jewel of West Coast modern architecture to the present day.

Erickson, like most of his early fellow architects, was deeply influenced by those demigods of modernism called Martin Gropius, Ludwig Mies van der Rohe, and Marcel Breuer, but in a thoroughly aesthetic sense minus the social commitment which originally went along with Bauhaus modernism. Another towering influence he shared with most architects of his generation was that of Le Corbusier, whose famous definition of architecture as "le jeu savant, correct, et magnifique des volumes assemblés sous la lumière" became the obvious source for the four corner pillars of this own architectural creed: "site—light—cadence—space." As a third generation modernist he did not feel compelled to adhere to the orthodoxies established by those early pioneers.[1] Modern architects he felt completely at home with were Louis Kahn and I. M. Pei, mostly because of the sculptural qualities of their oeuvre.

These are a few of the architectural prerequisites with which Erickson approached the site of the Smiths in West Vancouver. In his mind also worked the experience of his enthusiastic visit to Japan three years earlier where for the first time he carefully studied traditional Japanese house and landscape architecture. The Smith site is located on a strategic point of great natural beauty, above the sea where two side inlets of the Strait of Georgia unite and it offers views of breathtaking beauty.

Environment and landscape are of particular interest to Erickson, because they determine the conditions of light and henceforth the human perception of space:

> I wanted the Smith house to reveal the site in the same way it revealed to me when I first walked into it. Through the forest cleaning, one would discover the fern-covered rift between the rocks; then, at the end, the distant sea view through the vertical stems of young firs. To keep these inherent characteristics unspoiled demands the very careful placement of the building parts so that they occupied the least interesting parts of the site, thus saving the best parts for the enjoyment from the house. After the approach through the forest, stepping up to the entrance you see across the courtyard and under the living room bridge the light from the sea far away through the fir trees. The inner courtyard is an architectural reiteration of the forest cleaning—a monument of containment before the release of space into the surroundings.

---

[1] Cf. Peter Blake, Foreword to *The Architecture of Arthur Erickson*, 1988 (9-11).

Progressive discovery of the house and site is made possible by overlapping and stepping up each wing of the house in a kind of spiral. It starts at the *porte cochere*, climbs up to the kitchen dining wing, up to the living room, then to the bedrooms and continues outside, to the roof of the *porte cochere*, up to the roof of the kitchen and so on, intimating an endless spiral. At each corner is an anchor point—the studio at the entrance corner, the dining terrace at the viewpoint, the living room terrace into the forest, and a bedroom terrace edging the forest. Whereas the living room is a suspended box of rough wood and glass, the studio is a sky-lit solid enclosure with narrow slits of windows giving an even illumination to all the walls. (Erickson, 81)[2]

Rough fir and glass in unbroken sheets are the basic building materials of this house which thereby integrates into the environment, into nature. In a Miesian way of floating spaces the house opens up to nature, nature is drawn into the house. In his publications Erickson never speaks about the cultural ideas behind his buildings and what the owners made of them. Yet at closer observation, these ideas can be gradually revealed layer by layer.

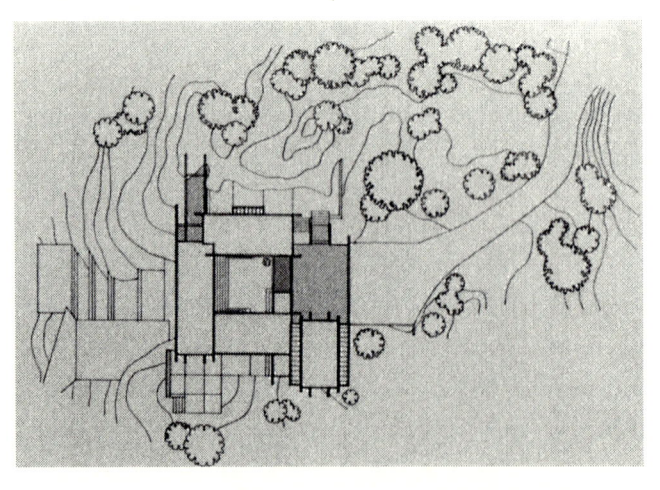

British born artists Gordon and Marion Smith, two culturally very conscious and alert but also very modest human beings together with Vancouver-born architect Arthur Erickson developed and practice a cultural concept here which could serve as a model for a Province still called 'British Columbia' and also for the entire Pacific North West.

---

[2] *The architecture of Arthur Erickson*, 1975 (81).

On a first level their home resembles the typical British fort, a bold statement placed into the wilderness, defendable on all sides and from the roof tops: "We are here and we take possession of this land, tame this wilderness." The house's rectangularity as well as that of the landscaping of the garden creates that typical gesture of modernity, yet also quotes elements of Japanese garden architecture. Already at second glance it becomes obvious how much their concept differs from that of earlier colonists who drove local cultures into the sea without ever reflecting upon their values and native rights.

Instead of taking a defensive attitude and shutting itself off against the environment, the house takes a conciliatory attitude. Its post and beam construction was used by Erickson's Swedish ancestors, by early settlers, native Haida and Kwakiutl Indians alike. Here, at the Pacific Rim, Japan is far west and Europe far east. The house is an outpost of western civilization and simultaneously it fuses influences of western Bauhaus and traditional Japanese architecture. Gordon Smith, the British Canadian painter, deliberately chose an architect who gave his studio the form of a traditional Haida Long House. The interior courtyard may reiterate the typical forest clearing, but the Smiths also turned it into a biotope, into an almost sacred place of worship to nature. The living room glass bridge and outlook at the same time is dominated by an immense sculptural fireplace of Arthur Erickson's which expresses its nature as both modern sculpture and archaic altar, the holy fireplace. The classical modernism of Corbusian and Marcel Breuer chairs and settees accentuates Modernist convictions, yet turned towards a harmonious coexistence with nature and native influences.

This is reflected in Gordon Smith's art collection as well. Despite his being one of the best Canadian landscape painters, there is not a single painting of his own to be found in his house. Smith turned the house into a small, but exquisite gallery of classical modernist art: Leger, Picasso, Klee, Matisse, delicate small originals from a time when they were still affordable, alongside Haida Bill Reid and Robert Davidson and little, native pieces of sculpture from around the world. There is no hierarchy, the only criterion is artistic excellence.

The Smiths breathed a soul into Modernist functionalism, thereby establishing a new cultural ideal and identity to a whole region, one that harmoniously consoles and combines western, eastern, and Native American characteristics. In the midsixties, this was almost as prophetic as were the paintings of Emily Carr, and it certainly contributed to a changing awareness of public opinion, education, and research in British Columbia. Gordon Smith, moreover, was for a long time deeply involved in the revival of Native American art, fighting alongside Bill Reid and Arthur Erickson for the recognition of native culture, the latter attaining international fame by designing—among many other public and private commissions—the UBC Vancouver's Museum of Anthropology (1972-1979). It stands out as one of the most brilliant museum buildings of the seventies, bringing Erickson's concepts of a new cultural identity of the North-West Coast into a unique form by turning the idea of the Haida Long House, built of huge cedar beams, into his magnificent Great Hall, constructed out of glass and concrete:

> Knowing the Native use of enormous split cedar logs and their exaggerated, luxurious effect, I felt that a similar ponderous weight and disregard for structural reality could pertain here. We could show the same generosity and flamboyant disdain for economy as the Native people in their potlatches and still suggest their reverence for nature; so we began the process of establishing supports for a deep-beamed structure.[3] (Erickson, 87-88).

Yet by that time Arthur Erickson, who designed a modern palace for his final student thesis, had discovered his taste for luxury and for concrete as "the stone of the 20th century." We had many arguments about his predilection for concrete, which, indeed, he used to treat with utmost care and which he intended to bring to a perfection comparable to the finest creations of Renaissance architecture. "Athenians had their Pentelic marble, we have our concrete," (Erickson, 97)[4] he used to say, a statement I could never agree with, because I thought about the long-term weather

---

[3] *The Architecture of Arthur Erickson* (87-88).
[4] The Architecture of Arthur Erickson (197).

effects on concrete which are so more visibly harmful, even damaging to constructions, than those on stone-clad buildings, especially in a moist climate like the North West's.

Twenty years after *Smith-House 2*, in 1983 Erickson, who now ran successful offices in Vancouver, Los Angeles, and Toronto, started designing another cultural statement near Tacoma, in terms of a private home on a little peninsula overlooking Puget Sound. Close to the prototypical little Western town Key, the old 200 acre farming estate of the Russell family became a playground for a mix of brilliant postmodern ideas. With the old farm building still on the site, looking down a slope to their private beach, the Russells wanted a new, more comfortable, luxurious home:

> Their property was a wonderfully diverse spread; grazing fields for their Arabian horses, berry patches, fruit orchards, a swampy glade, and a forest of conifers, broadleaf maples and arbutus on a cliff face spilling down to the beach. After my initial visit, I practically invented my own program, for I wanted the house to partake of all these special natural features and each room to capture a different light.[5] (Erickson, 199).

The Russells are a wealthy family who manage the pension funds of several big companies like Shell. Globalization, now a common phenomenon to almost everybody in business, was still in the early stages, but for the Russells it already meant everyday routine. Their main office is located in Tacoma, but at the heart of their new country home, already in 1987 a computer center was installed that connected them with stock markets around the globe.

Erickson managed to combine and synthesize a number of ideas, namely that of the farm forming a little village consisting of several buildings, that of a modern country villa, and that of a small country seat, with references dating back even to Greek temples, and Romanesque medieval ruins as shown in his skillfully disguised garage building.

---

[5] The Architecture of Arthur Erickson (199).

Again Erickson is trying to establish a new cultural identity for his native North West, which he regards as an ethnic and cultural entity divided by an artificial modern border between Canada and the US, which sooner or later will disappear

again. For the Native Americans the place was sacred, for its modern American owners it is just a place with a fine view, a home for relaxation which also could be used for work. In contrast to his early Vancouver houses, Erickson does not allude to West Coast first nations' culture here as he almost at the same time did in a nearby Seattle home of another rich client where he amalgamated the local post and beam construction with that of a modern villa in glass and concrete. Instead, he tried to endow the place with a new identity which is a compound of a kind of a universal Mediterraneity and the American West. Self-critically he had much earlier commented on his first architectural endeavors in the fifties:

> Like any young man beginning his profession I was still testing for a direction. I struggled with the light and the beauty of the Northwest Coast sites, but the lingering images of the great architecture on the shores of the Mediterranean had a subtle, subduing effect on my modernist enthusiasm.[6]

---

[6] Cf. Blake, "Preface" (8).

Here, once and for all, he could give free rein to his Mediterranean imagination. A variation of roof forms from flat roof to pyramidal tent roof, from saddle roof to gabled roof or to barrel vaulting in the entrance area, plays an important role in this game. A semi-Japanese bath, a quasi-monastic kitchen garden with many herbs and flowers, a ceremonial dining room under a vaulted roof, a fantastic view from the living room and master bedroom across Puget Sound prepare for the garden rest place and viewpoint which is the quasi-sacred center of the whole complex, equipped with columns, uniting earth and sea and skies, a place of worship to nature's beauty, of rest and of sheer aesthetic pleasure, inspired by Erickson's visit to the Acropolis shortly before. One of the characteristic features of Ericksonian elegance consists in the leveled water basins in front of bedroom windows. You wake up and you look across water planes in your garden in the extension of which the Pacific Ocean stretches out. Exquisite materials and perfect craftsmanship make the Russell House a place where landscape, environment, and culture form a union that claims a new identity for this westernmost position of our civilization. German-Canadian landscape architect Cornelia Hahn-Oberlander created a natural garden-landscape with meadows, flowers, and bushes for all seasons which makes this place a multi-sensory pleasure and enjoyment all year round.

From the point of view of architectural theory, Erickson fuses elements of modernism with historical references of postmodernism into a very elegant union, bringing the old rural farming tradition of the family to a contemporary level of postmodern, postindustrial living. He himself stated:

> It was 1983 (when I designed this house), and Postmodernism was swirling around with its historical contrivances. Here was also a chance to play teasingly with fashion and to show it up; so we have a house that looks like a house "should," with pitched roofs and lots of columns and slatted sliding. Anybody can provide that outline. The real lesson and attraction of history's archetype lie much deeper.[7] (Erickson, 199).

This game with archetypes refers right back to architectural dreams of Erickson's youth, but business clients like the Russells lack the specific cultural understanding for these intentions. A more striking contrast as that between the Smiths and their educated artistic sensibility and the Russells as prototypical successful American business people, frank, open-minded, but without major cultural pretensions, can hardly be imagined. Erickson nevertheless certainly reached them on a psychological level, where his sense for light, spatial rhythms coincided with their requirements for a family home and their pride and pleasure in this particular place with a family history behind it. And, of course, their home cost more than 50 times as much as that of the Smiths.

The third Erickson house I want to present is one that combines the American tradition of modernity with German craftsmanship and Canadian ingenuity. In 1953 the twin brothers Helmut and Hugo Eppich, both fitters, emigrated from Franconia to Vancouver. Their little trade soon began to flourish and became a typical 'from rags to riches'-success story. Thirty years later they were the most successful entrepreneurs in British Columbia, owning steel mills, furniture factories, and other

---

[7] The Architecture of Arthur Erickson (199).

mixed enterprises. Helmut built a residence with Erickson which won international fame in 1974. A couple of years later Hugo wanted one as well. It was originally designed in 1979, but its final completion took until 1991. Hugo wanted to act as his own general contractor, having all materials and furniture for his home produced in his own factories. It was the dream and the adventure of his life. Being a steel man, he wanted a house in glass and steel. But as a model Arthur Erickson took the ultimate icon of modern American architecture, Frank Lloyd Wright's *Fallingwater House* (1935-39). The *Eppich House* sits on a West Vancouver hill like a high-tech racing yacht, overlooking the Strait of Georgia, ready to go full speed every moment. It is a dramatic response to the challenges of the rugged, irregularly shaped site, sharply sloping towards a creek, surrounded by abundant stands of alder and scattered evergreens, and offering spectacular views of downtown Vancouver.

The building takes the L-shape from *Fallingwater*. The entry terrace and reflecting pool appear to be one with that of the mid-level on the west side, creating an effect as if the building is suspended above. The walls of these terraces are formed of fieldstone, uncovered at the site during excavation and placed on the outer surface of the formwork before pouring concrete. Water from reflecting pools on each level cascades and disappears behind continuous planters overflowing with trailing roses along the top of each wall. The water cascades, but the house cascades down to the water as well.

The interior, like the exterior, is a harmony of contrasts. The precise character of the building materials has created a somewhat reflective but sometimes transparent skin in which the ever changing natural surroundings are continually being mirrored. Similarly, inside, a palette of hard, reflective materials such as chromed stainless steel, brushed aluminum, and glass receive warmth from natural materials such as the blonde sandstone floor and a re-sawn hemlock board ceiling. Warm beige walls were chosen as a neutral background for the colorful primary accents of soft leather custom furnishings, carpets, and artwork.[8]

I accompanied this house from the laying down of the foundation stone to its completion. I experienced my friend Hugo's pride in the construction of the largest steel girders produced so far for a single house in North America and fitted with an exactitude of less than two millimeters clearance. Erickson designed them, but he and his German engineers and workmen actually manufactured and installed them. The same goes for the furniture designed by Erickson's partner Francisco Kripacz, custom made by Hugo and his cabinet makers.

The house breathes cool elegance, warmth radiates from Cornelia Oberlander's garden architecture. It is by no means to everybody's taste. Brigitte Eppich, Hugo's wife, heartily disliked it for quite some time. She missed her snug little wooden house filled with memories of Germany, Heino records, growing children, and gradual acclimatization to their new life in Canada. She in some ways lost her past when Hugo fulfilled his dreams by moving into their new home. Within one decade he repeated for himself what generations of pioneers had achieved as their life's work in the West. But this time it was executed on a high-tech level. I never met a person with greater reverence for the genius of his architect than Hugo Eppich. For him Erickson's plans and ideas were sacrosanct. Whatever he and Francisco designed, Hugo and his crew gave shape and substance to it and their dedication was the virtual stuff that souls are made of, thus giving life to cool materials like glass, steel, aluminum, and leather.

Home is, after all, where the soul feels at home, and the soul feels at home where the house has a soul. But people's tastes and souls, thanks to our genes, par-

---

[8] Cf. Arthur Erickson Architects, "Hugo Eppich Residence" (1992, 94.-105).

ents, education, and environment are very different. On a certain level there is only good, mediocre, and bad architecture.

The three Arthur Erickson houses presented in this article are certainly examples of good architecture. At the beginning of a new century we are able now to look back on the twentieth century as a whole and gradually developments are being put into historical perspective. From the point of view of architecture I think it is justified to talk about the previous century as the 'age of modernism'. From this perspective the three Erickson houses represent three characteristic variants of modernism, each endowed with a personal handwriting:

Smith House, a symbiosis of classical Bauhaus modernism, filtered by Japanese influences, both integrated with allusions to local, native Haida traditions of Long House post and beam construction; as such this house suggests a possible new modern identity for the Pacific Rim.

The *Russell House*, representing the postmodern variant of modernism, merging the traditions of Western farm houses and villages, modernizing them by simultaneously integrating historical influences from classical antiquity to medieval allusions in roof forms and hand built walls of carefully selected field stones to modern country residences: "All having differing views, compositions, scales and styles yet create among them a strange and compelling tension that is fundamental to our fascination with the whole [...] the result is a decidedly picturesque composition."[9] (Erickson, 197).

The new identity it creates is a truly postmodern one, indicating that modernism transforms itself into an immensely variable mix of composites which combines historical consciousness with local allusions and such of a refined tradition of European influences gone American with remarkable freshness and playfulness. As such it stands for another possible positive alternative for twenty-first century architecture.

The *Eppich House*, which originally was designed four years earlier than the *Russell House*, stands in the tradition of high-tech engineering which claims the genuine place in architectural art. Erickson, moreover, shows how it can achieve a symbiosis with regional landscape and garden architecture. Simultaneously he plays ingeniously with *the* icon of typical American modernism, namely Frank Lloyd Wright's *Fallingwater*, which, after all, was one of the buildings that have inspired him and many other architects until the present day.

Together the three residences demonstrate the mature craftsmanship and the width of the scale of artistic ingenuity in the *oeuvre* of a modern architect who links Canadian and American regional traditions with historical European influences and global contemporary developments.

Credits:

Picture 1 (p. 278). Smith House Ground Plan.
Picture 2 (p. 282). Russell House (living room at night). Photo by Wayne Fuji.
Picture 3 (p. 283). Russell House (sea view with garden temple). Photo by C. W. Thomsen.
Picture 4 (p. 285). Eppich House (terraces). Photo by C. W. Thomsen.

Bibliography

Blake, Peter. Foreword to *The Architecture of Arthur Erickson*. Text by Arthur Erickson. Vancouver/Toronto: Douglas & McIntyre, 1988. 9-11.

Erickson, Arthur. *The architecture of Arthur Erickson*. With Text by the architect. Tundra Books of Montreal, Quebec, 1975.

--- "Hugo Eppich Residence, West Vancouver, British Columbia." *Global Architecture, GA Houses*, 33. A. D. A. EDITA (Tokyo Feb. 1992): 94-105.

- *The Architecture of Arthur Erickson*

---

[9] *The Architecture of Arthur Erickson* (197).

Protecting Open Space:
The Urban Sprawl Discussion in the USA and in Germany

Bernd Streich, Carsten Hagedorn, Sabine Wolf

1. An Understanding of the City

The present physical structure of cities is a product of socio-political systems with diverse ideologies regarding the city. The conceptions of urban planning and design, location of services and facilities of all kinds as well as the principles of segregation of society differ greatly from one another (cf. Lichtenberger).

The definition of the term 'city' is difficult due the multidisciplinarity of its discussion. The primary differentiation lies in the distinction between a historical and a contemporary understanding of 'city.' The definitions of both the historical and contemporary 'city' make systematic as well as spatial references. The historical definition is determined by four factors—containment by an enclosing wall, intersection of streets, arrangement of the city in quarters and a special judicial status. In addition to these spatial criteria which make reference to the term 'city,' the contemporary definition of the term contains systematic criteria of size, density, and income structure of the population. Our understanding of mobility and the individual relationship toward this additional factor has grown in importance as well (Lichtenberger, 35ff.).

Today, the city is the human settlement form with the highest population. In Germany, the image of the compact European city with a historical core strongly influences the population's perception as well as the political and cultural discussion. However, the reality of the city is something else entirely, and has been so for some time: even in Germany the historical city core makes up only a fraction of the city's area. About 90% of a city's populated area lies outside of the core (cf. Sieverts).

The positive connotations of the historical city are countered by the perception of the periphery. Massive use of open space, sprawl, disjunction, etc. are the negative terms associated with a loss of clearly-defined urban structures. The hierarchical relationship and dependence between core city and surrounding area have changed drastically: the peripheral structures carry out distinctively urban functions and are no longer purely residential areas. Were they to disappear, they would leave behind a core without basis for existence. This dynamically spreading global phenomenon has, to date, not been termed consistently worldwide. In Germany, it is usually condensed in the term 'dispersed settlement' (*Zersiedlung*), whereas in the USA the term 'urban sprawl' is commonly used.

This paper is intended to serve as an introduction to the current discussion of peripheral growth in the US and in Germany, based on a description of American urban sprawl and a comparison with the development of suburban areas in Germany. The goal of this paper is to show the potential inherent in new methods of information and visualization to make the population aware of 'urban sprawl.'

2. Urban Sprawl

The diverging terms used in the US and in Germany shall briefly be introduced before defining 'urban sprawl,' as it is used in this paper, since no commonly accepted term for development in the area surrounding cities exists.

In the US, the development in the area surrounding cities is commonly termed 'urban sprawl': "It is a problem that affects urban, suburban, and rural communities. The results of sprawl range from the loss of farmland to the decay of older urban centers" (Senville). Simple definitions are hard to come by because there is no clear-cut distinction between sprawl and suburbanization. It is hard to say exactly where sprawl begins and ends (cf. Schmidt).

There is no universal definition for the development in suburban areas surrounding German cities; the terms most often used are 'dispersed settlement' and 'surface consumption.' Strategies with which one hopes to counteract the further spread of cities are termed 'sustainable urban development' and do not constitute a separate research category. The term 'urban sprawl' will be used in the following to categorize the processes of suburbanization in the US as well as in Germany. It is understood as follows: sprawl is dispersed and low-density development outside of compact urban and village centers along highways and in rural areas. Because of the low density of these settlements, cars are necessary in order to move. One of the most negative consequences of sprawl is the loss of land.

3. Models of Urban Development

The onset of industrialization radically changed the make-up of cities. Formerly compact cities spread into open space so that, presently, the suburbanization of living and working comprises the greater part of modern city development. The increase in the number and use of cars in society together with growing individual income brought about the first highpoints of this development in the 1960's in Germany, comparable to the development in the US 40 years earlier. A standstill has not been reached, rather, cities continue to spread (cf. Ronneberger, Lanz, and Jahn).

The English architectural critic, Cedric Price visualized the different historical phases of city development in a very comprehensible manner by comparing them with different methods of preparing an egg. Price argued that the cities of antiquity through history all the way to the cities of the absolutist late-baroque period which consisted of a center and an outer area within fortifying walls are comparable to a hard-boiled egg with yolk and shell. During industrialization, however, the city spread outwards. A loosely knit core is surrounded by suburban space and a freely flowing fringe. The industrial metropolis takes on the form of a fried egg. Today's city is similar to a scrambled egg with bits of bacon. Center and periphery are mixed and spread out in all directions—the urban sprawl (cf. Price). A further, empirically based model is proposed by van den Berg et al. on the basis of a research project concerning 189 city regions between 1960 and 1970. This model considers functional urban regions (FUR) and uses figures of population change in the core, ring, and functional urban region. This model suggests a patterned development of cities, postulating four phases based on the change in population and employment structure in the core and ring.

- Urbanization Phase: strong population increase in the core city
- Suburbanization Phase: relative stronger population increase in the ring
- De-urbanization Phase: population decrease in the entire area
- Re-urbanization Phase: relative population increase in the core city

It has as yet not been empirically proven whether the phase of re-urbanization will actually take place, and especially if the core city will grow while the population of the ring declines. In the US, the phase of de-urbanization led to urban sprawl. In Germany, cities are still categorized as being in the phase of de-urbanization with a continual population shift toward rural areas.

A key concept to the understanding of urban sprawl is mobility. Mobility is defined by four factors: activity, route traveled, duration, and distance. The amount of time spent per day on the move (one hour) as well as the number of routes traveled and activities carried out has remained constant over the past 30 to 40 years. The only variable which has changed is that of distance. The variable of distance has doubled, if not tripled. This has formed the basis for the shift of urban activities to the surrounding area. The relationship toward mobility, in particular, the choice of transportation, is considered to be a dominant factor in the development of urban sprawl.

4. Spatial Planning in the Context of Society USA/Germany

The key to understanding spatial planning in America lies in the political and cultural traditions which formed the American consciousness and values of its society. Important roots of American culture and American consciousness are utilitarian individuality and a puritanical rural set of ethics. Local autonomy, equality, freedom of the individual, and the protection of individual property thus have the highest priority and are directly manifested in the Constitution of the United States. Political and cultural traditions and values broke openly with structures of power of European example. No potential constriction of personal or individual desire or property was accepted. With the onset of the Cold War, anything restricting personal freedom was seen to be indicative of communist or socialist tendencies and, as such, not worthy of discussion. This fact emphasizes key differences between the political-cultural traditions and values of German and American society.

Characteristic for Germany is an interest in the well-being of society as a whole and a system of government which goes beyond the individual, rather than focusing on privacy and individualism. The values of German society are strongly influenced by a clearly hierarchical federal system of 16 states headed by the Federation (*Bund*). A tradition of planning exists in which concepts, ideals and projects of the 19th and 20th century were transformed into building laws and codes. The European tradition of urban planning has important roots in both the progressive reform-oriented movement to improve the living conditions of the working classes as well as the conservative ambitions of the Arts and Crafts or Home and Hearth movement. The German system of government uses the Federation as a regulative force with regard to social projects such as regional and city development, whereas, in the US, the power of the state is fragmented and the Constitution is not endowed with a mandate to foster regional or municipal growth.

4.1 Parameters of Planning Law in the USA

Concepts which are anchored in the Constitution of the United States weave a mesh of participants and create a culture of decision-making that diverges from the German system. Privatism, the concession that private and privately financed participants play a key role in city development, individualism, and pluralism are characteristic of federal-policy with regard to cities as well as regions. Thus, the influence of political participants on city development and infrastructure planning is weak. Federal laws governing city development in the entire country must be brought into effect by the individual states. The American planning system, in contrast, does not have a coordinated regional planning policy. Until 1998 less than a dozen of the country's 330 Metropolitan Areas had a regional government. On a communal level this means that the prosperity of individual cities and regions has always been more dependent on individual entrepreneurship than on communal planning. The public image of the city is thus much more the product of the economic goals of developers and builders than of city-planning. Existing planning is strongly influenced by economic interests and lobbyists (cf. Palm).

Nonetheless, since 1920, classical planning instruments exist which are comparable at least in scale with the German *Flächennutzungsplan* (plan governing land-use), the *Bebauungsplan* (plan governing built volumes), and the *Baunutzungsverordnung*. The two most established planning instruments are the Comprehensive Plan and the Zoning Ordinances. The Comprehensive Plan (a type of *Flächennutzungs-* and *Bebauungsplan*), concerned with the entire community, is established for a time of ca. 20 years and aims toward the total development of a city. The most common tool of regulating the use of land a city has is called 'zoning.' Similar to the German *Baunutzungsverordnung*, it governs the specific use of a building, its position on the plot of land and the possible use of the land. In addition, there are a number of instruments made for an individual state's political context and specific goals. Nineteen states have implemented Urban Growth Boundaries (UGB) to deal with the phenomenon of urban sprawl in reaction to the unhindered growth of American cities.

4.2 Parameters of Planning Law in Germany

In Germany, the use of land is coordinated by government planning, oriented toward the welfare of the majority and assisted by public planning law. The German Constitution (*Grundgesetz*) allots autonomy and communal self-government to communities and states, similar to the procedures in the US. It gives the Federation the right to pass laws if the equality of living-conditions beyond the border of an individual state so necessitate it. It also increases the Federation's power to pass regulations on spatial organization (*Raumordnung*) and laws regarding land within the bounds of competing legislation. The *Grundgesetz*—and here US and German procedures differ—governs the tasks as well as their allotment to either nation or state. The *Raumordnung* consists of three stages: federal, state (including the regional level) and municipal.

The Usage Plan (*Flächennutzungsplan*) is responsible for overall planning, specifically regarding the use of land, for the entire community within a time span of 10 to15 years. The communities as well as other bodies of planning are bound by this Usage Plan (cf. Schlichter and Stich, 280), whereas private persons are exempt from its regulations. The Plan of Built Volume (*Bebauungsplan*) contains the legally binding considerations of city planning.

5. A Comparison of Urban Sprawl Discussions

The discussion of urban sprawl differs considerably in Germany and the USA. In Germany, the public generally has not yet recognized the implications of widespread settlement, and thus discussions are held almost exclusively on a professional level. In the US, the discussion is far more controversial and broader due to the fact that the population is directly confronted with the effects of a more extensive urban sprawl and is thus sensitive to the topic.

5.1 State of the Discussion in the USA

The discussion in the US is of a rather emotional nature, and participants are, for the most part, private groups, initiatives, foundations, etc. In particular, local initiatives attempt to stop the sprawl in their area, but there are also regional and national groups that fight the sprawl:

In January 1999, Vice President Al Gore launched a comprehensive **Liveability Agenda** to help the nation seek a high quality of life and sustainable economic growth. The agenda focuses on strengthening the federal role in support of state and local efforts to build liveable communities. As the administration continues to work with and learn from states, municipalities, and other stake-holders, it will develop new tools and strategies to help them preserve open space, curb suburban sprawl, ease traffic congestion, and pursue other 'smart growth' activities.

The Smart Growth Network is an effort to design an approach to growth that identifies common ground where developers, environmentalists, public officials, citizens, and financiers can find ways to accommodate growth that is acceptable to each entity. The goal is not to stop growth, but to accommodate growth in sensible ways that preserve the integrity of the community, protect the environment, and enhance economic vitality. Smart Growth is about being fiscally responsible with tax dollars, investing in existing infrastructure, and eliminating obstacles to infill and the prohibitive costs of redevelopment.

Congress for the New Urbanism (CNU) is an urban-planning reformation movement which established itself out of critical positions toward urban sprawl and a call for alternatives. It is organized around a series of yearly conventions on various topics. It calls for "mixed-use, mixed neighborhoods, higher density, architectural diversity, orientation on historical city plans, orientation on regional architectural tradition, pedestrian friendliness, advancement of alternative transportation, a reduction of vehicular traffic, and [...] more time when realizing urban projects" (Bodenschatz, 24).

The Sierra Club, America's largest environmental group, has made stopping sprawl a top national priority. The Club published various reports with the subject urban sprawl, for example, the Sprawl Reports in 1998 and 1999. The objective of the Sierra Club's national challenge with the Sprawl Campaign is to provide materials, winning strategies, training, and funding to better equip the club's volunteers and staff for changing the sprawling suburban development patterns.

Sprawl, however, is not only considered to be negative. A number of initiatives see the potential to realize the American dream of a single family home with a large plot of land in urban sprawl. These groups consider the density of cities to be problematic enough for them to prefer urban sprawl:

1000 Friends of Oregon is a non-profit charitable organization, founded in 1975 by Governor Tom McCall and Henry Richmond as the citizens' voice for land use planning that protects Oregon's quality of life from the effects of growth. The organization promotes compact, liveable cities with affordable housing, green spaces, and transportation alternatives. These objectives are to be achieved through Oregon's pioneering state-wide program to plan for Oregon's growth in conjunction with other state, local, and regional land-use planning efforts.

The **Heritage Foundation** is a think-tank based in Washington, DC. Its program focuses on "defending property rights" and attacking government regulation.

The Los Angeles-based Reason Foundation is a conservative, libertarian national research and educational organization that advocates public policies based on a free-market approach. **Reason Public Policy Institute**, a division of the Reason Foundation, fuses theory and practice to influence public policies. RPPI publishes pro-sprawl reports such as "The Sprawling of America: In Defense of the Dynamic City," by Samuel R. Staley, which challenges the need for Clinton/Gore smart growth policies.

5.2 State of the Discussion in Germany

The professional discussion in Germany is top-down, being led by public institutions. Local initiatives that fight dispersal are unknown. 'Sustainable development' is the topic of numerous investigations, reports, and conferences. Dispersed settlement, however, while an important aspect, does not constitute a central issue.

The **Federal Government** has published numerous studies, reports, and positions on the topic of "Sustainable Development" through different ministries. According to the authors of the "National Plan of Action for Sustainable Settlement Development" and the "Sustainable City Habitat II," it is of central importance to charge the respective party with the ensuing ecological and social costs of disorderly settlement, in particular with regard to infrastructure. The Federal Research Institute for Geography and Spatial Order's (BfLR) city-planning report "Sustainable Development" deals more concretely with the subject of dispersal. The goal of the report is the "Defense of Natural Resource-Capital." In this regard, a five-point plan is introduced, advocating people to, for instance, "use non-renewable resources such as energy, material and space sparingly and conservatively." It favors "conservative land-use policy" through which "strategies for the reduction of the use of open space" are to be developed. In addition to these publications, the Ministry of Traffic, Building, and Housing held a national city-planning conference in November in cooperation with the Conference of the Ministry of Building, the

German City Congress, and the German City and Community Federation which was intended to ascertain future tasks and to serve as an inventory of German city-planning policies at the turn of the millennium.

The **Federation of German Cities** (*Deutscher Städtetag*) is composed of the city-states Berlin, Bremen, and Hamburg, all district-free cities, as well as 4,000 district cities with a total population of 44 million. At the National City-Planning Congress, the president of the Federation of German Cities, Hajo Hoffmann, gave a speech entitled "Inventory and Perspective: City Planning Policy from the Standpoint of the Cities" in which he described possible strategies to redirect city planning policy. Included in the ten tenets toward this goal are: halting segmentation of land, fostering careful densification, and obstructing the establishment of large-scale single-merchant commercial developments on undeveloped land. According to Hoffmann, further use of land will be necessary due to the developmental pressure in German cities. To prevent this from leading to an uncontrolled dispersal of non-core area he argues that government-controlled development of settlements is unavoidable. This dispersal is to be countered by the increased density of existing developments as well as by newly planned projects.

The **German Institute for Urbanism** (*Deutsches Institut für Urbanistik*), an independent municipal research-facility of the cities, supports communities in search of solutions to contemporary problems as well as long-term perspectives of urban development with practical research, continuing education, and advice. In the study "The Future City: Compact, Mobile, Urban," this institute examines the interdependent forces of traffic and the development of settlements and reaches the conclusion that cities which adhere to concepts and strategies of "the compact city" are also more successful than others in terms of economic prosperity. In order to regulate the development of settlement and traffic more effectively, the study suggests, among other things, a general tax on the use of resources.

The **Academy of Spatial Research and Regional Planning** (*Akademie für Raumforschung und Landesplanung*), an independent academic institution dedicated to servicing research facilities, assesses the continual use of open space, in particular for the purposes of settlement and traffic, as detrimental to open space and contrary to a sustainable development of settlements. In 1999, the task group "Policies of Spatial Use" published on trends and the results of the use of open space in 1999, describing the challenges of sustainable development and plausible strategies for influencing the future use of space on all levels of spatial planning. Included among these strategies are goal-oriented implementation of planning tools, the improvement and further development of legal and political tools, and their support through economic tools.

The **Task group Suburbanization** addresses decision-makers in politics and government as well as the general public in a paper entitled "East German City-near Regions Under the Pressure of Suburbanization." This paper specifies practice-oriented steps toward a balanced and sensibly governed development of non-core regions based on the research results of several East German institutions.

5.3 Comparison of the Discussions in Germany and the US

A comparison of the state of the discussion in Germany and the USA shows decided differences with regard to the protagonists of the discussion as well as the media used. In the US, numerous and diverse groups of different legal status and radius of action (local, regional, national) were founded explicitly for the purpose of dealing with urban sprawl, while in Germany the discussion is confined to professional circles.

Print media is dominant in Germany, with regard to the medium in which the discussion is held. In the US, however, a broad palette of communication tools ranging from radio, film, and television to the internet and newspapers are used as the forum for discussion. Specifically, Al Gore and his Liveability Agenda have incited news coverage of the subject by large multi-regional media organizations. Apart from very few exceptions, the spread of information in Germany is based entirely on typically factual and non-illustrated printed material. The US also primarily makes use of text, despite the one-time extensive media coverage. When illustrations appear in the printed materials, both in the US and Germany, simple graphics and photos, as well as ground plans spanning several years of development to show the growth of metropolitan regions can be found. Beyond this, and contrary to what is the norm in Germany, the US also makes use of the spoken word (in film, television, and radio) as well as motion pictures (in film and animation on the internet) to spread information. Neither country visualizes possible future developments based on different starting scenarios. A glimpse of the future is mainly confined to vague and non-specific general information. Possible change is not documented with the aid of animation or pictures, rather with columns of figures, if at all.

5.4 Outlook

Depending on the underlying logic of the site, the internet offers direct access to detailed background information through so-called links. Previous methods of information gathering beyond the original text had relied on complicated research based on specific keywords. Beyond simple numeric or written descriptions, the internet offers the opportunity to interpret data visually, an enormous improvement, in particular when it comes to geographical or topographical facts which cannot be sufficiently regarded in spatial planning.

The implementation of computer-assisted methods of visualization offers the opportunity to show planning in a realistic manner and improves flexibility and attractiveness beyond traditional methods of visualization. The possibility ensues to transport the spectator into the future world of planning, staged with the aid of a perfect model that is realistically lighted in front of a natural background including a backdrop of natural sounds (Streich, 1983; Streich, 2002). This increases understanding of the planned project and allows everyone the possibility to voice comments directly while the planning process is still underway. Computer animation can be produced with relatively simple computers programs by interested lay people while motion picture simulations require the work of experts due to the complexity and cost of production. This increases variation and flexibility and, at the same time, saves enormous amounts of time and money. A further advantage is the freedom to interpret the same set of data on numerous occasions with different programs and using different processes. One final asset is the opportunity to allow for interactive work. Previously dispersed and disconnected fragments of information can be presented together on the screen, thereby linking relevant data from different areas or subject matters. The internet can be considered the basis for the creation of a global network of any and all data, and, at the same time, allows for vertical exchange between planners and those impacted by the planning. In this way it is possible to create a transparent planning process.

The problems of using new methods and possibilities in information technology as well as in computer-aided visualization, connected with the accessibility, quality and usefulness of data and the cost of acquiring this data (cf. Höllriegl) shall not go unmentioned. Moreover, the possibility to manipulate as well as easily create an illusion of precision are points of criticism, as well as the danger that the technical possibilities or limits of the system used have an impact on the content.

6. Conclusion

If asked to describe the desirable state of the contemporary city, most would wish for the pattern of the compact historical city. The reality of our cities, however, is different. The urban sprawl, the dispersed and low-density development outside of compact urban and village centers, along highways and in the countryside, holds our cities tightly in its grip.

The phenomenon of urban sprawl which has become more and more apparent since the 1960's is the extreme velocity and unbelievable dynamic of its 'outward movement.' Noticeable is not a linear growth pattern which successively occupies space but rather that skipped-over open space occupation. This trend is the result of increasingly faster modes of transportation, especially the increased acceptance of and availability of motorized individual transportation such as the automobile which is capable of going great distances as long as the necessary infrastructure is available. German cities are close on the heels of America's cities, spilling over into open space. The influence of differences within the context of society on the structure of our cities is not directly verifiable, but should be considered as a given.

The discussion of urban sprawl is confined to a professional audience in Germany, generally under the headline of 'sustainable development.' A broad discussion held in the American media on the other hand shows the increasing influence of the so-called new media. It is a fact that information is primarily transmitted via the written word. The influential possibilities of different forms of transferring knowledge which computers have brought into existence remain largely ignored. In particular with the aid of computer-visualization and animation, it would be possible to show how the image of the landscape and settlements of one region changes dramatically over a period of time, following small previously unnoticed changes, making use of the potential of computers for recreation processes. The development of different scenarios by changing the determining factors is also feasible. This would be desirable especially in Germany, where urban sprawl has gone largely unnoticed outside of an interested audience of professionals. The communication opportunity that the 'new' medium offers may well be its biggest potential. One thing is certain: the problem of urban sprawl is not restricted to the individual cities of two countries. It is as global as the medium internet itself. It seems that global solutions must be found in a communal process. Alongside the necessary communication infrastructure, once again the political and social will to change is prerequisite for success.

Bibliography:

Berg, L. van den et al. *Urban Europe: A Study of Growth and Decline* Vol. 1. Oxford, 1982.

Bodenschatz, Harald. "New Urbanism." *Stadtbauwelt* 145 (December 2000): pages.

Bollier, David. *Land-Use Planning and Zoning.* http://www.sprawlwatch.org/zoningandplanning2.html. 1998. Washington, D.C., 1998.

---. *Urban Growth Boundaries.* http://www.sprawlwatch.org/ugb2.html. Washington, D.C., 1998.

Cox, Wendell. *The President's New Sprawl Initiative: A Programm in Search of a Problem.* http://www.heritage.rg/library/backgrounder/bg1263es.html. 1999.

Dollinger, F. and J. Strobl, eds. *AGIT III. Salzburger Geographische Materialien* 16, 1991.

Finkelnburg, Klaus und Karsten-Michael Ortloff. *Öffentliches Baurecht.* Vol. 1: Bauplanungsrecht. 5th rev. ed. München, 1998.

Gaebe, Wolf. *Verdichtungsräume.* Stuttgart, 1987.

Heinze, W. "Auf dem Wege zu einem neuen Leitbild für unsere Städte und ihren Verkehr." *dialog* (November 1996): pages.

Hesse, Markus und Stefan Schmitz: "Stadtentwicklung im Zeichen von 'Auflösung' und Nachhaltigkeit." *Informationen zur Raumentwicklung* 7/8 (1998): 435-453.

Hirche, M. "Modellsimulation – eine Möglichkeit der Architekturdarstellung." *Deutsches Architektenblatt* 3 (1982): 613 – 616.

Höllriegl, H.P. "Stand der Geoinformationstechnologie in Österreichs Landes- und Kommunalverwaltungen." *AGIT III. Salzburger Geographische Materialien* 16.

Kostoff, Spiro. *The City Shaped.* London, 1991.

Lange, Eckart. "Our Visual Landscape." *DISP* 139 (1999): pp

Lange, Eckart. *Realität und computergestützte visuelle Simulation.* ORL-Bericht 106. Zürich, 1999.

Lehmkühler, Stefan. *Computergestützte Visualisierungstechniken in der Stadtplanung – Bedingungen und Potentiale des Ersatzes traditioneller durch computergestützte Visualisierungstechniken in der Stadtplanungspraxis.* Dortmunder Beiträge zur Raumplanung 91. Dortmund, 1999.

Lichtenberger, E. *Stadtgeographie 1, Begriffe, Konzepte, Modelle, Prozesse.* Stuttgart, 1991.

Price, Cedric. "Das Ungewisse – Die Freude am Unbekannten." Cedric Price im Gespräch mit Philipp Oswalt. *Arch+* 109/110 (1991).

Ronneberger, Klaus, Stephan Lanz und Walter Jahn. *Die Stadt als Beute.* Bonn, 1999.

Schlichter, O. und R. Stich, eds. *Berliner Kommentar zum Baugesetzbuch.* Berlin, 1988.

Schmidt, Charles W. *The Specter of Sprawl.* http://www.plannersweb.com/sprawl/schmidt/ focus.html. 1998.

Schneider-Sliwa, Rita. "Politisch-kulturelle und Planungstradition in den USA." *RUR* 6 (1995): pages.

Schrenk, Markus: "Informationstechnologie als Instrument und als Gegenstand in der Raumplanung." *Computergestützte Raumplanung. Beiträge zum Symposium CORP '96. Institut für EDV-gestützte Methoden in Architektur und Raumplanung der Technischen Universität Wien.* Wien, 1997.

Senville, Wayne M. *Sprawl Guide: Introduction to the Guide.* http://www.plannersweb.com/ sprawl/sprawl1.html, November 1999.

Sieverts, Thomas. *Die Zwischenstadt, zwischen Ort und Welt, Raum und Zeit, Stadt und Land.* Bauwelt Fundamente, Vol. 118. 2nd ed. Wiesbaden, 1999.

Sprawl Watch Clearinghouse. *Research on Pro-Sprawl Players and Messages.* http://www.sprawlwatch.org/communications.html. Stand 2/2000.

Staley, Sammuel R. *The Sprawling of America: In Defence of the Dynamic City.* http://www.rppi.org/ps251.html. 1999.

Topp, Hartmut H. "Weniger Verkehr bei gleicher Mobilität?" Festbeitrag zum 60. Geburtstag von Prof. Dr. Hans Kistenmacher. Kaiserslautern, 1994.

Geography and Socio-Political Space

Charles S. Aiken and Kyle T. Rector

A friend, who recently retired, spent the last eight years of his professional career discussing the importance of scale in geography and the book manuscript which he was writing. When asked why he had not published his book on scale, the friend replied that after reading the manuscript several times, he concluded that everything he had written was obvious and known and that he did not want to be remembered as one who published a simplistic book.

Closely related to scale in geography is the concept space. Geography is a spatial science, and geographers frequently use spatial and geographical interchangeably. Since the end of World War II, geographers have explored and integrated into the discipline new approaches involving space, including diffusion of ideas, objects, and diseases across space; perception of space; allocation of space; and administrative structure of space.[1] However, in *American Geography*, with the exception of cartography, the fundamentals of space, including size, shape, depth, and content of space, like scale, are assumed to be so obvious and simple that relatively little has been written about them.[2]

In this article, we discuss one of the fundamentals, the shape of spatial units, or more specifically, the shape of space as defined for political purposes. The background of the ways in which many contemporary American geographers view space lies in the philosophical and methodological alterations that occurred in American geography during the quarter-century following the Second World War, the period from 1945 to about 1970. Although the alterations are frequently termed 'the quantitative revolution,' they involved much more than the mere application of mathematical techniques. Led by academic geographers who had served in the military and by the first generation of post-war graduate students, the philosophical

---

[1] For examples see Gould (1969), Soja (1971), Scott (1971), and Massam (1972).

and methodological alterations were an effort to give geography more intellectual depth by making research and university course content more rigorous.[3]

Among the changes was the abandonment of regional geography as the primary approach to both research and teaching. Prior to the Second World War American geography attempted to identify and study regions thought to be created by the natural environment and by cultural and economic processes. Regions are areas which have homogeneity based on one or more features. The philosophy accepted by many contemporary geographers holds that space termed a 'region' is a human construct. A region is a space on the earth's surface defined for a purpose. In *American Geography: Inventory and Prospect*, the first major evaluation of the status of geography in the United States following the Second World War, Derwent Whittlesey wrote:

> the committee, pondering the history and philosophy of regional study in geography, decided to undertake a fresh inquiry into the nature of regions [...] The committee came to see the region as a device for selection and studying areal groupings of the complex phenomena found on the earth. Any segment or portion of the earth surface is a region if it is homogeneous in terms of such an areal grouping. Its homogeneity is determined by criteria formulated for the purpose [...] So defined, a region is not an object, either self-determined or nature-given. It is an intellectual concept, an entity for the purpose of thought, created by the selection of certain features that are relevant. (Preston and Jones, 30)

Stated more concisely for present-day geography students, "regions are not naturally occurring phenomena awaiting discovery [...] Rather, regions are concepts

---

[2] Cartography is one facet of the discipline in which the fundamentals cannot be ignored, at least in a technical sense; for size, shape, depth, and content of spatial units are used in the construction of maps for research and illustration. Cf. Robinson et al. (1995).

[3] An overview of alterations in the discipline of Geography in North America and the United Kingdom can be found in Johnson (1983). Prunty Jr. gives insights into his graduate education at Clark University, which had one of the foremost programs in its School of Geography prior to 1940. Prunty, who built a strong graduate program at the University of Georgia, faults Clark „considerably for its limited emphasis on research, [...] particularly through problem-oriented seminars for doctoral candidates" (1979, 42-45). For the perspective that American Geography

devised in the human mind for some purpose, and they are useful only insofar as they serve that purpose" (McKnight, 104).

Fundamental to American democracy are electoral regions or districts. An electoral district is a space identified for political purposes. Under the United States Constitution, a census of the population is to be taken every ten years to reapportion the national Congress so that each Congressman or Congresswoman represents approximately the same number of persons. In *Baker v. Carr* the United States Supreme Court ruled that state legislative districts also must be equal in population.[4] The federal courts extended the *Baker* decision to all types of electoral districts. Equal number of persons, not equal size of electoral spatial units, is what is critical.

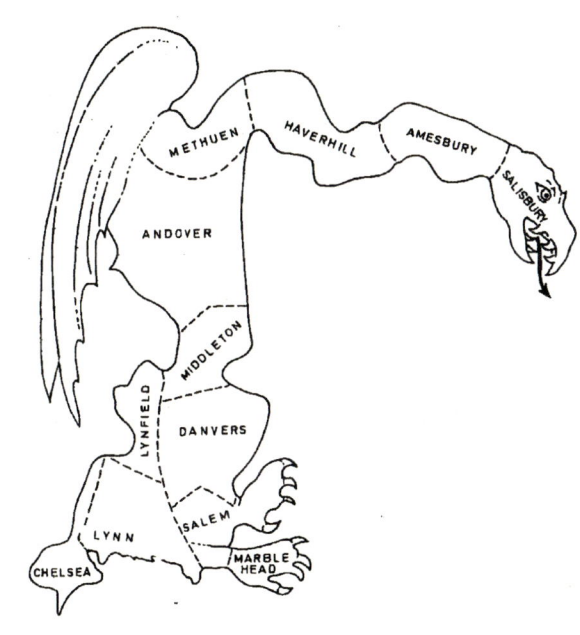

At an early date in the history of the United States the concept emerged that shape of an electoral district, Congressional, state, county, or municipal, can indicate a spatial unit that is unfairly drawn. In 1812, anti-Federalists in Massachusetts redrew the boundaries of a state senate district in Essex county in such a way that the Federalist vote was concentrated. Embellished by an illustrator into a monster, the cartoon was published in a Boston newspaper and was labeled a salamander [Fig. 1]. It later became

---

lagged behind other disciplines, especially in scientific methodology, see Ackerman (1963) and National Academy of Sciences-National Research Council (1965).

[4] *Baker v. Carr* (1962).

known as a 'gerrymander' after Governor Elbridge Gerry, who was instrumental in creating the district. The satirical term *gerrymander* entered the American language to mean, according to *Webster's New World Dictionary* (1972), "to divide a voting area so as to give one political party a majority in as many districts as possible." [5] That spatial shape of an electoral district identifies a gerrymander is central to the concept.

Blacks voted in large numbers in the South following their emancipation from slavery by the American Civil War. However, beginning in 1890 blacks were disfranchised by changes in election laws in the southern states. The principal devices used to disfranchise blacks were the requirements that voters had to pay an annual poll tax and had to pass a literacy test by correctly interpreting a passage from the state or the United States Constitution.[6] During the civil rights movement between 1954 and 1972 the United States Congress passed several potent acts designed to restore civil rights to blacks. A new era of voting began in 1965 with congressional passage of the Voting Rights Act. This act was one of the principal achievements of Martin Luther King, Jr., the primary leader of the civil rights movement.[7] Originally intended to restore the voting rights of blacks in particular southern states, provisions of the act soon were used by federal courts to protect other minorities, including Hispanics and native Americans. In 1982, Congress extend the Voting Rights Act to 2007, and additional states and voting districts within states were placed under the provisions of the legislation. The Voting Rights Act and interpretations of it by the federal courts require that any spatial changes that affect voting, including alterations in the boundaries of voting districts, must be approved by the Attorney General of the United States or by the Federal District Court for the District of Columbia.[8]

---

[5] Cf. Webster's New World Dictionary (1972). See also Morrill, (1981).
[6] Cf. Aiken (1998, 22-28). Until 1920 only men 21 and older voted in the United States. An amendment to the United States Constitution gave women the right to vote.
[7] Cf. Aiken (1998, 197-228). Voting Rights Act of 1965. Public Law 89-110, Stat. 437, *United States Code* at 486 (1965).
[8] Cf. Aiken (1998, 285-300). Voting Rights Act Amendments of 1982. Public Law 97-295, Stat. 96. *United States Code* at 131 (1982).

One of the most controversial aspects of the Voting Rights Act is its used by blacks and other minority groups to alter the boundaries of congressional and other types of electoral districts so that a racial or ethnic minority population is the majority. The argument used to create such districts is provision of the Voting Rights Act and subsequent federal court decisions to rectify past discrimination. No blacks from the South served in the United States Congress between 1901 and 1972. Also, blacks did not hold any elected office in the southern States (cf. Aiken, 300-305).

Historically, the construction of electoral districts and even minor changes in their boundaries, especially in rural areas, was an expensive, time-consuming task that involved field analysis. For this reason, counties were the spatial units usually used to construct electoral districts. A fundamental unofficial rule was that, outside of large cities, boundaries of Congressional Districts were to be drawn along county lines [Fig. 2].

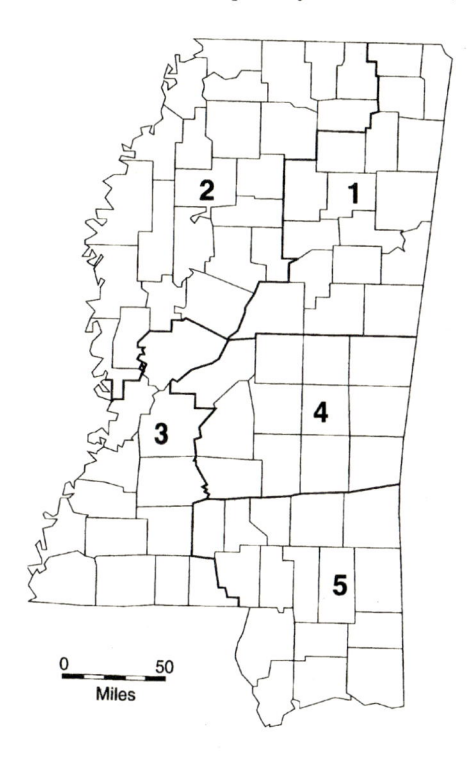

Ironically, three major technological advances that facilitated the ease of making minute spatial changes in boundaries of electoral districts followed the passage of the 1965 Voting Rights Act. One is inexpensive computers that can handle large data sets. The second is powerful computer cartography software that is easy to use. The third is spatially-detailed census maps and data for all rural areas, towns, and cities in the United States that reveal micro-scale population distribution by race and ethnicity. The first spatially-detailed block and block-group maps for rural areas and small towns were created by the Bureau of the Census for five states in 1980 and included Georgia and Mississippi. For the 1990 census, block and block-group maps and data were created for all territories in all of the 50 states. Only after the 1990 census did the full impact of the Voting including United Rights Act begin to be realized. Blocks and block groups are not political spatial units, but they permit the creation of more detailed boundaries for electoral districts, including United States Congressional Districts. Creation of block and block group maps and racial data for the 1990 Census of Population by the Bureau of the Census permitted the Mississippi Legislature to draw detailed boundaries for Congressional Districts. The boundaries for the 2nd Congressional District were drawn so that it had a voting-age population in which blacks were the majority.

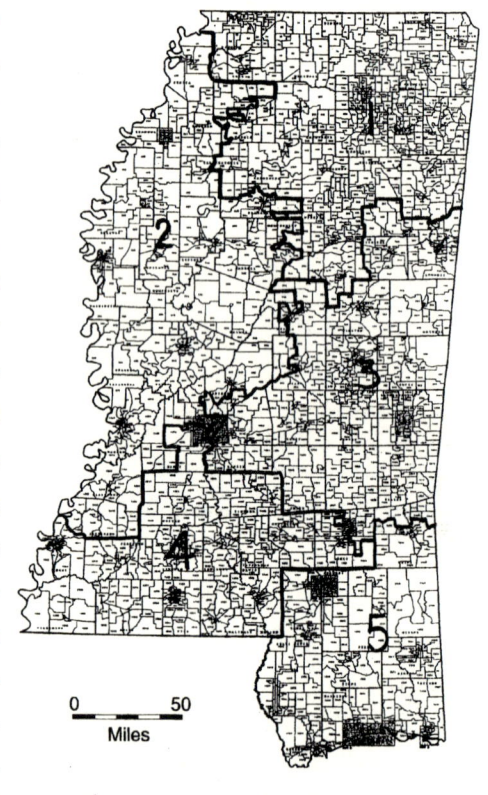

In 1986 the United States Supreme Court issued a decision under the Voting Rights Act that attempted to establish guidelines for the creation of voting districts in which a minority population is the majority.[9] First, the minority group must be sufficiently large and geographically compact to constitute a majority. Second, the minority group must be "politically cohesive." Third, the white majority votes as a block to defeat the minority's preferred candidate.

Altering the boundaries of Congressional Districts and creating districts in which blacks and other minority groups were the majority was relatively easy using the spatially detailed 1990 census data and maps. Because of court suits brought by blacks and pressure from the United States Department of Justice, southern state legislatures created new majority-black Congressional Districts under the Voting Rights Act.

Including the 18 black Congressmen and Congresswomen from the South, the number of blacks in the United States House of Representatives increased from 24 in 1989 to 38 in 1993. Many of the majority-black Congressional Districts were in inner-cities of metropolitan areas, but ten in the South combined rural territory, small towns, and metropolitan fringes to create districts.

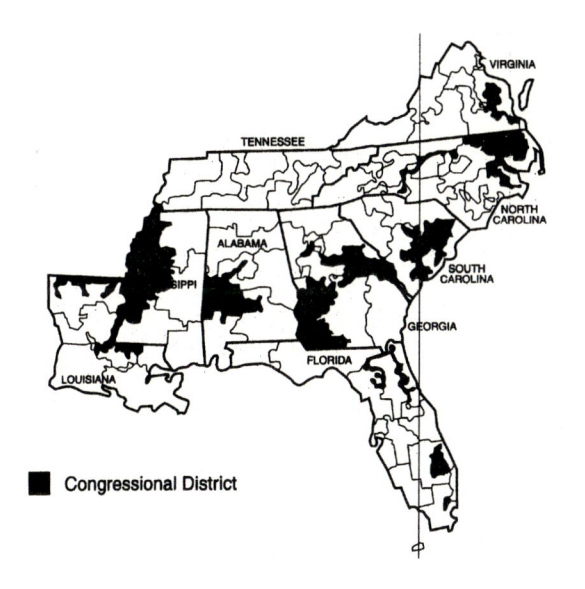

Of the majority-black Congressional Districts created following the 1990 census, the one that attracted the most attention as obviously gerrymandered was the Twelfth in North Carolina [Figure 4]. The United States Justice Department mandated that under the Voting Rights Act two majority Black Congressional Districts were to be created in North Carolina. The First Congressional District on the Coastal Plain contained a large black population, and relatively minor changes in

---

[9] Cf. *Thornburg v. Gingles* (1986).

the district 's boundaries made it majority black. The Twelfth Congressional District on the highly urbanized Piedmont was created by joining black residential areas in small and medium size cities in a district that stretched from Durham to Charlotte primarily along Interstate Highways 40 and 85 [Fig. 5].[10] A number of sarcastic comments were made about the long, narrow Twelfth District. H. M. Micheaux, an unsuccessful candidate to represent the Twelfth, said, "I love the district. It 's so narrow I can drive down Interstate Highway 85 with my car doors open and hit every voter" (Smothers, 1).

A group of whites in the Twelfth District brought a court suit to reconfigure it because it was a gerrymander. In 1993 in *Shaw v. Reno* the United States Supreme Court issued a 5 to 4 split decision that declared the Twelfth District unconstitu-

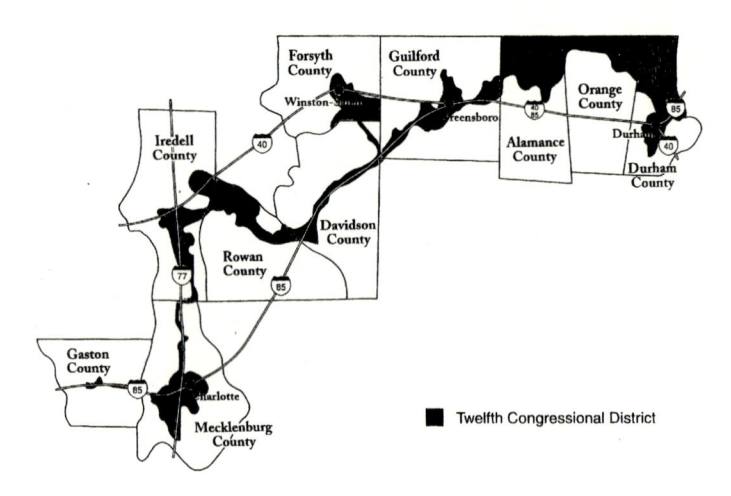

tional. In writing the majority opinion, Justice Sandra O'Connor warned in strong language that "reapportionment is one area where appearances do matter." A plan "that included in one district individuals who belonged to the same race, but who are otherwise widely separated by geographical and political boundaries and who

---

[10] Cf. Rector (1995).

may have little in common with one another but the color of their skin bears an uncomfortable resemblance to political apartheid."[11]

The Supreme Court based its Shaw decision on legal arguments rather than on an investigation of the geography of the Twelfth Congressional District. To determine if the long and narrow Twelfth District is truly gerrymandered, a comprehensive statistical analysis of the district's internal characteristics and spatial shape was conducted (cf. Rector). The Twelfth was compared with four samples from among the United States 435 Congressional Districts: the other eleven North Carolina districts, the other nineteen majority-black southern districts, a random sample of 50 southern districts, and a random sample of 50 districts from the nation. A total of 109 districts were compared with North Carolina's Twelfth. The Supreme Court's guidelines in *Thornburg v. Gingles* were employed in the analysis. Six variables were used to test for equal population and community of interest: number of inhabitants, educational attainment, percent of urban population, percent of home ownership, per capita income. The data were analyzed using a two-sample t-test, which is a modification of the student's t-test. The null hypothesis was that two sets of data are random samples from a normally distributed population. In a normally distributed population the observations coalesce around the mean.

A total of 24 tests were conducted. North Carolina's Twelfth Congressional District passed 15 of the 24. The Twelfth did not have one failure in the tests for equal population. Also, persons in the Twelfth, blacks and whites, have communities of interest that are as strong, or stronger, than the average sample district. The Twelfth District did not fail any of the batteries of tests for percent of urban population and per capita income. Even in the batteries where the Twelfth's performance was poorest, there were other districts in the group sampled that were equally low, or lower. Also, the Twelfth was far from being the "worst " district in any variable.

The Twelfth District performed poorly in the political boundary test, failing all four of the tests, which was expected, given its shape. However, the Twelfth is not the only Congressional District with poor spatial shape. Nineteen of the sample

---

[11] *Shaw v. Reno* (1993).

districts were as poorly shaped as the Twelfth North Carolina (cf. Rector, 78-113). The results indicate that there are no compelling statistical reasons to invalidate North Carolina's Twelfth Congressional District. To interpret the Twelfth as unreasonably constructed, the district should have failed the majority of the tests.

Only with respect to spatial shape are there statistical reasons to invalidate the constitutionality of North Carolina's Twelfth Congressional District. However, because space is an intellectual concept, what constitutes a properly configured electoral region changes through time. Recent alterations in the technology of communication and travel have practically negated shape among the important considerations in political space. Also, the spatial form of American cities has changed considerably since 1950. Urban areas sprawl along Interstate Highways in a linear form with the boundary of one municipality adjoining that of another. Various names have been given to the new urban areas including 'galactic city,' 'dispersed city,' 'edge city.'[12] One of these new linear cities is a rapidly growing one that spreads along Interstate Highways 40 and 85 from Raleigh to Charlotte, North Carolina (cf. Gade and Young, 251-255). The shape of the Twelfth Congressional District merely mimics politically an urban area that is already established on the central North Carolina landscape.

The Shaw decision opened the gates for numerous court suits challenging new majority-black and majority-Hispanic Congressional, state, county, and municipal electoral districts created to comply with the Voting Rights Act. Three decades after passage of this important legislation, Congress and the federal courts have reached an impasse in which they do not grasp the spatial context of voting by blacks and other minorities. Judicial confusion prevails concerning the creation of Congressional and other types of electoral districts in which minorities are the political majority. A review of the United States Supreme Court's 1999-2000 session concluded that "without direction from the Court racial-preference laws are enforced unevenly" (Turque and Brant, 18-25).

---

[12] Cf. Lewis (1995), Hays (1976), and Garreau (1991).

The impasse hinges on what is perceived as correct and incorrect spatial shape of voting districts. Justice O'Connor specifically stated in *Shaw* that "appearances do matter." Despite O'Connor's personal belief that shape of an electoral district is important, there are no Constitutional or federal laws regarding the form of space defined for political purposes. The fictitious spatial monster known as the gerrymander has haunted the creation of electoral districts and judicial decision far too long. If the federal courts merely accepted the Twelfth North Carolina and other minority electoral districts for what they really are, regions defined for a purpose under the Voting Rights Act, the confusion and the judicial deadlock over correct shape of space should disappear.

Credits

Figure 1 (p. 307). The original 'gerrymander'. Drawing of the 1812 Massachusetts state senate district created by Governor Gerry's Republican-Democrats to minimize the Federalist vote. *Boston Gazette* March 26, 1812. Reprinted in Morrill 1981.

Figure 2 (p. 309). Mississippi Congressional Districts in 1956. The Congressional District boundaries followed by county lines. Charles S. Aiken, 1998.

Figure 3 (p. 310). Mississippi Congressional Districts in 1991. Creation of block and block group maps and racial data for the 1990 Census of Population by the Bureau of the Census permitted the Mississippi Legislature to draw detailed boundaries for Congressional Districts. The boundaries for the 2nd Congressional District were drawn so that it had a voting-age population in which blacks were the majority. Mississippi State Election Commission.

Figure 4 (p. 311). Congressional districts with majority-black voting-age populations in 1993. Aiken 1998.

Figure 5 (p. 312). North Carolina's 12th Congressional District in 1992. Kyle T. Rector, 1995.

Bibliography

Ackerman, Edward A. "Where is a Research Frontier?" *Annals of the Association of American Geographers.* 53.4 (December 1963): 429-440.

Aiken, Charles S. *The Cotton Plantation South Since the Civil War.* Baltimore: Johns Hopkins UP, 1998.

Baker v. Carr 396 United States, Supreme Court 691, 7 L. Ed. 2d 663 (1962).

Gade, Ole and James Young. "North Carolina's Urban Crescent: A Vision of America's Urban Future." *Snapshots of the Carolinas: Landscapes and Cultures.* Ed. Gordon G. Bennett. Washington, D.C.: Association of American Geographers, 1996. 251-55.

Garreau, Joel. *Edge City: Life on the New Frontier.* New York: Doubleday, 1991.

Gould, Peter R. *Spatial Diffusion.* Commission on College Geography. Resource Paper 4. Washington, D. C.: Association of American Geographers, 1969.

Guptill, Stephen C. *Elements of Cartography.* New York: John Wiley & Sons, 1995.

Hays, Charles R. *The Dispersed City: The Case of Piedmont North Carolina.* Chicago: Department of Geography, University of Chicago, 1976.

James, Preston E. and Clarence F. Jones. *American Geography: Inventory & Prospect.* Syracuse, New York: Syracuse UP, 1954.

Johnson, R. J. *Geography and Geographers: Anglo-American Human Geography Since 1945.* London: Edward Arnold, 1983.

Lewis, Peirce. "The Urban Invasion of Rural America: The Emergence of the Galactic City". *The Changing American Countryside.* Ed. Emery N. Castle. Lawrence, Kansas: UP of Kansas, 1995.

McKnight, Tom L. *Regional Geography of the United States and Canada.* 3rd Edition. Englewood Cliffs, New Jersey: Prentice Hall, 2001.

Massam, Bryan. *The Spatial Structure of Administration Systems.* Commission on College Geography. Resource Paper 12. Washington, D. C.: Association of American Geographers, 1972.

Morrill, Richard. *Political Redistricting and Geographic Theory.* Resource Publication in Geography. Washington, D. C.: Association of American Geographers, 1981.

National Academy of Sciences-National Research Council. *The Science of Geography.* Report of the Ad Hoc Committee on Geography, Earth Sciences Division. Washington, D. C., 1965.

Prunty, Merle C., Jr. "Clark in the Early Years." *Annals of the Association of American Geographers.* 69.1 (March 1979): 42-45.

Rector, Kyle T. *Shaw v. Reno and North Carolina's Twelfth Congressional District: Testing the Constitutionality of a Majority-Minority District.* M. S. Thesis. Department of Geography, University of Tennessee, Knoxville, Tennessee, 1995.

Robinson, Arthur H., Joel L. Morrison, Phillip C. Muehrcke, A. Jon. Kimerling, and Stephen C. Guptill. *Elements of Cartography.* New York: John Wiley & Sons, 1995.

Shaw v. Reno. 509 United States, 113 Supreme Court. 2816, 125 L. Ed. 2d 511 (1993).

Smothers, Ronald. "Two Strangely Shaped Hybrid Creatures Highlight North Carolina's Primary." The New York Times. (May 3, 1992): 1

Soja, Edward W. *The Political Organization of Space.* Commission on College Geography, Resource Paper 8. Washington, D. C.: Association of American Geographers, 1971.

Thornburg v. Gingles. 487 United States 30, 106 Supreme Court. 2752, 92 L. Ed. 2d 25 (1986).

Turque, Bill and Martha Brant. "The Supreme Question." *Newsweek* (June 10, 2000):18-25.

Regional Uniqueness or Global Uniformity?

Edward M. Bergman

How do we account for the apparently contradictory facts of growing uniformity in global culture, consumer goods, media, etc. and the fact that some regions retain, sometimes intensify, their unique qualities while others become novel in quite unexpected ways? Two small adjoining cities in North Carolina provide a useful contrast. How has Chapel Hill maintained its singular focus on the University of North Carolina and closely-related academic functions for 200 years while its close neighbor Durham, known as 'Bull City' for its tobacco reputation until the 1970s, became the 'City of Medicine' in less than a generation?[1]

Do unique regional identities result from acts of intentional design, or is it simply a matter of selecting the most apt titles for places that naturally deepen historically beneficial roots and also for places that somehow morph from their past into a new present? Following a brief review of widely circulated views concerning globalization and global cities concerning evidence of regional uniformity vs. uniqueness, it will be argued that mixtures of path dependence, social capital, and capitalist competition are together most likely responsible for certain growing global uniformity and unique regional identities in the 21st century.

Globalization and Global Cities: Uniformity or Uniqueness?

Social and cultural scientists have gravitated toward evolving concepts of globalization, particularly after the events of 1989 reduced much of the capitalist vs. collectivist debate to intellectual rubble. Rapid expansion of capitalist logic and open trade throughout the world introduced familiar products to many places, which prompted predictable concerns about a fast-food homogenization of society and the globe: "McDonaldization [...] is the process by which the principles of the fast-food

---

[1] For an empirical account of changes in Durham's industrial, social and spatial structure through the mid-80s, see Bergman and Goldstein.

restaurant are coming to dominate more and more sectors of American society *as well as the rest of the world*" (Ritzer, 1, italics added).

Simplistic views of globalization abound, based essentially on the homogenizing effects of consumer culture (Alfino, et al.), at least those consumer products that enjoy global markets. More nuanced popular views of post-1980s globalization take account of its economic and technological tendencies toward homogenization of consumption patterns as well as tendencies toward deadly ethnic and nationalistic differentiation (Barber, Friedman). The profusion of books and articles that deal with all aspects of globalization continues to grow so rapidly that one is barely able to monitor available publications or track the swirl of debates across the internet.[2]

Global cities and regions have become a preferred framework for discourse and analysis among those who once debated the role of the nation state under advanced capitalism, as well as among meliorist progressives who prescribed activist roles for nation states and reminded its managers and political agents of policy obligations to the poor of its urban or rural subdivisions. The simultaneous collapse of collective economies, the market reconfiguration of social economies, and the burgeoning growth of liberal economies since the early 90s may also have helped to invigorate new critiques of capitalism—more culturally based versions and those termed the 'politics of identity'—which appear to have displaced more traditional class-based critiques.[3] At the same time, globalist perspectives might help account for the factors responsible for explosive growth among a subset of cities and regions throughout the U.S. and worldwide, although only certain of the largest cities are among those considered 'global'. While all of these pose interesting questions, the main point here is whether the forces of globalization are seen to produce unique or uniform regions.

---

[2] Because these points are directed toward questions of regional uniformity vs. uniqueness, other globalization effects concerning the relative position of industrial and developing countries, which have dominated many recent discussions, go unmentioned.

[3] A robust competition among capitalism's urban and regional critics is analyzed in Smith, particularly in the chapters of Part I.

Assuming one accepts the work of Saskia Sasson as reasonably representative of the concepts at play here,[4] they can be boiled down to these three:

1. Telecommunication advances and deregulation of financial or other markets now permit transnational corporations (TNCs) of all kinds to operate anywhere worldwide in an effort to maximize market share and total profits.
2. The need for rapid movements of capital and the ability to orchestrate investments and production have given rise to the financial and corporate services industry (FCS), which specialize in supporting TNCs.
3. The FCS are not equally distributed across national or international urban systems, but rather concentrate only in a few cities where highly skilled professionals and the necessary infrastructure are found in abundance in global cities.

Beginning with this simple scenario, a dense narrative is then woven around the significance of FCS in global cities, the interconnections among global cities, the flows of investment among these cities and other regions, the bi-polar salary/education received by workers in its extreme occupations, and most importantly the role played by FCS itself in the development of global cities.

These features come together to produce in global cities what Sasson sees as new development patterns:

> High-income gentrification is labor intensive, in contrast to the typical middle-class suburb that represents a capital-intensive process: tract housing, road and highway construction, dependence on private automobiles or commuter trains, marked reliance on appliances and household equipment of all sorts, large shopping malls with self-service operations. Directly or indirectly, high-income gentrification replaces much of this capital intensity with workers [...]. High-income gentrification generates a demand for goods and services that are frequently not mass produced or sold through mass outlets. Customized production, small runs, specialty items, and fine

---

[4] An alternative view, 'Transnational Urbanism', proposed by Smith begins with a critique of Sasson's position, which we will not examine further. In summary, "Structuralism, economism, and inattention to questions of culture and agency are identified as key weaknesses of their approach to urban theory" (50).

food dishes are generally produced through labor-intensive methods and sold through small, full-service outlets. (Sasson, 2000, 133-34)

If we summarize the globalization thesis with respect to uniformity vs. uniqueness of regions, we are led to conclude that global cities contain privileged communities of corporate officers whose demand for boutique goods and services are met by lower classes of service workers. An unspecified development dynamic and resultant urban pattern contrasts strongly with mass-produced houses and settlements of the middle class, who live elsewhere, and with those who provide menial and custodial services to FCS facilities or who cater to specialized consumer demands.

In short, Sasson apparently sees class-determined settlement patterns in global cities that differ from those of non-global cities and regions, due mainly to mixtures of class consumption unique to global cities. These class mixtures are in turn traced back to the servicing needs and professional or technical personnel employed by transnational corporations. However, there is no basis for knowing from this account whether class consumption interactions produce unique global city regions or how consumption of a specific class leaves its imprint on regions that lack global cities.

This account does not go far enough to provide much insight into our initial question. Indeed, there seems to be less here than routinely meets the eye almost anywhere one looks: the daily experience of international travelers includes close encounters with the identical brands of consumer and cultural goods worldwide, use of the same airline alliances, they are assaulted by the same logos, appealed to by the same ads, entertained by the same films and music, which are increasingly in one language, English. Airports, shopping centers, street signs, youth apparel etc. are all either comforting or disturbing, depending on one's perspective, but one message seems clear: there are aspects of global uniformity and continuing homogenization of consumption in places that the global cities scenario omits. The apogee of consumer uniformity is perhaps best exemplified by so-called 'edge cities', (Garreau, 1995) which differ only slightly from region to region.

'Edge Cities' and a host of other urban and regional morphologies do receive the attention of post-modern geographers who routinely reject modern theories of every type and associated concepts. Basing their new concepts on Los Angeles as a proto-region,[5] Flusty and Dear invite us to consider a post-modern urbanism driven by globalization and restructuring, which, they argue, is best dimensioned by the deliberately

> promiscuous use of neologisms [...][which] are employed when no existing terms adequately describe the conditions we seek to identify, when a single term more conveniently substitutes for a complex phrase or string of ideas, and when neologistic novelty aids our avowed efforts to rehearse the break.
> (I.e. the assumption that a radical break with modernism has already occurred. Flusty and Dear, 1999, 5, 38)

Among the elements of Flusty and Dear's post-modern urbanism most congenial to Sasson's vision of global cities are 'cybergeoise' (those who provide major corporate command and control functions), including lesser 'para-cybergeoise' and marginalized 'protosurps' that support both. All populate the collective world city 'Citistat,' of which global cities are a part. Citistat also contains 'Commudities,' which are defined as "commodified communities created expressly to satisfy (and profit from) the habitat preferences of the well-recompensed cybergeoise" (Flusty and Dear, 42). Other elements also promote urban and regional homogenization, particularly "Holsteinization," defined as the "process of monoculturing people as consumers to facilitate the harvesting of desires," (39). This poly-terminate account leaves one with the general sense that globalization is thought to produce a monoculture of uniform regions, but underlying mechanisms remain wholly unspecified and obscure.

---

[5] For a review and on-line debate of these propositions, see Miller.

These widely circulated accounts seem nearly as simplistic as the naive McDonaldization thesis[6] if we accept the notion that

> Globalism works at the surface of identity, while particularism defines what lies several layers beneath and is several degrees more essential: the traditions of language and history. Global change is scouring the face of the planet, but we have lived with it long enough to know that it is not going to scrub away the meanings encoded with the 5,000 languages on the globe. The particular is just as tenacious and resourceful as the global [...] the more globalism makes our consumption patterns converge, the more we defend the particularisms which remain." (Ignatieff, 60)

It is precisely these traditions and history that motivate people and institutions to behave in ways consistent with the best scientific theories. Indeed, Ignatieff continues: "The only intellectuals who have escaped this crisis of authority (i.e., retained intellectual's historical role of defending the universal against the violence and closure of tribal, national and ethnic) have been the scientists [...] The reason is simple: they appear to know something [actually the] command of the scientific method itself." (62) In reviewing the postmodernist themes now popular in geography, John Rees, himself a regional scientist and economic geographer, concludes that "it is not surprising that for most regional scientists postmodernism will only amount to an intellectual cul de sac" (106).

Regional Differentiation: Other Views

If we shift to some new perspectives of how the market economy functions in cities and regions, and how it has changed due to various globalist tendencies, we can answer the original question put forward in the title more precisely, while also ac-

---

[6] Perhaps the intellectual porosity characteristic of contemporary geography and urban studies has depleted them of reliable theories such that neologisms now substitute freely for testable hypotheses and serve equally well. To many "geography appears fickle, faddish and belligerent. The quantitative geographers of the 1960s, the Marxist geographers of the 1970s and the postmodern theorists of the 1980s are often the same people. One reaction is to admire the intellectual flexibility of geography [...] another is to shake one's head upon learning that the neighbor now has a fifth spouse and has joined yet another cult." Isserman, (280).

counting for some of the stylized narratives that arise in previously referenced work.

What should be made of brand name and product uniformity that we observe in cities of all sizes throughout the developed world, and even in far less developed places? Isn't this direct evidence that regional uniqueness is fading, to be replaced by a mass consumption culture of global proportions? Fukuyama disagrees, stating that "the underlying truth is that the global economy is still limited [....] institutions remain intensely local. Trade, for example, is still predominantly regional [...] Intra-European trade accounts for roughly 60% of all European trade" (14). In fact, very high proportions of trade involve brandless commodities and intermediate—not branded—consumer-goods. However, global trade of consumer goods, even if smaller than commonly imagined, permits previously isolated regions to consume a preferred import, rather than a more traditionally prepared regional good.

Imported products and services a city or region consumes matter far less than what regions require to produce for export. Put more succinctly, *acquiring the ability to produce and export goods competitively contributes more to regional uniqueness than is lost by the branded products a region happens to consume.* The productive ability of a region hinges on the generalized yet peculiar expertise of its workers and entrepreneurs, such that, in Marshall's famous dictum, "The mysteries of trade become no mysteries: but are as it were in the air" (Marshall, 271).

The practical process of skill-building in two regions is described best by Jane Jacobs, former journalist and architectural critic whose close observation of cities and subsequent writings have earned her a well-deserved reputation first as an urban theorist and later as an economist.

> When Tokyo went into the bicycle business, first came repair work cannibalizing imported bicycles, then manufacture of some of the parts most in demand for repair work, then manufacture of still more parts, finally assembly of whole, Tokyo-made bicycles. (Jacobs, 38)

Jacobs continues, this time reviewing observations of the Third Italy region firms by Charles Sable:

> A small shop producing tractor transmissions for a large manufacturer modifies the design of the transmission to suit the need of a small manufacturer of high-quality seeders. In another little shop a conventional automatic packing machine is redesigned to fit the available space in a particular assembly line. A machine that injects one type of plastic into molds is modified to inject another, cheaper plastic. A membrane pump used in automobiles is modified to suit agricultural machinery. A standard loom or cloth-cutting machine is adjusted to work efficiently with particularly fine threads. (39-40)

The 'mysteries of trade' Marshall detected in the air nearly a century earlier were—and still are—learned almost automatically in entrepreneurial settings by suitably-trained and perceptive workers whose surroundings and socialization are such that work in certain industries and technologies seems like the natural, logical outcome of simply living in the region. A key feature of regions that helps instill productive competence among its citizens is what Putnam and others identify as social capital or civil community. As political scientist who has studied the Third Italy region which focuses on good regional governance and economic performance, Putnam writes:

> Networks facilitate flows of information about technological developments, about the creditworthiness of would-be entrepreneurs, about the reliability of individual workers, and so on. Innovation depends on continual informal interaction in cafes and bars and in the street. Social norms that forestall opportunism are so deeply internalized that the issue of opportunism at the expense of community obligation is said to arise less often here than in areas characterized by vertical and clientelistic networks [...] It is no surprise to learn that these highly productive small-scale industrial districts are concentrated in those very regions of north-central Italy that we have highlighted as centers of civic traditions, of the contemporary civic community and of high-performance regional government. (161)

Important regional features that Putnam's work highlights are the tightly meshed interdependencies between civic virtues, the efficient and relevant services or facilities provided by competent regional government, and the extraordinary advantages that result, which accrue to a few highly specialized industries and technologies. The combination of local civic culture, unique infrastructure, and particularized policies leave distinctive imprints on a region's culture and physical morphology, enhancing its overall uniqueness. Krugman cites the carpet industry in Dalton, Georgia. From a geographer's point of view, it was certainly by chance that tufting technology was essentially invented there:

> In 1895 the teenaged Miss Evans made a bedspread as a gift. The recipients and their neighbors were delighted with the gift, and over the next few years Miss Evans made a number of tufted items, discovering in 1900 a trick of locking the tufts into the backing. She now began to sell the bedspreads, and she and her friends and neighbors launched a local handicraft industry that began selling items well beyond the immediate vicinity. Dalton became a leader in carpet production [....] scaley economies and externalities reinforced its lead, and the rest (as they say) is history. (Krugman, 60)

What sets off virtuous circles of concentrated expertise and productivity in highly specialized, successful regions? Three possible development paths will be mentioned briefly here. First are the purely historical accidents, upon which the concept of path-dependencies usually depends. As Paul Krugman illustrates, the handcrafting of a simple 19th century wedding gift led eventually to the highly specialized carpet-producing region of northern Georgia.

Second are intentionally designed regional features that result in highly specialized industrial or commercial development. A good example of this is the Research Triangle Park, which was originally conceived, designed, and launched in 1959, and which rode the technology wave that first surged in the late 1970s. (Luger and Goldstein). This profound change caught several surrounding communities and the state quite unprepared for the rush of barely controlled growth and its rippling consequences for towns in the region, including Durham and Chapel Hill, North Carolina.

Third are the episodic corporate or technological transitions that shift a region entirely away from one industrial or technological specialization to another. Durham exemplifies this transition, as it was dominated by the tobacco industry until the early 1970s, when its remaining patron firm was bought by a British conglomerate and ceased its Durham operations just as the Duke Medical Center and nearby pharmaceutical firms in Research Triangle Park began their rapid growth. (Bergman and Goldstein). Equally remarkable is a transition still underway in Finland brought on by the explosive growth of Nokia, which began as a forest products firm in the 19th century and which in 1980 still posted half of its sales from wood and rubber products, eventually selling these and all other unrelated product lines in 1995 to concentrate wholly on what became its core competencies: telecommunications equipment and mobile telephones (Ali-Yrkkö et al.).

The steadily paced historical development path of a continuously elaborated place that remains focused on its original functions, such as Chapel Hill, NC, contrasts strongly with the more rapid regional production transformations underway in Durham and Helsinki. The latter invariably reveal sharp changes in culture, governance and supporting features that are necessary to move away from one production regime to another.

Regional Imprints of Concentrated Production

Whatever the mechanism—historically dependent, intentionally designed, or technologically transitional industries—a productive region is usually good at very few, sometimes only one, major industries or technologies, and it tends to gravitate over time toward those few. The extreme case is a company town, where all production is doubly-concentrated in a single industry *and* a single firm. This is usually an unstable combination in competitive market situations and many regions have suffered when their sole patron failed to maintain its position. The Carolinas are familiar with this phenomenon, as early industrialization there was typically of this type.

However, specialization and concentration need not necessarily imply dominance by one firm, as the vibrant economies of many regions testify. What is necessary is that sufficient scale of output ensures efficient production and competitive prices that permit export to potential markets. This reintroduces the question of global markets, more specifically product markets, which are increasingly open to entrepreneurs worldwide. Products sold worldwide give a deceiving appearance of global homogeneity, until one looks more carefully at the extraordinary diversity of the regions producing widely purchased items. The key to greatly expanded markets is the practical possibility of world trade. NAFTA, the European Community, MERCUSOR, and other trading blocks have emerged to promote customs-free trade within their collective boundaries, while GATT and now WTO continue to reduce trade barriers between these blocks and unaffiliated countries wishing to export their production.

The growing volume of inter-regional and global trade steadily expands the possibilities for specialized, scale-efficient production in hundreds of cities and regions worldwide. Productive specialization lies at the very heart of why regions retain or sometimes intensify their uniqueness even while their goods are consumed worldwide. It can be argued that the concentrated production of traded goods gives a region its most visible and enduringly unique features. Obvious historical examples are port cities, whose concentration in port-based trade simultaneously produced an infrastructure uniquely configured to local topography and orientation. At the same time, the functions that give meaning to uniquely built environments also find particularistic expression in the language, habits, and tastes of its workers and citizens.[7]

Uniquely configured infrastructure is recognizable everywhere, if one is looking for it. Even after original functions cease, historically significant infrastructure and

---

[7] Others see strikingly similar parallels at work concerning the globalization of culture: "If the process of globalization implies increased contact among various territorial cultures, it is likely to produce geographically varied responses" (Nijman). If globalization is seen to intensify cultural nationalisms, then it "does not result in homogeneity, but in a deepening of particularity" (King cited in Nijman, 222).

buildings are often recycled for new regional functions, the combination of which is literally unduplicated anywhere else. A good example is Durham, NC, which is still in the process of recycling its large inventory of tobacco warehouses for other uses, including health and medical care facilities. Other cities and regions experience similar transformations.

Cities and regions that become specialized in certain industries and technologies tend to develop supporting public facilities and services that are advantageous for their local economy, and patterns of locally advantageous production shapes the urban morphology and features, including residential districts. This can be seen in Chapel Hill, home of UNC-CH. This small city has served a very nearly singular purpose during its 200 year history: it is a university town *par excellence*. Other university towns of comparably ranked institutions have grown or taken on new functions, particularly in the post-WWII period, but Chapel Hill retains its essential educational mission and has refined its features accordingly. It is essentially an attractive residential and knowledge worker environment where faculty in their most productive years are able to focus efficiently on their work in comfortable and secure living conditions. These same qualities are in part responsible for the attraction of similar knowledge-based industries to the town and surrounding region.

The seeming paradox of unique locations co-existing with the consumption of mass-produced goods requires only the familiar concept of scale economies. Mass-consumed products of many kinds, including highly specialized goods, are typically produced in relatively few specialized regions and sold worldwide at competitive prices. A city or region can become highly specialized in the production of some product, perhaps electronic equipment, pharmaceuticals, or major motion pictures. Research Triangle Park and a handful of other regions specialize in selected facets of the first two industries, while Hollywood specializes in the latter.

To the degree that expanded world trade regimes offer additional opportunities for regions to specialize in a few specific sectors for which they are particularly well-suited, the dynamic of scale-efficient production drives regions—consciously or not—to favor their most successful industries and technologies. This usually means advantageous development decisions, key investments in new or refurbished infrastructure, an efficient supply of key public services, and support of competence-specific education and community programs of all kinds. In short, regions around the world are busily trying to assess what they are good at doing and redesigning themselves to better suit those purposes. It is this process that has served to distinguish the underlying culture and morphology of cities that have traditionally engaged in trade and the process appears to continue unabated, each adding specific 21st century elements to their accumulation of earlier defining features.

Bibliography

Alfina, Mark, John S. Caputo and Robin Wynyard, eds. *McDonaldization Revisited.* Westport, CN: Praeger, 1998.

Ali-Yrkkö, J., L. Paija, C. Reilly and P. Ylä-Anttila. *Nokia: A Big Company in a Small Country.* Helsinki: The Research Institute of the Finnish Economy, 2000.

Barber, Benjamin R. "Jihad vs. McWorld." *Atlantic Monthly* 269.3 (March 1992): 53-65.

Bergman, Edward M. and Edward Feser. *Industrial and Regional Clusters: Concepts and Comparative Applications.* Morgantown: University of West Virginia Webbooks. (http://www.rri.wvu.edu/WebBook/Bergman-Feser/contents.htm), 1999.

Bergman, Edward M. and Harvey Goldstein. "Urban Innovation and Technological Advance: Durham's Economic Evolution in the Research Triangle Region." *Sustainability of Urban Systems. A Cross-National Evolutionary Analysis of Urban Innovation.* Ed. Peter Nijkamp. Aldershot: Avebury, 1990.

Feser, Edward J. and Edward M. Bergman. "National Industry Cluster Templates: A Framework for Applied Regional Cluster Anlysis." *Regional Studies* 34.1 (2000): 1-19.

Flusty, Steven and Michael Dear. "Invitation to a Postmodern Urbanism." *The Urban Moment: Cosmopolitan Essays on the Late-20th Century City, Urban Affairs Annual Reviews.* Eds. Robert Beauregard and Sophie Body-Gendrot. Vol. 49. 25-50.

Friedman, Thomas L. *The Lexus and the Olive Tree.* New York: Farrar Straus & Giroux, 2000.

Fukuyama, Francis. "Economic Globalization and Culture: A Discussion." Technology and Society, Globalization and Economics Forum. Merrill Lynch, 2000 (http://www.ml.com/woml/forum/global.htm).

Garreau, Joel. *Edge City: Life on the New Frontier.* New York: Anchor-Doubleday, 1992.

Ignatieff, Michael. "Where are they now?" Prospect (August-September 1997) (http://www.prospect-magazine.co.uk/highlights/where_are_they/index.html).

Isserman, Andrew M. "The history, status and future of regional science: An American perspective." *International Regional Science Review* 19: 37-48

Jacobs Jane. *Cities and the Wealth of Nations.* New York: Random House, 1984.

King, Anthony D. "Representing World Cities: Cultural Theory/Social Practice." *World Cities in a World-System.* Eds. Paul L. Knox and Peter J. Taylor. Cambridge: Cambridge UP. 215-231.

Krugman, Paul. *Geography and Trade.* Cambridge: MIT Press, 1991.

Luger, Michael and H. Goldstein. *Technology in the Garden. Research Parks and Regional Economic Development.* Chapel Hill: U of North Carolina P, 1991.

Marshall, Alfred. *Principles of Economics.* 1890; London: McMillan, 1978.

Miller, Donald W. "The New Urban Studies: Los Angeles Scholars use their region and their ideas to end the dominance of the 'Chicago School' in Research and Publishing Section." *The Chronicle of Higher Education* (18 August 2000) (http://chronicle.com).

Nijman, Jan. "The Global Moment in Urban Evolution: A Comparison of Amsterdam and Miami." Institute for Urban Research and Spatial Policy Lecture, Amsterdam Study Center for the Metropolitan Environment (October 1996). (http://www.frw.uva.nl/ame/pub/nijman.global.htm)

Putnam, Robert D. *Making Democracy Work: Civic Traditions in Modern Italy.* Princeton: Princeton UP, 1993.

Rees, John. "Regional Science: From Crisis to Opportunity." *Papers in Regional Science* 78 (1999): 101-110.

Ritzer, George. *The McDonaldization of Society.* Thousand Oaks, CA: Pine Forge P, 1993.

Sable, Charles F. 1982. *Work and Politics: The Division of Labor in Industry.* Eds. S. Berger, A. Hirschman, and C. Maier. Cambridge Studies in Modern Political Economies, Cambridge: Cambridge UP, 1982.

Sasson, Saskia. *Cities in a World Economy*, 2nd edition. Thousand Oaks, CA: Pine Forge P, 2000.

Smith, Michael Peter. Transnational Urbanism. Malden, MA: Blackwell Publishers, 2001.World Bank, "Globalization, Development and Poverty." Development Forum Debate, May 2000. (http://www.worldbank.org/devforum/ forum_globalization.html).

Notes on Contributors

Charles S. Aiken is Professor of Geography at the University of Tennessee, Knoxville. He has studied the southern United States for more than 30 years. Among Aiken's publications is *The Cotton Plantation South Since the Civil War* which was awarded the 1999 John Brinckerhoff Jackson Prize by the Association of American Geographers. His most recent book manuscript is a geographical interpretation of William Faulkner's fiction.

Edward M. Bergman is Professor and Director of the Department of City and Regional Development, Vienna University of Economics and Business Administration, Vienna, Austria. He also launched and directs NEURUS-Europe, an EU-U.S. funded six-university project to foster student research of comparative regional integration and development. He recently published *Innovative Clusters: Drivers of National Innovation Systems* with P. den Hertog and D. Charles.

Christian Berkemeier studied English, American, French, and Russian philology at Münster, Rouen, and Berkeley. He has just completed his dissertation on Donald Barthelme as parodist at the University of Paderborn, where he is now a Postdoctoral Fellow. He is co-editor of a collection of recent essays on Paul Auster and a special issue of *Amerikastudien* on Intermedia in Contemporarty American Fiction.

Hanjo Berressem is Professor for American Literature and Culture at the University of Cologne. He is the author of *Pynchon's Poetics: Interfacing Theory and Text* and of *Lines of Desire: Reading Gombrowicz's Fiction with Lacan*. His publications revolve around American literature, poststructuralism, cultural studies, and the relation between the hard and the soft sciences.

Cornelius Browne is Assistant Professor for American Literature at Oregon State University. He has published essays on John Steinbeck, Barry Lopez, John Muir, and Rachel Carson. He is at work on a book about Pragmatism, John Dewey, and American environmental writing.

Diana von Finck studied English, French, and Japanese. She taught at different high schools and works as a free-lancer. Her publications include *Ideen der Ordnung in der amerikanischen poetologischen Lyrik des 20. Jahrhunderts* and *Katastrophe - Trauma oder Erneuerung?*, edited with H.D. Becker and B. Domres.

Winfried Fluck is Professor and Chair of American Culture at the J.F. Kennedy-Institute for North American Studies of the Freie Universität Berlin. His publications include *Inszenierte Wirklichkeit. Der amerikanische Realismus 1865-1900*, *Das kulturelle Imaginäre. Funktionsgeschichte des amerikanischen Romans 1790-1900* and numerous essays on literary theory as well as American literature and American culture.

Richard Grusin is Professor and Chair in the Department of English at Wayne State University. He is the co-author of *Remediation: Understanding New Media*. He has recently published *Culture, Technology, and the Creation of America's National Parks* (2004), from which the essay in this volume is adapted.

Aurélie Guillain is a senior lecture at Toulouse-Le Mirail University, France. She wrote her doctoral thesis on William Faulkner's representation of the infant child's state of *Hilflosigkeit* and of its echoes in adult life. She published several articles on William Faulkner and translated some short stories by William Faulkner and Henry James for the Gallimard Pleiade Collection.

Carsten Hagedorn and **Sabine Wolf**, studied Spatial and Environmental Planning at the TU Kaiserslautern until 2000. They received the prestigious FRU Promotion Prize in 2001 for Spatial Research and Regional Planning (ARL) in Hannover, Germany. Today, Sabine Wolf is a graduate student at the TU Kaiserslautern and Carsten Hagedorn is working for the planning office 'R+T und Partner' in Darmstadt.

Gerhard Hoffmann is Professor Emeritus of American Literature at the University of Würzburg. Among his major books are: *Raum, Situation, erzählte Wirklichkeit* (1978), *Making Sense: The Role of the Reader in Contemporary American Fiction* (ed. 1989), *Indianische Kunst im 20. Jahrhundert* (1985), and *Im Schatten der Sonne: Zeitgenössische Kunst der Indianer und Eskimos in Kanada* (ed. 1988).

Lothar Hönnighausen is Professor Emeritus of British and North American Literature at the University of Bonn and Director of the university's Alumni-Office. Among his recent books are: *Faulkner: Masks and Metaphors* (1997), *William Faulkner: German Responses* (ed.1997), and *Regional Images and Regional Realities* (ed. 2000).

Frank J. Kearful is Professor Emeritus of English at Bonn University. "'Going Around in Circles': Wallace Stevens, Amy Clampitt, and Rita Dove" is the sixth essay in a sequence in progress on Healing Fictions in American poetry since 1954. James Mirrow, Robert Lowell, Shirley Kaufmann, Theodor Roethke, and Amy Clampitt have been the subject of other recent essays.

Pearl A. McHaney is Assistant Professor of English at Georgia State University, Atlanta, Georgia, specializing in 20th Century American literature. Her current projects include an edition of the contemporary reviews of Eudora Welty's writings and an anthology of Georgia literture and history. She is the co-editor of a *South Atlantic Review* special topic issue: The Worldwide Face of Southern Literature (Fall 2000) and editor of the *Eudora Welty Newsletter*.

Reingard M. Nischik is Professor and Chair of American Literature at the University of Constance, Germany. Among her recent publications are *New York Fiction, Margaret Atwood: Works and Impact, Uni literarisch: Lebenswelt Universität in literarischer Repräsentation*, Schwellentexte der Weltli-teratur, *American Film Stories*, and numerous articles on American and Canadian literature and culture. She is editor of the bookseries European Studies in American Literature and Culture.

James L. Peacock is Kenan Professor of Anthropology, Professor of Comparative Literature, and Director of the University Center for International Studies at the University of North Carolina at Chapel Hill. He received his B.A. in Psychology from Duke University and his Ph.D. in Social Anthropology from Harvard. His fieldwork includes studies of proletarian culture in Surabaja, Indonesia (see *Rites of Modernization*), of Muslim fundamentalism in Southeast Asia (see *Muslim Puritans*), and of primitive Baptists in Appalachia (see *Pilgrims of Paradox*). He is also the author of *The Anthropological Lens*.

Carina Plath is the Director of the Westfälischer Kunstverein Münster in Germany. She received her Ph.D. in Art History at the Ruhr-Universität Bochum with a thesis on California artists of the 1970s and from 1999-2001 did Curatorial Studies at Bard College, New York. Dr. Plath has been an art critic for *Das Kunst-Bulletin* (Zurich) since 1994.

Kyle T. Rector is a Ph.D. candidate in geography at the University of Tennessee, Knoxville. His doctoral dissertation is a comparison of the fall of legal segregation in the southern United States and the end of apartheid in South Africa.

Ulfried Reichardt is professor of American Literature and Culture at the University of Mannheim. Recent publications include *Alterität und Geschichte: Funktionen der Sklavereidarstellung im amerikanischen Roman*, essays on William Faulkner, cultural hybridity, and American Pragmatism; he also edited a special issue of *Amerikastudien* on "Time and the African American Experience" and co-edited "Engendering Manhood".

Sabine Sielke is Professor of American Literature and Culture and Chair of the North American Studies Program at the University of Bonn. Among her publications are *Fashioning the Female Subject, Reading Rape*, the (co-)editions *Theory in Practice, Gender Matters, Engendering Manhood, Making America, Der 11. September 2001, 18x15: amerikanische post:moderne,* as well as essays on poetry, theory, painting, photography, censorship, museum and popular culture.

Bernd Streich is Professor in the Department of Computer-Aided Design and Planning Methods in Urban Planning and Architecture at the University of Kaiserslautern. From 1997-2001 he worked at the Institute of Urban Planning and Design at the University of Bonn and has published widely on urban sprawl, computer supported planning processes, planning ethics, and experimental media design methods in architecture and urban design.

Christian W. Thomsen is Professor of English and American Literature and Media at the University of Siegen. He is director of FAM (Fortbildungsakademie Medien in Siegen) and for long years served as speaker of the only media research program of the Deutsche Forschungsgemeinschaft. He has published 27 books, edited more than 50 volumes and published 280 articles on literature, architecture, art, design, and the media.

Wolfgang Werth is Professor for American Studies at the University Duisburg – Essen. He also has a gallery for contemporary art in Düsseldorf.

Louise Westling is Professor of English at the University of Oregon. Recent publications include a 1996 book, *The Green Breast of the New World: Landscape, Gender, and American Fiction* and articles on Virginia Woolf, William Faulkner, and Green Humanism.

Heide Ziegler is the President of the International University in Germany which she co-founded in 1998. She also served as Vice President and Rector of the University of Stuttgart until 1996. Among her research interests are the works of William Faulkner and postmodern American literature. Her most recent publication is *The Translatability of Cultures* (ed. 2002).

Index

Abbey, Edward, 9, 101, 102, 104, 105, 106, 107, 108, 111, 112, 113, 114
Abish, Walter, 79
Acker, Kathy, 74
Adams, Henry, 50
Adcock, Craig, 251, 254, 261
Adorno, Theodor W., 143
Alfina, Mark, 330
Alighieri, Dante, 215, 216, 224, 229
Altoon, John, 249
Ammons, A.R., 69, 221
Anaya, Rudolfo, 117
Antheil, Gerald, 144, 154
Anzaldúa, Gloria, 117, 123
Appadurai, Arjun, 8, 13, 89, 99, 100
Asher, Michel, 252
Auster, Paul, 8, 165, 333

Babbage, Charles, 57
Bacall, Lauren, 193
Bachelard, Gaston, 211, 224, 225, 230, 263, 274
Baker, Peter, 242, 246
Banham, Reyner, 13, 247, 248, 261
Barber, Benjamin R., 319, 330
Barnes, Djuna, 77
Barnes, Trevor J., 171, 177, 183
Barth, John, 79, 153
Barthelme, Donald, 19, 29, 152, 166, 333
Baudrillard, Jean, 10, 44, 50, 51, 59, 85, 86, 115, 116, 117, 123, 151, 154
Beach, Joseph W., 143, 154
Beatles, 74
Beckett, Samuel, 150, 152, 154, 232
Beethoven, Ludwig van, 233
Bell, Daniel, 147, 154
Bell, Larry, 249, 250
Bellamy, Joe David, 152, 154
Bellow, Saul, 145, 147
Bengston, Billy Al, 249
Bergman, Edward M., 13, 318, 327, 330, 331, 333
Bernard, Claus, 46
Bigsby, Christopher, 153, 156
Bischoff, Peter, 185, 200
Bloch, Ernst, 63, 74
Booth, Wayne C., 143, 154
Bordwell, David, 24, 29
Borges, Jorge Luis, 9, 31, 32, 33, 34, 36, 38, 39, 40, 41, 151, 153, 154, 155
Bremer, Sidney, 164, 167

Breuer, Marcel, 277, 279
Bronson, Charles, 189
Brooke-Rose, Christine, 216, 230
Brownstein, Rachel, 21, 29
Buell, Lawrence, 101, 125, 135
Burroughs, William S., 79
Buscombe, Edward, 187, 200
Butler, Judith, 80, 82, 83, 84, 85, 86
Butler, Samuel, 174, 183

Cage, John, 11, 56, 59, 61, 232, 233, 234, 235, 236, 237, 244, 245, 246
Calder, Alexander, 46
Cardinale, Claudia, 188
Carlyle, Thomas, 140, 154
Carr, Emily, 280
Casey, Edward S., 8, 9, 13, 88, 99, 100, 101, 113
Cassirer, Ernst, 140, 154
Castells, Manuel, 91, 100, 171
Castillo, Ana, 9, 117, 118, 120, 121, 122, 123
Celant, Germano, 259, 261
Chambers, Ross, 137, 154
Cixous, Hélène, 83
Clampitt, Amy, 11, 216, 219, 221, 222, 223, 224, 227, 230, 231, 334
Cohen, Jack, 46, 59
Conley, Verona, 7
Conrad, Joseph, 143, 145, 146
Coover, Robert, 74
Costner, Kevin, 193, 194
Crane, Hart, 143
Crary, Jonathan, 57, 65
Cronon, William, 125, 126, 135

Davidson, Robert, 280
Davies, Sir John, 215, 216, 217, 229
Davis, Mike, 247, 248, 261
Dear, Michael, 322, 331
DeKoven, Marianne, 77, 86
Deleuze, Gilles, 9, 42, 48, 49, 50, 54, 60
DeLillo, Don, 8, 52, 165
Dembo, Lawrence S., 153, 155
Derrida, Jacques, 80, 178, 179, 183, 184, 216, 230
Dewey, John, 10, 16, 17, 18, 29, 102, 103, 104, 107, 109, 113, 333
Diaz, Juneau, 159, 167
Dick, P. K., 46, 60
Dillard, Annie, 48, 60, 114
Disney, Walt, 10, 115

337

Donne, John, 215, 228
Dos Passos, John, 147, 159
Douglas, David, 129, 136, 167
Dourish, Paul, 31, 40, 41
Dove, Rita, 11, 216, 224, 225, 227, 228, 230, 334
Dreiser, Theodore, 143, 147, 159, 160, 168
Duchamp, Marcel, 46, 264, 270
Duncan, James S., 171, 183
Durkheim, Emile, 205
Dydo, Ulla E., 217, 230

Eagleton, Terry, 216, 230
Einstein, Albert, 118
Elam, Keir, 178, 183
Elder, John, 69, 72
Eliot, George, 143, 155
Eliot, T. S., 75, 77, 141, 143, 217, 230
Elkin, Stanley, 10, 149, 155
Ellis, Bret Easton, 161, 162, 163, 164, 167, 168
Elsbree, Langdon, 185
Emmeche, Claus, 46, 47, 51, 54, 60
Engel, Leonard, 185, 186, 187, 200
Eppich, Brigitte, 286
Eppich, Helmut, 12, 284
Eppich, Hugo, 12, 284, 286
Erickson, Arthur, 12, 276, 277, 278, 279, 280, 281, 282, 283, 284, 286, 287, 288

Farr, Cecilia Konchar, 102, 113
Faulkner, William, 144, 145, 146, 333, 334, 335, 336
Federman, Raymond, 152, 155
Feser, Edward, 330, 331
Fitzgerald, F. Scott, 145
Flaubert, Gustave, 141
Flavin, Dan, 250
Flusty, Steven, 322, 331
Fonda, Henry, 188
Ford, John, 11, 186, 187, 192, 193
Forster, E. M., 145
Foucault, Michel, 8, 13, 63, 64, 75, 78, 79, 80, 82, 86, 171, 177
Frank, Joseph, 77, 78, 79, 80, 86, 141, 155
Frank, Robert, 76
Freud, Sigmund, 50
Friedman, Thomas L., 319, 331
Fukuyama, Francis, 324, 331

Gadamer, Hans-Georg, 65, 72
Garland, Hamlin, 143
Garreau, Joel, 314, 316, 321, 331

Gass, William H., 32, 152
Gates, Henry Louis Jr., 80, 81
Geis, Deborah R., 175, 183
Gelfant, Blanche Housman, 159, 167
Geronimo, 194, 195
Gerry, Elbridge, 308
Gibson, Andrew, 148, 155
Gibson, William, 8, 42, 43, 45, 51, 57, 60, 166
Giddens, Anthony, 147, 155
Goldstein, Harvey, 318, 327, 330, 331
Gombrich, E. H., 158, 167
Gore, Al, 295, 297, 299
Gropius, Martin, 276
Groys, Boris, 272, 274
Guattari, Félix, 9, 42, 48, 49, 50, 54, 55, 58, 60

Hackman, Gene, 190
Hahn-Oberlander, Cornelia, 284
Hall, James, 69, 227, 230, 265, 274
Hannerz, Ulf, 99
Haraway, Donna, 115, 116, 117, 124
Hardy, Thomas, 146
Harjo, Joy, 221
Harvey, David, 8, 13, 88, 91, 99, 100, 147, 148, 155
Hawthorne, Nathaniel, 145
Heisenberg, Werner, 118
Hejinian, Lyn, 233, 240, 241, 245, 246
Hemingway, Ernest, 75, 144, 145, 146, 147, 150, 155
Hiaasen, Carl, 48
Hill, Walter, 192, 195
Hoffmann, E. T. A., 46
Hoffmann, Wolfgang, 10
Hönnighausen, Lothar, 8, 14, 100
Hoover, Paul, 221, 230
Hopper, Edward, 27
Hopps, Walter, 249
Hornung, Alfred, 148, 155
Howells, William Dean, 159, 166
Hutcheon, Linda, 80, 85, 86
Hutson, Richard, 186, 200
Huyssen, Andreas, 63, 72, 74, 80, 86

Ickstadt, Heinz, 77, 86
Ignatieff, Michael, 323, 331
Irigaray, Luce, 80, 82, 83, 84, 86
Irwin, Robert, 11, 249, 250, 251, 252, 253, 259, 260, 261, 262
Iser, Wolfgang, 16, 21, 22, 23, 25, 29, 137, 140, 155

Isserman, Andrew M., 325, 331

Jacobs, Jane, 324, 325, 331
Jacquard, Joseph-Marie, 57
Jahn, Walter, 291
James, Henry, 65, 143, 145, 154, 155, 265, 274, 334
Jameson, Frederic, 9, 14, 32, 68, 69, 73, 75, 81, 85, 86, 87, 147, 148, 156
Jarmusch, Jim, 50, 192
Jaspers, Karl, 140, 156, 225
Jensen, Derrick, 113
Johnson, Barbara, 182, 183, 193, 194, 200
Joyce, James, 32, 77, 141, 144, 145, 147, 217, 220, 231
Judd, Donald, 250

Kafka, Franz, 141, 151, 153
Kahn, Louis, 277
Kant, Immanuel, 8, 140
Karl, Frederick, 101, 263, 272, 274
Kauffman, Craig, 249
Kaufman, Shirley, 221
Kerouac, Jack, 145
Kienholz, Ed, 249
King, Martin Luther, 308
Kircher, Cassandra, 112, 113
Kitses, Jim, 194, 197, 200
Klee, Paul, 279
Klotz, Volker, 159, 168
Kolb, Ellsworth, 128
Kolb, Emery L., 128, 135
Kolodny, Annette, 83, 87, 185
Kreutzer, Eberhard, 163, 168
Kripacz, Francisco, 286
Kristeva, Julia, 80, 83, 87
Krugman, Paul, 326, 327, 331

Lacan, Jacques, 54, 61, 333
Lanz, Stephan, 291
Laramée, Eva Andrée, 48, 56, 59, 60
Lawrence, D. H., 144, 145, 146, 200, 316
Le Corbusier, 277
LeClair, Thomas, 152, 156
Lefebvre, Henri, 66, 73, 171
Leger, Fernand, 279
Leider, Phil, 251, 261
Leipold, Tracy, 267
Leon Battista, 253
Leone, Sergio, 188, 190, 192, 193, 196
Lessing, Gotthold Ephraim, 77
Lévi-Strauss, Claude, 64, 73
Lichtenstein, Roy, 269

Limerick, Patricia Nelson, 126, 135, 185, 200
Lippold, Richard, 232
Lopez, Barry, 69, 333
Lowell, Robert, 221, 334
Luger, Michael, 327, 331
Lukács, George, 142, 156
Lurker, Manfred, 215, 231
Lynch, David, 163
Lyotard, Jean-François, 65, 73

Macy, William H., 178
Mallarmé, Stéphane, 80, 83, 87, 240, 241
Mamet, David, 11, 169, 170, 171, 172, 173, 175, 177, 179, 182, 183, 184
Marshall, Alfred, 324, 325, 331
Marx, Karl, 64, 66
Marx, Leo, 50, 51, 52, 60, 64, 66, 157
Matisse, Henri, 279
Maturana, Humberto, 46, 60, 73
Mayer, Bernadette, 11, 233, 243, 245, 246
McCaffrey, Larry, 217, 231
McCall, Tom, 296
McCartney, Paul, 74
McCaffery, Larry, 152
McClatchy, J. D., 221
McHale, Brian, 76, 77, 79, 80, 87
McInerney, Jay, 53, 60
McLuhan, Marshall, 128
McNiff, John, 161, 168
Melville, Herman, 145
Mendes, Sam, 164
Merchant, Carolyn, 130, 135
Merleau-Ponty, Maurice, 9, 102, 104, 106, 108, 110, 113, 117, 140, 156
Merrill, James, 129, 221, 224
Merrill, Keith, 129, 136
Meyrowitz, Joshua, 62, 73
Mies van der Rohe, Ludwig, 232, 276
Miller, Donald W., 322, 331
Milton, John, 215, 219, 228
Misrach, Richard, 132, 133, 136
Mitchell, W. J. T., 77, 78, 87, 156
Moore, George, 143
Morrison, Toni, 11, 74, 201, 202, 203, 206, 207, 209, 211, 212, 214
Moses, Ed, 249
Mozart, Wolfgang Amadeus, 222, 227
Mukherjee, Arun, 84, 87
Musil, Robert, 32

Nabokov, Vladimir, 151
Nicolson, Marjorie, 215, 231
Nijman, Jan, 329, 331

339

Nischik, Reingard M., 11, 186, 200, 334
Nordman, Maria, 12, 255, 256, 257, 259, 260, 261
Norris, Frank, 60, 143
Nye, David E., 52, 53, 60

Offray de La Mettrie, Julien, 46
Ortiz, Simon, 9, 117, 118, 121, 122, 124
Oursler, Tony, 12, 263, 264, 265, 266, 267, 268, 269, 270, 271, 272, 274, 275

Parmenides, 225
Pauline, Mark, 43
Peckinpah, Sam, 192
Pei, I. M., 277
Peper, Jürgen, 20, 28, 30
Perloff, Marjorie, 230, 237, 241, 246
Picasso, Pablo, 264, 279
Plagens, Peter, 249, 261
Plato, 215
Poe, Edgar Allan, 46, 145, 165
Poulet, Gorge, 215, 231
Pound, Ezra, 75, 141, 216, 230
Preminger, Otto, 27
Price, Cedric, 291
Price, Kenneth, 249, 261
Proust, Marcel, 32, 141, 147
Putnam, Robert D., 325, 326, 332
Pynchon, Thomas, 8, 42, 43, 45, 47, 48, 50, 51, 57, 60, 74, 79, 158, 165, 166, 168, 333

Raimi, Sam, 190
Rauschenberg, Robert, 11, 232, 264
Rawls, John, 66
Reed, Ishmael, 74
Rees, John, 323, 332
Reid, Bill, 279, 280
Retallack, Joan, 236, 237, 246
Rich, Adrienne, 74, 87
Richmond, Henry, 296
Rilke, Rainer Maria, 225
Ritzer, George, 319, 332
Robbe-Grillet, Alain, 148, 151, 156
Roethke, Theodore, 215, 229, 231, 334
Ronneberger, Klaus, 291
Roorda, Randall, 103, 113
Rorty, Richard, 9, 63, 66, 67, 69, 73
Rosenberg, Harold, 19, 30
Ross, Andrew, 121, 124, 132, 133, 136
Roudané, Matthew, 170, 175, 179, 184
Rousseau, Jean-Jacques, 147
Rucker, Rudy, 47, 61
Ruscha, Ed, 249

Rush, Michael, 268, 270, 271, 275
Rykwert, Joseph, 158

Sable, Charles, 325, 332
Sasskind, Saskia, 99
Sasson, Saskia, 320, 321, 322, 332
Satie, Erik, 233, 234, 246
Schmidt, Charles W., 290
Schwab, Gabriele, 25, 26, 30
Schwitters, Kurt, 264
Scott, Sir Walter, 142
Sennett, Richard, 9, 63, 66, 67, 68, 70, 71, 73
Senville, Thomas, 290
Serres, Michael, 58, 61, 148
Sherman, Cindy, 265
Shultis, Christopher, 56, 61, 237, 246
Silko, Leslie Marmon, 9, 117, 118, 119, 120, 121, 122, 124
Siporin, Ona, 113, 114
Slotkin, Richard, 185
Smetak, Jacqueline, 185, 186
Smith, Gordon, 12, 276, 277, 278, 279, 280, 281, 287
Smith, James F., 160, 168
Smith, Michael Peter, 319, 320, 332
Snyder, Gary, 9, 63, 66, 69, 70, 71, 73
Sobchak, Vivian, 24, 30
Soja, Edward, 64, 65, 66, 73, 171, 172, 184, 305, 317
Solinas, Rico, 133
Solnit, Rebecca, 9, 118, 122, 124
Sontag, Susan, 176, 184
Spencer, Sharon, 141, 156
Stafford, Barbara Maria, 43, 57, 61
Staley, Samuel R., 297
Stein, Gertrude, 75, 76, 77, 81, 86, 217, 242
Stein, Rachel, 77, 120, 124
Steiner, George, 146, 156
Sterling, Bruce, 42, 57, 60
Stevens, Wallace, 11, 216, 217, 218, 219, 220, 221, 222, 223, 229, 230, 231, 334
Stewart, Frank, 102, 114
Stewart, Michael, 46, 59
Stone, Sharon, 190, 200
Stoppard, Tom, 57
Sukenick, Ronald, 152, 156

Tabbi, Joe, 55, 61
Taggart, John, 11, 233, 242, 245, 246
Tennyson, Alfred Lord, 166
Thoreau, Henry David, 48, 61, 106, 135
Till, Emmett, 203, 209
Tinguely, Jean, 46

Todorov, Tzvetan, 141, 156
Tomlinson, Ray, 34
Tompkins, Jane, 187, 189, 200
Twain, Mark, 145
Tudor, David, 232
Turner, Frederick Jackson, 185, 191
Turner, Tina, 74
Turner, Victor, 80, 81, 87
Turrell, James, 12, 250, 251, 254, 255, 256, 259, 260, 261, 262

Updike, John, 163

van den Berg, L., 291
Varala, Francisco J., 60
Vaucanson, Jacques, 43, 45, 46, 47, 48, 56, 57
Vico, Giambattista, 217
Virilio, Paul, 7, 10, 14, 150, 151, 156, 272, 273, 275
Vonnegut, Kurt, 152
Vostell, Wolf, 270

Waldrop, Rosemarie, 240, 246
Weber, Max, 88, 93, 100, 158, 168
Webern, Anton von, 233
White, Richard, 126, 136
Whitman, Walt, 269, 270
Whittlesey, Derwent, 306
Williams, Raymond, 18, 30
Williams, Terry Tempest, 9, 101, 102, 104, 105, 107, 108, 109, 110, 111, 112, 113, 114
Williams, William Carlos, 75, 216, 219, 230, 231
Willis, Bruce, 192, 195
Willis, Hannah, 202
Winer, Helen, 249, 262
Wirth, Louis, 158, 168
Wofford, George, 202
Wolfe, Tom, 159, 160, 161, 168
Woolf, Virginia, 35, 144, 145, 147, 156, 336
Wortz, Ed, 251
Wright, Frank Lloyd, 276, 285, 288

Yeats, William Butler, 216, 220, 231
Yrkkö, J., 327, 330

Zimmer, Dieter E., 34, 38, 39, 41
Zinnemann, Fred, 193
Zizek, Slavoj, 53, 54, 61
Zola, Emile, 143